The Politics of Disenchantment

Bush, Clinton, Perot, and the Press

The Hampton Press Communication Series
Political Communication

David L. Paletz, Editor

Media Entrepreneurs and the Media Enterprise in the United States Congress: Influencing Policy in the Washington Community
Karen M. Kedrowski

The Politics of Disenchantment: Bush, Clinton, Perot, and the Press
James Lemert, William R. Elliot, William L. Rosenberg, and James M. Bernstein

Political Communication in Action
David L. Paletz (ed.)

Glasnost and After: Media and Change in Central and Eastern Europe
David L. Paletz, Karol Jakubowicz, and Pavao Novosel (eds.)

Germany's "Unity Election": Voters and the Media
Holli A. Semetko and Klaus Schoenbach

forthcoming

Journalism and the Education of Journalists in the New East/Central Europe
Jerome Aumente, Peter Gross, Ray Hiebert, Lisa Schillinger, and Owen Johnson

Mediated Women: Representations in Popular Culture
Marian Meyers, ed.

Global Communication, Local Cultures, and Intimate Coerseduction
René Jean Ravault

The Best Laid Plans . . . Strategic Failures in the Modern Presidency
Mary E. Stuckey

The Politics of Disenchantment

Bush, Clinton, Perot, and the Press

James B. Lemert
University of Oregon,
William R. Elliott
Marquette University
William L. Rosenberg
Drexel University
James M. Bernstein
Frank Magid Associates

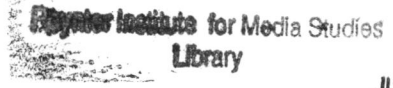

HAMPTON PRESS, INC.
CRESSKILL, NEW JERSEY

Copyright © 1996 by Hampton Press, Inc.

All rights reserved. No part of this publication may be reproduced, stored in a retrieval system, or transmitted in any form or by any means, electronic, mechanical, photocopying, microfilming, recording, or otherwise, without permission of the publisher.

Printed in the United States of America

Library of Congress Cataloging-in-Publication Data

The politics of disenchantment : Bush, Clinton, Perot, and the press / James B. Lemert . . . [et al.].
    p. cm.
    Includes bibliographical references and indexes.
    ISBN 1-57273-058-7 (cloth). -- ISBN 1-57273-059-5 (pbk.)
    1. Presidents--United States--Election--1992. 2. Campaign debates--United States. 3. Press and politics--United States. 4. Press--United States--Influence. I. Lemert, James B., 1935-
JK526 1992p
324.973'0928--dc20   95-51055
                                                                                                      CIP

Hampton Press, Inc.
23 Broadway
Cresskill, NJ 07626

Contents

Preface xi
About the Authors xiii

1. **THE POLITICS OF DISENCHANTMENT** 1

    Disenchantment with "Media as Usual"? 3
    Disenchantment with "Politics as Usual"? 4
    Disenchantment with Political Ads? 6
    Disenchantment with the 1988 Campaign? 10
    Disenchantment with the Party Candidates? 11
    Disenchantment with Perot? 11
    Purposes of this Study 12
    Convergent Research Approaches 20
    Organization of the Book 21

2. **METHODS** 25

    The Scope of the Present Study 26
    Advantages and Disadvantages of Each Design 27
    Journalistic Interviews with Campaign Decision Makers 29
    The Content Analyses 30
    The Survey Research Designs 35
    Conclusion 38

3. **THE USE OF NONTRADITIONAL MEDIA IN CAMPAIGN '92 AND ITS IMPLICATIONS** 41

    The Evolution of Nontraditional Media Use
       in Campaign '92 43

Contents

Perot Talks, the People Listen and the Mainstream Media Stew	47
Weird Talk Shows or Opportunities to Interact?	48
Possible Virtues and Drawbacks of the Nontraditional Media	51
Summary	53

4. TALK SHOWS AND THE NEWS: RESPONSE FROM TRADITIONAL MEDIA — 57

Background	58
Method	60
Analysis	64
Conclusions	69

5. THE AUDIENCE FOR CANDIDATE "TALK SHOWS" — 73

Criticisms of Candidate Talk Shows	74
Countering the Criticisms	75
The Audience for Talk Shows	78
Do Viewers Learn More?	86
Viewers React to Campaign Talk Shows	90
Voter Preferences	94
Conclusions	97

6. PEROT, THE "PEROT PEOPLE," AND THE PRESS — 101

Perot and the Media	102
Who Are These People?	110
Discussion	122

7. BACKGROUND AND FORMAT OF THE DEBATES — 127

History of Debates	128
The 1992 Election Context	131
The Bipartisan Commission on Presidential Debates Proposal	132
The Failure of the Original Debate Schedule	132
The Chicken George Strategy	133
The Two Campaigns' Strategy for the Debate about Debates	135
The Debate Compromise	135
Continuous Debates with Multiple Formats	138
Conclusions	140

8. DEBATE EFFECTS ON SURVEY RESPONDENTS — 143

| Debate Positives and Negatives | 144 |
| Debate Influences: Knowledge, Image, and Vote Choice | 146 |

	Methods, Variables, and Analyses	149
	Findings	153
	Summing Up	171
9.	**NEWS VERDICTS AND THEIR EFFECTS**	**175**
	Network Content	177
	A Verdict Effect?	185
	Summary and Conclusions	197
10.	**MEDIA AND MASS VIEWS OF THE PRESIDENTIAL DEBATES AS A POLITICAL INSTITUTION**	**199**
	How Deep the Roots?	200
	Three Things Debates Provide	200
	Legitimation Through Debates	201
	Purpose of This Chapter	201
	Study Methodology	202
	Results	205
	Discussion	231
11.	**RAPID RESPONSE TEAMS**	**233**
	Early Versions of the Fact Patrols and Response Teams	236
	The Clinton Rapid Response Team	237
	The Bush Response Team	239
	The Perot Response Effort	241
	Political Ads within the Rapid Response Team Function	241
	Summary	243
12.	**MEDIA AND VOTERS REACT TO THE 1992 PRESIDENTIAL ADS**	**245**
	Another "Echo Chamber" in 1992?	246
	Impact of "Attack" Ads	251
	Possible Weaknesses in Study Design	252
	Attack Ads in 1992	254
	Apparent Effects of the Ads on Candidates	257
	Analyzing Voting Intensity	260
	Panel Results	267
	Summary and Conclusions	270
13.	**THE ROLE OF POLLS AND POLLING IN THE '92 CAMPAIGN**	**275**
	Polling for the Campaigns	276
	News Media Polls	278
	A Major Flaw in National Presidential Polls	284
	The Future Role of Campaign Polls	285

14.	**SUMMARY AND CONCLUSIONS**	287
	Purposes of the Study	288
	Our Methodology	289
	The Findings	289
	Implications	294
	Future Research Needs: Preparing for 1996	297

Appendixes

A.	Wave 1 Questionnaire	301
B.	Waves 2-5 Questionnaire	315
C.	Wave 6 Questionnaire	333
D.	State-by-State 1992 Presidential Election Poll Results	343

Author Index	347
Subject Index	351

LIST OF TABLES

2.1	Basic Demographics for Panel and Trend Surveys	39
4.1	Portrayals of Hosts in Nontraditional Media by Period	65
4.2	Source Portrayals of Citizen Participation in Nontraditional Media	67
4.3	Source Portrayals of Quality of Information on Nontraditional Media	68
5.1	Mean Internal Efficacy Scores by Amount of Candidate Talk Show Viewing, October 11-22 Interviews	81
5.2	Influence of Talk Show Viewing on News Media Consumption	85
5.3	Debate and Talk Show Viewing as Predictors of Knowledge	85
5.4	Influence of Talk Show Viewing on Rating of Candidate Talk Shows	91
5.5	Comparison of Mean Ratings of Candidate Talk Shows and Changes in Those Ratings by "Latecomer" and 'Never-Viewer" Panelists, October and November Waves	93
5.6	Influence of Talk Show Viewing on Chance Respondent Would Vote for George Bush	96

Contents ix

6.1	For Whom Did Support for Perot Come? Party Identification and Intended Vote	112
6.2	Perot Voters and Four Efficacy Measures	114
6.3	Perot Voters and Feelings about "The Media"	116
8.1	Cross-Tabulation of Debate Performance by Party	154
8.2	Cross-Tabulation of Debate Performance by Party	156
8.3	Cross-Tabulation of Debate Performance by Party	157
8.4	Influence of Debate Exposure on Issue Knowledge	159
8.5	Influence of Debate Exposure on George Bush's Image	161
8.6	Influence of Debate Exposure on Bill Clinton's Image	163
8.7	Influence of Debate Exposure on Ross Perot's Image	165
8.8	Influence of Debate Exposure on Voting for George Bush	167
8.9	Influence of Debate Exposure on Voting for Bill Clinton	169
8.10	Influence of Debate Exposure on Voting for Ross Perot	172
9.1	Sources of Candidate Verdicts in ABC and CBS Evening Newscasts	183
9.2	Sources of Candidate Verdicts in ABC, CBS and NBC Post-Debate Specials	183
9.3	Time Since Debate and Rating for Perot as Debater	189
9.4	Post-Debate Analysis and Rating of Quayle as a Debater	192
9.5	Summary of Multiple Classification Analysis: "Town Hall" Debate Winner	194
10.1	Direction of Verdict About Debate by Year of Post-Debate Analysis Program	206
10.2	Object of Statements Made on Post-Debate News Specials by Year of Programs	207
10.3	Year and Importance of Presidential Debates	208
10.4	Print and Broadcast News Treatment of the 1992 Candidate Debates	210
10.5	Changes in Media Views from Before to After Vice Presidential and Richmond "Talk Show" Debate	211
10.6	Source by Direction of Verdict About the 1992 Debates	212

x   Contents

10.7A	First Presidential Debate, October 11 Summary of Multiple Classification Analyses	216
10.7B	Vice Presidential Debate, October 13	218
10.7C	Second Presidential Debate, October 15 Summary of Multiple Classification Analyses	220
10.7D	Final Presidential Debate, October 19 Summary of Multiple Classification Analyses	222
10.8	A Summary of Changes in Debate Support by Panelists Over Time	226
10.9	Survey Wave and Debate Format Preferences. Do Preferences Change as Experience Grows?	229
10.10	Debate Format Preferences	230
12.1	Number of Network News Stories Using Presidential Ad Sound Bites and Number of "Ad Watch" Segments in Those Stories, by Fall Campaign Year	250
12.2	Clinton, Bush and Perot Ads	256
12.3	Bush-Clinton Ad Exposure and Presidential Vote Choice	258
12.4	Political Ad Exposure and Probability of Voting for Bill Clinton	263
12.5	Political Ad Exposure and Probability of Voting for George Bush	264
12.6	Political Ad Exposure and Probability of Voting for Ross Perot	265
12.7	Attack vs. Positive Ad Tactics Comparisons for George Bush and Bill Clinton	267
12.8	October-November Changes in Value Placed on Presidential Ads	269

LIST OF FIGURES

2.1	Evening News Content Analysis Design	32
2.2	News Special Content Analysis Design	33
2.3	Survey Studies Design	37
7.1	Debate Schedule 1992	137
9.1	Percent Positive Verdicts by Debate and Candidate	180

Preface

This study of the 1992 presidential campaign, a follow-up to our 1988 campaign study, was once again funded by a grant from the family of Frank Allen, whose generous support, combined with matching grant support from the Dow Jones Fund, has made this study possible. Mr. Allen who, since awarding us the grant, has become the Dean of the School of Journalism at the University of Montana, also provided the bulk of the support needed for our study of the 1988 campaign.

The 1988 study resulted from an almost accidental coffee conversation between Jim Lemert and Mr. Allen, a graduate of the University of Oregon School of Journalism and then-Philadelphia bureau chief of *The Wall Street Journal*. The 1992 study resulted from an invitation from Mr. Allen to extend our campaign studies, an offer we accepted with almost unseemly haste! It is an understatement to say that this research would not have been done without Frank Allen.

The authors thank their respective computing centers, graduate students and home departments for their support and assistance in this project. We also want to thank Hampton Press President Barbara Bernstein and Political Science Editor David Paletz for their advice and encouragement.

The survey data were collected at each of our four locations, using questionnaires we developed in common, and then pooled. In that sense, each of us has contributed to every chapter that uses the survey data. The content analyses reported in some chapters generally were designed and executed by the respective authors of each chapter, sometimes in consultation with the rest of us.

As was the case for our previous project (Lemert, Elliott, Bernstein, Rosenberg, & Nestvold, 1991), each chapter generally is the responsibility of one of us.

- James B. Lemert wrote Chapters 1, 5, 6, 9, 12, and most of 10.
- William R. Elliott wrote Chapters 2, 8, and 14.
- William L. Rosenberg wrote Chapters 7, 11, and 13.
- James M. Bernstein wrote Chapters 3 and 4 and contributed the "Introduction" section of Chapter 10.

Bill Elliott did the difficult job of consolidating all our chapters into one word processing system. Bill Rosenberg managed data entry for Drexel, Oregon, and Indiana survey responses. Bill Elliott and Bill Rosenberg pooled the survey data from all four sites into a unified data set. Bill Elliott and Jim Lemert did final reorganizing, checking, and correcting of the data set.

Jim Lemert represented the group in contacting and negotiating with potential publishers. During revisions for Hampton Press, he also edited the complete manuscript.

Finally, all of us would like to express our love and gratitude to our patient and forbearing families.

REFERENCES

Lemert, J.B., Elliott, W.R., Bernstein, J.M., Rosenberg, W.L., & Nestvold, K.J. (1991). *News verdicts, the debates, and presidential campaigns.* New York: Praeger Publishers.

About the Authors

James B. Lemert is professor of Journalism and Communication at the University of Oregon. Dr. Lemert is author of two additional books and numerous articles about the media and politics, about journalists' craft practices, about using research to criticize media performance, and about public opinion measurement and conceptualization.

William R. Elliott becomes Dean of the College of Communication at Marquette University in January 1996, after serving as Associate Dean of the College of Mass Communication and Media Arts at Southern Illinois University, Carbondale. Dr. Elliott is a widely published author of research articles in academic journals.

William L. Rosenberg is Director of the Drexel Survey Research Center at Drexel University. A political scientist, Dr. Rosenberg has served as a media analyst during election campaigns, as well as a survey research consultant, and has written extensively about the media and politics.

James M. Bernstein, formerly on the Journalism faculties of both the University of Oregon and Indiana University, is Research Analyst with Frank N. Magid Associates of Marion, Iowa. Dr. Bernstein is the author of journal articles about audiences, economics, content, and effects of newspapers and broadcast news media.

1

The Politics of Disenchantment

James B. Lemert

This book represents the third in a series of studies on the media's role in presidential campaigns. One consistent purpose of our research has been to gather data to assess whether mass communication institutions have either enhanced or diminished citizen understanding and involvement in American presidential campaigns.

Included as well in all our research has been an examination of one specific political institution—the presidential debates. Our first study tested the impact of watching an early primary Republican debate on campaign knowledge and interest, demonstrating that one delayed effect of watching that debate was to stimulate Republicans' interest in who the Democrats were going to nominate for president (Lemert, Elliott, Nestvold, & Rarick, 1983). Our second study—and first book—looked from several perspectives at such questions as whether news verdicts about which candidate did better in a debate had as much or more impact than the debates themselves, whether over time the news media were undercutting the debates as a political institution, whether voters valued the debates, and whether presidential ads that attacked the opponent were as effective as ads that praised the sponsoring candidate (Lemert, Elliott, Bernstein, Rosenberg, & Nestvold, 1991).

The present study extends these interests to the Fall 1992 presidential campaign, but adds to them such questions as whether the so-called "talk-show campaign" and the Perot candidacy have fundamentally altered relationships among candidates, voters, and the conventional news media.

The eventful 1992 presidential campaign may mark the start of a new era in presidential campaigning, an era when conventional news media no longer exclusively control the flow of information to the electorate. The conventional news media found themselves having to make room for a tacit coalition of the candidates, the voters, and ambitious alternative media such as the talk shows. It was also a campaign in which:

- a third-party candidate seemed to have committed political suicide, yet came back from the dead;
- the presidential debates broke away from the old, joint-press-conference format;
- three contenders met together in television debates for the first time in any fall campaign;
- 1950s-style, program-length political commercials made a huge comeback;
- the political parties continued to lose control of how—even of whether—their conventions were televised;
- an incumbent president was punished by voters despite an apparent military—diplomatic triumph and an economy that may have been better than it looked; and
- after hitting a new low in the 1988 election, November voter turnout increased for the first time in the past six elections, despite unusually low turnout earlier in the 1992 primaries.

If the 1992 campaign does indeed mark a new era in presidential campaigning, historians may eventually say it was probably because the politics of disenchantment led to a reinvigorated politics of possibility, in which voters regained more control of their own campaign information resources and candidates found a number of new ways to reach voters without the intervention of the conventional news media. But even if historians eventually conclude that the 1992 campaign was just a temporary side trip off the beaten path, clearly voter disenchantment had a lot to do with that side trip. To say the least, there were plenty of signs that voters were ready for a different kind of presidential campaign—and they got it.

DISENCHANTMENT WITH "MEDIA AS USUAL"?

> The nightly news is out . . . talk shows are in. Mike Wallace of 60 Minutes (Lebel, 1993)

According to a Freedom Forum Media Studies Center (1993) analysis of the campaign, Bill Clinton (47 appearances), Ross Perot (33), and George Bush (16) made a combined total of 96 appearances on *Larry King Live*, Phil Donahue, and the ABC, NBC, and CBS morning news shows during the 1992 election year. These appearances were interpreted as both Clinton's and Perot's ways of getting their messages directly to voters without the intervention of political journalists. Bush's appearances generally were interpreted as a belated attempt to get to where the action was.

In an article highly critical of press performance, Ken Auletta (1992) suggested that Clinton had been given little choice but to do an end run around the media in order to reestablish his campaign themes. More important, many analysts declared that *voters* also wanted to hear more directly from the candidates.

Ironically, the conventional media were fairly quick to announce that this was going on. "This may be remembered as the year that the mainstream political press lost control," Jonathan Alter had already declared in the June 8 *Newsweek* (1992), just as the primaries were concluding. Writing a piece for Esquire that almost certainly was finished before the November 3 election, Auletta (1992, p. 112) asserted that "candidates and citizens alike rebelled against the media middleman."

This was not just a first impression either. Later reviewers seemed equally convinced that voters gratefully embraced ways of learning about the presidential candidates through talk shows, town hall meetings, and other, more "direct" contacts with the candidates. For example, *New York Times* executive Seymour Topping (1993, p.2) called it the "bypass syndrome"—the idea that the only way people could learn what they needed to know about the 1992 candidates was to "bypass" the conventional news media.

Writing in a series of analytical reports published by the Freedom Forum Media Studies Center, Edward Pease (1993, p. 137) said that "much of the public's attitude...seemed to be that the press not only couldn't be trusted to deliver untarnished political news, but had become irrelevant . . . once . . . less filtered avenues for political information became available." Writing nearly five months after the election, media analyst David Shaw (1993a, p. A18) declared that "the rise of Ross Perot . . ., the enthusiastic reception [given] Perot and President Bush . . . when they attacked the media—and the success that Perot and Clinton had in bypassing the traditional media" showed in 1992 that both voters and candidates had figured out other ways of reaching each other.

Far more critical and less optimistic appraisals of these trends were also offered by such journalistic notables as syndicated columnist Robert Novak (1992), magazine writer Elizabeth Drew (1992), and ABC's Ted Koppel (1993). In addition, political scientist W. Lance Bennett (1993), among other media scholars, characterized the "talk show" phenomenon as just a new way in which candidates could market themselves and fabricate a "false sense of intimacy" between themselves and the audience. Both journalists and some media scholars characterized questions asked of the candidates by voters as far too easy and lacking any followups (see Chapters 4 and 5).

Nevertheless, even all of these critics of the phenomenon concede that there was a phenomenon: Voters were using alternatives to conventional media coverage of the presidential campaign. (These perceived changes in the relative importance of "media as usual" also need to be placed in the context of a decades-old drop in per-capita newspaper readership, as well as more recent losses in ABC, CBS, and NBC network news viewership.)

Getting back to Campaign '92: Without implying anything yet about whether this purported trend away from "old media" actually took place, we organized this study to test several propositions, one of which certainly was that it did.

DISENCHANTMENT WITH "POLITICS AS USUAL"?

Ross Perot ran against "politics as usual," many analysts agreed. Perot brought "fresh air into politics," wrote columnist Leslie Gelb in a year-end review. "There is such hunger in the land for something different," David Gergen (1992) wrote after Perot said on *Larry King Live* February 20 that he would be available if people put him on the ballot in all 50 states.

Auletta (1992) suggested that one of the major consequences of Ross Perot's populist campaign was to energize voters, to remind them that they could be more than just passive spectators. Perot's "let's take back government" appeal rapidly gathered momentum from its tentative start in February, even though initially the mainstream media did not pay much attention. By May, Perot led both Bush and a badly trailing Clinton in some polls. By California's June primary, exit pollsters reported that voters in both the Democratic and Republican primaries favored Perot in a three-man race (Brownstein, 1992; Hines, 1992).

"Can you imagine how terrible this election [campaign] would have been without [Perot]? He really did serve as a catalyst," Lawrence

Grossman, former president of NBC News, remarked in a postelection panel discussion at the Freedom Forum Media Studies Center (Pease, 1993, p. 152). Ross Perot was probably "the last, best hope of putting the deficit on the political agenda," columnist Mary McGrory wrote after Perot's sudden withdrawal in July (McGrory, 1992).

Before his departure, as Perot shot into the lead in the media "horse-race" polls, the news media began investigating him. One magazine report termed him a possible "electronic Caesar" (Dugger, 1992). Among other developments, the media reported: (a) Perot had hired private investigators to look into the private lives of present and former employees (media wags dubbed him "Inspector Perot" in a pun on the bumbling Peter Sellers character in the "Pink Panther" films); (b) he had obtained an early release from his Naval service, a release earlier than Naval Academy regulations usually required of its graduates; (c) he had studiously avoided launching an investigation of a man living on the fringes of the law when that man could help his overseas business interests (Albright, 1992); and (d) he had apparently offended an audience of N.A.A.C.P. members by referring to them as "you people." Political journalists besieged Perot's as-yet undeclared campaign with requests for press conferences, interviews, and so on.

When on July 17 Ross Perot dropped out of the race, many analysts noted he did it because the news media were beginning to ask damaging questions about his record. When he reentered the race just before the debates, Perot became "the political version of Rosie Ruiz, the woman who did the same in the Boston Marathon . . . treated as a curiosity by the press, but not as a man who could have been president of the United States," *Boston Phoenix* media critic Mark Jurkowitz said after the election (Pease, 1993, p. 150).

If Perot were a political version of Rosie Ruiz, his dropping out and reentering were noted far more fiercely from the start, unlike the live coverage when Ms. Ruiz suddenly (re)materialized in the Marathon. By this time, journalists were much more interested in who Ross Perot was than in what the millions he represented wanted and believed. This focus on Perot, and not the interlocked hopes of his followers, may have contributed to journalists' apparent surprise when Perot's long "infomercials" continued to attract large audiences, even on rebroadcast. Clearly, Perot's antipathy toward the national press did not endear him to journalists, who cut him very little slack. But journalists' relative disinterest in exploring the wishes and hopes of the Perot followers helped contribute to a journalistic climate in which Perot was regarded as having no chance of winning, and even his qualifications to run a credible candidacy seemed not to be taken seriously.

To a certain extent, grudging recognition eventually was given

Perot's rise from the depths of his July withdrawal to a 19% vote in the election. Perot " did demonstrate the capacity to tap into the widespread voter discontent of 1992" (Germond & Witcover, 1993, p. 9A). That percentage of the vote was higher than any third-party presidential candidate since Theodore Roosevelt.

In Chapter 6, we argue that most pundits were slow to pay attention to Perot's February 20 appearance on *Larry King Live*, that they harshly attacked Perot when he suddenly withdrew in July, and that they grossly underestimated him when he returned in early October. Meanwhile, the Bush White House covertly fed journalists damaging leaks about Perot's military career, his personal background, and so on. It is no wonder, then, that Perot ran against the Washington establishment that had so chastised him. But, as many analysts were not reluctant to point out, Perot did so without admitting that he had himself used his money and contacts from the past to manipulate that very same establishment.

Did political journalists ever get a handle on Perot? As discussed in Chapter 6, many of them consistently underestimated his appeal. Chapter 10, describes Perot's witty and telegenic performance in the first televised debate, for which he was praised, but then undercut in news media verdicts. Significantly, verdicts of any kind about Perot had almost disappeared by the time of the final presidential debate. Perot accused the press of bias against him: Newsweek ran covers that called him "The Quitter" (Morganthau, 1992) when he dropped out in July and called his re—entry in early October an "Ego Trip" ("Ego trip," 1992).

What kinds of voters were most likely to identify with Perot? Did the debates help legitimize Ross Perot's candidacy, a conclusion asserted by many analysts after the election? Through our voter surveys, we help answer these questions.

DISENCHANTMENT WITH POLITICAL ADS?

In 1988, the conventional political wisdom was that people hate attack ads, but the ads nevertheless work. Perhaps because they believed that conventional wisdom, the television networks replayed with unprecedented frequency excerpts from 1988 presidential polispots (see Lemert et al., 1991, pp. 244—248; Jamieson, 1992, pp. 123—159). In 1988, the news media acted like a big echo chamber, extending the "reach" of the ads with almost no assessment of their accuracy. Bush ad replays outnumbered those of Dukakis. Bush campaign wizard Roger Ailes's "Revolving Door," "Tank," and "Boston Harbor" spots joined the Presidential Victory Committee's "Willie Horton" spot as attacks on Dukakis that were boosted by extensive replays on network news.

Our survey data from the 1988 campaign (Lemert et al., 1991, pp. 219-237) suggested clearly that the first part of the conventional wisdom was right: People hated attack ads, all right. It was the second part that was off the mark. Our results showed that attack ads backfired in 1988—with voters, at least, if not with the media.

Questions of Evidence

Not all of the scholarly literature on the 1988 Bush attack ads agrees, however. with our findings of a voter backlash. In a series of secondary analyses based on data collected by others, West (1993) depended on a 4-point scale of attentiveness to presidential ads to assert that Bush's attack ads worked in certain respects against Dukakis in 1988. According to West's findings, the more attention paid to presidential campaign ads in 1988, the less important to voters were issues of Bush's environmental record and his reputation for not caring about people.

However, there seem to be two basic questions about West's 1988 data. First, it is never quite clear whether his measure of attention to the 1988 ads is specific to one side's ads and not the other's; and second, even if it does focus attention on one side's ads, it lumps together all the ads for that candidate. Our 1988 results showed clearly that *only the attack ads backfired*. In contrast, the positive ads were more successful.

In an appendix to his volume, West (1993, pp. 170-173), reported ads that were most often recalled in each presidential year from 1984 through 1992. And, although he doesn't use specific ads often in his results, he did use the Bush "Revolving Door" ad to assert that the ad heightened voter concern about law and order as an issue: "among those not seeing the ad, only 5% cited [law and order]," whereas 12% of those seeing the ad cited the issue (West, 1993, pp. 112-113). Unfortunately, even this comparison pits only one of a large number of ads against its absence. Other ads for that candidate apparently were not considered in the comparison. Nor was there a comparison of positive versus negative ads for that candidate.

One has to be careful in assessing West's results, because in some years he seems to have had better measures of ad exposure than he seems to have had in 1988. For example, in West's analysis of the North Carolina Senate race between Jesse Helms and Harvey Gantt in 1990, he implies that he was able to separate attention to Helms ads from attention to Gantt ads, but his analyses at the presidential level sometimes avoid making it clear whether the amount of attention to ads means the ads of one or of all sides. Based as much on what he does not say as what he does, it seems likely that his measures of ad exposure did separate exposure to each of the candidates' ads in some campaigns and some years but not in other campaigns and other years. Dependence on data gathered by others can produce problems such as this.

Unlike West's analyses of his 1988 presidential data, our analyses during both presidential campaigns *always* explicitly and separately measure exposure to Republican, Democratic, and (in 1992) Perot ads. Furthermore, we were able both in 1988 and 1992 to distinguish between—and *compare directly*—"attack" and positive ads, something that apparently West was unable or unwilling to do.

What we are arguing here is that in our study of the 1988 ad wars we know we had sensitive measures of ad exposure that differentiated among the types of ads seen; because of the way his results were reported, we do *not* know how sensitive and discriminating West's measures were for that same year.

What West and We Have in Common

We agree with West that survey data of sufficient sensitivity can be used, after suitable controls to eliminate spurious or "mirage" effects, to make some pretty strong statements about the effects of presidential ads. These powerful control techniques are possible when samples are large enough to make them possible. Our largest 1988 and 1992 survey samples—more than 2,000 in 1988 and some 1,433 interviewed between October 11 and 22, 1992—are quite comparable to West's data sets. But where we are skeptical of West's conclusions is whether his measures of ad exposure are of sufficient sensitivity to warrant his conclusions about 1988.

Turning to 1992, West (1993, pp. 113-114) asserts that Perot's infomercials and Clinton's "How You Doing?" spot each succeeded in focusing people's attention on the economy and jobs. West also asserts that when Bush was blamed for the negativity of campaign ads, his attack ads in 1992 were associated with a voter backlash.

In Chapter 12, we continue to rely on recall of ads, as did West, to measure exposure to ads, but believe that comparing attack versus positive ads *for the same candidate* is a necessary component of any analysis. In addition, looking at apparent direct effects *on voting* will be a central component in our analyses, whereas West's analyses tended to emphasize more cognitive effects that presumably would indirectly affect voting through changes in criteria voters use to assess the candidates.

The 1992 Ad Police?

In 1992, the conventional wisdom about ads seems to have been that the news media were doing a better job as the Fact Police for political ads, a trend that began for some congressional and gubernatorial races in 1990 among some newspapers and a few local television stations. In Chapter 12, we extend our historical analysis of television news coverage of the ads.

Perot Rejects Conventional Ads

Conventional spots were not Ross Perot's thing. Thirty-minute and 60-minute political commercials are not regarded as cost efficient by most campaign managers because voters can too easily avoid them. Yet Ross Perot's folksy, 30- and 60-minute "infomercials" got astonishingly high ratings, outdrawing the average regular network programs (Carter, 1992). A.C. Nielsen ratings for Perot's 17 infomercial broadcasts *averaged* an estimated 8,000,000 (as cited in Lebel, 1993).

Although the conventional news media often referred, in a somewhat bemused and surprised tone, to the size of Perot's audiences, we can question whether these journalists ever absorbed the implications of this apparent audience thirst for new information in the 1950s-style "talking head" Perotmercials. Perhaps the size of his audience meant people wanted the kinds of information and analysis Perot was giving them. Perhaps, in other words, at least some of Perot's millions of viewers felt they could get something from these lecture-style infomercials that conventional "horse-race" coverage denied them. In any case, did Perot's unconventional tactics once again steal a march on the two major-party candidates? What advertising tactics did the Bush and Clinton campaigns use?

Clinton, Bush Go Their Own Ways

In the meantime, Clinton and Bush campaigns stuck almost entirely with the repetitively played 15-, 30- and 60-second spots.[1] However, as Chapters 11 and 12 argue, Clinton clearly went to school on what happened to Dukakis in 1988: He had "rapid response" teams ready to fire their messages to journalists to rebut Bush ads and to produce and run rebuttal ads very quickly. Meanwhile, Bush's 1992 ad campaign produced many more spots than were actually run, an ironic similarity to what happened with Dukakis in 1988. Nevertheless, two of an interesting series of "shopping mall" spots tried to create a favorable "spin" or "verdict" about how Bush had done in the previous night's debate.

Study Questions about the Ads

Some of the many questions we try to answer in Chapter 12 include: When voters tried to recall presidential campaign ads, whose ads were most likely to come to mind? Is it necessarily a good thing to have your ads come to mind first? If voters were disgusted with the 1988 ad campaign, did George Bush pay a price for 1988 in 1992?

DISENCHANTMENT WITH THE 1988 CAMPAIGN?

Both the news media and our own research reported considerable voter disenchantment with the way the *1988* presidential campaign was conducted. In general, the news media consensus seemed to be that Democrat Michael Dukakis ran a poor campaign that failed to stimulate voters and challenge Bush to even address the policies of the Republican administration. And, as we have already seen, the media consensus was both that Bush's attack ads against Dukakis worked like a charm, even though voters hated their negativity.

In our book (Lemert et al., 1991), we reported many signs of distress and unhappiness with the way the 1988 Bush—Dukakis campaign had been conducted. Among other signals, respondents said they hated the 1988 attack ads—but (contrary to media wisdom) they backed up that dislike by *punishing* the candidate whose attack ad they recalled. A second sign of unhappiness was this finding: The later in the 1988 campaign we asked about support for the presidential debates, the lower the regard for them. Third, respondents in our 1988 surveys overwhelmingly agreed that there had been too much "mudslinging" in the presidential campaign.

Meanwhile, journalists covering the 1988 campaign rarely seemed to have either voters or voters' interests in mind. Increasingly over time, network news specials most easily defined the debates as important if they had an impact on the ambitions of the candidates, not if they served voters (see especially Chapter 5 in Lemert et al., 1991).

What about 1992?

If voters did not like the way the 1988 campaign went, presumably they would be more receptive to the "new politics" of 1992. Certainly a "new politics" label encompasses many possibilities—the shift to "talk-show" politics, to "infomercials" instead of spot ads, to greater audience control of the information to which they were exposed, and to much more open and less rigid formats in the Fall debates.

DISENCHANTMENT WITH THE PARTY CANDIDATES?

It almost goes without saying, given that Bush lost, that voters were disenchanted with his handling of the presidency, especially his handling of the economy. According to the Gallup Poll Monthly of April 1992 (p. 10), "Bush receives higher negative ratings than any incumbent president" since World War II, "including Jimmy Carter and Gerald Ford, the last two incumbents to suffer defeat." As Lipset (1993) and others have reminded us, people's perceptions of how the economy was doing were more important in their disenchantment with Bush than was what economists would like to call "reality."

The striking fact, however, is that *Bush still led* Clinton by a comfortable margin in the preference polls in that Spring Gallup report. Clinton, too, suffered from extremely high poll "negatives" during the Spring primaries. That same Gallup Poll Report showed roughly 4 in 10 registered voters held unfavorable attitudes toward Clinton, and it showed 54% believed that party primaries and caucuses were not a good way of determining who were the best qualified nominees.

Along comes Ross Perot, a still undeclared candidate on the rise in the polls. Already, by early April, he and Clinton were neck and neck for second place in the horse race. By May, Perot actually took a narrow lead in some polls—all before he had formally indicated whether he would be a candidate. Perot's lead would continue to grow in the first half of June, with Bush still well ahead of Clinton.

DISENCHANTMENT WITH PEROT?

When H. Ross Perot suddenly announced in mid-July that he would not be a candidate, many supporters felt he had betrayed them because they were well on the way toward fulfilling their part of a bargain they thought they had with Perot. On the *Larry King Live* talk show February 20, Perot had promised to run a "world-class" campaign if his supporters put him on the ballot in all 50 states. By the time of his withdrawal, it was clear that Perot was going to be on the ballot in every state.

In the immediate aftermath of his withdrawal, network news gave heavy emphasis to both live and taped interviews with discouraged and disheartened Perot volunteers, some of whom said they did not believe he had actually withdrawn (Perot must have some new move in mind) whereas a smaller number of others bitterly accused him of not being able to "take the heat."

Lipset (1993) argues that Perot's July withdrawal gave Clinton the lead he would never relinquish. The argument goes something like this. It was easier for Republicans to move from Bush to Perot than it would have been to move from Bush directly to Clinton. Having initially decided to vote for somebody other than Bush, once Perot made his disenchanting withdrawal, these Republican refugees then had to look for somebody besides Bush.

When Perot returned in October, the argument continues, even people who might have favored him did not believe he had much of a chance. Unlike John Anderson in 1980, however, Perot actually gained support as the election neared. Was this because, unlike Anderson, the people who voted for Perot increasingly believed that he could win, or did their Perot vote have other motives? We try to answer these questions in Chapter 6.

PURPOSES OF THIS STUDY

One of our purposes in doing this study is to assess the accuracy of many sweeping claims about what was going on in Campaign '92.

The New Conventional Wisdom

Even if only some of these claims are supported by our extensive survey and content-analytic data, the 1992 presidential campaign will rank as perhaps the most unique one in this century. If any of these changes become institutionalized as characteristics of The New Campaign, this presidential campaign will have been a profoundly important one.

Finally, depending on which of these changes were to become institutionalized, and depending on what we find out about the meaning of these new developments, this presidential campaign might also be recognized as sending a profoundly hopeful message to us about the American electorate.

As we've seen, the idea that the 1992 campaign may have been the time when voters permanently shunted aside the once-dominant news media has, ironically, become the new conventional wisdom about the 1992 campaign, just as the conventional wisdom during the 1988 presidential campaign was that the Roger Ailes-produced Bush attack ads were killing Michael Dukakis in the eyes of voters.

One of the pleasures of bringing to bear the power of modern social analytic techniques upon the recent past is that we can test such conventional wisdom much more carefully and rigorously than do the media savants.

We don't yet promise how many bits of conventional wisdom our results will challenge about 1992; but we do promise to identify many of them for you—and give them as good a shakedown test as our combined imaginations and resources permit.

Building Knowledge about Campaigns

A second broad purpose of this book is to test what the scholarly research community believes to be our knowledge about presidential debates, campaign advertising and nontraditional media, as well as to trace certain changes since 1976 in mainstream media coverage of the campaign.

The Debates. The debates probably have been the single presidential campaign communication event most often studied by political communication researchers, especially the year they started (1960) and the year they resumed (1976). But the remarkable format changes and the uniquely compressed timing of them in 1992 provide a chance to see how much we think we know about the presidential debates will hold up in these unusual circumstances.

In 1992, the first debate (October 11) had the customary moderator-journalist panel format. As we noted in our previous book, the candidates had always insisted that they face a panel of journalists, in the belief that the panel actually protected them from being fully exposed if they ran into trouble (see Lemert, et al., 1991, pp. 8-10). After the October 11 debate, though, formats were very different indeed.

On October 13 a strident and direct confrontation took place between vice presidential candidates Dan Quayle and Al Gore, interrupting and challenging each other, while Perot running mate James Stockdale stood by, apparently bemused. Characterized by some as resembling a "food fight," this debate provided no panel of journalists to protect Republican Quayle and Democrat Gore from each other.

In the October 15 "town hall" or "talk show" presidential debate a pre-selected audience of "undecided" voters asked direct questions of the candidates, with one audience member asking Bush in effect to change debate tactics and another asking him repeatedly to demonstrate that he understood how hard times were hurting people like her.

"The resounding thud that greeted President Bush's apparent inability to appreciate the [recession's] human toll" came across more clearly to the electorate than to the media covering the debate, wrote analyst Gregory G. Lebel (1993, p. 31). If this is so, it would mark a decided change from 1988, when we found (Lemert et al., 1991, Chapters 6, 7 and 8) that many voters seemed at least temporarily dependent on media lysts to tell them who won—or lost. The audience-participation format of the October 15 debate, however, may have made it much easier for viewers to discern who was in trouble, a case we and others have argued might happen with debate format changes (e.g., Lemert et al., 1991). Lebel (1993, p. 31) also implied that journalists had much more mixed views toward the quality of the October 15 debate than did voters. Our content analyses and survey data will allow us to assess these claims.

On October 19, a final debate provided a "half 'n half" mixture of the moderator-only format followed by the conventional moderator-panel format. Given 1992's remarkable variations from the debate format used in the Fall campaigns from 1976 through 1988, did voters become more positive about the debates over time in 1992 rather than less so—as happened in our 1988 study?

Here are some of the research questions we will be asking:

- Over time in 1988, voter interest in, and expectations for, the presidential debates declined as the debates proceeded. Did the same pattern happen in 1992? We have asked many of the same questions about the debates as a political institution as we asked in 1988, so we can trace change in support for the debates in the same way over time in 1992.
- Although the news media generally have either ignored or downplayed the effects of the debates in informing the audience, most of the research (e.g., Lemert, 1993; Sears & Chaffee, 1979) on debates suggests that they do, indeed, contribute to voter knowledge, and some research (Lemert et al., 1983) suggests that they can stimulate interest in the campaign. We know that the audience was quite large for the unusual 1992 debates; did they contribute to voter knowledge?
- How did journalists and viewers react to 1992's radical variations on, and departures from, the conventional journalist-panel format used in Fall campaign debates since 1976? At the end of the campaign, was respondent support for the debates as a political institution higher than in 1988? Which debate format received "better press" among journalists? Which was preferred by the most survey respondents?
- Given 1992's emphasis on "talk-show" politics and voter-driven media, did 1992 see a shift by journalists back toward more concern about how voters made use of the debates? Compared with previous presidential years, did television coverage of the 1992 debates display greater awareness that audience use of the debates could make debates important, whether the debates affected any candidate's electoral ambitions?

- If voters in 1992 learned to bypass journalists and communicate directly with the candidates, then shouldn't *news verdicts* about who did well in the debates have less power to influence voters than they did in 1988?

Much of our 1988 study was designed to study whether there was a "news verdict effect." A verdict effect occurs when people who have watched both a debate and subsequent news analysis interpret the debate more along the lines of the news analysis than do people who have watched only the debate. In 1988, we found a verdict effect after each of the three debates (Lemert et al., 1991, Chapters 5, 6, and 7; also see Elliott & Sothirajah, 1993). The verdict effect was most striking and most long-lasting after the Quayle—Bentsen debate in 1988: People who watched post debate news analyses that criticized Quayle's 1988 debate performance were much more likely to say Quayle did poorly than people who had watched only the debate. Similarly, Lloyd Bentsen's debate performance was regarded more favorably by those who watched postdebate analysis than by those watching only the debate.

This verdict effect sat on top of, and modified, up or down, a stronger "wishful thinking effect," in which people tend to think the debater they are rooting for does better than the debater(s) they are rooting against. In other words, historically the best single predictor of who the individual thinks did well in the debate is whom he or she is rooting for. Nevertheless, it was clear that the verdict effect was an important supplementary influence on who people thought did well. In the case of Dan Quayle, the verdict effect clearly influenced people who thought of themselves as Republicans as well as those we would expect—Democrats.

As we did in 1988, we designed our surveys to capture a verdict effect if it occurs. This *time-series* survey design requires that we do our best to interview as many people as we can just after the end of the debate—presumably before they could have been exposed to postdebate analyses—and then interview other groups of people on successive nights after the debate.

The peculiarly compressed character of the 1992 debates may make it hard to demonstrate a verdict effect because the aftermath of one debate often overlapped with the aftermath of an earlier one. This could well interfere with the strength and longevity of a potential verdict about the earlier debate. As the reader will recall, four 1992 debates were crammed into a total of nine October days. In contrast, the three 1988 debates were on September 25, October 5 (Quayle-Bentsen), and October 13, separated by more than a week in every case.

So, if we find evidence of a verdict effect in 1992, it would most likely be despite the timing of the debates. From the point of view of media attention spans, the timing of these debates presents a formidable challenge to a media verdict effect because we expect each debate to have a very short life span as the center of media attention. Therefore, there will be very little chance for verdicts about who did well in a given debate to be repeated by the news media long enough for the verdict to diffuse among the population. We think that one of the reasons the Quayle verdict in 1988 seemed to last so long was that the Bush campaign's decision to "hide" Quayle after the debate gave network journalists an easy opportunity to repeat, over an extended period of time, the negative verdict as the explanation for Quayle's absence. Meanwhile, Dukakis and Bentsen were inseparable over the same extended period. Nevertheless, media attention to Quayle-Bentsen began to fade a few days before the upcoming final debate between Bush and Dukakis.

Additional reasons why we might find a much weakened news verdict effect in 1992 have already been implied earlier: Maybe voters were rebelling against media-imposed verdicts; maybe debate formats made it easier for people to see who was in trouble.

The 1992 Ad Wars. The three-way ad wars were a mixture of the old, the previously discarded, and the new. It is worth remembering that an ad tactic that may have been successful in the past—or one that previously backfired, for that matter—may not necessarily have the same effect in the next campaign, in which the candidates, the context, and what is on people's minds may be different. In any case, here are some of the research questions we ask about 1992's presidential campaign ads.

- Whose campaign ads were recalled best? Did "attack ads" backfire as they seemed to do in 1988?
- Because journalists in 1988 believed the battle of the attack ads to be so devastating to the Dukakis campaign, they seemed to fall victim to what the research literature (e.g., Davison, 1983; Lasorsa, 1992) calls *the third-person effect.* Did the same thing happen in 1992?

The third-person effect occurs when an observer of a message believes that the message will have a powerful persuasive effect on the masses. Whereas the observer (journalists, in this case) feels personally invulnerable to the effects of that message, he or she actually changes his or her behavior in anticipation of that persuasive effect. In the case of journalists in 1988, they gave unprecedented (and uncritical) airplay to the 1988 attack ads and made Roger Ailes a national media figure. Never before had network television news rebroadcast presidential campaign ads so many times. The Vanderbilt Television News Index showed that network television news carried more than three times as many excerpts of 1988 presidential ads as in 1980, the year with the previous high.

Arguably, another sign of an ad-based third-person effect was the expectation by journalists that, with slightly more than three weeks left in the Bush-Dukakis campaign, the only remaining chance Dukakis had to beat Bush was the final debate. Both before and immediately after that October 13 debate, journalists said that the debate was the only remaining arrow in Dukakis's bow. In other words, Dukakis was presumed to be hopelessly outclassed in the Battle of the Attack Ads. The Bush ads seemed far superior to journalists, who proceeded to assume that they therefore were more persuasive (see Lemert et al., 1991 Chapters 10 and 11). When in the debate Dukakis failed to score a "knockout" (an alternative metaphor was "hit a home run"), the game was over—with three weeks left in the campaign. Granted, Dukakis was trailing badly in the polls by that time. Nevertheless, journalists' perceptions that the Bush ads worked probably changed how they covered the 1988 campaign. So, did the news media continue to cover the advertising campaign the same way as they had in 1988, or did they downplay the ads in 1992?

Alternative Media. As we have seen, 1992 was widely declared to be the campaign in which voters and candidates figured out ways of eliminating the conventional news media as the only way of communicating with each other. Because we are examining talk shows and other alternative media in only one campaign in this book, we will need to observe later campaigns in order to make a more complete assessment of how long-lasting and fundamental this change is going to be.

We strongly suspect that the key indicator of how profoundly changed presidential campaigns have been is not so much what the candidates do as it is what the audience and the conventional news media do. Although what candidates do is always important, candidates have always sought ways to get around the conventional news media. From their perspective, the major difference is that there are many more ways to do that now.

Perhaps never before have the conventional news media shown as many signs of awareness that the audience wants something it has not been getting from them. As discussed earlier, *Newsweek's* Jonathan Alter in June (1992) declared that the mainstream news media "lost control" of the 1992 campaign agenda. Furthermore, also before the 1992 campaign was over, the morning news shows—*Good Morning America, Today,* and *This Morning*—frequently shifted into what might be called a "town-hall/talk-show" format with, for example, Bush answering questions from a group of surprised tourists on the grounds of the White House. It is one thing to be aware of what is happening, however, and quite another to make wholesale changes in what you are doing, especially when you do not feel you can alter long-planned news resource allocations. In other words, even if they wanted to make changes, could the ABC, CBS and NBC evening newscasts, with their much more rigidly constrained formats and extremely limited time of approximately 22 minutes for the news, do what the two-hour morning news shows did? As for the print media, although the *Charlotte Observer* and *Wichita Eagle* showed that they were both willing and able to make very great changes in the way they organized their campaign news operations, those changes were planned well ahead of the campaign, not in the middle of it. Also, the closest a newspaper could come to a "town hall" meeting would have been to sponsor one—which several did.

Given the emergent nature of the shift away from the conventional news channels in 1992, then, perhaps massive changes would have been too much to expect of the conventional media *during* the campaign. Because of these time- and media-related constraints, we actually may have to wait until the 1996 presidential campaign to see how many lessons from 1992 have led to actual changes by the conventional news media in their presidential campaign coverage.

Nonetheless, we *can* take a close look at how key news media personnel—the journalists who covered the 1992 presidential campaign—were reacting to the shift away from "media as usual." If they reacted with hostility—especially if they remained hostile to the phenomenon after the campaign was over, and they presumably had taken time to reflect on the situation—we may be able to conclude tentatively that the odds are poor that these journalists, will be interested in changing the way they do things in 1996. Chapter 4 takes a close look at the way the conventional news media characterized the phenomenon during, and after, the 1992 campaign:

- Did national political journalists react defensively to the "talk-show" movement?
- What criticisms did conventional news media make of talk shows and other alternatives as ways of learning about the candidates?
- Were journalists more likely than anybody else to criticize the quality of information produced by these alternative communication channels?
- Did the amount of hostility in the news toward the alternative campaign media diminish after the campaign was over?

One of the reasons that presidential debates are beginning to become institutionalized is that candidates know they are expected to debate. Clearly, even though the Bush campaign was unenthusiastic about doing the debates, it did them. Goading from demonstrators, most especially from a voter dressed up in a "Chicken George" suit, clearly flustered and embarrassed Bush (see Chapter 7). But, in comparison to the debates, how deeply rooted did the talk shows become in voter's information-seeking habits? Arguably, both debates and talk shows allow viewers to observe the behavior of the candidates and to hear their policy views at far greater lengths than the notorious 9-second TV news sound bite.

The following are some of the questions we ask that may tell us a lot about voter use of, and reliance on, candidate talk-show appearances:

- As direct-observation methods of finding out about the candidates, how did the talk shows compare with the debates in viewers' evaluations?
- If "talk-show politics" were popular with our survey respondents, was the October 15 audience-participation debate also popular with viewers? If so, can we sort out whether that debate, in turn, helped boost the perceived value of the talk shows?
- In comparison to a variety of more conventional ways of finding out about the presidential candidates, how did our survey respondents rate candidate talk shows? Did they give them better or worse marks than for example, news interview shows?
- Was exposure to talk shows as nearly universal as it was to the debates? Who seemed to be the heaviest viewers, and what were they like?
- Was there any single candidate talk show appearance that garnered the most viewers? Did Ross Perot's appearances get a larger audience than Bill Clinton's? Than George Bush's?

Ross Perot. Ross Perot received a higher percentage of the presidential vote than any third-party candidate since Teddy Roosevelt. Another way of putting this is that the absolute number of popular votes he received was higher than any third-party candidate in U.S. history. Beyond the raw numbers, though, we need to know a lot more about the role Ross Perot played in the 1992 election: What kind(s) of voters were most likely to support Ross Perot? Perot's "take charge" rhetoric and his calls for citizens to retake control of government suggest that Perot supporters will have higher "internal efficacy" and lower "external efficacy" compared to Clinton supporters (Craig, Niemi, & Silver, 1990).

Political scientists have long been interested in the study of feelings of political efficacy. In general, the more positive the efficacy feelings, the more likely the person is to vote and engage in other political activity. More recently, it has become apparent that one needs to distinguish between two senses of efficacy: *internal*, which roughly corresponds to the amount of confidence a person has in her or his own personal political skills and effectiveness; and *external*, which generally corresponds to whether or not the person feels government and its officials are responsive and concerned about how citizens feel. In principle, all possible combinations of the two senses of efficacy are possible. Our reasoning is that people with high internal but low external efficacy would have enough faith in their own judgment to consider Perot—and enough cynicism about "politics as usual" to make that leap:

- If Perot supporters have faith in their personal ability to understand politics, yet are cynical about "politics as usual," will they be more receptive to direct-observation experiences like the debates and talk shows, and will their cynicism decline over the campaign if they regard the debates and talk shows as valuable to them?
- From whom did Perot seem to drain away more votes, Bush or Clinton?
- How was Perot treated by the news media in Campaign '92? Did he have a case that the media were biased against him and his cause?

CONVERGENT RESEARCH APPROACHES

These are some of the questions we try to answer using a powerful combination of these research approaches:

- several analyses of media content during the Fall campaign—the *content analyses*,
- survey interviews with separate samples of respondents just after Labor Day and October 11—22, the time of the debates and their immediate aftermath, which we call the debate *time series*; and
- a series of interviews with a smaller number of respondents three times during the campaign: just after Labor Day, once during the October 11—22 period, and just before the November 3 election day, which collectively we call *the panel*.

Increasingly, when social researchers have the resources to do it, we see them challenging, sifting, and refining their conclusions through a series of independent but convergent observations. In our case, instead of relying exclusively on surveys of voter reactions to the campaign, we collect and measure the media campaign content that may contribute to those reactions. Then we organize our time-series surveys to capture reactions to certain kinds of content at the times that the content we identified ought to have its greatest impact. Furthermore, by interviewing both a panel (the same people repeatedly) *and* an independent, daily-changing sample of respondents, we gain both the sensitivity to daily events provided by a large-sample time series and the panel's sensitivity to changes that an individual might experience over time. If we find that reactions by the panelists at any given time are the same as those displayed at that time by time-series respondents, we have gained reassurance from the time series that the changes shown by panelists are not the result of having been interviewed before. By showing changes taking place among panelists, the panel also can reinforce conclusions about the dynamics of the campaign that have been based on the single-interview time series.

ORGANIZATION OF THE BOOK

Chapter 2 provides a much more detailed description of these convergent methodologies. The reader should know we applied a similar convergence of methodologies to the 1988 campaign, allowing us both to draw a number of strong (and occasionally surprising) conclusions and to provide the most convincing and sensitive evidence for some more conventional conclusions about the debates and the media's role in the presidential campaign. Chapter 2 describes our study methodology. The general reader should read enough of Chapter 2 to pick up our vocabulary and to get a sense of why we think we have an extraordinarily strong and sensitive design.

This first chapter provided a general overview of our project. It, together with Chapter 2, comprises an introduction to what we are doing—and why. The remaining chapters are divided into four more sections.

In the first of these four parts, we consider the phenomenon of "talk show" or "new media" politics from a variety of points of view, including (a) the attitudes, goals, and expectations of the campaigns and TV producers concerning candidates' appearances on talk shows (Chapter 3); (b) mainstream journalists' treatment of the phenomenon (Chapter 4); (c) audience attention, learning, and attitudes toward talk shows (Chapter 5); and (d) the Ross Perot phenomenon (Chapter 6).

The second section focuses on the debates. Through the years, it appears that televised presidential debates have become institutionalized—people expect the candidates to debate, and the price of refusing to debate is seemingly becoming very high. The maneuvering prior to the 1992 debates clearly suggests that neither an incumbent president nor his challenger wanted to be blamed for the potential cancellation of the Fall debates (Chapter 7). Chapter 8 concentrates on what the debates add to the campaign process, which may certainly include acting as "teacher" of the electorate (e.g., Lemert, 1993; Lemert et al., 1983; Sears & Chaffee, 1979; Zhu, Milavsky, & Biswas, 1994). Chapter 9 asks whether we had another news "verdict effect" in the 1992 campaign. Chapter 10 describes how firmly supported the debates are in media coverage and in our surveys of potential voters.

The book's third section groups together chapters about each campaign's "quick-response teams" (Chapter 11), the effects of their advertising strategies (Chapter 12), and the role of media polling in the campaign (Chapter 13).

The final section of this book summarizes our findings and speculates about whether Campaign '92 represents the beginning of a new era in presidential campaigns.

ENDNOTE

1. Clinton did use a biographical film first played during the Democratic Party convention for a 30-minute paid program on the eve of the election. Other than that, his ads were in the much harder to avoid short format.

REFERENCES

Albright, J. (1992, June 29). Perot didn't probe one partner's scandals. *Houston Chronicle*, p. B-8.

Auletta, K. (1992, November). How the politicians and the public stopped reading newspapers and listening to Sam Donaldson and learned to loathe the media: An election-year anatomy of an institution in decline," *Esquire*, pp. 107, 112, 177, 179, 181, 182.

Bennett, W.L. (1993, November). *Talk show democracy*. Paper presented to the Speech Communication Association, Miami Beach.

Brownstein, R. (1992, June 3). Both parties favored Perot, exit poll shows. *Los Angeles Times*, p. A1.

Carter, B. (1992, October 13). Networks fret about loss of prime-time viewers. *The Register-Guard* (Eugene, Oregon), p. 8D.

Craig, S.C., Niemi, R.G., & Silver, G.E. (1990). Political efficacy and trust: A report on the NES pilot study items. *Political Behavior, 12,* 289-314.

Davison, W.P. (1983) The third-person effect in communication. *Public Opinion Quarterly, 65,* 91-106.

Drew, E. (1992, October 17). Interviewed by Daniel Schorr on *Weekend Edition,* National Public Radio.

Dugger, R. (1992, June 15). Electronic Caesar? Who is Ross Perot?, part one. *The Nation,* p. 813.

Ego trip: From the moment Ross Perot quit the race in July, he began planning his 'October surprise' return. The inside story of how he did it and how he might change the debate on the issues." (1992, October 12). *Newsweek* cover.

Elliott, W.R., & Sothirajah, J. (1993). Post-debate analysis and media reliance: influence on candidate image and voting probabilities. *Journalism Quarterly, 70,* 321-335.

Freedom Forum Media Studies Center (1993). *The finish line: Covering the campaign's final days.* New York: The Freedom Forum Media Studies Center at Columbia University.

The Gallup Poll Monthly (1992, April), No. 319.

Gelb, L. (1992, December 28). Those who deserve praise in '92. *The Register-Guard* (Eugene, Oregon), p. 10A.

Gergen, D. (1992, March 29). Ross Perot as nation's man on horseback; Outsider: A self-made billionaire seems poised to launch an independent presidential campaign, and the public has been encouraging." *The Los Angeles Times,* p. M1.

Germond, J., & Witcover, J. (1993, January 13). Perot's 'crazy'—crazy like a fox. *The Register-Guard* (Eugene, Oregon), p. 9A.

Hines, C. (1992, June 3). Primary Finale sets up three-man race; Clinton, Bush win as Perot shows political muscle. *The Houston Chronicle,* p. A1.

Jamieson, K.H. (1992). *Dirty politics.* New York: Oxford University Press.

Koppel, T. (1993, February 10). Dial-in democracy: Clinton's town meeting," *Nightline.*

Lasorsa, D.L. (1992). Policymakers and the third-person effect. In J.D. Kennamer (Ed.), *Public opinion, the press, and public policy* (pp. 163-175). Westport, Ct.: Praeger.

Lebel, G.G. (1993, January). Pop go the weasels. *Campaign,* pp. 30-32.

Lemert, J.B., Elliott, W.R., Bernstein, J.M., Rosenberg, W.L., & Nestvold, K.J. (1991). *News verdicts, the debates, and presidential campaigns.* New York: Praeger.

Lipset, S.M. (1993, March). The significance of the 1993 election. *PS: Political Science & Politics, 26,* 7-16.

McGrory, M. (1992, August 10). After Perot, candidates steer clear of the deficit. *The Register-Guard* (Eugene, Oregon), p. 9A.

Morganthau, T. (1992, July 27). The quitter: Why Perot bowed out. *Newsweek,* pp. 28-30.

Novak, R. (1992, October 17). Review of the presidential debates. *The Capital Gang*, CNN Transcript #41-1.

Pease, E.C. (Ed.). (1993, January). The media scoreboard, final round: lessons of campaign '92. In The Research Group, The Freedom Forum Media Studies Center, *The finish line: Covering the campaign's final days* (pp. 137-153). New York: The Freedom Forum Media Studies Center. January 1993.

Sears, D.O., & Chaffee, S.H. (1979). Uses and effects of the 1976 debates: An overview of empirical studies. In S. Kraus (Ed.), *The great debates: Carter vs. Ford, 1976* (pp. 223-261). Bloomington: Indiana University Press.

Shaw, D. (1993a, March 31). Trust in media is on decline. *The Los Angeles Times*, pp. A1, A14, A15, A17, A18.

Shaw, D. (1993b, April 1). Distrustful public views media as 'them'—not 'us.' *The Los Angeles Times*, pp. A1, A18, A19.

Topping, S. (1993, April). A note from the president. *The Bulletin of the American Society of Newspaper Editors*, pp. 2, 20-21.

West, D.M. (1993). *Air wars: Television advertising in election campaigns, 1952-1992*. Washington, D.C.: Congressional Quarterly, Inc.

Zhu, J.H., Milavsky, J.R., & Biswas, R. (1994). Do televised debates affect image perception more than issue knowledge? A study of the first 1992 presidential debate. *Human Communication Research, 20*, 302-333.

2

Methods

William R. Elliott

This is our third study of presidential candidate campaign debates. In 1980, we (Lemert, Elliott, Nestvold, & Rarick, 1983) used a quasi-experimental design to test the influence of primary campaign debates during the 1980 campaign year. Over the years, the research team and the scope of the research have changed. For the 1988 campaign, we expanded our study to include Carbondale, Illinois, and Philadelphia, Pennsylvania, in addition to Eugene, Oregon (Lemert, Elliott, Bernstein, Rosenberg, & Nestvold, 1991). Not surprisingly, when the 1992 campaign was being planned, we joined to look at media influences on presidential campaigns and decision making. For 1992, we added a fourth location—Indianapolis, Indiana. In addition, we conducted more of our interviewing in the rural areas surrounding Carbondale, Illinois, giving that sample a less urban demographic.

Our previous studies, particularly the study of the 1988 campaign, relied primarily on two mass communication research strategies: content analysis and survey research. For this study, we extended our range of methods to include more extensive interpersonal interviews with campaign decision makers in addition to content analysis and survey research. This three-method attack overcomes some of the problems that have limited the use of many mass communication research efforts typically fail simultaneously to include message production, message content, and the joint impact of message content and media exposure.

By interviewing decision makers, we have been able to learn more about the strategies and decisions that shape the messages reaching voters. Next, by closely examining the content of campaign advertising and news reports, we are able to understand the campaign messages created by campaign decision makers and the press. And by looking at voter exposure to campaign messages, news reports, and events, we are able to determine the impact of messages on the attitudes, knowledge, and intended voting behavior of the people we interviewed. Thus, we hope we have remedied some of the concerns raised by Shoemaker and Reese (1991) about studies that look only at some segments of the communication process, rather than all of them.

THE SCOPE OF THE PRESENT STUDY

We designed and conducted a study that uses several methodologies to broaden our understanding of the relationships between the creation of media messages, the media messages themselves, and the influence of these messages on an audience. In making this attempt, we brought together three research traditions and methodologies: the journalistic interview, content analysis, and survey research.

In Chapter 3, "The Use of Nontraditional Media in Campaign '92 and Its Implications," we combined historical narrative with journalistic interviews to explore what was different about the "nontraditional" media and how the campaign participants—candidates, staff, media personnel—viewed the changes in political campaigning. Here the tradition is decidedly qualitative, an attempt to both read between the lines of the campaign rhetoric and to integrate the rhetoric with what we have learned elsewhere. We attempted, throughout the book, to merge qualitative synthesis with traditional "objective" sources of information about Campaign '92.

We also relied on quantitatively based content analysis. Although content analysis extends beyond the strictly qualitative, quantification remains an important element within the mainstream of content-analytic studies. In this book, the quantitative approach (Stempel, 1989) is used to investigate the media "verdicts" regarding candidate "winners" and "losers," to analyze how the media evaluated the debates as an institution, and to investigate the mainstream media response to the rising use of nontraditional media by campaigners and voters.

Our third methodology—survey research—allows us to tie media use to the attitudes, knowledge, and behaviors of the audience. By analyzing the responses of adults sampled from four sites, we are able to see how the campaign media, which we characterized as traditional and nontraditional, influenced the mass public in 1992. Bringing our three methods together, we can provide a picture of the structure, content, and effects of the 1992 campaign for President of the United States.

ADVANTAGES AND DISADVANTAGES OF EACH DESIGN

Journalists collect information by talking with people, taking careful notes, and working from their notes to construct the "facts" surrounding an event. We used the same techniques when we interviewed campaign staff members to construct our "facts" about how the campaigns were put together. No one can discount the importance of this way of gathering information in getting at the reasons why things happen as they do. Elite interviewing allows us to talk directly to people who formulate policy, who develop the strategies for a political campaign, who create messages, who decide where and when to hold a town meeting, and who decide when, where, and how many debates will take place.

Interview information provides depth and substance for our research. However, the journalistic interview, by itself, is flawed. Among its problems is the possibility that elite "insiders" may have their own agendas in mind when describing their decisions. The journalistic interview, which thus depends on the selective memory of the people being interviewed, can only provide a restricted set of information. It can give us part of the answer but, by itself, it is not enough.

Content analysis has proven its worth many times. For example, Herman and Chomsky (1988) used content analysis to document what they felt was a pro-U.S. government bias by the mainstream press in its coverage of Central America and Eastern Europe. Content analysis can often make us aware of how the media portray some segment of reality. It can be a powerful tool. Still, content analysis cannot tell us of the motives of the message creators. It cannot tell us about the impact of a message. It cannot even tell us if the message has been read, seen, or heard. As valuable a tool as content analysis is, by itself it provides only a portion of the story. In something as fluid and fast-changing as a presidential political campaign, at its best content analysis can only provide a snapshot view of some of the information that is available to the electorate. By itself, that snapshot is not enough.

Survey analysis allows us to go directly to the people who vote—the ultimate political decision makers. By using complex survey designs, as we have done in this study, details of media influence on the electorate become visible.

By using a *panel* design in which we interview the same people at several different times during the campaign, we can determine if and how they change their ideas, attitudes, and behavior over the course of the campaign. Did the people interviewed in September change their ideas of the candidates by the time of the first debate? The vice presidential debate? The second debate? The third debate? The election? Did people's knowledge of the issues change as the campaign progressed? A panel study, of the type we used, can provide some of the answers.

By designing our survey around the presidential candidate debates and looking for changes in audience response, it becomes possible to determine the influence of the debates and post-debate analysis on the audience. When a survey is designed to track changes in the population over time, as we did over the period of the debates, it is called a *trend* study (Shoemaker & McCombs, 1989). A trend study (often referred to in this book as a *time series* or the *debate time series*) has many benefits that complement the *panel* design. A time series interviews respondents just once, but spreads the interviews over a series of days. Although identifying specific individuals who changed (e.g., their viewing habits, knowledge, candidate preferences) is not possible because the respondents were interviewed only once, nevertheless each day's separate samples can suggest trends taking place in response to specific events such as the debates, because we can compare what people are saying the day before the event against what another, comparable group of people is saying right after the debate, 24 hours later, 48 hours later, and so on. If each day's sample is large enough, we can get a fairly stable estimate of how people are reacting that day. When interviews with a large enough sample take place each day, a time series can sensitively pick up reactions to events that took place almost immediately before the interview, while memories (and reactions) are relatively fresh.

We use what Cook and Campbell (1979) call a "simple interrupted time series design." A communication event such as a debate is the "interruption" whose effects may play out over a series of days. The lay reader may be familiar with the term *tracking polls*, run day by day by both the campaigns and the news media, which represent a subtype of the time series. Tracking polls are meant to provide sensitive measures of reactions to specific developments during a campaign.

One possible disadvantage of a panel is that the way respondents react to a second and third interview might in several ways have been changed because we had already interviewed them at least once before.

The time series protects against that possibility by allowing us to compare how panelists are reacting at any given time with how trend/time-series respondents respond to the same questions. If there was no difference between the panelists and single-interview time-series respondents, then panelists most likely were not "sensitized" by a previous interview. On the other hand, a trend study implies change over time, but cannot demonstrate it directly because nobody is interviewed more than once. So each survey design compensates for the weakness of the other.

Panel studies like the one we have done are costly. In panel studies, attrition is an unavoidable problem. In a panel study of the 1992 election (McLeod et al. 1993), only 65% of the 202 potential voters interviewed in August 1992 were available for reinterview between late October and election day. In our own study, just 71% of our 209 panelists were interviewed the ideal of three times. Panel studies, with consequent attrition, require higher initial samples and higher resulting total costs.

Like the journalist interview and content analysis, survey research is best combined with other approaches. But the survey designs we have used—the panel study and the cross-sectional trend study—are expensive. Between the first debate on October 11 and our last debate-period interview on October 22, we interviewed 1,433 respondents. On average, that is about 120 per night. We were fortunate to have financial support from the Frank Allen family and the Dow Jones Fund. Without that support, this study could not have been completed.

Given the various disadvantages, it might seem futile to attempt such large studies. Obviously, we do not agree. We feel that the procedure used in this study, a procedure combining three methodologies and using the results from each of the methodologies as a tap on one part of the campaign process, represents a significant improvement over many studies that use only one technique. More details about how and when each of these methodologies was applied are presented next.

JOURNALISTIC INTERVIEWS WITH CAMPAIGN DECISION MAKERS

People involved directly in the campaign can provide information about campaign activities and strategies that is impossible to gather any other way. During the 1988 campaign, we used such interviews only with two officials of the League of Women Voters to illuminate the League's decision not to sponsor the final debate (Lemert et al., 1991, pp. 101-106). Chapter 3 presents results from interpersonal interviews with a major figure from each 1992 campaign organization. We talked with Torie Clark, the communication director of the Bush-Quayle campaign; Jeff

Eller, political consultant for the Clinton campaign; and Sharon Holman, press secretary for United We Stand, the organization behind Perot's candidacy. These interviews add to our understanding of why the candidates either used or avoided television talk shows, radio talk shows, electronic town meetings, and popular-culture programs such as MTV, *Donahue*, and *Arsenio Hall*.

THE CONTENT ANALYSES

We conducted several quantitative content-analytic studies. In Chapter 4, "Talk Shows and the News," we employed content analysis to look at the way traditional news media responded to how the candidates used television talk show programs to bypass them, sending their message directly to the voters. We were interested in the way journalists characterized the questions asked by "regular" people on the talk shows, how the performance of talk show hosts was described in the mainstream media, and how media professionals evaluated the quality of the information from the talk shows.

Content analysis also plays a significant role in Chapter 9, "News Verdicts and Verdict Effects." Separate analyses were done of network evening newscasts and of postdebate news specials. We analyzed network news coverage of the debates in terms of the "verdicts" concerning candidate performance. The effect of these verdicts on our survey respondents (and the consequent integration of survey analysis with content analysis) is also analyzed in Chapter 9. Because we had asked similar survey questions in 1988, we were able to make comparisons as well between the 1988 and 1992 campaigns.

The third chapter that presents content-analytic results deals with media responses to the presidential and vice presidential debates as a political institution (Chapter 10). As is true of the "verdicts" chapter, content analysis and survey results both were used. Two samples of content—network news specials after the debates and a combined print-broadcast sample—were drawn and examined to see how the media portrayed the debates as a part of our political culture. For the network news specials, we actually have similar content-analytic results going back through the 1976 campaign, thus allowing us to trace campaign-by-campaign changes. Among other advantages given us by our second content sample—the combined print-broadcast sample—we can compare how the media treated a given 1992 debate before as well as after it occurred. Some very revealing before versus after discrepancies emerged.

Traditional Media React to the Talk Shows (Chapter 4)

Determining the reaction of the traditional media to the use of nontraditional media during the 1992 campaign required a method for locating mainstream media stories about the use of talk shows, MTV, *Arsenio Hall*, *Donahue*, *Larry King Live*, *Oprah*, and so on, in the campaign. Using keywords such as *talk show*, we looked for relevant articles and news stories in major papers, broadcast transcripts, wire services, and magazine files as listed with the Nexis database service.

We restricted the time frame to a 13-month period running from December 1991 through 1992. This time frame was divided into four segments. The first, which covered the entire primary season, ran from December 1991 through June 10, 1992. The second period ran through Summer 1992 to the day before Labor Day—from the end of the primaries to just before the start of the traditional campaign. The third time frame went from Labor Day—the "official" start of the campaign—through election day. The final period started on the day after the election and ran through the end of the year. Coverage of this final period allowed us to investigate the postcampaign analyses assessing the impact of nontraditional media on the campaign outcomes. Presumably, journalists would have had the chance to reflect on the impact after the campaign was over.

One dozen stories were randomly selected from each time period. These were then analyzed for the number of assertions dealing with nontraditional media. More than 900 such assertions were identified. These assertions were coded along a number of attributes, including how journalists characterized citizen participation and the talk show hosts, how they evaluated the quality of information available from nontraditional media, and how the media addressed questions of control and citizen empowerment resulting from the rise of nontraditional media in campaign '92.

News Verdicts in Newscast and News Specials (Chapter 9)

In our previous book, we reported network news "verdict" results from each of two separate samples: the regular evening newscasts and the news specials following each debate. Both of these samples stretched from the 1988 campaign through 1976, thus allowing a number of historical comparisons. By including the data collected in 1992, we are now able to look at the changes taking place over five presidential campaigns, not to mention being able to compare what was happening from debate to debate in 1992.

For the 1976, 1980, 1984, and 1988 newscast content study we analyzed evening newscasts by ABC and NBC one and four days after each debate. This technique allowed us to determine immediate newscast response (the first regular newscast after the debate) and then after enough time has elapsed so that summary judgments regarding the debates would be possible (four days after the debate).

Because of the more compressed timing of the debates in 1992 (presidential debates on October 11, 15, and 19 and a vice presidential debate on October 13), we performed our newscast content analyses for 1992 one and three days after each presidential debate. This provided measures of media response to the debates on the day after each presidential debate (October 12, October 16, and October 20) and the networks' delayed response three days after the debates (October 14, October 18, and October 22). The study design and dates when data for the evening news content analysis were collected are presented in Figure 2.1.

	First Presidential/VP* Debates Oct. 11, Oct. 13*		Second Presidential Debate Oct. 15		Third Presidential Debate Oct. 19	
Network	Oct. 12	Oct. 14	Oct. 16	Oct. 18	Oct. 20	Oct. 22
ABC	X		X	X	X	X
CBS		X	X		X	X

Figure 2.1. Evening news content analysis design

The 1992 news stories for this study were obtained from the Vanderbilt Television News Archive (CBS news) and from transcripts of the ABC newscasts (Lexis/Nexis). Missing newscasts resulted from baseball (CBS, October 12) and other preemptions (ABC, October 14; CBS, October 18). In all, we content-analyzed five nights of ABC network news and four nights of CBS news. This produced 1,070 "verdict" cases for our analysis. Intracoder reliability (test-retest) was .85.

We were also interested in how the news networks responded to the debates in postdebate news specials. We looked at network coverage by ABC, CBS, and NBC immediately after each 1992 debate. In addition, ABC's "Nightline" regularly programmed debate analyses the night of the debate and/or on the night following the debate. We analyzed the news programs listed in Figure 2.2. Stories for this portion of the study

	Debate 1 October 11	VP Debate October 13	Debate 2 October 15	Debate 3 October 19
Network				
ABC	X		X	
'Nightline" Oct. 12	Oct. 14	Oct. 16	Oct. 19-20
CBS		X	X	X
NBC		X	X	X

Figure 2.2. News special content analysis design

came from our own taping of ABC postdebate analysis (including *Nightline*) and from CBS and NBC tapes from the Vanderbilt Television News Archive. Intracoder reliability (test-retest) was .90. We used this set of content analyses to determine news media verdicts and judgments about the candidates, references to "spin doctors," the level of conflict in the debate, and other content categories.

This specific design gave us the potential to measure journalistic reaction to each debate, immediately after the debate during postdebate analysis, the day after the debate in newscasts and sometimes on *Nightline*, and three days later, after the pundits had time to reach consensus on the meaning of each presidential campaign debate. Our design also allowed us to compare the press's response in 1992 with its response in 1976, 1980, 1984, and 1988.

Debates as a Political Institution (Chapter 10)

Two samples were used for the content analyses here. One used the same postdebate news specials from 1976 through the 1992 campaign that were part of the verdicts studies. The second was a special print-broadcast sample drawn by a computer keyword search. By using the word *format* in combination with other debate-related words, the keyword search allowed us to screen out all stories focusing exclusively on the candidates' performance in the debates and to select only those print and broadcast stories with content concerning the debates as an institution. This search identified a population of 319 broadcast and print stories. Our next step was to randomly select a sample of these story items. To do this, we broke the debate period into six time periods, the first two before any debates had been held, the next four following each of the debates. The six periods are described in the sections that follow.

Period 1. Before the October 2 agreement to hold the debates. This marks the time in the campaign before the two major candidates reached agreement and offered an invitation to Ross Perot. Although the candidates did not agree to the debates and debate formats until October 3, news stories about possible dates for candidate debates began appearing in early 1992. Most of the debate stories during this period, however, appeared in the few weeks preceding the agreement.

Period 2. October 3 until the start of the first debate. Because the October 11 first debate used the old format, candidates, reporter and commentators were accustomed to the format, so perhaps coverage focused on speculation about the possible debate outcome.

Period 3. After first presidential debate but before the October 13 vice presidential debate. As mentioned, the October 11 debate was most familiar to the audience and to the media personnel because of its use of the traditional presidential debate format—moderator and panel. But, because advance stories about the vice presidential debate were included in this subsample, this sample of stories also marked the transition to a new format for the debates—a format with a single moderator, no panel, and a chance for the vice presidential candidates to address each other directly.

Period 4. After the vice presidential debate but before the October 15 "town hall" debate. It was during this period that commentators and audiences had a chance to think about the vice presidential debate in retrospect, to anticipate the upcoming second presidential debate whose format would allow members of the audience to question the candidates.

Period 5. After the Richmond debate but before the October 19 final debate. Over this time period the media had a chance to evaluate the effectiveness of the new "town hall" format, to comment on the accumulated impact of the two presidential and one vice presidential debates, and to prepare for the third and final presidential debate.

Period 6. Immediately after the final presidential debate through the month of October. From the end of the debates until almost the election, the media had the opportunity to evaluate the debates individually or jointly, to speculate on their possible impact, and to move to new areas of discussion as the nation prepared to vote on November 3, 1992.

Seven stories were randomly selected from each of the six time periods. This provided us with a sample of 42 stories about the debates, selected from early 1992 to the end of October 1992. The stories generated 1,162 assertions for analysis with a test-retest reliability coefficient of .83.

THE SURVEY RESEARCH DESIGNS

We used two survey designs in completing our research methodology. Survey methodology, unlike content analysis or journalistic interviews with message creators, allows us to look at how audiences react to the campaign messages they receive. Our primary concerns were with the influence of the debates, postdebate analyses, talk shows, and campaign advertising on the knowledge, attitudes, and intended behaviors of our respondents. As explained earlier, we used two basic survey designs—a panel study and a cross-sectional trend study. The study was broken down into six waves:
1. post-Labor Day (September 7-18)
2. the first presidential debate (October 11-12)
3. the vice presidential debate (October 13-14)
4. the second presidential debate (October 15-18)
5. the third presidential debate (October 19-22)
6. and the preelection period (November 1-2)

The Survey Instrument

We used the same format for the survey questionnaire across all six sample waves.[1] The questionnaire, approximately 14 pages in length for the third presidential debate, averaged about 20 minutes for completion. Our extensive questionnaire focused on exposure to television news, presidential campaign ads, ad content, exposure to television talk shows featuring presidential and vice presidential candidates, exposure to televised town meetings, reading of the main news section of the newspaper, the utility of campaign information sources, party affiliation, political ideology, voting intention, campaign activity, exposure and evaluation of the debates and debaters, issues raised in the debates, presidential candidate image, campaign interest, internal and external political efficacy, debate attitudes, debate format preference, campaign issue knowledge, and demographic information.

The Panel Study

Any study that interviews the same people more than once qualifies as a "panel" study. The prototype of all campaign panel studies was done on the 1940 presidential campaign between Democrat Franklin Roosevelt and Republican Wendell Wilkie (Lazarfelds, Berelson, & Gaudet, 1948). Panel subjects in this study of 2,400 Erie County, Ohio residents were interviewed six times over the course of the campaign beginning in June

1940. Three fourths of the subjects served as controls and were interviewed only once. The remaining one fourth of the sample was interviews all six times.

The use of a panel design made it possible for these researchers to track changes in people's media use and voting intentions. Early interpretations of the results of the 1940 study were that media had limited influence on voting choice, and the results have often been advanced as evidence of a "minimal effects" model of media influence.

We also adopted a panel as part of our survey design. Our survey design, which includes the panel study and the cross-sectional trend or time-series study, is presented in Figure 2.3.

The panel began with 478 respondents during the post-Labor Day period (Wave 1). Of the 478 respondents, 377 (78.9%) agreed to continue as part of the panel. We contacted 290 of our potential panel subjects, 76.9%% of the original pool of 377 potential panelists. During interviewing Waves 2 through 5—the debate period—we were able to contact 259 panelists, 89.3% of the 290 respondents who finished in our panel. During the final Wave (Wave 6, preelection), we interviewed 237 panelists.

We tried to interview each panelist three times: first during the post-Labor Day interviews, once over the course of the campaign debates (October 11-22), and a final time just before the election (November 1-2). Such a design allows us to make comparisons between the post-Labor Day period and after the first presidential debate, the vice presidential debate, the second presidential debate, the third presidential debate, and then during the final interviewing period just prior to the election.

Two hundred and six of the panelists (71.0% of the 290 panelists) were interviewed three times: during Wave 1, during Waves 2 through 5, and during Wave 6. Fifty-three were interviewed only twice: during Wave 1 and during Waves 2 through 5, whereas another 31 were also interviewed only twice—but during Wave 1 and Wave 6. The completion rates for the first panel study interviews, post-Labor Day, were 56.2% in Illinois, 50.7% in Oregon, and 54.5% in Indiana.

Cross-sectional Trend Study

Unlike a panel study, a cross-sectional trend study randomly selects members of the population to be interviewed at various time points. These respondents are interviewed only once. We began collecting information from our cross-sectional trend sample immediately after the first presidential debate on October 11. We interviewed each night from October 11 through October 22.

By combining the panel and cross-sectional trend study respondents, we were able to look at the campaign debate period and how the

Methods

Post-Labor Day Sept 7-18 Panel N = 290 Total N = 478			
First Pres Debate Oct 11 Panel N = 19 Trend Study N = 85	First Debate + 1 Day Oct 12 Panel N = 33 Trend Study N = 100	VP Debate First Debate + 2 Days Oct 13 Panel N = 23 Trend Study N = 92	VP Debate + 1 Day First Debate + 3 Days Oct 14 Panel N = 23 Trend Study N -= 92
Second Pres Debate Oct 15 Panel N = 6 Trend Study N = 45	Second Debate + 1 Day Oct 16 Panel N = 30 Trend Study N = 92	Second Debate + 2 Days Oct 17 Panel N = 21 Trend Study N = 98	SecondDebate + 3 Days Oct 18 Panel N = 18 Trend Study N -= 95
Third Pres Debate Oct 19 Panel N = 26 Trend Study N = 107	Third Debate + 1 Day Oct 20 Panel N = 24 Trend Study N = 109	Second Debate + 2 Days Oct 21 Panel N = 22 Trend Study N = 130	SecondDebate + 3 Days Oct 22 Panel N = 15 Trend Study N -= 128
Pre-Election Nov 1-2 Panel N = 237			

Figure 2.3. Survey studies design

various debates, discussions about the debates, and respondents' attitudes, knowledge, and behaviors were influenced by campaign information. Taken together, we interviewed 1,433 respondents between October 11 and October 22. The completion rates for Waves 2 through 5 were 57.7% in Illinois, 53.0% in Oregon, and 52.6% in Indiana.

The basic demographic characteristics of the panel and trend/time-series studies are presented in Table 2.1. As you can see, for the most part the comparisons are quite close between the two samples. Party affiliation is roughly the same, with 31.0% of the panelists who consider themselves to be Republicans, compared with 26.9% of the trend study respondents. For Democrats, the percentages were 41.0% in the panel and 41.3% in the trend study.

The average age for the panelists was 40.5 years and for the trend study 41.6 years. The mean number of years of school completed was 14.5 for the panelists and 14.3 for the trend study. Nearly the same percentage was employed full time in the panel study (51.0%) as in the trend study (46.7%). The modal income range was the same for both samples, $30,000 to $50,000 annually, although there were more in this category (32.8%) for the panel than for the trend study (21.4%). There was a higher percentage of whites in the panel (85.9%) than in the trend study (78.1 %), with approximately same percentages of blacks (9.7% panel; 10.8% trend). For the panel, 54.2% were female and 45.5% male. For the trend there were 51.1% female and 43.8% male. (These don't add to 100% because gender was not recorded in a few cases.)

Overall, the demographics indicate two very similar samples.

CONCLUSION

No method or set of methods can ever provide all of the reasons about "who," "what," "when," "where," and especially "why." But, by using a number of independent but convergent methods, we think we are in a good position to make some sense of the presidential campaign of 1994. If we are able to accomplish that, then most of our goals will have been met.

Table 2.1. Basic Demographics for Panel and Trend Surveys.

Variable	Panel Study % ($N = 261$)	Trend Time Series Study % ($N = 1,172$)
Location		
Illinois	29.0	23.4
Pennsylvania	24.1	29.0
Oregon	21.0	30.9
Indiana	25.9	16.6
Political Party		
Republican	31.0	26.9
Democrat	41.0	41.3
Independent	23.4	22.0
Other	3.8	5.6
Don't know/refuse/missing	0.7	4.3
Mean age (years)	40.5	41.6
Mean schooling completed (years)	14.5	14.3
Employment		
Full time	51.0	46.7
Part time	12.1	9.8
Student	15.9	15.4
Retired	12.4	14.8
Homemaker	6.2	4.9
Unemployed	2.4	3.8
Don't know/refusal/missing	0.0	4.7
Family income (annual)		
< $10,000	15.2	16.5
$10,000 to $20,000	15.5	16.3
> $20,000, < $30,000	13.8	18.3
$30,000 to $50,000	32.8	21.4
> $50,000	19.3	17.3
Don't know/refuse/missing	3.4	10.2
Race		
White	85.9	78.1
Black	9.7	10.8
Asian	1.7	2.8
Hispanic	0.7	1.2
Native American	0.3	0.3
Other	0.7	1.4
Refuse/missing	1.0	5.3

Table 2.1. Basic Demographics for Panel and Trend Surveys (cont.).

Sex		
Female	54.2	51.1
Male	45.5	43.8
Refusal/missing	0.3	5.1

ENDNOTE

1. The complete questionnaires can be found in the appendices. The questionnaire for Wave 1 (post-Labor Day, September 7-18) is in Appendix A; the questionnaire for Waves 2 through 5 (the debate period, October 11-22) is in Appendix B; and the questionnaire for Wave 6 (preelection period) is in Appendix C.

REFERENCES

Cook, T.D., & Campbell, D.T. (1979). *Quasi-experimentation: Design & analysis issues for field settings.* Chicago: Rand McNally.

Herman, E., & Chomsky, N. (1988). *Manufacturing consent: The political economy of the mass media.* New York: Pantheon.

Lazarsfeld, P.F., Berelson, B., & Gaudet, H. (1948). *The people's choice: How the voter makes up his mind in a presidential campaign* (32nd ed.). New York: Columbia University Press.

Lemert, J.B., Elliott, W.R., Bernstein, J.M., Rosenberg, W.L., & Nestvold, K.J. (1991). *News verdicts, the debates, and presidential campaigns.* New York: Praeger.

Lemert, J.B., Elliott, W.R., Nestvold, K.J., & Rarick, G.R. (1983). Effects of viewing a presidential primary debate. In *Communication research* (Vol. 10, pp. 155-173). New York: Praeger.

McLeod, J., Guo, Z., Daily, K., Steele, C., Huang, H., Horowitz, E., & Chen, H. (1993, November). *The impact of traditional and non-traditional forms of political communication in the 1992 presidential election.* Paper presented to the Midwest Association for Public Opinion Research, Chicago, IL.

Shoemaker, P.J., & McCombs, M.E. (1989). Survey research. In G.H. Stempel III & B.H. Westley (Eds.), *Research methods in mass communication* (2nd ed., pp. 150-172). Englewood Cliffs, NJ: Prentice-Hall.

Shoemaker, P.J., & Reese, S.D. (1991). *Mediating the message: Theories of influences on mass media content.* New York: Longman.

Stempel, G.H. III. (1989). Content analysis. In G.H. Stempel III & B.H. Westley (Eds.), *Research methods in mass communication* (2nd ed., pp. 124-136). Englewood Cliffs, NJ: Prentice-Hall.

3

The Use of Nontraditional Media in Campaign '92 and Its Implications

James M. Bernstein

In Chapter 1 we pointed out what to many readers is well known: What has become known as "talk-show campaigning" was prevalent during the 1992 presidential campaign. In this chapter, we focus on several issues at the center of the emergence of "talk-show campaigning." First, how did the talk shows emerge as one of the critical elements of communication in the 1992 presidential campaign? Second, what are the reasons for the dominance of talk-show campaigning throughout 1992, dominance both as a medium of communicating with voters and as a focal point of coverage by the mainstream news media? Third, in using talk shows so prominently for the first time in a national campaign, what purposes and expectations did the politicians have in mind? Were those expectations realistic, based on what we know about the political goals that may be accomplished through communications technology?

Campaigning on talk shows and televised town meetings would not have been possible, let alone widespread, had candidates and their campaigns not been willing and able to take advantage of communication technology. The willingness, we believe, came from a desire to deliver to voters a direct message, one that was not filtered through nightly network newscasts, daily newspapers, and weekly news magazines. The ability to do this had existed for some time. Most of the technology that the talk shows and town meetings incorporated—satellite and cable technology, for example—had been available for several years. In fact, the technologies had previously been used in local, state, and regional government and politics; increased simplicity of use and accessibility resulted in their national application in 1992.

Many of the principles that underlie the development of media technology in politics and government are relevant to this study, and so our discussion goes beyond development of the 1992 talk-show campaign to explore how these principles might provide a framework for studying the impact of what we have been calling talk-show campaigning. The campaign practitioners—both the politicians and the media practitioners—also had principles and assumptions guiding their use of the communication technology. In this chapter, we recount portions of personal interviews we conducted with those responsible for creating and covering the campaigns in order to explore their ideas as well. We also raise research questions that emerged from both the principles and events of the 1992 campaign.

Before going any further, we want to change the vernacular somewhat. Thus far, we have been referring to talk-show campaigning and talk-show politics, terms we have assumed are familiar to the reader—indeed, a dictionary definition of the terms would allow us to justify using them throughout this book. Still, we would be the first to acknowledge that the term *talk show* is perhaps too narrow for what we intend to convey, discuss, and study.

For one thing, we compare and contrast the uses and effects of different types of conventional campaign media with those we have been calling talk-show media. Using the term *talk show* implies a contrast with *non-talk shows* not merely conventional campaign media. So, for example, the *Arsenio Hall* program is a non-talk show, but it is certainly not a conventional campaign medium or program. It and its relatives (*Donahue*, MTV, and other cable outlets in which candidates have appeared) have been called *new media* and *nonmainstream media* as opposed to *old media* and *mainstream media* (e.g., network television news and daily newspapers). But old and mainstream media, we believe, would also include local television and radio news, two channels that had seldom played important roles in national campaigns, but did in the 1992 campaign.

Many of the programs we refer to included some element of candidate-voter interaction, so we thought the interactive/noninteractive dichotomy might be appropriate. But that, too, left out other areas that had contributed importantly to campaign communications in 1992 but rarely before.

That is why we settled on the distinction between traditional and nontraditional media. *Traditional media* are those on which presidential candidates and voters have relied for many campaigns, primarily network television news (regularly scheduled news programming on ABC, CBS, NBC and, now, CNN). We also include as traditional daily newspapers (especially elite papers such as *The New York Times*, the *Washington Post*, the *Los Angeles Times*, and the *Wall Street Journal*) and weekly news magazines (*Time, Newsweek*, and *U.S. News and World Report*). *Nontraditional media* include televised town meetings, appearances on so-called popular-culture media (e.g., MTV, *Arsenio Hall*, and *Donahue*), and both radio and television call-in talk shows.

THE EVOLUTION OF NONTRADITIONAL MEDIA USE IN CAMPAIGN '92

When we embarked on this project midway through 1992, the primaries were coming to an end and the presidential field had, for all intents and purposes, been narrowed to three candidates—George Bush, Bill Clinton, and Ross Perot. It was our principal intent to replicate our study of the 1988 presidential campaign and the influence of the televised debates, media coverage of the debates, and campaign advertising (Lemert, Elliott, Bernstein, Rosenberg, & Nestvold, 1991). It was also clear, however, five months from Election Day that media campaigning in the 1992 presidential campaign was going to be unique. Indeed, it had already been.

Once again, a presidential candidate had suffered political wounds from allegations that he had had an extramarital relationship. But unlike Gary Hart in 1987, Bill Clinton survived. What is important to our study, however, is not so much that Clinton did survive, but how the Gennifer Flowers story emerged and how the candidate survived it. In retrospect, the episode signaled the changes in the roles of the candidates, the media, and the public in the 1992 campaign.

The story first emerged in tabloid newspapers, then on local television news, not in the mainstream news media. However, the traditional, national mainstream campaign press corps could not completely ignore the allegations of Clinton's affair with Flowers, so they "backed into" the story by publishing a piece on media coverage of the brewing scandal—a story about the story—not on the scandal itself[1] and by reacting to the coverage of their local affiliates. Still, within these media critiques, the mainstream news media had to provide background of the allegations in order to provide context for the media story. That background then provided the mainstream news media the rationale to legitimately report the scandal.

Why is this episode and the way the national mainstream news media handled the story important for our study? Because the national mainstream news media's reporting of *The Star's* payments to Flowers for her story, of the Clintons' Super Bowl Sunday response on *60 Minutes*, and of Flowers' counter-response on *A Current Affair* were among the first public signs that mainstream news media were losing control of the political agenda. Signs of who was gaining control of the political agenda would not become apparent until a short time later.

We argue that, up to the point of the Gennifer Flowers story, the national news media had both been in solid control of the campaign agenda, and coverage had improved. Inspired by the lessons they learned from their failures in 1988 and by the postmortems of that campaign—particularly David Broder's oft-cited column of early 1990[2]—the traditional news media during the winter of 1992 were paying greater attention to substantive issues than they had in 1988, talking more to actual voters, relying less on candidate photo opportunities, and scrutinizing candidate television advertising more. Certainly the new vigilance by the news media during the early parts of the campaign took a respite when the Gennifer Flowers story broke. Ironically, though, even before the Flowers allegations, the very notion of an aggressive, skeptical, issue-oriented news media in control of the campaign agenda was in fact forcing candidates to discover alternative methods for communicating their messages without media filters.

The assertion here is that vows by the mainstream news media after 1988 not to be taken in by media events, themes of the day, and sound-bite strategies planted the seeds of ideas among candidates and their campaigns to explore the possibilities of using alternative channels for communicating unfiltered political messages. Those ideas took root during the early days of campaign 1992, but fully blossomed when Bill Clinton found that he needed a way to speak to primary voters without having to deal with a mainstream news media pack that had rediscovered political scandal.

In essence, we assert that despite their best attempts to avoid the mistakes of the 1988 presidential campaign, the mainstream news media would have lost control of the political agenda regardless of the Gennifer Flowers story. In fact, we believe that a primary reason the mainstream news media would have lost control of the political agenda in 1992 was because of their success in avoiding a repeat of 1988. The promise of new vigilance by the news media forced candidates to look for other channels through which to communicate relatively unfiltered messages—talk shows and call-in shows among them.

Does this loss of control by the mainstream news media mean the candidates had regained control of the political agenda halfway through 1992? In part, yes, although in no way like the control they exercised in 1988. Bill Clinton's effective use of call-in shows and talk shows during the weeks leading up to the New York primary allowed him to sufficiently deflect attention away from the tabloid-like stories and toward material and issues with which he felt more comfortable. His appearance before the April New York primary on the New York radio show of Don Imus—a frequent Clinton antagonist—may not have won over Imus, but it did appear to charm him and his listeners. Clinton's success in wresting control of the political agenda from the mainstream news media, however, came with assistance from citizens, who also managed to gain a share of control.

During the final days leading up to primary day in New York, Clinton appeared on the *Donahue* show twice—in a half-hour segment by himself on April 1 and in an hour-long segment with Jerry Brown on April 6. In the first appearance, host Phil Donahue's persistent questioning of Clinton about the Gennifer Flowers allegations provoked not only resistance from the candidate but a sharp rebuke from audience members. As media critic Jay Rosen (1992a, 1992b) pointed out, here was a case of a person (Donahue) serving the role that a mainstream journalist would: asking tough questions about an issue that had been in the news and on the agenda of the news media. Clinton was clearly displeased with the questioning and expressed his displeasure to Donahue. But it took the severely negative reaction from the audience to demonstrate that mainstream journalists—here with Donahue as representative—were pursuing an issue agenda that was not salient to the public. Although Clinton refused to answer Donahue's questions about the character issue, it took the studio audience's reaction to allow the candidate's issues—and apparently the public's issues—back on the agenda. On the April 6 joint appearance with Clinton and Jerry Brown, Donahue stepped back and allowed the candidates to discuss between themselves substantive issues such as the economy and health care.

Although the Imus and Donahue episodes occurred several months into the primary portion of the campaign, they demonstrate the sophistication with which the Clinton campaign operated its communication plan. These incidents were not seat-of-the-pants, spur-of-the-moment appearances merely designed to stop the hemorrhaging that was occurring from a focus on the character question: Certainly that was the result and to some extent the purpose. They were also part of a campaign-long communication strategy. That strategy, according to Jeff Eller, political communication director for the Clinton campaign, was to identify and use channels for communicating a message free from journalistic filters, brevity, and interpretation. "The bottom line in all of [Clinton's appearances on talk shows and televised town meetings] was to give people a more full and expanded view of Bill Clinton," Eller said. "We always thought that if we could show Bill Clinton in a longer form, and that they would have a chance to not see just a 30-second sound bite, that we would win" (Eller, personal communication, January 6, 1993).

The candidate himself articulated this view shortly after he had finished the primary campaign season. "What we're finding," Bill Clinton told *The Los Angeles Times* in June, "is the more I can directly communicate with the people, the better I do" (Chen, 1992, p. A16).

The real key to the use of the nontraditional media, at least for the Clinton campaign, was delivering an unmediated message that might reach potential voters who typically were not interested in information about national politics that came from traditional news media, network news and daily newspapers in particular. (Chapter 5 discusses how realistic that campaign assumption was.) "It's touching a whole group of voters who have never been touched before," Eller said. "We think there's an opportunity . . . for more voters to get information from the candidates" (Eller, 1992).

What is interesting is that, although the use of the nontraditional media was commonplace among Democrat candidates throughout the first half of 1992, this shift failed to gain the rapt attention of the mainstream, traditional news media in a way that it would later in the year. Stories about Jerry Brown's 800 number and Paul Tsongas's monograph on the economy appeared, and those stories did indeed portray those communication efforts as "different." But the traditional, mainstream press did not seem to take these efforts seriously, nor did it characterize them as important.

Why? One reason has to be that the press did not consider these candidates "electable," so they did not take these candidates or their techniques and strategies seriously, Brown in particular. References to "Governor Moonbeam" persisted throughout the campaign, and the candidate's own irreverent style when reciting the phone number left one wondering how serious he was about using it. Yet another reason is that these candidates were still making themselves available to the traditional media, despite their use of nontraditional media to communicate directly to voters. As long as journalists who worked for the traditional news media were able to have access to candidates and their campaigns, they would find it easy to tolerate, if not ignore, the communication methods designed to avoid them. That toleration and inattention to the non-traditional media by the traditional media changed once Ross Perot demonstrated that he not only could launch a successful campaign without traditional news media outlets, but he could actually gain public support by doing so.

PEROT TALKS, THE PEOPLE LISTEN, AND THE MAINSTREAM MEDIA STEW

Perhaps no candidate ever controlled information as much and as well as Ross Perot. His strict avoidance of press conferences, interviews, and other trappings of dealing with the mainstream national news media became legendary. Instead, Perot communicated to voters through talk shows and satellite-transmitted political rallies. The Texas billionaire also enthusiastically advocated the concept of national electronic town meetings.

Although Ross Perot received a great deal of credit for the use of new or nontraditional media during the 1992 campaign, we believe basic changes in the way candidates communicated with the electorate were occurring several weeks before Perot became an "undeclared" presidential candidate February 20 on *Larry King Live*. Nevertheless, the story of new media technologies and nontraditional media use in the campaigns manifested itself only after the Perot phenomenon took hold of the country and members of the mainstream news media began to rankle over Perot's use of the technology to bypass and evade them.[3]

We suggest an additional explanation for the traditional news media's inability to recognize the story. Our research on news media coverage of televised debates (see Lemert et al., 1991) shows the elite press covers the debates in terms of what is at stake for the candidates rather the voters. Likewise, the horse-race coverage, with polls, handicapping, and discussions of campaign strategies, tends to create coverage that fascinates and benefits insiders and political junkies, whereas the majority of eligible voters are reduced to becoming spectators. By all means, public opinion polls are designed to measure the attitudes of "ordinary" citizens, but the modern-day use of polls in campaign journalism has not only detached journalists from real people, but it has also created a sterile form of political "participation" that has, in essence, removed people even further from the political process than was the case before the proliferation of polls.

In the case of the 1992 campaign, the mainstream news media, despite their best efforts to talk to actual voters, failed to understand that people wanted to participate in the political process at a more active, meaningful level than voting, talking to reporters, and answering survey questions. The mainstream news media were reluctant to acknowledge that someone (Ross Perot) could conduct a viable campaign without them and were hesitant to cede control of the political agenda to someone intent on bypassing them. The mainstream news media were also oblivious to the mass public's inclination to associate them with the very politicians they were covering, as well as its desire to express its own views in its own way, through nontraditional media channels.

We believe, therefore, the traditional media were unable to recognize the story of the nontraditional media and their impact in the initial stages of the campaign, coming to a belated recognition only after feeling threatened by a candidate both willing and able to ignore the normal channels of political communication. Additionally, we suggest that a reason for the increased use of nontraditional media is an understanding by the candidates of the mass public's frustration with being reduced to spectators, its desire to be a greater part of the process, and its frustrated willingness to associate mainstream news media with a failed old process.

Journalist William Greider offers a similar explanation and several compelling arguments in his indictment of the media for their contribution to the failure of the democratic process. Industrial and organizational changes in major metropolitan daily newspapers, he says, have resulted in new journalistic standards and practices, ones derived primarily from the need to increase profit through advertising. Advertising comes from the ability to deliver large audiences to advertisers, audiences that can be attracted only with bland, neutral news coverage. Journalists typically generate this type of coverage from contacts with the political power elite: expert government officials, academics, and politicians. The process, in turn, has decreased the distance between the political power elite and the newspapers and the journalists who work for them, while increasing the distance between the nonelite and journalists (Greider, 1992; see also Bagdikian, 1993). Reminiscing on the early part of his career in Cincinnati, Greider said the "angle of vision" among Midwestern reporters of the 1950s was often representative of their working-class audience. Years later at the Washington Post, Greider wrote, the newspaper seemed "to look downward on its subject matter" (p. 295).

Television offers the promise of allowing people to connect with the political process, transporting audiences in a way that allows the "pictures inside our heads" (Lippmann, 1922) to become the pictures inside our living rooms. Paradoxically, however, the same industrial/organizational structures that have affected newspapers also influence television, Greider said. He wrote: "Broadcasting is inescapably populist in its quick accessibility yet also elitist in its organizational structure" (p. 308).

WEIRD TALK SHOWS OR OPPORTUNITIES TO INTERACT?

All of the major campaigns in 1992 found ways to take advantage of the strengths of television—its populist nature and accessibility—while minimizing its weaknesses, although some embraced these characteristics more readily than others. Bill Clinton discussed these very aspects of television and the campaign during an appearance on the *Today* show. During a June 9 call-in segment on the program, a caller wanted to know what Clinton thought about the effect of talk shows on the political process. Clinton focused on the accessibility element and the opportunity the shows presented voters to interact with candidates. Talk shows, he said, had helped remove the artificial nature of the media campaign and the remoteness of the candidates. "The way campaigns have been run (in the past)," he continued, "people haven't been able to relate. Being able to talk to candidates alleviates that." Again, however, only one of the campaigns—Clinton's—did so with an organized strategy in mind.

In contrast, so reluctant was President Bush "to plunge into the talk-show circuit" that it was not until October that his campaign increased its effort to "personalize its approach" (Black, 1992). Throughout the campaign the president referred to 1992 as "a weird political year" characterized by "weird talk shows" (Devroy, 1992). The president's reluctance, said Torie Clark, communication director of the Bush-Quayle campaign, came from a concern that using non-traditional media would appear undignified. "There were quite a few people—most in the White House—who did not think that the talk-show route was the way to go," Clark said, "thinking it was nonpresidential and that it somehow put the office of the presidency in a less-than-dignified light" (personal communication, August 31, 1993).

President Bush always had a very strong feeling that it was his obligation to protect the office of the Presidency—the office that had come before him, the office that was going to come after him. He did not want to do anything that he thought would somehow lessen the importance of that office. "And then there were certain people within the strategic camps who said one of the only advantages we had over Bill Clinton was that we were President and he wasn't, and that we should try to maintain some stature and distance between yourself and the other guy" (Clark, personal communication, August 31, 1993).

The irony, said Clark, is that when President Bush ultimately did appear on nontraditional media—especially the morning news programs and *Larry King Live*—he performed well. "When he did do them he was quite relaxed and enjoyed them, and he would entertain a hostile question from a real person much better than a hostile question from a reporter," Clark said. "Because he believed they were citizens and they had a right to their opinions and attitudes and all that. He would give them benefit—a real person at a town hall meeting—more than, say, a reporter."

For Ross Perot's campaign, using nontraditional media was a matter of what the candidate wanted to do rather than what he felt obliged to do; at the outset, at least, his appearances on nontraditional media were more by comfort and instinct and less by long-term design. Sharon Holman, press secretary for United We Stand, the organization behind Perot's candidacy, suggested that initially Perot's use of nontraditional media was merely happenstance.

"None of us had ever been involved in politics before," Holman said. "We didn't know what was happening. We were not even aware, initially, for several weeks after that [February] Larry King appearance, that it was happening on the scale that was nationwide. And so it was like being one foot away, or one foot in front of a tidal wave throughout the whole campaign" (Holman, personal communication, July 12, 1993).

Were the motivations for the candidates to appear on the nontraditional media purely altruistic? Were the candidates merely acting in the best interest of the public and the democratic process? Perhaps, but many, especially journalists from the traditional media, believed the candidates, like all politicians, were motivated primarily by what was in their best self-interests. (See Chapters 4 and 5 for other criticisms made by journalists.)

Questions from ordinary citizens may have been a way for them to relate to candidates. But to the extent that nontraditional media appearances substituted for appearances on traditional media, they allowed candidates to avoid the potentially embarrassing "gotcha" questions that are typical of Sunday morning pundit programs. Relatively long, unfiltered explanations of candidate issue positions may have provided citizens information that was superior to a sound bite. However, in previous campaigns, these sort of candidate-controlled messages occurred mainly in paid advertising. In 1992, the nontraditional media, particularly the talk shows and call-in shows, provided free opportunities with few limitations.

By the fall, all three campaigns understood that it was in their best interests not only to appear on the nontraditional media, but to do so as often as possible. The media practitioners also discovered benefits of nontraditional media appearances, benefits that addressed the public interest in the literal sense. That is, once the producers of the non-traditional programs realized how much audience interest and ratings increased when the candidates appeared, they made certain the candidates appeared frequently.

The interaction that was occurring between the voters and the candidates—even a reluctant George Bush—gave the appearance of voters being involved in the political process in a way that did not and probably could not exist in traditional campaigning and traditional media. Even if a voter him- or herself could not actually speak with the candidate, the fact was that a real voter somewhere was asking the candidates questions that voters cared about, questions that addressed issues voters cared about. All too often journalists in the traditional media focused on tactics and strategies of the campaigns and candidates, political arcana that could only interest other journalists and politicians.

Were the interaction and voter involvement indeed merely a perception? What would we expect the effects should be of the interaction and the potential for increased voter involvement? In the next section, we discuss the concept of interactivity and its relevance to the mass media. We also discuss research on the uses in government and politics of what we have been calling nontraditional media, a discussion that provides a framework for questions we ask in this book about the nontraditional media during the 1992 presidential campaign.

POSSIBLE VIRTUES AND DRAWBACKS OF THE NONTRADITIONAL MEDIA

One of the primary virtues of the nontraditional campaign media and the technologies that support them (primarily satellite and cable technology) is that they allow a greater volume of information to be available than do traditional forms of campaign media (Abramson, Arterton, & Orren, 1988; Freedom Forum Media Studies Center, 1992). The technologies have also brought a proliferation of nonnews programming to compete for audience members already disinclined to pay attention to, or show interest in, politics.

A related benefit of the nontraditional media and their technologies is the accessibility of information to people who may not have had access previously (Abramson et al., 1988; Freedom Forum Media Studies Center, 1992; Meadow, 1991). Some have referred to this as the "democratization" effect of the new media technology, in which not only does the amount of political information increase (in this case, information about the candidates), but the places where the information appears varies. For example, traditionally, the candidates would appear primarily on network television newscasts or in metropolitan daily newspapers. Satellite and cable technology and the nontraditional media provided opportunities for people to see the candidates where they had rarely, if ever, appeared: on, for example, MTV, The Nashville Network, and televised local town meetings. In principle, this would make the candidates and information about them available to many people who may not have previously paid attention to presidential politics. The novelty of seeing political information in a nontraditional form and the unique accessibility of the information could also increase campaign interest among those previously indifferent about elections and election coverage.

It is also possible that despite the novelty and accessibility, people would find the information more than they want or need and reject it.[4] Additionally, this kind of narrowcasting or targeting could also reduce accessibility to information for those who are not among the target audience or who do not have access to the technology itself.

In this case, the nontraditional media would increase the amount of sender control over the message and where it appeared, although not necessarily at the expense of receiver control. In fact, audience members would, in principle, become increasingly active in two ways. First, despite targeting and narrowcasting, audience members would increase their ability to control when and what messages they receive because of the increased volume and variety of available information. For example, a candidate may deliver a message via a traditional channel, such as network television news, but because of recent advances in satellite technology, the message could also appear in a local TV newscast. The audience member would have an option of either channel. Second, the technology would allow (and, in fact, did in 1992) an increase in interaction between the candidate-sender and the audience-voter-receiver. In essence, the audience member could ask questions of the candidates, reducing—perhaps eliminating—the need for a surrogate such as the traditional news media.

When increased receiver control exists due to the nontraditional media, implications occur for learning about politics, in particular about candidate issue positions. Although the evidence showing knowledge effects from media that incorporate interactivity is not strong, research has indicated acceptance, satisfaction, and preference for media that allow interactivity (Rafaeli, 1988). In Chapter 5, we present new results on talk shows and learning effects.

This notion of interactivity between candidate and voter assumes what researchers have called the "conversational ideal" (see Avery & McCain, 1986; Rafaeli, 1988; Schudson, 1978). That is, the "conversational ideal" assumes that face-to-face conversations (and by implication any interpersonal communication) are superior to mass communication. It also assumes that mass communication actually improves when it includes elements of face-to-face conversations. One of our objectives was to determine the relative influence of traditional and nontraditional media on a number of factors, including what people knew about the candidates and their positions, how much interest people had in the presidential campaign, and how people felt about the political process and their ability to participate in it. To what extent did the nontraditional media contribute to feelings of involvement with the political process among the public? What effect did the nontraditional media have on campaign interest among the public? What was the relationship between exposure to the nontraditional media and frustration with and hostility toward the traditional media? What other characteristics were related to use of the nontraditional campaign media? What relationship existed between use of the nontraditional media and traditional media? Did people use just a few nontraditional media sources or did they use several? Many of these questions are answered in Chapter 5, which looks closely at the audience for nontraditional media.

Other issues have resulted from the evolution of the nontraditional media and the changes they affected in traditional sources of campaign information. As audience members exercised increased control over the messages they received, the amount and the nature of the information they received could also change. This could happen in several ways. First, the audience member who opts for information from a nontraditional source such as a local television newscast may not be getting complete information from the most knowledgeable or analytical source.[5] And those watching or participating in a televised town meeting may feel more connected to a candidate, but, by and large, they are receiving unfiltered, uncritical, unanalyzed information. On the other hand, as nontraditional sources of campaign information became available, traditional sources, such as daily newspapers and network television news, found their roles changing from one of a simple conduit of information to one that involves increased interpretation and analysis.[6] This change in the traditional media may, therefore, produce an increased richness in information that is available only in the "old" media.

SUMMARY

In this chapter, we discussed the evolution of candidates' use of the nontraditional media during the 1992 campaign. We suggested that the candidates, particularly the Democrats and independent candidate Ross Perot, turned to nontraditional media because they frequently allowed the dissemination of unfiltered messages to the public. This held wide appeal among the candidates, who desired to communicate with voters without the intervention of traditional news media. Some of the candidates also recognized a public desire to make closer connections with the candidates themselves, and some forms of the nontraditional media provided that. The proliferation of the nontraditional media during the 1992 presidential campaign raises questions about their impact on public interest in and knowledge of the campaign. It also draws attention to questions about the quality of information from the nontraditional media, both in an objective sense and through the lens of the traditional media. Chapter 4 looks at how the traditional news media viewed the nontraditional media. As Chapter 4 suggests, what was seen through that lens seemed to vary, depending on when the lens was raised to the eye. Chapter 5 then looks at who was in the audience for the talk shows, what voters thought of the talk shows and the traditional media, and whether the talk shows contributed to voter knowledge.

ENDNOTES

1. Newsweek senior editor Jonathan Alter wrote about this technique of reporting the Gennifer Flowers story and himself confessed to doing it (see Alter, 1992).
2. In that column of January 1990, *Washington Post* columnist David Broder (1990) called on colleagues in political journalism to take a more active role in shaping the agenda in future elections than they did in 1988.
3. Journalist Paul Taylor says Perot "helped inspire" the use of new media, which may "be the most lasting contribution of his candidacy." He also said that some uses "predated" the Perot entry into the race (Taylor, 1992). What we are suggesting is that the mainstream news media were typically self-absorbed and only considered the "talk-show" campaign a story when it had a direct effect on them.
4. This is an assertion political scientist Austin Ranney (1983) has made about television news in a traditional form.
5. The question of whether local reporters can be as effective as the national press corps in covering a campaign is not resolved. Anecdotal evidence suggests that although local journalists often ask tough, critical questions of candidates, they lack the background knowledge and expertise to follow up effectively. One study of the 1988 campaign found local television news was not any different from network news in coverage of Super Tuesday (Entman, 1990).
6. As yet, no formal content analysis of traditional media exists to confirm this role, but comments throughout the fall campaign indicate that this was the case (see, e.g., Freedom Forum Media Studies center, 1992, pp. 99-101).

REFERENCES

Abramson, J.B., Arterton, F.C., & Orren, G.R. (1988). *The electronic commonwealth: The impact of new media technologies on democratic politics.* New York: Basic Books.

Alter, J. (1992, June). How Phil Donahue came to manage the '92 campaign. *The Washington Monthly,* pp. 11-14.
Avery, R.K., & McCain, T.A. (1986). Interpersonal and mediated encounters: A reorientation to the mass communication process. In G. Gumpert & R. Cathcart (Eds.), *Intermedia* (pp. 121-131). Oxford: Oxford University Press.
Bagdikian, B. (1993). *The media monopoly.* Boston: Beacon Press.
Black, C. (1992, October 3). Candidates make effort to reach out, touch voters. *Boston Globe,* p. 8.
Broder, D. (1990, January 3). Democracy and the press. *Washington Post,* p. A15.
Chen, E. (1992, June 13). Clinton faces voters on own talk show. *Los Angeles Times,* p.A16.
Devroy, A. (1992, July 1). Anxious Bush hunts for key to reelection; course unclear in 'weird' political year. *The Washington Post,* p. A1.
Eller, J. (1992, October 2). Panel on the news media and the 1992 campaign. Joan Shorenstein Barone Center, Harvard University, Cambridge, MA.
Entman, R.M. (1990, June). *Presidential campaigns and the future of television news: Super Tuesday on local TV.* Paper presented to the International Communication Association, Dublin, Ireland.
Freedom Forum Media Studies Center. (1992). *The homestretch: New politics. New media. New voters?* New York: Author.
Greider, W. (1992). *Who will tell the people?* New York: Simon & Schuster.
Lemert, J.B., Elliott, W.R., Bernstein, J.M., Rosenberg, W.L., & Nestvold, K.J. (1991). *News verdicts, the debates and presidential campaigns.* New York: Praeger.
Lippmann, W. (1922). *Public opinion.* New York: Macmillan.
Meadow, R.G. (1991, May). *New campaign technologies: How will the videocassette recorder and cable affect visual campaign communication in the 1990s?* Paper presented to the International Communication Association, Chicago.
Rafaeli, S. (1988). Interactivity: From new media to communication. In R.P. Hawkins, J.M. Wiemann, & S. Pingree (Eds.), *Advancing communication science: Merging mass and interpersonal processes* (pp. 110-134). Newbury Park, CA: Sage.
Ranney, A. (1983). *Channels of power.* New York: Basic Books.
Rosen, J. (1992a). Politics, vision, and the press: Toward a public agenda for journalism. In *The new news v. the old news: The press and politics in the 1990s.* New York: The Twentieth Century Fund.
Rosen, J. (1992b, November/December). Discourse. *Columbia Journalism Review,* pp. 34-35.
Schudson, M. (1978). The ideal of conversation in the study of mass media. *Communication Research, 5*(3), 320-329.
Taylor, P. (1992). Political coverage in the 1990s: Teaching the old news new tricks. In *The new news v. the old news: The press and politics in the 1990s.* New York: The Twentieth Century Fund.

4

Talk Shows and the News: Response From Traditional Media

James M. Bernstein

The purpose of this chapter is to follow up, elaborate on, and test some of the ideas we raised in the previous chapter. For example, we have suggested that throughout the campaign of 1992, a sense existed that the role of the traditional media had changed from that of previous campaigns. Some would argue, in fact, that the traditional media's role had diminished, as candidates sought and discovered other avenues through which to communicate their messages, and voters sought and discovered different channels through which to receive information about candidates. Although the campaign was only a few months old when at least some of the traditional news media showed some signs of awareness that voters and candidates were shifting their attention to the nontraditional media, perhaps it would have been unrealistic to expect immediate and wholesale adjustments to be made in the ways the traditional news media organized and implemented their already-laid plans to cover the 1992 campaign. The adoption of call-in formats on morning network news shows notwithstanding, most mainstream news media could not or would not make massive changes in their practices while the campaign was going on. Absent such easily observable changes, then, we need to look instead at how the new forms of campaign communication were treated by the traditional news media. If (say) reporters and editors consistently treated these phenomena with hostility, that may serve as an indicator of how willing these news personnel would be to reconsider how they cover the *next* presidential campaign. It is for this reason that this chapter considers how the mainstream news media treated the rise of the talk shows and other nontraditional campaign media.

BACKGROUND

In the previous chapter, we asserted that although these changing roles were evident in the early stages of the 1992 campaign, most members of the traditional media did not recognize either the changes or their impact until almost midway through 1992. Only then, when the changes—particularly the influence of nontraditional media—directly affected the traditional media, did reaction come. To borrow a phrase that feminists and other opponents of George Bush made popular, "They just didn't get it."

Interesting parallels exist between the traditional media and the Bush campaign when it comes to not getting it. For example, Germond and Witcover (1993) suggested a certain tone-deafness on the part of George Bush and his campaign. President Bush wanted the campaign to be about Bill Clinton, they wrote, but that is not what the voters wanted. The voters, they quote Democratic National Chair David Wilhelm as saying, wanted the election "to be about them—their problems, their hopes, their dreams, their economy."

Perhaps to a similar extent, the traditional media were also not able to see right away that this would be an election like no other in recent memory. For example, previous campaigns had been based in large part on personalities, personal attacks, and negative campaigning, so campaign coverage often had taken its lead from these elements. In addition, the traditional news media had served not only as watchdog during the election process, they had also taken on the role of mediator between voters and candidates. Patterson (1993) has asserted that since 1972, the news media have become coalition builders, much in the way political parties had been prior to that time, even though it has been a role for which the media are ill suited.

In the intervening elections (Patterson, 1993, p. 51), the responsibilities of mediating and building coalitions collided with the media's watchdog responsibilities and created information about presidential candidates "more likely to sour the electorate on its choices than create an understanding of the nature of those choices." When, in 1992, elements of the campaign changed, however, the traditional media seemed not agile or adaptable enough to change with them. But other elements—both candidates and nontraditional media—were able to, giving voters a voice they had not had in recent elections.

It could be that even though "the media were not designed" for "organizing presidential choice in a meaningful way" (Patterson, 1993, p. 51), the traditional news media did not recognize this. As the system searched for and discovered other ways to organize the choice in 1992, the mainstream press became resentful that other institutions were infringing on its territory. In essence, then, a role the traditional media had played since 1972 had been usurped by voters, candidates challenging an incumbent president, and the nontraditional media.

There are other ways that the media's tone-deafness in 1992 manifested itself. In Chapter 6, we argue that the traditional media equated Ross Perot with the nontraditional media campaign, not only making the two synonymous, but also suggesting that Perot was largely responsible for the advent of the use of nontraditional media. Although Perot frequently did use nontraditional media, often to the exclusion of traditional media, we indicated earlier that the Democratic candidates in particular were using nontraditional means throughout the New Hampshire primary campaign. The difference with respect to reaction from the traditional media is that the use of town meetings, "ask the candidate" forums, and 800 numbers by Democrats was *in addition* to the use of the mainstream press; Perot's use of appearances on *Larry King Live* and satellite town meetings was often instead of the mainstream press. We believe Perot's displacement of the mainstream press was the first clear signal the traditional media fully understood that they could be replaced, thus contributing to the resentfulness and scorn the traditional media showed toward the nontraditional.

As we indicated in the last chapter, the nontraditional media allowed candidates to avoid mainstream journalists and the kind of coverage they had provided over the last several elections, coverage that tended to focus on strategy and tactics rather than ongoing issues. Even when the traditional media did focus on issues, the coverage was not always beneficial for candidates, which compelled the candidates to use nontraditional media to communicate their positions on issues without the filter of mainstream journalism. Initially, this could create some bitterness toward the nontraditional media; ultimately, though, perhaps mainstream journalists may have discovered that "talk-show" campaigning not only was something new, it was also a new strategic element that they could incorporate into stories on campaign strategies.

What about the reaction of the traditional media toward voters within the context of nontraditional media use? After all, the use of nontraditional media was not only an attempt by candidates to bypass the mainstream press, it was also in large part an attempt to include voters in the process to a greater extent than they had been previously. Part of this dynamic came from the fact that the mass public felt alienated toward the mainstream press and no longer responded to the kind of coverage traditional news media were providing. Members of the mass public were becoming spectators in presidential campaigns rather than participants, in part because the traditional media provided them no outlet for reacting to candidates, news stories, or other voters. All at once, the talk shows, 800 numbers, morning show call-ins, and town meetings did provide and encourage opportunities to react, propose, respond, and participate like never before. For voters, the nontraditional media were everything that the traditional media were not. For all their attempts to find out about voters,[1] much of the traditional media may have been slow to understand either the extent to which the mass public resented typical campaign coverage or its desire for increased connectedness with candidates and the election process.

These observations frame the research questions we explore in this chapter. How did the traditional media cover the nontraditional media in 1992? What was the critical response by the traditional media to the nontraditional? Did they perceive a threat? How did they respond to the hosts of talk shows, whose roles had become increasingly important? How did they respond to candidates using the nontraditional media? How did the traditional media respond to citizens who were talk-show participants? As we argued earlier, how the traditional media eventually acted toward the nontraditional in 1992 is important as a signal of what we may expect regarding their willingness to change in 1996.

METHOD

Search Strategy

We conducted a quantitative content analysis of mainstream news media coverage that dealt with the nontraditional media. The content analysis was based on a computer search[2] that centered on media coverage of nontraditional media throughout 1992. The search used a subject keyword approach in order to include only those stories whose main focus was talk-show campaigning or nontraditional media, or stories that included candidates' use of nontraditional media as a campaign strategy. Our strategy was to include general campaign stories that might, for example, mention some future appearance by a candidate on a talk show or discuss how a series of appearances on morning news programs fit into an overall campaign strategy. We tried to exclude stories about the content of an individual candidate's appearance on a talk show.

For example, on an appearance on *Larry King Live* during the summer of 1992, Vice President Dan Quayle acknowledged that were his daughter to get pregnant and consider an abortion, he would not necessarily stand in her way. Ensuing stories in the mainstream media focused on the apparent contradiction between Quayle's policy position on abortion and his personal position, which he had revealed through a nontraditional media channel. This type of story would not have been included in our sample. Using these criteria, the database search revealed 596 broadcast and print items that dealt with the idea of the nontraditional media in the 1992 presidential campaign. A stratified random sample was drawn from this population of print and broadcast news stories through the creation of four distinct time periods during the 13-month stretch from December 1991 through 1992 and then the random selection of stories from each of the four time periods. Each of the time periods represented a distinctly different set of circumstances, ranging from the early period, when some journalists were just beginning to recognize that there was something new going on in this campaign, to the final period, at the end of the campaign, when journalists had a chance to reflect on the meaning of what they had witnessed. We wanted to make sure that each of these distinctly different time periods was thoroughly sampled and represented in our data, so we sampled 12 stories from each time period, resulting in a total sample of 48 print and broadcast news stories.

One of our major analytical plans is to compare the news treatment of the nontraditional media across these time periods, with special attention paid to the final period, when journalists had the time to consider the implications of the new alternative campaign media. The 48 stories produced a total of more than 900 assertions dealing implicitly or explicitly with the nontraditional media in the 1992 campaign. A description of each of the four time periods follows.

The first period started in December 1991 and encompassed the entire primary season, through June 10, 1992, a period when the new media phenomenon was first becoming apparent. This period contained the second largest number of stories from which to choose the sample, in part because it was the longest period of time among the four periods, but also because traditional media organizations discovered that candidates' use of nontraditional media provided fresh, new angles for covering the long, primary campaign. The nontraditional media use during this period not only was something new in presidential politics, it also provided the mainstream media with new ways to report and analyze strategic, tactical elements of the primary campaign.

The second period ran from the end of the primary season to the day before Labor Day, the traditional start of the Fall campaign. This period had the second lowest number of relevant stories, due no doubt to the dominance of the party conventions during the summer. It was also the time when the Democratic candidates embarked on bus tours through the Midwest and East, when Bill Clinton did televised town meetings on local television stations, when Ross Perot dropped out, and when George Bush began making Rose Garden appearances on morning news programs.

The third period went from Labor Day through Election Day and had the highest number of stories that dealt with the nontraditional media. Not only did this period have a large number of candidate appearances on nontraditional media, it also contained the Richmond televised debate, the debate that most resembled a televised town meeting. Additionally, the period saw the re-emergence of Ross Perot into the race and Perot's use of unconventional means—long-form infomercials—to communicate with voters.

The final period started the day after the election and extended through the end of 1992. Although the campaign was over, the traditional media continued, of course, to cover the campaign, mostly with post-election analyses, many of which considered the impact of nontraditional media, talk-show campaigning, the news media, and so on. During December, then-President-elect Bill Clinton led a televised economic summit meeting in Little Rock that some journalists likened to his use of nontraditional media in the campaign. It was during this period that, we expected, journalists would reflect on the implications of the new campaign media.

Coding

After randomly selecting a dozen stories from each period, one of the authors and a graduate student assistant coded assertions from the stories. We coded for a number of variables, including the news outlet in which the story appeared and the source of the assertive statement. Among the possibilities for source were the journalists themselves who produced the stories, journalists quoted within a story, a talk-show host or moderator, an academic expert, or a politician. Politician sources included candidates for president or vice president, party officials, campaign staff members, members of Congress or other office holders, and so on.

Previous observation allowed us to identify prevalent attitudes of some traditional, mainstream media toward nontraditional media in 1992. For instance, journalists often recognized the degree to which voters were able to question candidates about issues. Some were also critical of the tenor of the questions from citizens, calling them "easy" or "softballs." We were interested, therefore, in how stories characterized citizen participation.

Likewise, how were the abilities of talk-show hosts characterized? And, in the eyes of mainstream media, were the hosts able to recognize when candidates were being evasive?

As we mentioned earlier, candidates used the talk shows and other nontraditional media partly because they allowed opportunities for candidates' messages to reach voters without the filter and sound-bite mentality of mainstream media. On the other hand, the unfiltered information from talk shows often went without analysis or criticism. One of our tasks, then, was to code statements for what they said about the quality of information from talk shows, especially in comparison with information from traditional media. We also coded for whether the statements in stories referred to the candidates' abilities to use nontraditional media to elude tough questions.

Three other variables addressed the apparent change in control and empowerment that resulted from the proliferation of nontraditional media in 1992. They tapped into whether the traditional news media were referring to and making judgments about the change. Did they address the increased voter empowerment that nontraditional media allowed? Did they address the decreasing impact of the mainstream media during the campaign, a decrease that could have come from the increasing amount of talk-show campaigning? Finally, did their stories refer to the disenchantment with Washington, the federal government, and politics as usual?

We should note that not all coding categories were applicable or relevant to every assertion. For example, not all assertions contained comments about the quality of citizen participation or the ability of a talk-show host to recognize a candidate's evasion. In these instances, we coded the statements as "not applicable." We also excluded them from the analyses we performed. That is, we included in the analyses statements for which there were comments on the relevant topic. Our task, then, was to determine the nature of the commentary on, and reaction to, nontraditional media.

Intercoder agreement for each of the variables was at least 76%, in most cases greater than 80%. Intercoder reliability estimates using Scott's *pi* (Scott, 1955) were greater than .60 for all variables, and in most instances greater than .70.

ANALYSIS

In our analysis we developed two primary strategies. First, you will recall that we suggested earlier that the traditional mainstream media were slow to react to the rise of the nontraditional campaign media. Thus, our first analytical strategy was to see whether changes occurred over time in stories about the nontraditional media. Once the traditional media figured out that so-called talk-show campaigning would be a part of the 1992 election landscape, was their response to this change positive or negative? Another way of asking this question was to see whether mainstream news portrayals of the nontraditional campaign media changed over time, as either or both the visibility of the phenomenon and time for reflection and reconsideration varied. Our second analytical strategy was to explore differences among sources with respect to what they said about the new ways of communicating with voters. To the extent that journalists felt threatened by the phenomenon, we might expect that when journalists were sources of assertions about the nontraditional media, those assertions were more often negative than when other sources made assertions.

The Relationship Between Time Period and Assertions

Timing does seem to play a part in the nature of the reaction from traditional media toward nontraditional media, but it does not seem to be an issue of change over time or a question of the traditional media becoming increasingly negative as the campaign went on. Instead, statements in stories about nontraditional media reflect the relationship between time period and campaign activity. That is, portrayals of nontraditional media during the primary campaign period and the Fall campaign were different from portrayals from the aftermath of the primary and, especially, the aftermath of the election.

The data in Table 4.1 provide a good example of this. During Period 4—the aftermath of the November election—very few assertions were made that "softball" questions were asked the candidates during the talk shows and town halls. Similarly, assertions that the hosts' questions were intelligent and well informed dominated the coverage after the Fall campaign was over. Yet, during the Fall campaign (Period 3) "softball" assertions dominated news coverage of the nontraditional media, and very few statements were made that hosts' questions were intelligent and well informed. Thus, there was a remarkably clear distinction between what was said about the nontraditional campaign media while the Fall campaign was going on, as compared to after it was over.

Table 4.1. Portrayals of Hosts in Nontraditional Media by Period.

Period[a]	Easy, softball %	Ill-Informed %	Difficult, hardball %	Intelligent, well-informed %	Persistent %	(N)
Period 1	18.7	42.7	34.7	2.7	1.3	(75)
Period 2	32.1	7.1	20.2	33.3	7.1	(84)
Period 3	55.5	17.9	16.7	3.8	6.4	(78)
Period 4	6.4	8.5	10.6	66.0	8.5	(47)

$\chi^2 = 139.773$, $df = 12$, $p < .001$.
[a]Period 1 = December 1, 1991 to June 10, 1992
Period 2 = June 11 to September 7, 1992
Period 3 = September 8 to November 2, 1992
Period 4 = November 3 to December 31, 1992

Now look again at Table 4.1. To a lesser extent there may also have been a similar difference between Period 1—while journalists were covering the primaries—and the aftermath of the primaries (Period 2), although the differences are not as great and as easily interpreted. After the primaries were over, exactly one third of all the assertions said hosts' questions were intelligent and well informed, compared to less than 3% of all the assertions in stories written during the primary season. Similarly, that the questions asked were ill informed often was a statement made during the primary season, but hardly ever made during the postprimary period. On the other hand, the pattern of more favorable coverage during the postprimary period was muddied by results for the "softball" and "hardball" columns in the table, in which assertions were less favorable in those categories during the postprimary period.

Some of our other findings, however, tend to support differences between primary and postprimary periods as well as between the Fall campaign and its aftermath (data not tabled). The following are some highlights:

- Favorable assertions about the traditional media's losing control as a result of the rise of the nontraditional media were most likely to occur after the primary and after the election.
- Claims that talk shows and other nontraditional media provided the audience less analysis and interpretation happened most often during coverage of the Fall campaign.
- Positive assertions about nontraditional media content—those that suggested the nontraditional media provided substance and eliminated sound-bite campaigning—were most likely to appear after the November election.
- Favorable assertions about how the nontraditional media had empowered voters appeared most often after the November election.
- Statements decrying the loss of control by mainstream news media were made most often during the primary season.
- Statements that the rise of nontraditional media signified a harmful and misguided revolt against Washington were *least* likely to be made after the primaries and after the November election.

Sources and Assertive Statements

A clear delineation exists in how sources within the stories in our sample evaluated the nontraditional media campaign. As might be expected, talk-show hosts and politicians viewed the nontraditional media in a more positive light than did journalists and academic expert sources. The hosts of talk shows cited in our sample stories and the politician sources (candidates, staff members, etc.) were consistently more positive and supportive of the nontraditional media as a campaign communication mechanism than were journalists and academic experts, who tended to be skeptical of the usefulness of the nontraditional media.

Academic experts were especially critical of the nontraditional media in stories from our sample, even more so than were journalists. For example, Table 4.2 shows that journalists and academic experts were equally as likely to assert that citizen participants in talk shows asked easy, softball questions of the candidates. But academic experts (several of them political communication scholars) were most likely among all types of sources to term questions from citizen participants "ill informed." Fully one fourth (25.6%) of the statements from academic experts suggested citizen questions were ill informed. The next highest proportion was among politicians, who said the questions from citizens were ill informed about 1 out of 10 times (9.8%). Table 4.2 also clearly shows that when talk-show hosts and politicians referred to the quality of questions from citizens, they usually portrayed them as intelligent and well informed.

Results on assessments of the questions from talk-show hosts reflect similar portrayals, although perhaps not as extreme. Talk-show hosts tended to view their questions and those from colleagues as intelligent and well informed (47.2%), whereas a fourth of the statements from academic experts (26.5%) saw talk-show hosts' questions as ill informed. Roughly the same proportions of statements from journalists (24.2%) and politicians (22.7%) implied that the hosts' questions were ill informed. (Data not tabled.)

Table 4.2. Source Portrayals of Citizen Participation in Nontraditional Media.

Source	Easy, softball %	Ill-Informed %	Difficult, hardball %	Intelligent, well-informed %	(N)
Journalists	29.0	2.8	10.3	57.9	(107)
Talk-show hosts	6.8	4.5	11.4	77.3	(44)
Politicians	3.3	9.8	9.8	82.0	(61)
Academic experts	32.6	25.6	0.0	41.9	(43)

$\chi^2 = 53.848$, $df = 9$, $p < .001$.

Table 4.3 shows a greater negativity among academic experts than journalists toward nontraditional media again in statements that evaluate the substantive quality of the nontraditional media. More than half the statements from academic experts (50.7%) portray nontraditional media as less interpretative and analytical than the traditional media; a third of the statements from journalists do so. In contrast, nearly two thirds of the statements from talk-show hosts (65.3%) say nontraditional media provide more substance and less process-oriented coverage than traditional media do. A majority of statements from politicians (60.6%) say the nontraditional media have helped to eliminate sound-bite journalism in the campaign.

Academic experts are also more critical than other groups when it comes to the ability of candidates to avoid questions from mainstream journalists, although the difference is not statistically significant. More than one fourth of the statements from academic experts (28.4%) suggest that candidates did indeed use the talk shows to avoid answering tough questions from journalists. Interestingly, reaction from politicians and journalists were similar on this variable: Politicians (23.3%) were just as likely as journalists (22.9%) to say that talk shows allowed candidates to avoid tough questioning from journalists. (Data not tabled.)

Further analysis of the data reveals that campaign staff members accounted for the politicians acknowledging candidate circumvention of tough questions. For example, none of the 36 statements attributed by coders to the actual candidates for office asserted that the talk shows allowed the candidates to avoid tough questions, but more than 30% of the statements from campaign staff members made the acknowledgment. A typical statement would have a campaign staffer acknowledg-

Table 4.3. Source Portrayals of Quality of Information on Non-Traditional Media.

Source	More substance, less process %	Eliminates filtered information, sound bites %	Less interpretive %	No follow-ups %	(N)
Journalists	31.9	31.0	33.9	3.2	(248)
Talk-show hosts	65.3	13.9	19.4	1.4	(72)
Politicians	24.8	60.6	13.8	0.9	(109)
Academic experts	11.3	35.2	50.7	2.8	(71)

$\chi^2 = 91.899$, $df = 9$, $p < .001$.

ing the candidate used nontraditional media or talk shows to avoid getting grilled over personal issues. "Sure enough he goes on the *'Today'* show for one solid hour and does not get one personal question," said Clinton media consultant Frank Greer. "He gets only questions about what people really care about . . . it is just the opposite of what the press wants to dwell on" (Rosenstiel, 1992, A1).

Journalists and academic experts were much less judgmental than others on issues dealing with voter empowerment and the relevance of traditional media in the campaign. Nearly half of the statements from talk-show hosts (44%) and politicians (48.9%) suggested that the ability of the nontraditional media to empower citizens was positive, whereas less than a third of the statements from journalists (26.1%) and academic experts (32.4%) did so. However, journalists and academic experts were no more likely than talk-show hosts and politicians to say the ability to empower voters was negative, and they were much more inclined to acknowledge the ability of nontraditional media to empower voters without making a judgment.

The findings are similar with respect to statements that address the possibility that the traditional media's influence was decreasing as the nontraditional media's increased. For example, talk-show hosts and politicians were more likely than journalists and academic experts to assert the decrease was positive, yet just as likely to say the decrease was negative. Meanwhile, journalists and academic experts were more likely to make no judgment at all about the mainstream media's decrease in influence.

CONCLUSIONS

Our results show that stories that dealt with the portrayal of nontraditional media during 1992 were different with respect to both when they appeared and who was making the portrayals. During the primary and Fall campaigns, the tone of stories tended to be negative about characteristics of nontraditional media. Especially after the campaign was over, stories portrayed much more positive reactions to the unconventional new campaign media.

This suggests that a resentment toward nontraditional media and their various participants existed during periods of heavy campaigning, as talk shows, call-in programs, and televised town meetings threatened to usurp the role of the mainstream media. After all, the nontraditional media did indeed provide elements of campaign communication that traditional media did not.

Despite the downsizing of convention coverage by the networks, the traditional media still dominated the convention season to the extent that they would feel less threatened by the nontraditional media during this postprimary period. As for the candidates, the dominance of the conventions as the news story would seem to have precluded any significant opportunities for them to deal with nontraditional media during this time or for the media to cover them.

After the election, the traditional media were typically reflective in their political coverage, providing analysis of election results and interpreting the meaning and impact of the various campaign elements. Within this context it stands to reason that the mainstream media coverage would treat talk-show campaigning more kindly than before. Stories could provide perspective and insight about how and why talk-show campaigning worked, particularly in light of the fact that the successful candidate was a proponent and beneficiary of the nontraditional media. An optimistic interpretation of the lack of hostility toward talk-show campaigning in this period of increased reflection is that it may portend a willingness by traditional news media to accept the changes in 1992's media campaigning and to expect further changes in 1996, and perhaps even to both rethink and implement changes in their own ways of covering the next presidential campaign.

Regardless of when the coverage of nontraditional media was positive or negative, our evidence shows that the reactions often came from sources other than journalists. This is consistent with our previous work on media coverage of debates (see Lemert, Elliott, Bernstein, Rosenberg, & Nestvold, 1991, especially Chapter 3); in order to adhere to a standard of journalistic objectivity, journalists will avoid making judgments themselves about the value of certain types of campaign communication. In the case of debates, journalists relied more often on polls, focus groups, and person-in-the-street interviews to provide judgments about candidates' debate performances and about the debates themselves. In the case of the nontraditional media, journalists frequently used academic experts to provide criticism of the various characteristics of the form, criticism that served to balance the positive reactions that one could expect from participants in nontraditional communication.

ENDNOTES

1. During a postelection panel analysis, *Washington Post* columnist David Broder (1992) indicated that his paper had conducted hundreds of interviews with voters throughout the year leading up to the campaign. Broder indicated the interviews did indicate strong concern about issues such as the economy and health care, but they

apparently did not reveal the strong desire to participate in the process that would manifest itself in 1992.
2. The search for stories focused on nontraditional media, using keywords such as *talk show* and *presidential campaign*. We restricted the search to a period that ran just more than a year, from December 1991 through 1992. The search used the major paper, broadcast transcript, wire service, and magazine files of stories on the Nexis service.

REFERENCES

Broder, D. (1992, December 12). Panel on the news media and the campaign, Annenberg School for Communication, University of Pennsylvania, Philadelphia, PA.

Germond, J., & Witcover, J. (1993). *Mad as hell: Revolt at the ballot box, 1992*. New York: Warner Books.

Lemert, J.B., Elliott, W.R., Bernstein, J.M., Rosenberg, W.L., & Nestvold, K.J. (1991). *News verdicts, the debates, and presidential debates*. New York: Praeger.

Patterson, T.E. (1993). *Out of order*. New York: Knopf.

Rosenstiel, T. (1992, June 13). Call-in shows question tempo of political beat. *Los Angeles Times*, p. A1.

Scott, W.A. (1955). Reliability of content analysis: The case of nominal scale coding. *Public Opinion Quarterly, 19*, 321-325.

5

The Audience for Candidate "Talk Show"

James B. Lemert

This chapter describes the audience for "talk show" appearances by members of the Bush-Quayle, Clinton-Gore and Perot-Stockdale teams. It is based on both the time-series and the panel surveys. In this chapter, we tend to use the term *talk show*, even though some of these television appearances, strictly speaking, were more alternatives to the evening news than they were talk shows (see especially Chapter 3, this volume). Nevertheless, we use that term, sacrificing precision for common usage and convenience, much the way that we use the term *debates* to refer to what many would prefer (with some justification) to call *joint appearances*.

According to a count made by a Freedom Forum research team (Freedom Forum Media Studies Center, 1993, p. 16), the three presidential candidates made a total of 96 appearances from January through Election Day on five shows: *Larry King Live, Donahue,* NBC's *Today,* ABC's *Good Morning America* and CBS's *This Morning*. At 47 appearances, Clinton used the five talk shows most often, followed by Perot (33) and Bush (16). These 96 appearances apparently do not include those in which the vice presidential candidate alone appeared, and of course they do not count talk shows other than the five. Because even a very large total of 96 appearances very likely greatly underestimates the total, 1992's shift to a "talk show" campaign strategy certainly did not go unnoticed.

Two *Times Mirror* polls, several books, and a scattered academic literature so far have had much to say about the phenomenon. A summary follows.

CRITICISMS OF CANDIDATE TALK SHOWS

As the preceding chapter showed, some journalists as well as some nationally prominent academics were sharply critical of the quality of information provided by the talk shows, especially while the campaign was going on. Although we do not look beyond the survey data in this chapter, it is important to take account of the arguments about the talk show campaign because these arguments have strong implications concerning how the audience used talk shows—and what that audience was like. First we review the criticisms and then the defenses made of the talk show campaign.

Several prominent national journalists, for example, ABC's Ted Koppel, Chris Bury (1993), and Robert Novak (1992), have criticized the quality of the questions asked by citizens in such formats. Among other quality problems given by Koppel and some other journalists was the *amateurism* factor: Citizens are not used to framing questions, and this is the first time they have been on national television, looking directly at somebody who either is, or might be, President of the United States, so naturally they are going to stammer and ask imprecise questions. "They (presidents and other politicians) get easier questions from average Americans than they do from us," according to National Public Radio correspondent Mara Liasson (1993). Referring to the Richmond "town hall" format debate, elite columnist Robert Novak erupted on CNN's *Capital Gang* with the following: "That's a terrible format to have—I mean, it looks like the Phil *Donahue* show. That didn't have the feel and texture of a presidential debate. I mean, I thought the questions were stupid" (Novak, 1992). Discussing the Richmond debate on a National Public Radio program, Elizabeth Drew (1992), Washington correspondent for *The New Yorker* magazine, agreed: "The problem with this format is the candidates don't get pressed on the flaws in what they are saying."

Another related criticism emerging about the 1992 campaign appearances on talk shows seems to be that candidates like Clinton "play the studio audience like a saxophone," in the words of ABC correspondent Chris Bury (1993). Not only are the questions easy, this argument asserts, but the audience can be led to believe there is more to the answer than there really is. In a *Nightline* piece, Bury (1993) used a sound bite from political scientist Michael J. Robinson to make this point: "So what you've got in a town meeting is simply this: people standing up and talking about their personal problems, and the President saying, either as psychotherapist or as minister or as close friend, 'There, there, now. I'll try to make it better for you.'" In essence, this criticism says that *audiences are duped.*

In a related vein, political scientist W. Lance Bennett (1993) said that Bill Clinton used talk shows *to market himself* to voters, using the talk-show format to create a *false sense of intimacy* between himself and audience members. According to Bennett, the Clinton campaign found that matters they previously had tried to cover up—for example, the problems and personal histories of Bill Clinton's father and brother—actually helped create sympathy for the candidate when he "revealed" them on the talk shows. "Far from drawing people into issue discussions, talk shows were more a way of marketing Bill Clinton," Bennett asserted.

On the other hand, Germond and Witcover (1993, pp. 275-278) asserted that talk show hosts can be "electronic bully boys" or "the scandalmonger masquerading as a journalist." Yet they concede that the studio audience chastened Phil Donahue for his persistent questions about Clinton's personal life.

A final, and very obtrusive, theme was that talk shows allow candidates to do an *end run around journalists* and their tough, informed questions (Bennett, 1993; Drew, 1992; Koppel, 1993; Novak, 1992).

COUNTERING THE CRITICISMS

With all this criticism of the talk shows, why did a 1992 *Times Mirror* poll ("Voters say thumbs up," 1992) show slightly higher ratings being given talk show hosts than the press for "the way they handled themselves during the [1992 presidential] campaign"? Why did the same poll show much higher percentages believing they knew more about the issues in 1992 than was the case when a similar poll was done in 1988?

Many content studies have repeatedly shown that the news media provide very little coverage of presidential campaign policy issues (e.g., Patterson, 1980, 1993; Patterson-McClure, 1976), stressing tactics and performance rather than matters voters might care about (e.g., Lemert, Elliott, Bernstein, Rosenberg, & Nestvold, 1991). "The public saw the traditional press as snide, frenzy-driven trivializers who were contributing to the erosion of their democracy," wrote talk-show host Larry King (1993, p. 6) in his book about the 1992 campaign. If voters have not been well served by the way the news media customarily cover presidential campaigns, this argument goes, why shouldn't voters try other ways of finding out about the candidates? Furthermore, even if the "talk show experiment" turns out not to be as good a way as (say) presidential debates, American journalists have had about two centuries to settle on the basics of what to them seems "the best" way to cover a presidential campaign, so American voters are entitled to a little more than one election cycle to sort out what works for them.

Preliminary support for this argument comes from Ridout (1993), who compared network news and talk show coverage of the campaign in June 1992, when Clinton was running third in the polls and appearing on many talk shows in an effort to reach the voters and alter his poll standing. Ridout concluded that the news once more had "failed" to provide issue coverage, whereas the talk shows provided plenty of it: "Talk shows provided an alternative form of communication which contributed to a substantive dialogue between candidates and the voters" (p. 715).

As for whether the questions asked by citizens match up well with those asked by journalists, a study by Miller (1993) compared questions asked at the "town hall" debate against those asked by journalists in the other presidential debates. Miller found that, although voter questions may not have been as elegantly worded as those from journalists, the three candidates actually answered voter questions much more often than they did questions from journalists. "When 'better' is defined by whether the topic of the question matched that of the answer . . . nonjournalists . . . appeared to be much more effective in getting straight answers" (pp. 17-18), she concluded. A similar study by Eveland, McLeod, and Nathanson (1993) found that journalists asked more concise questions than voters, but the questions from journalists also were more likely to be argumentative, accusatory, and leading.

Like the writers of these research papers, political scientist Thomas E. Patterson observed (1993, pp. 55-56) that voters and journalists seemed to be preoccupied by remarkably different concerns when they asked questions of candidates. Instead of comparing questions asked at the debates, Patterson compared questions asked on television call-in programs with those asked by journalists at a Bush campaign press conference. Voters called in questions about problems (e.g., would you give money to Russia?), Patterson concluded, whereas press conference questions were about strategy and tactics—"the game," as Patterson put it.

A study by Sandell, Mattley, Evarts, Lengel and Ziyati (1993, p. 27) concluded that voters are forced to try to make sense out of campaigns along lines that depart considerably from the frames provided by conventional news coverage: "these persons in many cases made sense [of the campaign] in spite of media coverage. They eagerly sought out opportunities to view the candidates and decide on their own, watching the debates, the infomercials and the talk show appearances" (emphasis added).

Polar Opposites

Taken to their extremes, we have two almost completely opposed views here of candidate talk shows and their audiences. The first view claims that their content reveals nothing that voters need to know, yet can dupe and deceive voters by giving them the false impression that they have actually learned something. By implication, this view says talk-show viewers are not savvy enough about politics to see through what candidates are, and are not, saying on the talk shows. These viewers are thought to be so dependent on the candidate talk shows to follow the campaign that they lack the background information to recognize when hosts ask "softball" questions of the candidates. Implicit in this argument is the assumption that people following the campaign through the talk shows are not following it in any other way.

The opposite viewpoint is that political talk shows represent a logical first step by voters toward regaining more control of the information resources they need to decide who should be their next president. Candidate talk-show viewers have recognized that journalists are not giving them the information they need to have about the presidential campaign. This argument also implies that the talk shows have enlarged the numbers of Americans who are interested in following the campaign. The further implication of this is that, like the "polar opposite" view presented earlier, at least some of the people following the presidential campaign via the talk shows are not following it in any other way.

This chapter looks at the survey data to test the merits of these two contending viewpoints, both where they disagree about the nature of the 1992 presidential talk-show audience and on the few occasions where they seem to agree. When we examine our survey results, we first look closely at who was in the audience for the candidates. In the second section, we examine whether the talk shows imparted information about the candidates to the audience. In the third section, we take a look at how respondents evaluated the talk shows. The final section concerns how and whether exposure to talk shows seemed to influence anybody's candidate preferences.

THE AUDIENCE FOR TALK SHOWS

Audience Size

Some (Michael Schudson, as cited by Asard, 1993) assert that the audience for 1992 campaign talk shows was too small to be of much importance. What does our survey evidence tell us about how big the audience was? First, it is important to realize that no single appearance by a given candidate on a given show commanded a very large share of the audience. Nevertheless, based on our survey results, cumulatively a very large share watched at least some candidates on some talk show somewhere.

September Audience. Just after the traditional Labor Day start of the Fall campaign, slightly more than a third of our Wave 1 respondents reported already having seen Bush, Quayle, Clinton, or Gore on a talk show (recall that Perot had not yet reentered the race, so we did not ask about him). At only 8.1%, Clinton's appearance on the Arsenio Hall Show, complete with saxophone, had the single most often recalled early season viewership.

Audience by October. By the time of Waves 2 through 5 (October 11-22), almost 45% said they had seen a presidential or vice presidential candidate on a talk show (but recall that the candidates now include Perot and Stockdale). During this time period, the largest single reported viewership was Perot on *Larry King Live* (9.6%), but this number does not distinguish among Perot's several appearances on King during 1992, possibly even including his February 20 hint that he could be "drafted" to run. Bush on Larry King (he also made more than one late-campaign appearance with King) finished second among specific shows at 7.1%. A number of respondents remembered seeing one or more of the presidential candidates on a TV talk show, but they could not recall anything about what show it was. If we include these mentions, Clinton would have exceeded Bush on Larry King, with 7.7% of our Wave 2-5 sample, but there is no reason to suppose that everyone had the *same* show in mind—whatever that was!

Attention to the candidates on talk shows thus seemed high but extremely diffuse during Waves 1 and 2-5, having sprinkled itself lightly over a huge variety of viewing opportunities. Already we can sense that this finding differentiates between the much scarcer presidential debates, which had very large audiences for a few debates, and the talk shows, which had a substantial audience spread thinly across many shows. In any case, even though the overall talk show audience was large, did it seem to get larger as the election neared?

Audience by November. Because Wave 6 included only panelists, it would be risky to compare their November 1 and 2 reports of talk-show viewing against everybody we interviewed during the September and October waves. But we can compare viewing rates only among panelists, and the key result is that reported viewing of candidates on talk shows increased from just under 35% in early September to *almost 65%* in our November questionnaire, a very large (and statistically significant) increase. In addition, even starting with the October height of the campaign, the number of panelists reporting that they watched a candidate talk show increased from the October 11-22 period to November by a 5 to 1 over the decreases (also a statistically significant increase). In general, then, an increasing number of viewers saw the candidates on talk shows. Who was in this audience? What were they like?

Characteristics of the Audience

In a sense, both sides of the argument about campaign talk shows and their audience tend to assume that the people following the campaign through the talk shows are somehow not using conventional news coverage of the presidential campaign. But after that they diverge somewhat. Critics of the talk-show campaign say this avoidance of conventional news coverage reduces the talk-show viewers' information resources and makes the talk-show audience much less able to detect sophistry and "softball" questions. Also implied is the picture of an audience that has relatively low feelings of political self-confidence. What is fairly clear is that the critics seem to be assuming low information or low attention to the conventional news media as well as low political confidence among talk-show viewers.

Proponents of the talk-show movement tend to say that viewers have made a reasoned decision to look to the talk shows for the information they have not been getting from the conventional news media. In this vision, the talk-show audience would tend to be knowledgeable and self-confident regarding its own ability to judge—and process—campaign information. Whether that reasoned choice of talk shows would lead to actual *avoidance* of conventional news coverage perhaps is not as clearly implied as it is for the audience envisioned by the critics, but we think this viewpoint does imply that at least some members of the audience have made a reasoned decision to forget about conventional news accounts and to rely instead on alternative ways of learning about the candidates.

We asked our respondents a number of questions about their political attitudes and demographic characteristics (age, education, and so on). Let's see how talk show viewers differ from nonviewers.

Efficacy Feelings. As we saw in Chapters 1, 3, and 4, many journalists interpreted the audience's interest in talk-show politics as a kind of revolt against politics as usual, including conventional media portrayals of the presidential campaign. Furthermore, scholars such as Bennett (1993) have implied that following the campaign through talk shows may feel psychologically less alienating than following it through more conventional media. We have ourselves (Lemert et al., 1991, Chapter 5) reported that news media coverage of the debates has tended toward elitist disinterest in the concerns of run-of-the-mill voters. Perhaps, then, conventional news coverage of presidential campaigns may simultaneously undermine the political self-confidence of voters and help alienate them from conventional media coverage of the campaign, thus driving them toward the talk shows. Our measure of political self-confidence is termed *Internal Efficacy* by those developing these scales (Craig, Niemi, & Silver, 1990). We also report results for a second type of efficacy—External Efficacy—which is meant to reflect the belief that the political system is interested in, and responsive to, citizen input.

In our survey we asked everyone two questions as Internal Efficacy measures and two as External Efficacy measures. Each set of two items included one in which agreement with the item resulted in a high efficacy score and one in which disagreement also resulted in a high efficacy score.[1]

When we checked to see whether the two Internal Efficacy items correlated with each other, we found that they had a surprisingly low correlation. The same was true of the two External Efficacy items—how somebody responded to one of the items did not particularly predict how he or she responded to the other. Given these results, we decided to use and test each of the four items separately, rather than to compute overall Internal and External Efficacy scores.

Thus, our results are reported separately for each scale, although we still indicate here which of the two types of efficacy each was supposed to represent:

- Internal Efficacy: "Sometimes politics and government seem so complicated that a person like me can't really understand what's going on" (abbreviated as "Complicated"), and "I feel I could do as good a job in public office as most other people" ("Do Good Job").
- External Efficacy: "If public officials are not interested in hear-

ing what the people think, there really is no way to make them listen" ("No Way"), and "Under our form of government, the people have the final say about how the country is run, no matter who is in office" ("Final Say").

These four items were interspersed throughout a number of other items about other topics. Respondents used a 5-point scale running from Strongly Agree to Strongly Disagree to each of the long series of items. Because "Disagree" responses to two of the four efficacy items—"Complicated" and "No Way"—were actually the high-efficacy response, we reversed the scoring of the responses when needed so that the higher the number, the more positive the efficacy feelings.

Results for the efficacy measures were more than a little eye-opening: In general, the more candidate talk shows watched, the more positive the Internal Efficacy feelings, regardless of whether we are talking about the "Complicated" or the "Do Good Job" scales. The results for each of the Internal Efficacy items are presented in Table 5.1. Thus the results for Internal Efficacy went in precisely the opposite direction from the hypothesized pattern. Furthermore, contrary to the notion that candidate talk-show viewers were more alienated from "normal" poli-

Table 5.1. Mean Internal Efficacy Scores[a] by Amount of Candidate Talk Show Viewing, October 11-22 Interviews.

Reported viewing of Candidates on Talk Shows	Internal Efficacy Measures	
	Good job in public office**	Politics too complicated for me***
None Seen (N = 842)	2.71	3.05
One Seen (N = 199)	2.69	2.97
Two Seen (N = 136)	2.69	3.18
Three Seen (N = 114)	3.06	3.27
More (N = 71)	2.86	3.52

**$p < .05$.
***$p < .01$.
[a]The full efficacy measures are: (a) I could do as good a job in public office as most people; (b) Sometimes politics seems too complicated for people like me. Responses ranged from 1 (strongly disagree) to 5 (strongly agree). The higher the score, the more positive the efficacy feelings. When the item is worded negatively (e.g., politics too complicated to understand), scoring is reversed to give higher scores to disagree responses.

tics, the viewing audience for talk shows had scores for each of the *External* Efficacy scales that were essentially the same as scores for the nonviewers. People were less willing to endorse the "Final Say" item than to reject the "No Way" item, but the amount of candidate talk-show viewing made no difference. Scores for the "No Way" item ranged from 3.10 to 3.70, with an overall mean of 3.14, slightly above the midpoint of the efficacy scale. Scores for "Final Say" ranged from just under 2.40 to 2.60—all well on the low side of this 5-point efficacy scale.

Interest: Besides high Internal Efficacy, viewers of the most talk shows also expressed the highest amount of interest in the presidential campaign (data not tabled, probability of this result occurring by chance was less than 1 in 100: $p < .01$). Talk-show viewers were more interested in the presidential campaign than everybody else.

Demographics: When we examined whether any demographics related to the number of candidate talk shows, it was striking how few of them did. The number of candidate talk shows seen was significantly related (we defined "significant" as $p < .05$) only to years of education. Given the results for each of the Internal Efficacy scales, it perhaps no longer is quite as surprising to say that heavier viewers of candidate talk shows had more years of education than lighter viewers. Meanwhile, gender, occupation, income, marital status, and race—all of them—did not predict the number of candidate talk shows seen.

Let's turn now to some other aspects of the argument about the talk-show audience. Our analyses and tables will be more complicated than what was done in Table 5.1, as we explain next.

Use of Mainstream Media: Before we present these and other results, we should explain a little about how to read the tables and what to look for. Many of our tables present the results of a statistical procedure called Multiple Classification Analysis (MCA). What MCA does is test whether each of a series of many predictors actually relates to the "dependent" variable. In the case of "mainstream" media use, there are actually two such dependent variables: the number of days per 7-day week that each respondent reads the newspaper, and the number of evenings per 7-day week that each respondent watches the network news.

MCA does more than just simultaneously test whether there are relationships between predictors and a dependent variable. It allows us to "control"—to eliminate from further consideration—the predictors in which we are less interested but must take into account, such as education level. When those controls are exerted, we in effect extract from the dependent variable every ounce of variability that can possibly be attributed to those control variables, leaving only whatever variance remains. Only then is the key communication variable in which we are interested allowed any chance to predict what happens. In the case of this chapter, exposure to candidate talk shows is the key predictor that is not allowed to explain the dependent variable until after all the controls are exerted. Obviously, then, this approach gives the benefit of the doubt to the control variables rather than talk-show exposure.

What rivals to talk-show exposure do we need to control before we allow the talk-show experience to explain anything? Education generally predicts media exposure, so we ought to extract whatever influence it might have. As we already saw, education was the only demographic variable to predict exposure to talk shows.

Our results and perhaps those by Newhagen[2] (1993) show that high Internal Efficacy predicts larger numbers of candidate talk shows seen, so we should introduce as controls each of its two scales—"Complicated" and "Do Good Job." Although we already saw that neither External Efficacy scale ("No Way" and "Final Say") was particularly related to attention to talk shows, each may very well be related to attitudes toward talk-show politics and certain other aspects of the campaign that will serve as dependent variables later in this chapter.

Finally, we wanted to consistently control for three other variables: presidential campaign interest, political party identification, and whether respondents were part of our panel survey or the single-interview, time-series sample. Interest in the presidential campaign could easily be a powerful predictor of political message attention, political knowledge, and numerous other dependent variables that we use in this chapter to describe what talk-show audience members are like. Political party identification is a good indicator of some attitudinal predispositions of respondents—presumably existing prior to any of the talk-show communication experiences we are concerned with in this chapter, so we give it priority over talk-show exposure. Finally, because for certain purposes we wanted to combine panelists with single-interview time series respondents, we needed to protect against the possibility that panelists, having been interviewed before, might have been sensitized by a previous interview.

Although we hope that the logic of the analysis is clear now, we fear that the lay reader may find these MCA tables a bit mind-boggling at first. The reader will come across two terms in the table that need a bit more explanation: *regressions* and *adjusted means*. When the control variable is a "continuous" one (e.g., years of education or a 1 to 5 efficacy or campaign interest scale), the term regression will appear. A regression figure describes whether the predictor is positively or negatively related to the dependent variable: If positive, the values of the predictor and dependent variable rise and fall together, and if negative, the value of one rises while the other falls. For lay readers, the numerical value taken by the regression figure is not important. When the predictor variable assumes categorical values (e.g., did the respondent watch a debate or not?), then the tabled figures are *adjusted means*. The means for each category have been adjusted for the influence of all preceding predictors listed above this variable in the table. This is how the influence of all the controls is extracted before our talk-show variable is given any chance to explain things.

In this section, we test whether, as both critics and supporters of the talk-show trend seemed to believe, talk-show audiences had turned away from the mainstream news media. Once again, our results (Table 5.2) challenge this widely shared belief about Campaign `92. Even after we had controlled for the eight other variables that could rival talk-show exposure as predictors of the frequency of newspaper reading and of newscast viewing, we find that the more talk shows watched, the more days the evening news is watched and the newspaper is read. A clear cutting point for both network news viewing and newspaper reading once again appears to be at three or more candidate talk shows. In the middle column of the table, when we look at newscast viewing, viewers of three or more candidate talk-show appearances bunched around five evenings a week of network newscasts, well above the rest of the respondents. Mean days reading all were well over four days a week for people reporting three or more exposures to candidates on talk shows, and less than four days a week for those reporting two or fewer talk-show exposures. Overall, respondents averaged slightly fewer days of newspaper reading than network news viewing, a finding consistent with widespread reports that network TV news has become the medium of choice for following the presidential campaign.

Before we leave Table 5.2, we should also point out an interesting finding concerning whether the respondents were panelists. Note that the adjusted means show that panelists read and watched the news *fewer* days per week than did our other respondents. This finding, in a way, is rather reassuring: It suggests that people who agreed to be panelists were *not* stimulated by our first interview with them so as to pay more attention to the news. In any case, though, whether respondents were panelists will continue to be controlled throughout the analyses in this chapter.

In general, then, heavy viewers of candidate talk shows also were heavier viewers and readers of the news. We know as well that, even after we controlled for the same eight control variables, heavy viewers of candidate talk shows also evaluated presidential campaign coverage by a variety of conventional news media as more useful to

Table 5.2. Summary of Multiple Classification Analyses: Influence of Candidate Talk Show Viewing on News Media Consumption; Adjusted Mean Scores and Regression Coefficients.

Predictors[a]	Days Watching Network TV News $M = 4.04$		Days Reading Newspaper $M = 3.84$	
Regressions[b]				
Education	-.070**		.200***	
Efficacy				
"Too complicated"	---		.275***	
"Do good job"	---		---	
"No way"	.122*		---	
"Final say"	---		---	
Campaign Interest	.122*		---	
Adjusted Means[c]				
Party Identification	---		---	
Panel Member				
No	4.12***		4.01***	
Yes	3.62		3.02	
Number of Candidate Talk Shows Seen				
None (N)	3.62***	(581)	3.72**	(722)
One	4.63	(144)	3.95	(177)
Two	4.61	(78)	3.54	(121)
Three	5.03	(73)	4.28	(100)
More	5.09	(43)	4.75	(64)

*$p < .10$.
**$p < .05$.
***$p < .01$.

[a] The predictor variables are listed in order of analytical priority.
[b] The lay reader should pay attention to whether the sign before the regression numbers is + or -; that tells you whether the relationship between the control variable and the dependent variable is positive (as education increases, days reading the newspaper increases) or negative (as education increases, days watching network TV news decreases).
[c] The "adjusted means" represent the mean scores for each category of political party, panel membership, and number of candidate talk shows seen after adjusting for the influence of all preceding control variables in the multiple classification analysis. Basically, these "adjusted means" represent what the mean scores would be if all of the people interviewed were equivalent on the other variables. These procedures are followed for Tables 5.3, 5.4, and 5.6.

them than did lighter viewers of candidate talk shows. These results are not tabled, but include such mainstream campaign news sources as newspapers and television as well as such elite interview shows as *This Week with David Brinkley*. Furthermore, as campaign talk-show viewing increased, viewing of all three presidential debates also increased. Viewing of the Quayle-Gore-Stockdale debate apparently did not.

What is beginning to emerge here is a portrait of a self-confident, media-savvy, well-educated audience for campaign talk shows. Clearly, talk-show viewers were interested, educated, and used the talk shows as only one of a wide repertoire of campaign information sources. The high education and interest of talk-show viewers tends to undercut critics of the talk shows as a campaign vehicle. The very wide use of all media by talk-show viewers undercuts an assumption common to both critics and supporters of the talk-show movement. Given the findings so far, we should expect another finding that critics should find uncomfortable: *The more talk shows viewed, the more respondents should know about the campaign.*

DO VIEWERS LEARN MORE?

Ideally, we would like to argue, if our prediction about knowledge differences is correct, that viewing more talk shows causes respondents to learn more about candidate stands and presidential campaign issues. Because we would like to test that argument, we use the MCA once again. Assuming that we do find that more frequent candidate talk-show viewers know more, at least two explanations of this finding are possible. Viewers know more because they are more interested, they consume more of all media content, they watch the *presidential* debates more often, they have higher Internal Efficacy and more years of education. In effect, this explanation asserts that both viewing of talk shows and knowledge are effects of other factors. Second, whereas all the relationships listed here may be true, even after we extract the influence of these factors, talk-show exposure still predicts knowledge. In effect, the campaign talk shows are added to a list of determinants of voter knowledge.

Even if "only" the first explanation were supported, we would again have evidence against any talk-show criticisms that assume a helpless audience. If we find that the second explanation is supported, we can perhaps make an even stronger assertion about the talk show phenomenon, that is, that some or all of these shows must have contained campaign information that is learned by viewers.

During the October 11-22 phase of the study, we asked respondents to identify for us which presidential candidate or candidates had endorsed three policy proposals: a constitutional amendment prohibiting most abortions (Bush), a higher income tax for persons with annual income of $200,000 or more (Clinton), and 10-cent-per-gallon increases in gasoline taxes each of five consecutive years (Perot). In each of these three policy areas, well over half our October 11-22 respondents were able to recognize which candidate favored the proposal (abortion, 66%; higher taxes for higher-income people, 85%; gas tax, 64%). Correct matches on each question were scored 1, incorrect ones 0, and the scores were added across all three items, thus yielding a total information score that could range from 0 to 3.

Knowing the answers to these questions would mean that the respondent had begun clearly to differentiate among the candidates and that this knowledge might be of considerable help in making a voting choice. If, after controlling for the competing predictors, heavier talk-show viewing continues to predict the learning of information such as this, a strong case can be made that at least some of the campaign talk shows contained the kind of information that would assist viewers to make a voting choice.

For this key test, we gave analytical priority to education, campaign interest, the number of days per week spent watching network news and reading the newspaper, each of the two Internal Efficacy scales, political party affiliation, whether the respondent had been interviewed in September as a panelist, and debate viewing. Only then was the amount of candidate talk show viewing allowed to account for knowledge.

Table 5.3 presents the results, which were organized for the aftermath of each debate. Although our talk-show viewing predictor may be applicable across the entire Fall campaign, the debate viewing variable was specific to each presidential debate, so the MCAs in Table 5.3 were completed using the smaller numbers of interviews following each of the three presidential debates. In these analyses, there was no overlap in samples: People interviewed after the first debate constituted our first sample, people interviewed after the October 15 Richmond debate our second, and people interviewed after the October 19 debate our third.

Education, campaign interest, days per week of network news viewing, and one Internal Efficacy scale ("Complicated") were positively related to knowledge in each of the three separate samples. Newspaper reading was more weakly related ($p < .10$ twice, $p < .05$ once). Only in the aftermath of the final debate did panelists differ from single-interview respondents.

Regardless of which presidential debate it was, in general the adjusted means showed that the more of the debate watched, the higher the knowledge score. In two cases (Debates 1 and 2), people who said

Table 5.3. Summary of Multiple Classification Analyses: Debate and Talk Show Exposure as Predictors of Knowledge (Range = 0 - 3) of Candidates' Policy Proposals Adjusted Mean Scores and Regression Coefficients.

	Debate I Knowledge	Debate II Knowledge	Debate III Knowledge
Overall Means	2.00	2.04	2.06
Predictors[a]			
Regressions[b]			
Education	.117****	.115****	.099****
Campaign Interest	.089**	.109***	.124****
Network News	.053***	.062****	.050***
Newspaper Reading	.031*	.052*	.051****
Internal Efficacy			
"Do Good Job"	---	---	---
"Too Complicated"	.149****	.136***	.148****
Adjusted Means**			
Party Identification	---	---	
Panel Member	---	---	
No (N)			2.03**(407)
Yes			2.24 (72)
View Debate?			
No	1.90*** (220)	1.87*** (216)	1.84*** (220)
A Little	1.77 (17)	1.78 (17)	1.92 (19)
Some	1.88 (36)	2.05 (28)	2.19 (45)
Most	2.10 (54)	2.22 (56)	2.15 (78)
All	2.28 (85)	2.42 (83)	2.32 (117)
Campaign Talk Shows			
None	1.88*** (266)	1.95*** (204)	1.99*** (324)
One	2.21 (74)	2.20 (62)	2.19 (62)
Two	2.44 (38)	2.63 (26)	2.43 (38)
Three	2.01 (23)	1.97 (31)	2.14 (36)
More	2.02 (11)	2.03 (17)	2.00 (19)

*$p < .10$.
**$p < .05$.
***$p < .01$.
****$p < .001$.
[a] The predictor variables are listed in the order entered.
[b] See explanation for "regression" and "adjusted means" in Table 5.2.

they did not watch had slightly higher means than people who said they watched just a little. In this chapter, however, our primary interest is in the talk-show campaign. We use the debates here as a control because heavy viewers of talk shows also were heavy viewers of the presidential debates, as we reported earlier. (See Chapter 8 for analyses of the debates and learning.)

Even after controlling for debate exposure, the talk shows seemed to have an independent effect, although the adjusted means show what looks like a curvilinear effect: The highest scores were for those who watched one or two such candidate appearances, followed by those who watched three or more, followed by those who did not watch any. Although it is tempting to dismiss as a byproduct of small, unstable sample sizes the dip taken by those with the highest talk show exposure, the fact remains that nearly identical dips occurred in each of these three independent samples.

One clue in interpreting these results can be found by looking at the means for the talk-show exposure groups *before* they have been adjusted for the influence of the other predictors. For each of the three independent samples, the effect of adjusting for other predictors disproportionately reduced the scores for the two highest exposure groups, while either minimally reducing or actually raising the adjusted knowledge scores for the no-exposure, one-exposure and two-exposure groups. Recall that we already reported earlier in this chapter that the two heaviest talk-show exposure groups were the most heavily exposed as well to both the presidential debates and to mainstream news coverage, and had more interest, more years of education, and more positive Internal Efficacy feelings. Because the score adjustments were caused by the extraction of the influence of these other predictors, if practically everyone in the two highest exposure talk-show groups possessed these other characteristics, the adjustments arguably would severely and disproportionately reduce their scores, especially in comparison to the no-, one- and two-exposure groups, larger proportions of whom would lack one or more of the highest values taken by education, interest, reading and viewing the news, Internal Efficacy, debate viewing, and so on.

Based on this reasoning, what we conclude about the information effects of viewing candidate talk shows is that, at the very least, the candidate talk shows provided useful and relevant information to people who might otherwise, our other predictors tell us, not have acquired it. Roughly a fourth of each sample was comprised of people who watched either one or two presidential talk shows—a substantial number of people. In general, the heaviest viewers of campaign talk shows seemed to be well-informed, self-confident, media-savvy, and perhaps not so dependent on the talk shows for their information because of the other sources available to them. But the finding in Table 5.3 concerning those who watched a lower number of campaign talk shows is the first to suggest that there might be something to the claim that the talk shows served a real purpose for those who were not quite campaign news "junkies." One can easily imagine a talk-show host reminding a given candidate (and the audience) of some of the candidate's past policy proposals in the course of asking questions. As Patterson (1993) argued, voters can use such information as this to judge what each candidate would do if elected, even in areas not explicitly related to the policy proposal itself.

VIEWERS REACT TO CAMPAIGN TALK SHOWS

One obvious way to see how people reacted to their experiences with candidate talk shows would be to ask them to evaluate the usefulness of talk shows as an information source in helping them decide among the presidential candidates. Table 5.4 presents the MCA results for talk-show ratings by the October respondents. Interestingly, education was *negatively* related to these ratings. In other words, as years of education increased, ratings of talk shows went down. None of the four efficacy scales predicted talk-show ratings at the $p < .05$ level. As campaign interest increased, so did how favorable ratings were of candidate talk shows. Note as well that those who thought of themselves as Democrats gave the most favorable ratings to candidate talk shows as a campaign information source.

Even after all controls, the more talk-show appearances seen, the more favorable the rating given talk shows "where the audience can ask the candidates questions," as our question put it. Note that ratings climbed in virtually an unbroken upward line as the number of reported talk shows also climbed.

So, perhaps we can conclude that the talk-show experience was an increasingly satisfying one for those who watched candidate appearances on them most often. Nevertheless, a skeptic might argue that should not be too surprising. After all, if the experience were frustrating, viewers would drop out—therefore contributing to the lower ratings given by those watching relatively few talk shows. In other words, the findings in Table 5.4 do not rule out the possibility that people who were disappointed by the talk shows dropped out early after watching at most one or two shows.

In order to test this "contrarian" interpretation of Table 5.4, let's therefore use other ways to examine what happens to support for campaign talk shows.

Table 5.4. Summary of Multiple Classification Analysis: Influence of Candidate Talk Show Viewing on Rating of Candidate Talk Shows as a Campaign Information Source; Adjusted Mean Scores and Regression Coefficients.

Predictors[a]	Rating as a Campaign Information Source Range: 0 (lowest) to 10 (highest)	
Regressions[b]		
Education	-.122***	
Efficacy		
"Too complicated"	---	
"Do good job"	---	
"No way"	.173*	
"Final say"	---	
Campaign Interest	.221***	
Adjusted Means[c]		
Party Identification		
Republican (N)	5.05***	(329)
Democrat	5.62	(491)
Independent	5.04	(276)
Panel Member	---	---
Number of Candidate Talk Shows Seen		
None (N)	4.50***	(647)
One	5.70	(168)
Two	6.48	(118)
Three	7.03	(99)
More	7.50	(64)

*$p < .10$.
**$p < .05$.
***$p < .01$.
[a]The predictor variables are listed in order of analytical priority.
[b]See explanation for "regression" in Table 5.2.
[c]See explanation for "adjusted means" in Table 5.2.

Latecomers versus Never Viewers

We already know from our panel data that viewing of candidate talk shows increased from the October waves to the November wave. What this means is that, by November, 65% of the panelists—far more than had watched any candidate talk shows in October—had been introduced to candidate appearances on a talk show. In other words, a substantial number of panelists had watched their first candidate talk show between their second interview in October and their final one in November. For convenience, let's call these panelists *latecomers* to the viewing of candidate talk shows.

The "contrarian" interpretation of Table 5.4 would be in trouble if we found that latecomers had much more favorable ratings of talk shows in November than they did in October. The "contrarian" dismissal of Table 5.4's results would be weakened even more if we also found that latecomers had much more favorable ratings of the candidate talk shows in November than did *never viewers*—those who never did watch any candidate talk shows. How would this reasoning proceed?

Ideally, talk-show ratings by latecomers and never viewers would be the same in the October interview. This would imply that, if self-selection were behind each group's low ratings of talk-show appearances, latecomers and never viewers started out with the same aversion to these appearances. But if, by the November interview, latecomers then gave more positive ratings of talk shows, this would strongly imply that the recent experience of viewing one or more candidate talk show appearances had produced the ratings change.

This package of results is exactly what happened. As Table 5.5 shows, the mean October talk-show ratings were low—and nearly identical—for both latecomers and never viewers. Furthermore, the ratings improved significantly for latecomers in November, while there was hardly any movement at all for the never viewers.

Of course, there were other panelists besides latecomers and never viewers. Did ratings of talk shows improve among all panelists from October to November? Yes, and by a substantial amount—nearly a full rating point on that 0-10 scale (data not tabled; $N = 178$ who provided ratings both times; $p = .001$ by t test). The overall ratings' improvement was driven largely by the latecomers, as we would expect, because only they had the newer experience of watching candidates in a talk show.

Impact of the "Town Hall" Debate

Another analysis suggests itself for a rebuttal of the "contrarian" interpretation of Table 5.4. The October 15 "town hall" debate in effect was a talk show, with questions asked by the audience. A huge audience watched it, even people who still had not watched an "ordinary" candidate visit to a talk show. Within the entire October sample, we can separate ratings of talk shows by wave so that we can compare talk show ratings obtained before the "town hall" debate with those obtained afterward. So we reran the data in Table 5.4 by adding another predictor to

Table 5.5. Comparison of Mean Ratings of Candidate Talk Shows and Changes in Those Ratings by "Latecomer" and "Never-Viewer" Panelists, October and November Waves.

Panelist Group	Mean Talk Rating (Oct.)	Number of Cases[a]	Did Means Differ?	Mean Change in Talk Rating (Oct. to Nov.)	Number of Cases	Did Means Differ?
Late-comers	4.33	40	No, by t-test	2.31	39	Yes, by t-test
Never viewers	4.51	59		.04	54	

[a]The number of cases will vary between tests of October scores and change scores because of missing data.

the batch—wave number. All the other controls remained in place: Were ratings of talk shows more favorable after the Richmond "town hall" debate? Yes, they were. The mean talk show ratings, adjusted for the impact of all the control variables in Table 5.4, were: Wave 2 (October 11 and 12), 4.72; Wave 3 (October 13 and 14), 4.98; Wave 4 (October 15-18), 5.38; Wave 5 (October 19-22), 5.50. These mean differences could have been the result of chance only .011 of the time.

Despite the wave number's importance as an influence on ratings of talk shows, adding it as a variable in the MCA had no discernible impact on talk-show exposure, which remained a highly potent ($p = .000$) predictor of talk-show ratings. Given the overlap with, and lack of change in, the Table 5.4 results, we did not table these MCA results with the wave number introduced into the analysis.

Talk Shows versus Other Media

Compared to other sources of campaign information, how did talk shows rate? When we looked at our large October 11-22 sample, we found that only the televised presidential debates ($M = 6.7$) rated higher on a 0-to-10 scale of usefulness than did the candidate talk shows ($M = 5.3$). Television news coverage of the presidential campaign received a rating (5.1) that was very slightly below that for talk shows. All the other sources—newspaper coverage (4.98), network TV news specials (4.96), TV journalists' interview shows with the candidates (4.91), and televised political advertising (3.4)—received mean ratings that were significantly lower than for the talk shows.[3]

VOTING PREFERENCES

We ran MCAs for each of the four talk-show exposure measures against each respondent's self-declared probability of voting (1) for Clinton, (2) for Perot, and (3) for Bush. The four talk-show exposure measures were: (1) total shows mentioned in which Perot was the guest, (2) total for Clinton as a guest, (3) total for Bush as a guest, and (4) total number of all presidential candidate talk shows.

We therefore had $4 \times 3 = 12$ opportunities to get a significant voting result for a talk-show variable. We found only 3 of the 12 MCAs showing a talk-show relationship that reached at least the $p < .05$ level for the large October sample. At 1 in every 4 tests, that is slightly higher than the chance prediction of almost one significant result out of the 12 tests, but not enough higher to be completely convincing.

However, a little more convincing was some evidence of a pattern in the few results that did reach statistical significance. The pattern was this. The only talk-show variable that predicted odds of voting for Clinton was the one that was specific to Clinton: When we used the number of Clinton talk shows seen, odds of voting for Clinton rose as the number seen increased. Similarly, when we looked at the odds of voting for Perot, it was only an increasing number of Perot talk-show appearances that accompanied a rise in the odds of voting Perot. However, even if we believe these two results to be stable and reliable, they certainly do not conclusively demonstrate that viewing the talk shows caused viewers to want to vote for that candidate. The picture was both further muddied and made more interesting, however, when we looked at odds of voting for Bush. Unlike the other two, it was not the number of Bush talk-show appearances that predicted the Bush vote. Instead, it was the total number of appearances by any of the candidates. Intriguingly, odds of voting for Bush went *down* as the number of all candidate talk shows seen increased.

These MCA results did withstand controls for education, each of the Internal and External Efficacy scales, campaign interest, party identification, and whether the respondent was a panelist. As we will see in more detail in Chapter 6, Bush supporters had lower Internal Efficacy feelings than did Perot and Clinton voters. In Table 5.6, the lower the "Complicated" and "Do Good Job" Internal Efficacy response, the higher the odds of voting for Bush. As we will also see in Chapter 6, Bush voters tended to have higher External Efficacy than Perot voters. Table 5.6 is also consistent with this finding. As agreement that people have the "Final Say" goes up, odds of voting for Bush also rise.

As might be expected, party identification always was very strongly related to the intensity of support for each of the candidates (p = .000 in all cases). The control for party identification did provide some protection against all this being a "less-than-meets-the-eye" apparent effect of the talk shows. That apparent effect would have been produced by self-selection: Perot adherents watched Perot talk shows; Clinton adherents watched Clinton talk shows. Additional assurance came from the fact that Bush's support went *down* as the total number of talk shows by *any* of the candidates went up and was completely unrelated to the number of Bush talk-show appearances seen, unlike Clinton and Perot. Certainly there were plenty of chances for Bush supporters to have watched Bush on talk shows. (By October, 316 of our 1,433 respondents reported watching Bush make one or more talk-show appearances. Yet these self-selected viewers did not especially support Bush.) The results for the number of candidate talk shows seen and the probability of voting for Bush are in Table 5.6. However, when we move from a rating

Table 5.6. Summary of Multiple Classification Analysis: Influence of Candidate Talk Show Viewing on Rating of Chance Respondent Would Vote for George Bush Adjusted Mean Scores and Regression Coefficients.

Predictors[a]	Rating of Chance of Voting for George Bush Range: 0 (lowest) to 10 (highest)	
Regressions[b]		
Education	-.060*	
Efficacy		
"Too complicated"	-.299***	
"Do good job"	-.214***	
"No way"	---	
"Final say"	.330***	
Campaign Interest	---	
Adjusted Means[c]		
Party Identification		(N)
Republican	6.98***	(349)
Democrat	1.24	(532)
Independent	2.87	(280)
Panel Member	---	
Number of Candidate Talk Shows Seen		(N)
None	3.34**	(707)
One	3.68	(170)
Two	3.74	(120)
Three	3.01	(100)
More	2.51	(64)

*$p < .10$.
**$p < .05$.
***$p < .01$.
[a]The predictor variables are listed in order of analytical priority.
[b]See explanation for "regression" in Table 5.2.
[c]See explanation for "adjusted means" in Table 5.2.

measure to a ballot-like question that asked respondents to choose among Bush, Clinton, and Perot, none of the talk-show variables ever did predict the choice, either among the October respondents or the November panelists.

CONCLUSIONS

Regardless of whether and how much they viewed talk-show politics, all our respondents placed talk shows second only to the presidential debates as useful information sources in the 1992 presidential campaign. The talk-show campaign had a large audience, but it was sprinkled over a large number of talk-show appearances by the candidates. Unlike the debates, which had a huge audience for a very small number of viewing opportunities, in the case of the talk shows a very large cumulative audience gradually was assembled over lots of viewing opportunities. By November, 65% of our panelists said they had watched at least one talk-show appearance by a candidate or candidates. This percentage still was not as high as the viewing of at least one of the four debates by our panelists (92%), but it is very high, nevertheless.

Heavier viewers of talk shows were not at all like some of the critics' mental pictures of them. They were highly educated, had strong feelings of Internal Efficacy, had far more than casual interest in the campaign, knew more about candidate policy proposals than did lighter viewers, and used talk-show appearances as only one of a large number of campaign information sources. Critics who assumed that the candidate talk-show audience was composed of helpless souls, unable to evaluate independently what they were seeing and hearing, must find another set of assumptions if they remain intent on decrying the 1992 talk-show campaign.

Advocates for the talk shows, although not contradicted as thoroughly by our results, need to take into account the fact that heavy viewers did *not* desert mainstream media sources, even though the mainstream news media were perceived as less valuable campaign information sources than the talk shows.

Viewers of one or two candidate appearances were the ones who seemed to learn the most from the talk shows. This finding is consistent with the interpretation that the talk shows reached—and informed—people who were not chronic "campaign junkies," an argument that suggests that at least some of the talk shows contained substantive information that allowed voters more clearly to differentiate among the presidential candidates. On its face, knowing the connections between candidates and their policy proposals is precisely what the civics books say voters ought to be able to do.

Candidate appearances on talk shows seemed to be associated strongly but very selectively with the self-declared odds that respondents would vote for Clinton or Perot. The more Perot appearances seen, the higher the odds the respondent would vote for Perot. Similarly, the more Clinton appearances watched, the higher the odds of voting for

Clinton. In October, slightly more people reported seeing a George Bush than a Ross Perot talk show appearance, yet seeing Bush on a talk show bore no relation to the odds of voting for him. Instead, the more talk shows seen—regardless of who the candidate was—the *lower* the odds of voting for George Bush.

Although the popular wisdom about the rise of the candidate talk-show campaign has been as a sort of consumer revolt against the mainstream news media, we think the evidence suggests it is more complicated than that. Viewers of candidate talk shows want to continue to use the conventional news media, and we expect them to do so in 1996. But—and this is a big but—for the first time they are equipped to consider an alternative to conventional network and newspaper coverage and to compare the two alternatives. Some of that comparing they are already doing, as President Clinton takes advantage of many of the alternative ways of sending—and receiving—messages to Americans without the intervention of the conventional news media. Certainly, in the 1992 campaign, conventional media coverage of the presidential campaign both literally and figuratively was tried and found wanting in this comparison.

Obviously, in the long run this does not bode well for the conventional news media, especially if they do not make the effort to think through their many highly questionable campaign coverage practices.

ENDNOTES

1. After each of the efficacy items was read to the respondents, who were asked to rate the extent of their agreement with the item on a 5-point scale that went from Strongly Agree (5), Agree (4), Neither (3), Disagree (2), to Strongly Disagree (1). The two Internal Efficacy items were: "Sometimes politics and government seem so complicated that a person like me can't really understand what's going on," and "I feel I could do as good a job in public office as most other people." Notice that the high efficacy response would be to disagree with the first of these two statements and to agree with the second. The two External Efficacy items also were split between a positive and a negative item and scored in the same way: "If public officials are not interested in hearing what the people think, there really is no way to make them listen" (negative), and "Under our form of government, the people have the final say about how the country is run, no matter who is in office" (positive). The four efficacy scales were intermixed with a larger set of questions about other matters, all in the same Strongly Agree to Strongly Disagree format.

2. In an interesting study conducted near Washington, DC, Newhagen created a "talk show index" that appears to have combined both attention (watching, listening) and activity (actually calling in). Calling in, like any other act of political participation, always has been predicted by efficacy feelings. Unfortunately, not separating attention from calling in does not allow us to know for sure whether our finding about Internal Efficacy predicting attention is unique.
3. These data were based on t-test paired comparisons. Because of missing data for some comparisons, the number of available cases for these comparisons ranged from 1,223 to 1,289. The means reported in the text were based on the maximum available number of cases.

REFERENCES

Asard, E. (1993, November). *Talk show democracy*. Paper presented to the Speech Communication Association, Miami Beach.

Bennett, W.L. (1993, November). *Talk show democracy*. Paper presented to the Speech Communication Association, Miami Beach.

Bury, C. (1993, February 10). Report on *Nightline*.

Craig, S.C., Niemi, R.G., & Silver, G.E. (1990). Political efficacy and trust: A report on the NES pilot study items. *Political Behavior, 12*, 289-314.

Drew, E. (1992, October 17). Interviewed by Daniel Schorr on "Weekend Edition," National Public Radio.

Eveland, W.P., Jr., McLeod, D.M., & Nathanson, A.I. (1993, November). *Reporters vs. undecided voters: An analysis of the questions asked during the 1992 presidential debates*. Paper presented to the Speech Communication Association, Miami Beach.

Freedom Forum Media Studies Center. (1993). *The finish line: Covering the campaign's final days*. New York: The Freedom Forum Media Studies Center at Columbia University.

Germond, J.W., & Witcover, J. (1993). *Mad as hell: Revolt at the ballot box, 1992*. New York: Warner Books.

King, L., with Stencel, M. (1993). *On the line: The new road to the White House*. New York: Harcourt Brace.

Koppel, T. (1993, February 10). Dial-in democracy: Clinton's town meeting. *Nightline*.

Lemert, J.B., Elliott, W.R., Bernstein, J.M., Rosenberg, W.L., & Nestvold, K.J. (1991). *News verdicts, the debates, and presidential campaigns*. New York: Praeger.

Liasson, M. (1993, February 10). Dial-in democracy: Clinton's town meeting. *Nightline*.

Miller, C.B. (1993, August). *Questions vs. answers in the 1992 presidential debates: A content analysis of interviewing styles*. Paper presented to the Radio-Television Journalism Division, Association for Education in Journalism and Mass Communication convention, Kansas City, MO.

Newhagen, J.E. (1993, August). *Self efficacy, class, race, and call-in political television show use*. Paper presented to the Association for Education in Journalism and Mass Communication convention, Kansas City, MO.

Novak, R. (1992, October 17). Review of the presidential debates. CNN's *The Capital Gang*, Transcript #41-1.

Patterson, T. E. (1980). *The mass media election: How Americans choose their president*. New York: Praeger.

Patterson, T. E. (1993). *Out of order*. New York: Alfred A. Knopf.

Patterson, T., & McClure, R. D. (1976). *The unseeing eye*. New York: G.P. Putnam's Sons.

Ridout, C. F. (1993). News coverage and talk shows in the 1992 presidential campaign. *PS: Political Science & Politics, 26*, 712-716.

Sandell, K. L., Mattley, C., Evarts, D. R., Lengel, L., & Ziyati, A. (1993, November). *Media and voter decision-making in campaign 1992*. Paper presented to the Political Communications Division, Speech Communications Association, Miami Beach.

Voters say thumbs up to campaign, process & coverage. (1992, November 15). *Times Mirror* Center for The People & The Press, Survey XIII.

6

Perot, the "Perot People," and the Press

James B. Lemert

"Who are these people, anyway?" That is the way one article about Ross Perot's supporters put the question in *Campaigns & Elections: The Magazine for Political Professionals* (Hamilton & Mealiea, 1993). That is also partly what this chapter is about: What were the Perot supporters in our samples like? Where did they come from? How did they differ from Clinton and Bush supporters? What can we tell about what they might do in the future?

Some of the same questions, of course, could have been asked about Ross Perot himself. We look briefly at the way the news media first virtually ignored Perot, then tried—and once again failed—to come to grips with who and what Perot, for better or worse, represented. A qualitative examination of media coverage strongly suggests that underestimating him seemed to have been the most visible and consistent error the news media made about Ross Perot in 1992.

We also speculate briefly about why the Clinton and Bush campaigns treated Perot with kid gloves. Then we briefly contrast that treatment with the markedly different way Vice President Al Gore treated Perot in the 1993 NAFTA Great Debate.

PEROT AND THE MEDIA

It has often been remarked that Perot seemed reluctant to do conventional campaign appearances before crowds, instead preferring to use the mass media. Having turned down the restraints on spending that would have been imposed if he had accepted federal matching funds for his campaign, he spent more money on campaign ads than any presidential candidate in history.

Although it is true that voters had no trouble finding Ross Perot in the media in 1992, it is also true that, over time, Perot became very selective in which media he used. At a press conference following the October 19 debate, Perot accused journalists of wishing he were not in the race: "You guys hate that I'm in the race. What a bunch of jerks. . . .You guys have less respect in this country than Congress" (Rosenstiel, 1993, p. 336). Although Perot did not make quite as many appearances as Clinton did on the morning news shows, *Larry King Live* and *Donahue* (Freedom Forum Media Studies Center, 1993, p. 16), nevertheless his campaign since his October 1 reentry seemed largely to be visible on the debates, the talk shows, and his paid commercials.

Reporters and editors certainly noticed this, but so little time remained between his reentry and election day that relatively few either began or restarted the hard, investigative work that had been shelved when Perot withdrew July 16. Another factor that discouraged investigative reporting was the mistaken belief that Perot was merely an eccentric billionaire who had completely destroyed his electoral prospects by withdrawing in July. Newsweek ("Ego trip," 1992), in fact, greeted his October 1 return with the words "ego trip" superimposed in large letters on Perot's picture.

Indeed, underestimation of Perot seemed to be the most common mistake that journalists made. Although in June and July and after his October 1 return Perot made no secret of his hostility to questions from journalists, journalists seemed to assume that the mass audience wanted them to ask him those questions. Whether that was so still remains an open question. In any case, despite Perot's inability to hide his hostility toward the press, he might very well have understood the media better than the media understood him.

In July, given the talkative Ed Rollins's departure and given a rising tide of investigative reporting about his personal history, Perot might well have decided that the best way to control the damage was to withdraw until early October, in the meantime both continuing to build up an organization that he could control and getting on the remaining state ballots. As long as these efforts were kept relatively quiet, Perot, his stories about himself, and his personal history would all be "old news" to the restless news crowd. If this were what Perot expected would happen, he was largely correct. We present now a qualitative study of Perot's coverage at the various turning points in his 1992 campaign career.

"I'm Available"–Larry King, Feb. 20

Almost no attention was paid by the mainstream news media to Perot's initial statement that he would be available if put on each state's ballot. A computer search[1] of national news media turned up only a single, 133-word *Los Angeles Times* article during the rest of February about Perot's statement. In the first week of March, there were brief references to Perot's statement on CNN's March 5 *Inside Politics* and a brief March 6 item on *The Hotline*, an "insider" newsletter used by many political journalists. It was not until David Gergen wrote a lengthy piece on Perot for the March 16 *US News & World Report* that reporters and editors began to show some interest.

When Perot appeared March 24 on *Donahue*, his toll-free 800 number generated 18,000 calls in the first 30 seconds (King & Stencel, 1993, p. xiv). Even then, the next items to be found were not until March 29, and both were boiled-down op-ed versions of Gergen's longer magazine article that ran in both the *Los Angeles Times* and *Washington Post* (1992). Gergen's articles suggested the possibility that Perot might represent something important and might add something to the campaign, should he summon the nerve and will to enter.

As is so often the case, the Gergen articles in three prestige media probably had at least as much impact on journalists (and perhaps talk-show producers) as on voters. *Time Magazine* weighed in on April 6 with an article buried in the middle of the magazine ("Plutocratic populist," 1992, p. 19): "Given his record of stirring things up, it is not so surprising that Perot, 61, has embarked on . . . his self-appointed mission . . . to restore power to average people." As seemed to be true of most media coverage throughout 1992, the story seemed to concentrate on who Perot was rather than what he might represent.

Sign On, Sign Up-Larry King Again

By the time Perot appeared again on Larry King's mid-April show, Perot's toll-free number reportedly had already received startlingly high numbers of calls urging him to run. Political reporters were beginning to assess Perot's chances. By the end of the month, a piece in *The Christian Science Monitor* by John Dillin (1992, p. 1) asserted that Perot "now seriously threatens" the chances of both Bush and Clinton, according to the polls and to political insiders. Dillin's article cited a Dallas newspaper report that Perot had already met ballot requirements in 15 states. Only relatively deep in the story was pollster George Shipley quoted describing Perot as "very adroitly" capturing "the anger that Americans feel toward politics as usual." Even here, the quote focused on his ability to capture the anger, not the anger itself.

Although during this period there was a relative shift of press focus toward Perot's following rather than Perot himself, the shift nevertheless represented an assessment of the size and organizational strength of his following, not really what the Perot followers believed. For the time being, a little less attention was being paid to Perot the man (although the term *billionaire* hardly ever escaped the use of the journalist) and more attention was paid to Perot—The Political Force.

Newsweek combined a focus on both The Political Force and on Perot himself in an April 27 feature article that presented his standing (20%) in its presidential "horse-race" poll along with a biography and interview: "What kind of man would spend $100 million of his own money to run for president? Only someone as rich, outspoken and messianistic as Ross Perot" ("The wild card," 1992, p. 21).

The Political Force

During May and early June, the news media seemed preoccupied with Perot's standing in the polls. That this preoccupation, combined with Perot's performance on *Meet the Press*, ultimately would lead to intense efforts to scrutinize Perot's background and character was almost a certainty. Meanwhile, a *Time*-CNN poll May 13 and 14 found Perot with 33% leading Bush (28%) and Clinton (24%). Electoral College projections suggested Clinton would have trouble winning more than Arkansas's six electoral votes. In California's June 2 primary the combined network exit poll showed Clinton able to hang onto only 51% of the Democrats in a November three-way race (Hines, 1992). In addition, the exit poll suggested Perot would have won both the California Democratic and Republican nominations if he had been listed and had a slate of delegates.

By mid-June, several polls showed Perot with something of a "gender gap" problem: Women were starting to feel uneasy about him. By June 17, the first poll was published that showed Perot's support was down slightly.

Who Is Perot? Journalists Start Digging

Perot's May 3 appearance on *Meet the Press* reinforced journalists' belief that he—and his idiosyncracies—was the story. Helped by leaks and tips from the White House and other insiders, media investigations began in earnest. For example, we were told that Perot wanted to be released from the Navy a year earlier than specified by the terms of his Naval Academy education agreement. Undoubtedly this information was leaked to the news media. Eventually, in the aftermath of stories about his hiring investigators to check the backgrounds of business associates and of some volunteer supporters, journalists and other insiders started using the tongue-in-cheek "Inspector Perot" label to refer to him. A June 15 article in *The Nation* termed Perot an "Electronic Caesar" (Dugger, 1992). A June 29 Cox News Service piece by Joseph Albright (1992, p. B8) even found it newsworthy when Perot did not investigate a business associate, one Abolfath Mahui. Albright strongly implied that Perot resisted his "compulsion to investigate people [such as Mahui]" because he needed someone in Iran who was able to operate "on the edge of corruption."

Additional unfavorable coverage followed Perot's allegedly insensitive speech to the NAACP, his dismissal of an advertising firm for his campaign, leaks about growing friction between Perot and hired guns Ed Rollins and Hamilton Jordan, and declining poll standings. Once again, this coverage tended to emphasize Perot's idiosyncratic character and/or his inability to delegate authority to his campaign aides.

By this time, the people covering the Perot campaign were now operating on familiar journalistic grounds. Can we tell what kind of president he would be by looking at his tactics and campaign decision-making style?

The "Quitter"

Hours before Bill Clinton's July 16 acceptance speech in New York City at the Democratic National Convention, Ross Perot announced he would not run for president, citing his concerns that, if he ran, the race might be thrown into the House of Representatives to decide the winner.

Across the country, media commentary about Perot's sudden July withdrawal was venomous:

- *Newsweek* not only labeled Perot "The Quitter," but writer Tom Morganthau (1992) asserted that Perot's "boy-scout preconceptions" (p. 29) about what it would take to win had led him to believe that all he had to do was "schmooze his way to the White House." When forced to confront political reality, he seemed to "suffer a catastrophic failure of nerve" (p. 30).
- "Ross Perot betrayed his legion of followers . . . and revealed himself as the self-centered tycoon many had been painting him to be" ("Perot escapes," 1992), one Western editorialist wrote.
- *Newsday's* David Firestone (1992, p. 4) wrote that Perot's "stunning announcement devastated . . . millions of volunteers. . . . Many said they were furious at their hero." He noted the irony of a man whose campaign had already been "the most disruptive force" in many campaign years withdrawing while saying he wanted to avoid being disruptive.
- Network newscasts featured extensive footage of dismayed, occasionally disbelieving, often angry, interviews with Perot's volunteers. Rollins told the *Los Angeles Times* ("Ex-chairman says," 1992) that Perot could not stand press scrutiny, was unwilling to spend the money needed to win, and was temperamentally unfit either to run or to be president.

Quickly, attention shifted (e.g., Yang, 1992) to whom would be helped and hurt by Perot's withdrawal. Underlying this shift was the common media assumption that Perot was "History"—over and done with. In a way, this quick dismissal of Perot was similar to the unsympathetic treatment given the League of Women Voters' withdrawal from sponsorship of the final 1988 debate (Lemert et al., 1991, pp. 101-107). The League's blast at the campaigns for trying to limit and control how that debate would be run received minimal attention on the network news, with no second-day followups. Much of the print and broadcast coverage seemed more concerned with whether the third debate would be held than with whether the League's charges had any merit. The League was "History."

Despite the fact that both the Bush and Clinton campaigns were trying to position themselves to pick up Perot supporters by expressing sympathy with the perceived "take government back" views of the Perot movement, journalists rarely looked beyond Perot to the disenchantment that he and his followers represented. One exception would be columnist Anna Quindlen (as quoted in *USA TODAY*—Keen, 1992, p. A9), who said "Mr. Perot was never a candidate; he was a wake-up call with ears." Interviewed the night of Perot's withdrawal, Bill Moyers made similar remarks (CNN News, July 16, 1992): Flawed as Perot was,

"I'm sorry to see him go.... Millions of Americans are now left wandering in the wilderness.... You have enough disaffected ... Americans who, if they disappear, can cost this system some legitimacy—and it has too little legitimacy as it is, already."

What Does This Man Want?

Even though the news media reported in passing that Perot was continuing to be placed on the ballot in an increasing number of states, they remained dismissive of his intentions. Soon after his withdrawal, Perot's attempt to organize the "United We Stand" movement to pressure Congressional and presidential candidates for the November election was framed in many news reports either as Perot's attempt to save face or a way to have influence without risk.

Late in September, as Perot hosted visits from representatives of the Bush and Clinton camps, the media now framed the visits mostly as humiliations the egoistic Perot was inflicting on the visitors. Often Perot was portrayed as having complete control over his followers' reactions to these visitations. As Ted Koppel put it on the September 28 "Nightline," "This was the day he held court ... and [Perot] loved every minute of it" ("Perot plays footsie," 1992). By this time, Koppel and his guests all seemed to assume that Perot would get back in.

Well before then, by mid-September, speculation had resumed that Perot would find a way to get back in the race: "He hates the fact that people called him a quitter," the ubiquitous Rollins told R.W. Apple, Jr. (1992). "The only way he saves his reputation is to jump in again."

He's Back!

As noted, Perot's return had been the subject of dismissive media speculation for weeks. Headline writers and editorialists across the country used the phrase, "He's Baaackk!" in a mocking reference to the words of a little girl in a horror movie who had gotten up in the wee hours of the morning to peer between the lines of an apparently empty television screen. Although it quickly became apparent that Perot would be invited by the Clinton and Bush campaigns to participate in the debates, the invitation certainly did not result from media pressure.

Once again, media attention focused only on what impact Perot's return would have on Clinton and Bush. Given only 7% in the polls ("CNN *Inside Politics*," October 1, 1992), the media agreed that Perot must have gotten back in only to show he was not "chicken."

The Debates

The conventional wisdom is that lesser known candidates have the best chance of gaining from debates with previously established opponents. As reported in our chapters on the debates, Perot certainly gained in popular support over the period of the debates. Network verdicts about Perot's performances in the first debate were both highly favorable and curiously constrained: His one-liners and easy command were praised but were also diminished in importance because, in essence, Perot was to be enjoyed—but had no chance to be elected president.

Stockdale's bewildered performance in the vice presidential debate often was taken to be a "character" reflection on Perot's insensitivity in putting a good man into a position he could not handle. (Once again, this reasoning may reflect journalists' apparent belief that campaign decisions reflect the way candidates would govern.)

As our content analysis of debate verdicts (Chapter 9) shows, favorable verdicts about Perot's performance occurred increasingly less often in his second and third debates. In fact, debate verdicts of any kind about Perot—favorable, unfavorable, or neutral—occurred less often over time as journalists seemed increasingly to focus only on the Bush versus Clinton battle.

Yet even mainstream journalists (e.g., Rook, 1992) conceded that Perot's poll percentages continued to increase over the course of the debates, so it would appear that the way voters framed Perot's role in the debates did not correspond entirely to the increasingly inattentive way national political journalists did.

Perot's Infomercials

Four themes emerged in the media coverage of Perot's campaign advertising. These themes mostly concerned his "infomercials," not his short spots:

1. The infomercials attracted an amazingly large audience, even when they were being shown a second or third time.
2. The infomercials were extremely expensive to run (actually, not nearly as expensive per minute as the shorter spots), but used simple, low-budget, 1950s-style television production techniques.
3. Perot had complete control of infomercial content and thus, through them, was doing another end-run around journalists. (Despite this assertion, very few attempts seemed to have been made to do fact checking on these lengthy political ads.)

4. Perot's reliance on televised infomercials continued a pattern of avoiding face-to-face campaigning.

For the most part, this coverage did not address itself to the actual content of the infomercials, except for occasionally slapping labels on them (e.g., "the economy," "the deficit," etc.). Arguably, the audience for these infomercials was boosted because voters had learned not to expect news coverage of their substance. If, indeed, perceptions of what *not* to expect of mainstream campaign journalism helped increase the audiences for the infomercials, the thought did not seem to occur in news stories about the surprisingly large audiences for these Perot infomercials.

Perot and His Debate Rivals

Although the news media seemed repeatedly to underestimate Perot, to some extent Perot was protected by his two rivals, each of whom had reason both to fear alienating him and his followers and to ?.hope that they would inherit his following if Perot self-destructed. Neither wanted to be accused of excluding him from the debates, so they immediately invited Perot at a time when his support in the polls was less than 10%. Because no one at the time was sure how many Perot votes might come from Bush and how many from Clinton, both could imagine that helping Perot might help themselves if he *did* stay in the race. As we will see, for George Bush that turned out to be a mistake because our survey data show that Perot's support seemed to have come largely from people who voted for George Bush in 1988.

During the debates, Bush and Clinton seemed to focus on each other, not Perot, who sometimes directly intervened on Clinton's behalf to rebut an attack by Bush or remind viewers bluntly that Bush had a lot of explaining to do about helping Iraq's Saddam Hussein before the Gulf War.

About a year after the election, a remarkable transformation occurred in the way Perot was challenged by the Clinton camp in a debate—the November 9 NAFTA debate between Vice President Al Gore and Ross Perot on *Larry King Live*. Gore interrupted Perot, pressed him for specific solutions, and generally frustrated him enough that Perot's anger turned into nastiness, according to the usual spate of media postdebate performance "verdicts." For example, CNN correspondent Jean Meserve (1993) asserted that "the pundits and the public agreed that Gore came out on top." Hearst newspaper correspondent Marianne Means (1993, p. C4) bluntly concluded that "Gore made mincemeat of Perot. . . . It is not often in politics that we see such a knock-out blow."

Of course, the Clinton team was not facing two other debaters, as was the case in the 1992 debates, so obviously there was not an opportunity to concentrate their fire this time on somebody besides Perot. However, the way Gore handled Perot was markedly more abrasive than the way Clinton, at least, handled the opponent he did concentrate on—Bush—in 1992. Treating Perot with kid gloves in the 1992 debates probably was a smart tactical decision for the Clinton campaign, and taking those gloves off in 1993 also seems to have worked out well in the short run, judging by media and public opinion poll feedback about who "won," and judging by the reaction of Congress in approving the NAFTA treaty proposal. The long run may or may not be another matter.

Perot and the Talk Shows

In the previous chapter, we saw that heavy viewers of Perot's talk-show appearance were more likely than others to be Perot voters. We also saw that, whereas people often used and valued the candidate talk shows as part of their campaign information resources, talk-show viewers cannot and could not be reduced to merely being followers of Ross Perot. In our sample, heavy viewers of Bill Clinton's talk show appearances tended to vote for him, and the number of Clinton's heavy viewers greatly outnumbered the number of Perot's. As Clinton pointed out in the Richmond debate, he had been a practitioner of "town hall" and candidate talk-show TV appearances longer than Perot. On the other hand, long before Clinton's candidacy, and long before he became a potential candidate, Perot had been a frequent guest on talk shows.

Despite Clinton's claim to an earlier campaign talk-show start, both early media portrayals and preliminary analyses of the 1992 campaign tended to equate Perot with the campaign talk-show phenomenon. Perhaps this oversimplification reveals something about media and intellectual treatment of Perot: "the larger story for the press was Perot's personality and his unconventional strategy of bringing his message to the people via talk shows" (Patterson, 1993, p. 65). We return in the next section to the question asked at the start of this chapter.

WHO ARE THESE PEOPLE?

The Gallup organization interviewed 754 registered voters on April 15 and 16, 1992. Based on this sample, *Newsweek* ("Who are the Perot supporters?" 1992) reported the following findings: Perot supporters were more likely to be male, upper income, regard themselves as political

Independents, and from the Western states. Given the timing of this poll for *Newsweek*, we probably could regard this poll as describing the characteristics of Perot's first group of supporters—supporters before his July 16 withdrawal.

Although we did ask a few questions about Perot in the September wave, that is, before his October 1 reentry, our October interviews produced the largest, most stable indicators of what Perot's supporters were like. Thus, many of our descriptions of Perot voters are based on our October question about whom respondents intended to vote for. People saying they intended to vote for Perot will generally be contrasted against those intending to vote for Bush or for Clinton. We also use our panel data set to talk mostly about changes taking place among Perot, Clinton, and Bush voters.

Demographic Comparisons

In comparison with Bush and/or Clinton voters, Perot voters were considerably younger (mean $2\frac{1}{2}$ years younger than Clinton voters, 5.6 years younger than Bush voters); had fewer years of education; like Bush voters, were highly likely to be white; like Bush voters, had relatively higher incomes; were more likely to be male (60%) than Bush (49%) and Clinton (40%) voters; and were, like Bush voters, more likely to be presently married.

Political Ideology

Ideologically, both Bush (55%) and Perot voters (39%) came heavily from those who classified themselves as conservatives. However, like Clinton, Perot also appealed strongly to those who thought of themselves as moderates. Both Perot and Clinton drew about 44% of their votes from self-described moderates. Liberals were outnumbered slightly by moderates among Clinton voters, but as one would expect, Clinton voters were far more likely to describe themselves as liberals (43%) than were either Perot (17%) or Bush (8%) voters.

Given earlier speculation in the media about whether Clinton or Bush would be hurt the most by Perot's reentry, the data strongly suggest that Bush was hurt more. Table 6.1 shows that Perot's support came more often from Republicans than from Democrats. Bush was able to hang onto only two of every three Republicans, whereas Clinton held onto 87% of the self-identified Democrats. The numbers of Republicans straying to Perot in October almost equalled the number abandoning Bush for Clinton.

Table 6.1. From Whom Did Support for Perot Come? Party Identification and Intended Vote.

	Intend to Vote For				
Party I.D.	Bush (%)	Clinton (%)	Perot (%)	Other (%)	Total (%)
Republican (N = 359)	67	16	15	2	100
Democrat (N = 553)	4	87	7	2	100
Independent (N = 284)	17	50	27	6	100
Other (N = 57)	19	43	24	14	100

Another way to examine the damage Perot did to Bush is to look at our respondents' reported vote in 1988. In October 1992, George Bush was hanging onto only 53% of the nearly 500 people who said they voted for him in 1988, whereas Clinton hung onto slightly more than 90% of the people who said they had voted for Dukakis. Perot garnered three times as many former Bush voters as Dukakis voters, so once again it is apparent that Perot was doing more damage to Bush than to Clinton. More than half the people who intended to vote for Perot had voted for Bush in 1988; only one in six had voted for Dukakis. The remaining Perot voters did not vote, were not eligible, or voted for another third-party candidate in 1988.

Political Knowledge

In October, we used two tests of political knowledge. The first was the total number of issues respondents could name as important to them in the campaign. We asked respondents to name two; if they were able to do so, we then asked them to name some more. Scores could range from 0 to 9 on this item. The second test asked respondents to match candidates with their policy proposals: Perot's gas tax proposal, Clinton's higher tax on upper income Americans, and Bush's early 1992 proposal to pass a Constitutional amendment banning abortions. Adding across all three items, scores could range from 0 to 3.

Clinton voters had the highest mean scores on both tests, with Perot and Bush voters trading second and third places, depending on the test. Perot voters finished in the middle on the total number of issues (mean score of 2.21, compared to 2.41 for Clinton voters and 2.05 for Bush voters; mean differences significant at $p < .001$). On the proposal-matching task, Clinton voters correctly matched 2.24 out of 3 items, compared to 2.14 for Bush and 2.07 for Perot voters ($p < .05$).

Efficacy Feelings

In Chapter 1, we argued that Perot voters would most likely have higher Internal Efficacy and lower External Efficacy feelings than either Clinton or Bush voters. How did the results turn out? Analysis of the individual scales revealed that neither the two Internal nor the two External Efficacy items correlated particularly well with the other in its group. Thus, we decided separately to analyze each of the four efficacy scales. Because two of the efficacy scales were worded negatively, we reversed the scoring for them so that a higher score always meant higher efficacy. Table 6.2 presents these results.

Because education generally is correlated with efficacy, and because we already know that Perot voters had fewer years of education than did either Bush or Clinton voters, we decided statistically to control for education by using a procedure called Multiple Classification Analysis (MCA). What MCA does is allow us to extract any apparent influence of education on efficacy responses before we allow presidential voting to predict those efficacy scores. (See Chapter 5 for more details about MCA and how to read MCA tables.)

As Table 6.2 shows, education almost always predicts the efficacy response at the usual level of statistical significance ($p < .05$). Interestingly, the more years of one's education, the more positive the efficacy response, *except* in the one case that just barely missed the $p < .05$ level, which was: Under our form of government, the people have the final say about how the country is run, no matter who is in office. It may be that the last words in the item—*no matter who is in office*—turned off those with more education. Perhaps consistent with this interpretation is the finding that Perot voters also independently had the lowest agreement with this item. Because Perot voters clearly had deserted the two major party choices in favor of the charismatic Perot, one might expect them to object to the "no matter who is in office" aspect of this one External Efficacy item.

Table 6.2 shows modest support for our hypotheses about Perot voters having confidence in their own political abilities and distrust in the system. This support occurred for one of the two Internal Efficacy scales and one of the two External Efficacy items. Regarding Internal Efficacy, Perot voters expressed more confidence that they could do as

Table 6.2. Summary of Multiple Classification Analyses: Perot Voters and Four Political Efficacy Measures.[a]

Predictors	Good job in public office	Politics too complicated for me	Officials not interested, won't listen	People have final say, no matter
Regressions[b]				
Education	.065***	.131***	.081***	-.024*
Adjusted Means[c]				
Voting Intention				
Bush	2.57***	3.04NS	3.23NS	2.58**
Clinton	2.77	3.14	3.16	2.49
Perot	2.92	3.17	3.03	2.32

NS = not statistically significant.
*$p < .10$.
**$p < .05$.
***$p < .01$.

[a]The full efficacy measures are: (a) I could do as good a job in public office as most; (b) sometimes politics seems too complicated for people like me; (c) if public officials are not interested in hearing what the people think, there is really no way to make them listen; (d) under our form of government, the people have the final say about how the government is run, no matter who is in office. Responses ranged from 1 (strongly disagree) to 5 (strongly agree), but scores for items (b)—politics too complicated—and (c)—not interested—are reversed so that higher scores always reflect higher efficacy.
[b]For an explanation of what the regression figure means, see note b in Table 5.2.
[c]For an explanation of what the "adjusted means" is, see note c in Table 5.2.

good a job in public office as "most other people" ($p < .01$). Bush voters were the least likely to express such personal confidence, although in truth most people were reluctant to express unbounded self-confidence in response to this item. For the second Internal Efficacy item ("too complicated for people like me"), although the mean response for Perot voters was marginally higher, the three adjusted means were very close together.

As was true for the two Internal Efficacy items, both the External Efficacy scales had means for voter groups that fell in the predicted direction (Perot voters with the least faith in the political system), but once again only one of the two means approached statistical significance (a chance probability of exactly .05, when the usually acceptable level of significance is anything just under .05). In any case, the results for efficacy show modest support for our two predictions about the nature and direction of Perot voters' efficacy feelings.

Attitudes Toward the News Media

Performance Ratings. In our November wave, as the campaign drew to a close, we asked panelists a series of four questions about how they rated news media performance in the presidential campaign. Although in general Perot voters expressed the most resentment of news media performance, Bush voters often were very close behind. Clinton voters were relatively favorably disposed toward the news media. It seemed apparent that the problems Clinton had with the news media during the primaries were not as salient to Clinton voters in November as were Bush's and Perot's more recent media "bias" complaints to their respective voters. These MCA results are summarized in Table 6.3.

Because our primary focus in this chapter is on Perot voters, we added to education the number of Perot talk show appearances seen as a control for these analyses of attitudes toward the news media. (Scores ranged from no Perot appearances watched to four.)

Presumably, viewing Perot talk-show appearances might reflect an underlying dissatisfaction with the job the conventional media were doing, but this control variable did not predict responses to any of the four media scales. (Recall that in Chapter 5 we saw that heavy candidate talk-show viewers were "news junkies," so in retrospect we should perhaps have expected Perot talk-show viewing not to predict hostile attitudes toward the mainstream news media.) The education control variable predicted scores for the only media attitude measure with which Perot voting showed no relationship at all. As years of education increased, *dis*agreement increased that people could learn more from talk shows than from daily news about the candidates.

The item with the highest agreement from everybody was that the media use the polls too much for "horse race" reasons and not enough to explore why people feel as they do. In fact, agreement was so widely shared that differences between Perot voters and the other two voter groups might have been held down by a "ceiling effect," because on the average people were already using 4- on a 5-point scale of agreement. Journalists who believe "horse-race" polls attract audiences should take note of this finding.

Judging by the means and variances, much more mixed agreement and disagreement characterized responses to the second and fourth items in the table: that the media had done a good job, and that people can learn more about the candidates from the talk shows than the daily news. The results for neither scale can be taken as a vote of confi-

Table 6.3. Summary of Multiple Classification Analyses: Perot Voters and Feelings About "The Media"[a]

Predictors	Media Rating Measures			
	Too much concentration on horse race	Media have done a good job	Press more concerned with dirt	People learn more from talk shows
Regressions[b]				
Education	negNS	negNS	negNS	neg***
Perot Talk Viewing	negNS	posNS	negNS	negNS
Adjusted Means				
Voting Intention				
Bush	4.20*	3.09***	3.73***	3.03NS
Clinton	3.90	3.59	3.24	3.10
Perot	4.28	3.01	3.97	3.25

NS = not statistically significant.
*$p < .10$.
**$p < .05$.
***$p < .01$.

[a]The full media rating measures are: (a) When they report the polls, the media concentrate too much on who is winning and not enough on the reasons people feel the way they do. (b) Generally the media have done a good job in covering this campaign. (c) The press seems more concerned about dirt than they are about the substance of the campaign. (d) People can learn more about the candidates from talk shows than they can from daily news reports. Responses ranged from 1 (strongly disagree) to 5 (strongly agree).
[b]The *neg* and *pos* terms refer to the direction of the regression figure describing the relationship between this control variable and the rating of news media performance. Note that higher agreement means a more critical attitude toward media performance for three of the four items in the table.

dence in the conventional news media, but at least they imply a willingness to compare news and alternative media performance in at least one more presidential campaign.

Usefulness Ratings. During the October period, we asked our largest group of respondents to evaluate on a 0 to 10 scale how useful various media sources were to them in following the presidential campaign. Of most interest to us here are usefulness ratings of TV news, newspapers, and TV talk shows. We introduced education, each of the four efficacy scales, and viewing of Perot talk-show appearances as controls in the MCA. After controlling for each of these predictors, we then introduced whether the respondents intended to vote for Bush, Clinton, or Perot.

Perot voters gave the lowest ratings to *newspaper* coverage of the presidential campaign (an adjusted mean of 4.45), whereas Clinton voters gave by far the highest (M = 5.43), with Bush voters (4.62) again much closer to Perot than to Clinton voters (p = .000). As education and scores on three of the four efficacy scales increased, the value placed on newspaper coverage also grew (p < .05, in every case). The only individual efficacy scale not to predict the newspaper rating was the feeling that "I could do as good a job as most people."

A similar pattern occurred for ratings of TV news coverage of the campaign. Once again, Clinton voters rated TV news much more highly (5.46) than Bush (4.99) and Perot (4.74) voters (p = .005). Only one of the four efficacy scales ("people have the final say") significantly predicted TV news ratings, whereas the number of Perot talk-show appearances watched was also positively related to these ratings.

In marked contrast to the ratings of the two mainstream news media, the three groups of voters rearranged themselves when they rated the *usefulness* of talk shows. This time, Perot (adjusted M = 5.56) and Clinton voters (5.63) grouped together in giving campaign talk shows higher ratings than did Bush voters (4.96; mean differences significant at p = .026). Education was negatively related to these ratings. For every additional year of education, the ratings went down by just under 0.10 of a unit on this 0 to 10 scale. The more confident respondents were that they could do as good a job in office as other people, the higher the ratings given campaign talk shows. Perot talk-show viewing had easily the biggest relationship to perceived usefulness of candidate talk shows: for every additional Perot appearance seen, the rating went up a whopping 1.4 units on that 0 to 10 scale! Although all the relationships described here reached at least the p < .05 level of significance, the Perot talk-show relationship was so strong that the odds that it could have been due to chance were only about 1 in 10,000.

Because we also obtained media usefulness measures in November, we can group panelists by their November voting preferences and examine whether their media perceptions changed between the October and November 1 or 2 interviews. Because we interviewed the same people each time, we concentrated on simple tests of change within each voting group.

In brief, Clinton voters' evaluation of talk shows improved substantially (p < .01, by t test) from October (M = 5.2) to November (6.2 on that 0 to 10 scale). A similar increase for talk shows among Bush voters (from 4.3 to just under 5.3) just missed the customary p < .05 level of statistical significance (p = .051). In contrast, talk-show ratings by Perot panelists were already high in October (just under 6.2) and were just over 6.3 in November—no change, in other words. So both Bush and

Clinton voters thought better of the talk shows in November than they did in October. Neither ratings of newspaper nor network news coverage changed significantly within any voting group.

Attitudes toward the Debates

Historically, if we ignore for the moment the chronic problem of postdebate analyses by the news media, the presidential debates were one of the first ways that candidates could get around the news media and speak at length directly to the American people. If disenchantment with the news media were a factor in 1992, thus causing Perot and Clinton voters to look on talk shows as a way around the mainstream news media, we might therefore expect the debates to be valued as another way of observing the candidates at length. We already know that, despite a growth among them in appreciation of the talk shows, the Bush voters valued the talk shows least, so we might therefore expect that they valued the debates less than the other two voter groups.

Not very surprisingly, we found in Wave 1—the period after Labor Day but before Clinton and Bush had agreed on debate arrangements—there were no differences among the three groups of voters in their responses to three questions about the presidential debates: (a) the debates are the best way to find out about the candidates, (b) the candidates always seem to avoid answering the questions asked them on the debates, and (c) the debates are a waste of time. Responses to these items ranged on a 5-point scale from Strongly Agree to Strongly Disagree. In the October interviews, we added a fourth Agree-Disagree item about the debates: I could hardly wait for the debates to begin. In addition, we asked respondents to rate, on that now-familiar 0 to 10 scale, the usefulness to them of the presidential debates. When there were no differences in September, there often were in October after the debates had started.

In October, Perot voters were most likely to agree that the debates were one of the best ways to find out about the candidates, that they could hardly wait for the debates to start, and that candidates always seemed to avoid answering questions in the debates. Even though the last item indicates some reservations about the debates among Perot followers, by November our Perot panelists showed a large drop in those reservations, having become no more likely than anybody else to agree that the candidates avoided answering questions in the debates. Not only was there a decline in their cynicism about candidates ducking debate questions, but Perot panelists' agreement both that they had been waiting with anticipation for the debates and that the debates were one of the best ways of finding out about the candidates increased significantly. Support for the debates also grew significantly for Clinton panelists, who were more likely to agree in November that they had been waiting for the debates and to disagree that the debates were a waste of time. Bush voters, already by October generally more skeptical about the debates, showed no changes from October to November.

A fifth indicator of support for the debates comes from the 0 to 10 ratings of their usefulness. Both Perot and Clinton voters gave substantially higher ratings in October than did those intending to vote for Bush. In addition, Perot and Clinton panelists also had in common an improvement from October to November in usefulness ratings of the debates. Like Perot panelists, Clinton panelists' ratings—already high—increased even further over time. Clinton panelists went from a mean of 6.6 in October to 7.1 in November ($p = .018$ by t test). Perot panelists went from 6.2 to 7.6, a very large increase ($p = .003$). Note that by November, Perot panelists were giving the televised presidential debates even higher ratings than were the Clinton panelists. Once again Bush panelists showed no increase in their rating of the debates, actually dropping very slightly from 6.0 in October to 5.98 in November.Unlike the 1988 campaign, interest in and support for the debates seemed to grow over the campaign—especially among Clinton and Perot voters.

Attitudes toward the Campaign

Interest. Even after we had controlled for education and efficacy, during September the Perot supporters expressed significantly less interest in the presidential campaign than did Bush and Clinton voters. Obviously this was the period just before Perot reentered the race. Interest in the presidential campaign was measured on a 5-point scale that ranged from 1 (extremely low interest) to 5 (extremely high interest).

With Perot's return, all three voter groups had essentially similar interest scores in October. They also did in November, but of course only panelists were interviewed then. When we looked only at change among panelist groups, each of the three groups of voters experienced significant increases in interest from September to November, with Perot voters showing the largest gain—almost all of their gains taking place in October.

Too Much Mudslinging? A second item about the presidential campaign was asked everyone we interviewed in September, October, and November. The item asserted that there was too much mudslinging going on in the presidential campaign and was one of the many that offered the respondent five choices, ranging from Strongly Agree (5) to Strongly Disagree (1).

In our study of the 1988 campaign, we found that agreement with this item climbed steadily during the campaign. The same thing happened in 1992. Agreement in October was higher than in September among all respondents. Among panelists agreement was higher in October (3.94) than September (3.71) and even higher in November (4.12). All these differences reached at least the $p < .01$ level of statistical significance.

Despite the general growth in feelings that too much dirt was being thrown, were Perot voters more likely than the others to feel that way? Not in September, the period in which Perot ostensibly remained sidelined, having been knocked out of the race by "dirty tricks," according to Perot. But by the October 11-22 time series, Perot supporters expressed substantially higher distaste (adjusted mean score of 4.21) than Clinton voters (4.05) and, especially, Bush voters (3.76). However, this difference had disappeared in November—at least among panelists, the only people we interviewed. Interestingly, the more Perot talk-show appearances seen, the *lower* the November agreement that too much mud was being slung.

Attitudes toward Perot's Return

In October and November, we asked two items about Perot's return, each with that 5-point Strongly Agree (5) to Strongly Disagree (1) scale following it. They are: Now that Ross Perot is a candidate again, this is a better campaign; and I agree with many of the things Perot has said.

It was no surprise to find that Perot voters most strongly agreed with each of these items. What was mildly surprising, though, was to find that it was the *Clinton* voters who were the least willing to concede that Perot's return had made it a better campaign. In the October interviews, the adjusted mean for Clinton voters actually fell slightly on the "disagree" side. The same was even more strikingly true for the November panelists: Bush voters mildly agreed (adjusted mean of 3.23) that Perot had made it a better campaign; Clinton voters disagreed (2.87). Another way of putting this is that this may be another indicator of Bush's greater vulnerability to Perot's appeal; the Clinton voters almost seemed determined not to be tempted by Perot as the campaign neared its end. Perhaps this apparent refusal by Clinton voters to consider Perot was because Perot's July 16 withdrawal absolutely turned off Democrats who might once have been tempted.

Overall, Perot gained considerable strength among all panelists between September and the October 11-22 debate period. Nevertheless, even by November, the mean self-estimated odds that any respondent would vote for Perot had risen from slightly more than 2 in September to a mean of only slightly above 3 on a 0 to 10 scale. Almost certainly, the September odds were greatly lowered by the fact that Perot was no longer a candidate—officially, at least.

Intensity of Support. The odds of voting for Bush slumped significantly among all panelists from September (3.7) to October (3.3). No significant changes were observed for Clinton, whose mean remained slightly above 6.0 among all panelists throughout the study period. Consistent with the idea that campaigns tend to reinforce choices voters already had made, the odds of voting for Clinton went lower among Bush panelists over time, and the odds of voting for Bush went up ($p < .05$ in both cases). Half of the same pattern held true of panelists who were Clinton voters: Odds of voting for Clinton went up over time among them ($p < .05$), but the odds of voting Bush—already extremely low—did not go down any further.

The biggest gains in intensity, however, occurred among people who said they would vote for Perot. The mean probability of voting for Perot went from less than 7 in September to more than 9 out of 10 in November among the Perot panelists ($p = .000$). Nevertheless, in November, Clinton panelists remained slightly more intense in their preferences for Clinton (9.5) than Perot panelists did for Perot (9.1). Intensity for each group was significantly higher for their respective chosen candidate than for Bush voters, who were at 8.1 in November.

Motives for Vote Choice. In the November interviews, we offered panelists a series of four voting motives, asking them to indicate all that applied. Only one of the four—"my vote for president is a protest vote"—differentiated significantly among the three groups of voters. One in every 3 Perot voters said that their vote could be described as a protest, compared to less than 1 in 7 Clinton voters and 1 in 16 Bush voters ($p < .01$ by chi-square test). Consistent with the protest motive was the fact that even Perot supporters did not expect Perot to win. Despite the widely observed tendency to believe that the candidate you favor will win— it's called the "Looking Glass" effect (see Lemert, 1986)—3 of every 4 Perot voters said the odds were against a Perot victory.[2]

Speculations About the Future

Perot may very well have understood the mainstream media better than they did him. Since the 1992 election, Perot has been able to command news attention whenever he wanted it, although the attention, to put it mildly, certainly has not always been favorable. If Perot wants to continue playing a high-profile role on the national stage, but does not want to run again for president—that he does not want to run again would be our bet at this stage—he nevertheless will delay as long as possible any firm announcement that he will not run. As soon as he becomes "History" again by withdrawing, media interest will shut down. If Perot were to occupy center stage until mid-1996, however, the prospect that some other third-party candidate could mount a real challenge would be virtually nonexistent.

This is the dilemma Perot faces if he means what he says about changing the way the federal government performs and continues to believe that neither the Democrats nor the Republicans have the answers or the will to make those changes.

DISCUSSION

To be sure, Perot gave journalists reasons to be suspicious of both his motives and his grasp on reality. Nevertheless, if Perot had been the nominee of one of the major parties, the media would still be defending themselves against bias charges levelled by hot-eyed party loyalists. Hordes of academics would be writing content-analytic papers testing whether, and how much, unequal treatment there was, instead of papers examining Perot's rhetoric for what it revealed about him.

Consistently, the mainstream news media belittled and downplayed Perot, increasingly ignoring his role in the debates after the first one. After Perot's return, he was consistently portrayed as a candidate whose principal importance was as a spoiler, ignoring his claims that he represented the legitimate aspirations of a social movement. Although impressed and surprised by the size of the Perot infomercial viewership, journalists did not seem to recognize that the size of the audience might have reflected a perception by the audience that, given the failures of mainstream journalism, nowhere else in the media could they hear an extended, uninterrupted presentation about how bad the country's deficit and economic problems were and what needed to be done about them (see also Chapter 12).

Both Perot and Bush voters shared a dislike of conventional campaign news coverage. It is not new that resentment and (perhaps) scapegoating of the news media occur among voters who realize that their major party candidate is about to lose. But can we dismiss as easily the resentment felt by the almost 1 in every 5 voters who probably expected from the start that their third-party candidate had at best only an outside chance to win? Here are some reasons to worry:

- Our survey results suggest that Perot voters were on the whole considerably younger than voters for the two major party candidates—something of a surprise given the apparent age of most of the Perot "volunteers" whom we saw being interviewed on television. Those younger people are going to

be around for a while, and they are not pleased with the way the conventional print and broadcast news media covered the presidential campaign.
- In 1992, Perot supporters produced a 19% vote for a third-party candidate, in absolute numbers the largest ever for an independent candidate and, in relative terms, the highest percentage since Theodore Roosevelt ran against Taft and Wilson in 1912. These predominantly male voters seem to have as much disposable income as did the Bush voters—even if they had fewer years of education. They also had relatively high confidence that they could do as good a job of running things as most anybody else—even if their political knowledge tested out as relatively low. This volatile combination of resentment, confidence, energy, resources, and, perhaps, limited educational background and political information could be a tinderbox waiting for another match.

On the other hand, Perot supporters felt good about the debates and about talk shows, and, over time, their approval of those two "unconventional" institutions may ultimately help legitimize for them American election campaigns. Clearly, they are not likely to feel better about presidential elections based on conventional news media handling of them. Viewing of Perot's talk-show appearances, in fact, seemed to reduce cynicism about the mud throwing in the campaign, which coincided with the return of Perot voters to a more "typical" November level of such cynicism. Meanwhile, Perot voters also showed a spectacular growth over the campaign in their ratings of how useful the debates were. Furthermore, just as in November they no longer were more cynical than Clinton and Bush voters regarding the "mudslinging" item; Perot voters also became more like everybody else concerning whether the debaters always seemed to avoid answering the questions.

Danger signals for the news media certainly were not restricted to Perot's supporters. At best, our surveys showed rather tepid support for the way the conventional news media cover presidential campaigns. Among all respondents, the conventional news media suffered by comparison with both talk shows and the debates. As national politicians continue to exploit a rich variety of ways to reach citizens other than through the conventional news media, it is very much worth remembering a lesson from Chapter 5. The people who have the most exposure to these alternative media also tend to be the more reliable members of the conventional news media audience, *yet they seem to be finding the new alternatives superior* to what they have been getting from conventional news media. In our data, easily the most unpopular media predilection for all our respondents was using polls for "horse race" purposes. Yet year after presidential year, the "horse race" is easily the dominant frame that conventional national journalists impose on presidential campaigns.

Although his voters may have forgotten the way the news media covered him in the 1992 primaries, President Bill Clinton undoubtedly has not. As more and more new and direct ways of bypassing conventional journalism are brought on board at the White House and in modern campaigns, we can be very sure that Bill Clinton and perhaps Ross Perot will continue to exploit these new electronic forums. Future politicians—and voters—have learned some lessons about the conventional news media from the 1992 campaign. One wonders whether the conventional news media have.

ENDNOTES

1. The search, using the Lexis-Nexis "Campaign" electronic library, used the keywords Perot and (within three words) Larry King Live.
2. Perot supporters, however, gave a significantly higher odds of winning than did those supporting Bush or Clinton, so there was a "Looking Glass" effect for Perot voters (and, in separate analyses, for Bush with Bush voters and Clinton with Clinton voters). In the case of Perot, 95% of Bush voters and 91% of Clinton voters said the odds were against his winning, compared to 75% of Perot's voters. These data come from the November interviews with panelists.

REFERENCES

Albright, J. (1992, June 29). Perot didn't probe one partner's scandals. *The Houston Chronicle*, p. B8.
Apple, R. W., Jr. (1992, September 13). Noncandidate still, Ross Perot could still be a spoiler. *The New York Times*, p. 38.
CNN News. (1992, July 16). Live Report, Democratic Convention, Transcript #82-8.
CNN *Inside Politics*. (1992, October 1). Poll as cited on show.
Dillin, J. (1992, April 30). Bush and Clinton may both hear Perot's footsteps. *The Christian Science Monitor*, p. 1.
Dugger, R. (1992, June 15). Electronic Caesar? Who is Ross Perot? (Part 1). *The Nation*, p. 813.
Ego trip: From the moment Ross Perot quit the race in July, he began planning his 'October surprise' return. (1992, October 12). *Newsweek*, pp. 26-45.

Ex-chairman says Perot lost will to run campaign. (1992, July 20). *The Register-Guard*, p. A5.
Firestone, D. (1992, July 17). Why I quit. *Newsday*, p. 4.
Freedom Forum Media Studies Center. (1993). *The finish line: Covering the campaign's final days.* New York: The Freedom Forum Media Studies Center at Columbia University.
Hamilton, B., & Mealiea, W. (1993, August). 'Perotistas': Who are these people anyway? *Campaigns & Elections: The Magazine for Political Professionals*, pp. 20-23.
Hines, C. (1992, June 3). Primary finale sets up three-man race; Clinton, Bush win as Perot shows political muscle. *The Houston Chronicle*, p. A1.
Keen, J. (1992, July 20). Mourning in America, post-Perot. *USA Today*, p. A9.
King, L., with Stencel, M. (1993). *On the line: The new road to the White House.* New York: Harcourt Brace.
Lemert, J.B. (1986). Picking the winners: Politician vs. voter predictions of two controversial ballot measures. *Public Opinion Quarterly, 50,* 208-221.
Lemert, J.B., Elliott, W.R., Bernstein, J.M., Rosenberg, W.L., & Nestvold, K.J. (1991). *News verdicts, the debates, and presidential campaigns.* New York: Praeger.
Means, M. (1993, November 28). Gore revives interest in debates. *The Register-Guard*, p. C4.
Meserve, J. (1993, November 14). Report. *The week in review*, CNN.
Morganthau, T. (1992, July 27). The quitter: Why Perot bowed out. *Newsweek*, pp. 28-30.
Patterson, T.E. (1993). *Out of order.* New York: Knopf.
Perot escapes. (1992, July 17). *The Register-Guard*, p. A14.
Perot plays footsie. (1992, September 28). *Nightline.*
Plutocratic populist. (1992, April 6). *Time Magazine*, p. 19.
Rook, S. (1992, December 27). *Year in review: The political year.* CNN, Transcript #40-1.
Rosenstiel, T. (1993). *Strange bedfellows: How television and the presidential candidates changed American politics, 1992.* New York: Hyperion.
Who are the Perot supporters? (1992, April 27). *Newsweek*, p. 27.
Wild card: Who is Ross Perot: (1992, April 27). *Newsweek*, p. 19.
Yang, J.E. (1992, July 27). Clinton woos voters in "Perot country"; California seen as being up for grabs. *The Washington Post*, p. A8.

7

Background and Format of the Debates

William L. Rosenberg

The 1992 Presidential debates could be characterized as an on-and-off process, due primarily to the reluctance of George Bush, who initially did not want to debate. However, political realities led to eventual negotiations between the Bush and Clinton campaign teams that brought the debates about. This chapter first seeks to provide a brief history of the debates, so that an historical perspective can be applied when we later discuss the maneuvering prior to the 1992 debates agreement. From a contemporary standpoint, candidate debates seem like a central fixture of Presidential campaigns, but they have not always been so. Even after the televised presidential candidate debates began in 1960, they have not always been held. And even when held, it has often been touch and go whether they would be held.

HISTORY OF DEBATES

The history of debates in American elections, according to Anne Groer (1992), goes back at least to the founding fathers. The political debates of that time were said to be conducted over differences in issue positions that were presented to the legislatures and debating societies of the time. According to Groer, in 1788, James Madison and James Monroe ran for Congress and conducted the campaign by holding debates across Virginia. Madison initially resisted the debates, but later told Thomas Jefferson that the debates were the only way to answer the positions taken by Monroe. In the end Madison won that election. Almost 50 years later, another famous political debate was kicked off in Illinois for a U.S. Congressional seat between Stephen A. Douglas and John T. Stuart, who debated in every county seat in their congressional district. Stuart prevailed on election day.

In contrast, presidential races of the time were often contests highlighted by debates between surrogates for each of the candidates, never the candidates themselves. These representatives of each candidate crossed the country, directly debating each other while the candidates themselves generally stayed at home or in their offices, presenting themselves as dignified and "presidential." Abraham Lincoln, himself later to be a candidate for president, served as a surrogate for John C. Fremont's 1836 Whig candidacy for president, with John I. Calhoun representing Democratic nominee Martin Van Buren, the eventual winner. This pattern of debating by proxies continued at the presidential campaign level, according to Groer, until the mid-20th century.

At lower levels of political office, debates often were between the contenders themselves. One of the most famous of these was between Illinois Senate candidates Abraham Lincoln and Stephen A. Douglas, each of whom would later run for president. The Senate rivals jointly carried their debates throughout Illinois. Douglas won that Senate race, but not much later the election outcome was different when Lincoln was elected President, defeating Douglas.

Presidential debates essentially entered the media age in 1948 when the Republican primary candidates for President, Harold Stassen and Tom Dewey participated in an Oregon radio debate. The issue for the debate was whether the Communist Party should be outlawed. Stassen said it should, Dewey said it should not. Dewey won the primary but lost the general election to Harry Truman.

A debate between Estes Kefauver and Adlai Stevenson was broadcast before a Democratic presidential primary on radio and television in 1956. The first major televised debate took place in 1960 between John Kennedy and Richard Nixon. This debate, which had Kennedy as the clear winner in the public's mind, really provided the window to the future of presidential debates. However, in 1952, an attempt was made to launch the modern era of televised presidential debates. Senator Blair Moody of Michigan called on the networks to host a series of debates between Dwight D. Eisenhower and Adlai E. Stevenson. Neither candidate would agree to the debates. This situation foreshadowed much of the debate about debates that has taken place over the next 40 years. However, even if Eisenhower and Stevenson had agreed, Section 315 of the Federal Communications Act of 1934 (which includes the "equal-time" rule) would have prevented the debate from occurring unless all candidates would have been allowed to participate, including all minor party candidates.

In 1959, the FCC waived the equal-time rule for *bona fide* news coverage. When Stevenson suggested that Presidential debates be held in 1960, Frank Stanton, then the head of CBS News, told Congress that if Congress could waive the equal-time provision of the Act for news, they could also waive it for a special event such as a presidential debate. Congress agreed and invited both Kennedy and Nixon to debate, both of whom accepted. However, these debates were not really debates but rather side-by-side press conferences. According to Kraus (1988), although Nixon was considered the winner by the radio audience, most watched the debate on television and felt that Kennedy was the clear winner in the first debate. All told, there were four debates. Kennedy went on to win the election by the narrowest of margins.

The question of winning the debate serves to raise the next question: Does the debate winner necessarily win the election? As Peter Jennings (1992a) stated, there is an "important difference between picking the winner of a debate and deciding which candidate to vote for." In evaluating the debates we must keep that in mind.

Bush in 1992 had to try and make this calculation in determining whether to debate Clinton. From Bush's perspective, he might lose the debate on issues to Clinton, but Clinton might lose his front-runner status with voters due to what Bush hoped would be their unease with Clinton the person. Ultimately, because Bush continued to trail in the polls and had made little or not progress since at least the Republican convention, Bush's apparent reluctance to debate yielded to political reality. This was hardly the first time since the 1960 debates that at least one of the presidential candidates resisted the threat or opportunity to debate before a watching nation.

Martin F. Nolan (1992) cited the legend of the proposed 1964 Presidential debates. As the story goes, Kennedy and Goldwater were having drinks together in 1963 and agreed to hold a modern-day Presidential version of the 1858 Illinois Lincoln-Douglas Senatorial debates. Kennedy and Goldwater planned to debate each other 22 times at different sites, traveling together in the same airplane, with no reporters, no moderators, and few handlers. This personal agreement happened without a debate on debates. Unfortunately, the assassination of Kennedy prevented these proposed debates.

Instead, there were no debates in 1964 between Lyndon Johnson and Barry Goldwater. The incumbent Johnson did not want to share the spotlight with Goldwater and decided not to debate him. Given Johnson's control of Congress, it saw no reason to waive the equal-time provision. In the 1968 election, whereas Humphrey wanted to debate, Nixon had already had his "bad" experience and was unwilling to join. Congress sided with Nixon. In 1972, President Nixon chose not to debate George McGovern.

In 1976, Jimmy Carter faced off with Gerald Ford in three debates. President Ford was willing to debate because he was trailing in the polls, in part due to the Watergate pardon of Nixon and the sentiment for change sweeping the country. By this point the FCC had ruled that presidential debates, especially if sponsored by nonmedia groups, were *bona fide* news events and thus the equal-time provision would not apply. Given the climate in the post-Watergate era, Ford could not hide behind the equal-time provision, even if he wanted to. The two eventually debated three times. The American public also got its first taste of a vice presidential debate that featured Senator Bob Dole and Senator Walter Mondale.

In 1980, whereas President Carter and Ronald Reagan did debate, it was not until after Reagan and John Anderson, the Independent candidate for President, had already debated without Carter. President Carter had declined to debate with Anderson on the stage.

In 1984, Ronald Reagan became the first incumbent President who, while leading (by 15 points) in the polls, agreed to debate. He debated challenger Walter Mondale twice. We also saw the return of the vice presidential debates, this time between George Bush and Geraldine Ferraro.

The 1988 election found George Bush debating Michael Dukakis twice. Most scored the first debate a victory for Dukakis and the second for Bush after Dukakis responded without emotion to what he would do if his wife had been raped and murdered. In negotiations before the debates, Bush in 1988 showed that his campaign was effective in manipulating the debates to his advantage. Dukakis had four demands in 1988. They were to debate early, to have three presidential and one vice presidential debates, to have risers under him due to his short stature, and finally to have a one-on-one debate with no panel of reporters asking questions. Except for the risers, Bush prevailed over Dukakis on all of the major format items. This experience undoubtedly affected the way Bush and his campaign approached the question of whether to debate in 1992 and, if so, how the format should be structured.

THE 1992 ELECTION CONTEXT

The 1992 presidential election provided the opportunity for each candidate to offer his perspectives to the American electorate. Each came to the contest with both personal and political strengths and weaknesses that they wished to manage.

At first, George Bush was viewed as almost invincible. With the apparent major victory in the Gulf War and with the public opinion polls giving him approval ratings through the roof, he was virtually unchallenged by Republicans and Democrats alike. The only serious Republican challenger that eventually emerged was Pat Buchanan.

In the Democratic camp, many of the likely suitors chose to sit on the sidelines, figuring that they would bide their time, deciding instead to consider entering the 1996 race to potentially face Dan Quayle rather than Bush. With his strong position, Bush felt that he could walk to victory with little challenge. He did not consider any of the opponents as true contenders. This perspective eventually led Bush to a position that showed him to be isolated and out of touch with much of the American public. Eventually, even he felt that his message was not being received well. However, Bush was much more reluctant to enter into the public media arena—including debate settings—in the same manner as his rivals, Clinton and Perot.

In contrast, Bill Clinton was able to capitalize on his strengths as a communicator in attacking both Bush and Perot. Clinton welcomed the opportunity to interact with both the public and reporters. His approach was to engage in discussion, to put his positions on the table and work toward an understanding. His comfort with an open, free-flow exchange contrasted sharply with George Bush, who preferred a more controlled setting. Clinton's campaign style essentially was to hold public meetings with himself as the moderator. This allowed Clinton to discuss his positions with the audience in a framework comfortable to his own personal style.

Although Clinton was certainly relaxed and at ease with the public and the media, Perot essentially changed the name of the game in political communication in the 1992 presidential election. Perot decided to appear on the *Larry King Live Show* as a guest. The first appearance was to talk about the political and economic conditions in the United States. He later appeared as a guest in which he in effect unofficially announced his candidacy for the presidency. Perot was very comfortable with the alternative media and their free-flow formats.

Each of these personal campaign styles would come together in several political debates; however, the pathway was not direct. The Bush campaign team essentially dodged the debate process because it perceived the debates to not be advantageous to the President. The Bush campaign sought to place the candidate, if he were to participate in the debates, in the best format for his particular strengths and at the most opportune time during the campaign. It was not until the 1992 Bush campaign realized that it had to engage in the debates, because it was far behind in the polls, that the likelihood of the debates really emerged.

THE BIPARTISAN COMMISSION OF PRESIDENTIAL DEBATES PROPOSAL

On June 11, 1992, the Commission on Presidential Debates announced its proposed debate schedule. Three presidential and one vice presidential debates were proposed. The major difference between the Commission debate proposals in 1988 and 1992 was the replacement of the print and broadcast journalist panels by a single moderator. In early June, Clinton himself had proposed that there be 21 debates between the candidates. At that point in the campaign it was unclear whether Ross Perot would be invited to participate. The Commission had proposed a series of criteria for inclusion of Perot that related to such issues as whether he had a national organization; was placed on enough ballots in enough congressional districts to win enough electoral votes to win the election; was eligible for federal matching funds; had declared his candidacy in major conventions, party primaries, or state conventions; and had a significant level of popular support among the electorate. The Bush campaign suggested that decisions about Perot's inclusion should wait until after the Republican Convention in August.

By the early Fall, Perot was not a factor in the debate about the debates since he had withdrawn from the election. However, even when it was apparent that he might return, he was essentially locked out of the negotiations that were conducted between the Bush and Clinton campaigns.

THE FAILURE OF THE ORIGINAL DEBATE SCHEDULE

The first presidential debate between Clinton and Bush turned out to be a solo performance. Bush decided not to participate in the Commission's scheduled debate on the campus of Michigan State University because an agreement on format and structure had not been reached. Clinton decided to go to the debate anyway. This act would in effect embarrass Bush and capitalize on free press coverage. This was a tactic that John Anderson used in 1980—debating an empty podium.

Originally, Louisville, Kentucky was the proposed site for the vice presidential debate between Al Gore and Dan Quayle. However, in seeking to resolve the debate impasse and get the presidential debates started, the Commission proposed that the presidential candidates instead use the Louisville site for their first debate and switch the San Diego site to the vice presidential debate. However, the second proposed presidential debate in Louisville was canceled on September 23 as Bush and Clinton continued to insist that they wanted to debate, but each made no moves to resolve their differences over the format and structure of the debates. Clinton again showed up at the Louisville site, highlighting his presence and the absence of Bush. The next scheduled debate was proposed for Sunday, October 4, in San Diego, whereas the final Commission-proposed debate site was proposed for Richmond, Virginia, on October 15.

By the time the Kentucky debate failed to materialize, Clinton had agreed with the Commission's format that would have the two candidates, Bush and Clinton, squaring off against each other with a moderator. However, Bush was still insisting on a panel of journalists to ask questions. Clinton's campaign continued to assert that it would accept any debate format that the Commission proposed, whereas Bush insisted that the negotiations be held between the campaigns alone.

Beyond the debate about the debates were practical considerations that had to be considered as well. First, it takes about five days of round-the-clock activity to stage a debate. Second, the World Series was coming and would affect both the audience size and the ability of the network carrying the series to also broadcast the debates.

THE CHICKEN GEORGE STRATEGY

The watershed for Bush deciding to engage in debates resulted in large part from a ploy hatched by two Detroit-area men in a bar: Derrick Parker, a Navy veteran who had to drop out of college due to a lack of federal funds to support his education, and Corbett O'Meara, a college student who had to abandon his goal of attending law school due to the loss of a paralegal position that was helping him earn money to attend law school. These two men initiated what became known as the "Chicken George" strategy. This strategy, plus his lack of progress against Clinton, eventually led Bush into the debate fold. Both of the

Detroit men went to a public rally for George Bush with one dressed in a chicken suit and the other serving as his interpreter. "Read my beak," squawked the Chicken, "Chicken George is afraid to debate." Bush responded, "You talking about the draft dodging chicken or are you talking about the chicken in the Arkansas River? Which one?"

The first reference dealt with the issue of Clinton's alleged draft evasion. Bush's second reference implied that Clinton had a weak environmental record, allowing chicken parts from a slaughter house to be dumped into the Arkansas River. What was remarkable about the repartee was that the two hecklers did not really expect Bush to engage in "debate" with them, a chicken and his "interpreter," but he did! Bush again called attention to them, "Get out of here!" he said. Of course, the Chicken did not leave.

The Clinton campaign saw media coverage of the Chicken George event and thought that it was an effective image to promote against Bush, the reluctant debater. The Democrats began baiting the Bush campaign at many of his public appearances, chanting the Chicken George line. In effect, having within the public's mind the question, "Is Bush Chicken?"—afraid of debating. Eventually this tactic, coupled with falling figures in public opinion polls, led George Bush to call in his chief advisor, James Baker III, to discuss what bold step Bush could take to turn his failing campaign around. On September 29, at a rally in Clarksville, Tennessee, Bush got out in front of his campaign's own strategy and challenged Clinton to a series of debates, by saying, "Let's get it on."

Bush, then 10 points behind in the public opinion polls, challenged the Clinton campaign to four consecutive Sunday debates, ending just prior to the election. He agreed to two debates with a format he favored. At one of these two debates, they would have questions from a panel of journalists. The other two debates would be held with a single moderator, a format favored by the Commission and Clinton himself. Although the challenge was made, it was then up to Bush's own campaign to work out the details with the opposition in a manner that would still suit their best interests. After that challenge, Bush rejected the Clinton campaign's request to meet at the offices of the Presidential Debate Commission, insisting instead on meeting directly with representatives of the Clinton campaign, whereas the Clinton campaign sought to have the Commission involved. However, when the counterpunch came from Bush to debate on the four consecutive Sundays, Clinton's response was not direct. He wanted to discuss the matter at the Commission's Offices, but Bush was unwilling to do so. The next day Clinton suggested that perhaps the two candidates should both go on *Larry King Live*, and have one moderator—King. Bush did not agree.

This led to a series of negotiations between Bush's negotiator, James Baker, and Clinton's representative, Mickey Cantor, with the Bipartisan Commission tangentially involved.

THE TWO CAMPAIGNS' STRATEGY FOR THE DEBATE ABOUT DEBATES

The Bush campaign sought a format that would maximize their man's strengths and minimize his weaknesses. The Bush team wanted a panel of reporters serving as a buffer between the candidates. Initially, the Bush campaign felt that they had little to gain by participating in the debates, even though they were trailing in the polls. Because Bush was not closing the gap, they felt that they had to try something. Conventional wisdom states that incumbents and those in the lead avoid debates because they have the most to lose. The "stature gap" is often the ground that the incumbent wishes to preserve. A Republican official stated that "once Bush and Clinton get on the same stage, they become equals. If we give up something, we need to get something back" (Marelius, 1992). Thus, most incumbents avoid debate settings if they can. However, Ronald Reagan may have changed all this by being the first President who was leading in the polls—by 15 points at the time—to agree to debate.

Likewise, the candidate leading in the polls tends to avoid debates because of the possibility of making a blunder. Although Bush was the incumbent, he was trailing consistently throughout the later stages of the campaign and felt that his message was simply not getting through. He had to do something to avoid an apparently inevitable loss. Clinton, on the other hand, by virtue of his personality and style, sought debates in order to express himself. Clinton seemed to enter every public fray, talk show, public meeting, and debate that he could to hammer home his message of "change."

David Gergen (1992) quoted Richard Nixon about some advice Nixon was given in 1948, "If you debate you may lose, but if you don't debate, you're sure to lose." That seemed to be Bush's dilemma.

THE DEBATE COMPROMISE

Presidential debates had become a centerpiece of every campaign from 1976 through 1988, so it was no surprise that much pressure was brought to bear to have them in 1992. In effect, expectations that there would be debates are a mark of the institutionalization of the debates (see Chapter 10 for further discussion of this point).

Eventually, the Bush and Clinton teams agreed to meet and resolve their disagreements about debate formats. At the insistence of the Bush camp, the bipartisan campaigns made it clear that Ross Perot would be invited to participate in the debates, but he also was excluded from the negotiations. Perot's exclusion from the negotiations may have resulted from his on-again, off-again candidacy and late return to the campaign. The James Baker (Bush) and Mickey Cantor (Clinton) negotiating teams in effect dictated to the Commission—the only organization with an institutional commitment to always hold presidential debates—that Perot would be invited, the number and timing of the debates, and what their formats would be. Clearly, James Baker (and perhaps George Bush) did not want to help institutionalize the Commission as a kind of permanent, ongoing spokesperson for the debates. They seemed to want to make it very clear that it was up to the campaigns—and only the campaigns—as to whether presidential debates would be held. In 1992, in 1996. Whenever.

As they entered the negotiations, the campaigns each wanted something different. Bush, when he eventually decided to debate, asked for four debates—all within an 11-day period. His negotiating stance was to have a panel of reporters asking questions. The Clinton campaign favored a debate structure that had a single moderator and a live audience. (Perot, with his sharp wit and ability to provide provocative banter, preferred the more open debate formats as well.) The position of the bipartisan Commission was that they wanted a single-moderator format. On the basis of the 1960 debates between Kennedy and Nixon, the Commission felt that the single-moderator format was more informative than the reporter format, which was essentially a joint news conference. However, the Commission clearly indicated in late September that they were willing to sponsor the debates under any formats that the Bush and Clinton campaigns would jointly agree to.

The eventual compromise bought about three presidential and one vice presidential debates, all occurring within 11 days of one another. The structure was a compromised one. Figure 7.1 presents the original bipartisan Commission proposal and the actual debate settings that occurred in 1992. The first debate was to be conducted using a panel of reporters to question the candidates. This was the format sought by the Bush campaign. The vice presidential debate would use a single moderator asking questions and structuring the debate. The second presidential debate would rely on a single moderator and an audience that could ask questions, a format Clinton wanted. The third and final presidential debate would adopt a combination of formats. In this debate the first

Background and Format of the Debates   137

Commission Proposal   Incidents   Actual Debates
(June 11, 1992)

First Presidential Debate
East Lansing, Michigan
September 22, 1992
Moderator Only

       "Chicken George" initial incident
       September 29, 1992

Vice-Presidential Debate
Louisville, Kentucky
September 29, 1992
Moderator Only

       "Let's Get It On" statement by Bush
       September 29, 1992

Second Presidential Debate
San Diego, California
October 4, 1992
Moderator Only

               First Presidential Debate

               St. Louis, Missouri
               October 11, 1992
               Moderator and Panel

               Vice-Presidential Debate

               Atlanta, Georgia
               October 13, 1992
               Moderator Only

Third Presidential Debate   Second Presidential Debate
Richmond, Virginia   Richmond, Virginia
October 15, 1992   October 15, 1992
Moderator Only   Moderator and Audience

               Third Presidential Debate

               East Lansing, Michigan
               October 19, 1992
               Moderator 1/2 and Panel 1/2

Figure 7.1. Debate schedule 1992

half would use a moderator only, a format preferred by Clinton, and then the second half would use a panel of three journalists, a format preferred by Bush.

CONTINUOUS DEBATES WITH MULTIPLE FORMATS

The First Debate

The first actual general election presidential debate of the campaign was held on October 11, 1992, at Washington University in St. Louis, Missouri. This was the first debate in the modern era that presented three candidates for the presidency during the Fall campaign. Multiple candidates in the past and in 1992 have shared the stage during the primary season. This first debate featured Jim Lehrer of PBS as the moderator. Accompanying Lehrer were panelists John Mashek of the *Boston Globe*, Ann Compton of ABC News, and Sander Vanocur—a freelance journalist and member of the 1960 reporter debate panel. All of these participants were jointly approved by the Bush and Clinton campaigns. The format for the debate included a drawing to determine who would receive the first question, no opening statements, a single topic for each round of the debate, and no restrictions on content or subject matter. The panelists would be given 15 seconds to ask each of their questions. Then each candidate would have 2 minutes to answer the question posed. The other candidates would have 1 minute each to rebut the statement. Each candidate would have 2 minutes for a closing statement at the end of the debate. According to ABC News (Jennings, 1992a), the first presidential debate produced an audience of approximately 81 million, with about 60% of those who were watching television tuned to the debate.

The Vice Presidential Debate

The vice presidential debate was held on the campus of Georgia Tech in Atlanta, Georgia on October 13, 1992. The participants were Senator Al Gore, Vice President Dan Quayle, and James Stockdale. The format of the debate had Hal Bruno, political director of ABC News, serving as the moderator. The ground rules were that each candidate would have 2 minutes for an opening statement. The moderator would then present the issues to be discussed in the debate. For each topic presented, the candidates would each have 75 seconds to respond. After each of their comments, there would be a 5-minute session that permitted them to ask each other questions. The order of response was initially decided by a drawing and was rotated with each new topic. At the conclusion of the debate, each candidate was provided with the opportunity of presenting a 2-closing statement. The allocation of seating in the auditorium was evenly distributed between the campaigns so that they could each have an equal number of supporters present. According to ABC News (Jennings, 1992b), the vice presidential debate produced an audience of more than 70 million people.

The Richmond Debate

The second Presidential debate used a single moderator, Carole Simpson of ABC News, for the 90-minute debate. In her introduction to the debate, Simpson described her role as taking "care of the questioning, asking questions myself if I think there needs to be continuity and balance—and sometimes I might ask the candidates to respond to what another candidate may have said." There were no limits placed on the topics to be debated. The location of the second Presidential debate was the University of Richmond in Richmond, Virginia. Rather than the traditional lecterns on the podium, three stools were present, facing a 209-person audience of uncommitted voters. The stools allowed candidates to get up easily and approach the audience if and when they wished to. As events were to show, this more informal and intimate format was more advantageous to Clinton and Perot than to Bush. At the conclusion of the debate all three of the candidates were permitted the opportunity to make a closing statement.

What was also unique about the arrangements for the second presidential debate was that the persons in the audience were selected by the Gallup Organization. Gallup was charged with the responsibility of identifying and recruiting undecided voters for the audience. In essence, the audience was an extremely large focus group that was presented to the American public during prime time. Each of the candidates was equipped with a lavaliere microphone so he could move freely about, interacting with each other, with the moderator, and with the audience. Those in the Richmond audience were also connected to "peoplemeters" that essentially monitored their reactions to the debate on a minute-to-minute basis.

The Final Debate

The third presidential debate was held on the campus of Michigan State University in East Lansing, Michigan and used a combination of two formats. While millions watched the debate on television, some 900 guests, divided among supporters, invitees of the Commission, and about 200 MSU students, sat in the audience. The debate started with a single moderator, Jim Lehrer of PBS, for the first 45 minutes. This was the format favored by the Clinton campaign. Then the moderator, Lehrer, was joined by three journalists—Helen Thomas of UPI, Jean Gibbons of Reuters and Susan Rook of CNN—for the remaining 45 minutes. This moderator-panel format was the one favored by the Bush campaign.

CONCLUSIONS

The 1992 presidential election campaign saw the continuation of the debates as a primary focal point. Although new alternative media, such as talk shows and town meetings, became prominent, the debates remained a compellingly central feature of the campaign for the candidates, the media, and the people. The debates served as a primary means to evaluate the candidates.

Candidates will always seek to maximize their strengths and minimize their weakness. Initially, George Bush sought to avoid the debates because he saw little to gain and much to lose. Thus, when the bipartisan Commission on Presidential Debates proposed the debates and format, he resisted. It was not until Bush felt that he had to debate that the debates of 1992 become a reality. Even then, the debates did not occur without intense negotiations between the Bush and Clinton campaigns. With the large investment that the public makes in federally funding elections, one would think that this could be used as leverage to require that the candidates for the presidency debate. However, it is clearly evident that, in 1992, even making the debates a requirement for receiving federal funds would not guarantee compliance. With the presence of Ross Perot and his immense commitment of personal wealth to his own campaign, he could not be compelled by the carrot of federal funds. Although this may have been a unique situation, other candidates might well choose to raise funds privately if the requirements placed on federal funds are perceived by them to be too high.

The League of Women Voters, sponsors of every Fall presidential debate from 1976 through 1984, never could gain the upper hand in negotiations about format because the candidates always held the cards—they could always refuse to debate if the League were stubborn. Then, in 1988, the Bush and Dukakis campaigns and the two political parties created the Commission on Presidential Debates, which seemed designed to replace those persistent League negotiators. When the Commission offered the League nominal sponsorship of the final 1988 debate—only if the League would accept all the format rules negotiated by the two campaigns (many of them dictated by the Bush campaign to an increasingly desperate Dukakis campaign)—the Commission seemed to serve as the agent of the campaigns, not of the debates (see Lemert, Elliott, Bernstein, Rosenberg, & Nestvold, 1991, pp. 101-107). However, in the nearly four years during which the Commission's staff could do homework and reflection on the debates as an institution, something seemed to happen: At least part of the Commission's loyalty seemed to shift to the debates, with a little less support going to the parties and their candidates. It is in the context of this development that many of the same men (James Baker especially) who had insisted that the Commission be the agent for the debates in 1988 now wanted to make sure that everyone knew the Commission could sponsor the debates only if the real decision makers—the campaigns—allowed it to.

Perhaps ultimately, then, the pressure to debate will have to come from the electorate. Candidates certainly did not miss the huge audiences for the 1992 debates and the very large cumulative audience for the talk shows and alternative media (more on these points in Chapters 10 and 5, respectively). As voters became acquainted with the many opportunities to observe the candidates directly themselves through both the debates and alternative media, it may be that gradually the candidates will fear antagonizing voters if they refuse to debate even more than they will the risk of having to debate. Clearly, the news media can play a role here in challenging reluctant candidates to face off, but what voters expect a presidential candidate to be willing to do ultimately may be decisive. It is for these reasons that we examined both media and mass support for the presidential debates (Chapter 10).

Even if it becomes more and more difficult for candidates to evade the presidential debates, questions about debate format will continue to create delays and uncertainties. To a certain extent, these delays and uncertainties must be expected and tolerated because candidates have a legitimate vested interest in the rules of combat. That legitimate self-interest in the rules should not be allowed to supersede the larger public interest in holding the debates.

REFERENCES

Gergen, D. (1992, September 30). *A quote by Richard Nixon.* MacNeil/Lehrer News Hour.
Groer, A. (1992, October 11). *Orlando Sentinel Tribune*, p. A11.
Jennings, P. (1992a, October 12). *ABC World News Tonight.*
Jennings, P. (1992b, October 15). *ABC World News Tonight.*

Kraus, S. (1988). *Televised presidential debates and public policy.* Hillsdale, NJ: Erlbaum.
Lemert, J.B., Elliott, W.R., Bernstein, J.M., Rosenberg, W.L., & Nestvold, K.J. (1991). *News verdicts, the debates, and presidential campaigns.* New York: Praeger.
Marelius, J. (1992, September 24). Focus turns to San Diego for Presidential debate. *The San Diego Union-Tribune,* p. A1.
Nolan, M. F. (1992, October 11). Goldwater pointed way to gentlemanly fight in politics. *The Boston Globe,* p. 24.

8

Debate Effects on Survey Respondents

William R. Elliott

Many people, Richard Nixon included, "knew" why Jack Kennedy won the 1960 presidential election. Kennedy won because of the country's first televised presidential debates. Kennedy won because he took advantage of changing information technology and consequent changes in the style of political campaigning. From Nixon's perspective, the debates emphasized a candidate's appearance, not the substance of a candidate's position on the issues, not the strength of the candidate's political philosophy, but the candidate's ability to project a favorable "image." Appearance failed Richard Nixon during that first critical debate in 1964 (Spear, 1984).

Second-hand evidence seemed to support this interpretation. Most polls, a few studies, and commentator "intuition" suggested that Richard Nixon's haggard appearance (he was sick) and Kennedy's apparent excellent health tipped the scales in favor of Kennedy. Jack Kennedy, who appeared confident, rested, and able, was at least Richard Nixon's equal in that first encounter. That's what many said.

Hard evidence, the type you could defend in court, was missing. The truth is, it is difficult to "prove" that the presidential candidate debates of 1960, or any of the subsequent presidential candidate debates, exerted a great influence on the outcome of campaigns. After decades of experience with debates and scores of studies, we still cannot say, with certainty, that any debate "caused" an election to go one way or another. Partly this is because social science is far from exact. Mostly this is because the process of electing our political representatives is very complex.

We are still learning how the process works, including how debates influence our voting decisions. In this chapter, we will look at how exposure to the presidential debates influenced people's knowledge of the campaign issues, their images of the candidates, and the probability they would vote for the candidates. In Chapter 9, we look at how verdicts regarding debate performance, as presented by journalists and other "experts," influenced this unusual presidential campaign.

DEBATE POSITIVES AND NEGATIVES

We do know many things about presidential candidate debates (Meadow, 1983). Debates offer a way for candidates to bypass traditional media gatekeepers and present their ideas and visions directly to the voters. Debates allow voters to learn where candidates stand on the issues, although evidence for this influence is mixed. Debates are part of American politics, allowing us to affirm our commitment to the democratic process. For television networks, the debates are one of their most important symbols of network public service. Debates can give an air of legitimacy to lesser known candidates and, for better known candidates, they can reinforce a candidate's positive image with partisan supporters.

In spite of their potential for good, debates have serious limitations (Jamieson, 1987). The very format of the candidate debates makes detailed and thoughtful answers impossible. In 1984, Walter Mondale had 150 seconds to present his position on the extent of Soviet domination in Eastern Europe and how he would help to achieve the Helsinki Accords human rights goals for the people under Soviet control. With only one campaign winner, candidates fear telling too much. They avoid answering specific questions, often preferring to cite facts rather than relating facts to broader issues. For journalists, the temptation to ask questions they personally find interesting rather than following up on questions that would allow honest comparisons between the candidates must seem overwhelming.

Debates force oversimplification; being articulate replaces being thoughtful. Most of us feel that there is more to leadership than the ability to answer quickly. Debates can penalize candidates who ponder, consider, and speak slowly. The way a candidate looks or dresses can detract from meaningful discussions of ideas and positions. Some examples will help.

In 1976, when President Ford was debating Jimmy Carter, he mistakenly suggested that Eastern Europe was not under Soviet control. It was the type of mistake that anyone might make when they are nervous and under stress. Gerald Ford knew that the Soviet Union controlled Eastern Europe with an iron hand. He was momentarily confused. His "gaffe" was costly, and many, particularly in the press, saw that "gaffe" helping Jimmy Carter.

In 1980, candidate Ronald Reagan was instructed to "chuckle" whenever Carter would begin to attack him (Kraus, 1988). Reagan not only chuckled in the debate held in Cleveland, but added "there you go again" to campaign debate rhetoric. Carter was derailed.

Reagan tried the same tactic in 1984 in his debates with Walter Mondale. When Reagan said, "there you go again," Mondale answered by pointing out that Reagan had used the same tactic to stop Carter's claim that Reagan had proposed cutting Medicare. Mondale used the opportunity to point out that Reagan had cut Medicare by $20 billion (Dye & Zeigler, 1986).

Perhaps the most notorious debate question came during the 1988 debates. In the final presidential debate, Bernard Shaw of CNN asked Michael Dukakis how he would feel if his wife Kitty were raped and murdered (the "dead Kitty" question). Dukakis's response was seen as "unfocused, unaggressive, unimpressive" (Donaldson, 1988, p, 104). We are not sure how anyone could answer that question and be "focused, aggressive, and impressive." It is not the type of question that would bring out the best in any candidate.

The best remembered debate comeback took place in 1988 when vice presidential candidates Dan Quayle and Lloyd Bentsen confronted each other in their televised debate. Lloyd Bentsen cast considerable doubt on the ability of Dan Quayle and, by reflection, on George Bush, with his "you're no Jack Kennedy" response after Dan Quayle noted similarities between himself and the late president. Donaldson (1988) reported that the "you're no Jack Kennedy" response was rehearsed in advance.

Presidential candidate debates, subject to influences outside of the control of the candidates, the press, and the voters, are imperfect. Yet, given their imperfections, given that journalists may ask pointless questions, that candidates may often respond with "canned" answers, that interpretation of debate performance may turn on a single failed fact or misstatement, debates still provide the most important campaign information for voters. Debates give voters a chance to watch and listen to the candidates, to judge them *before* television and newspaper editors have interpreted their ideas and thoughts, and to form and modify their own perceptions of the candidates.

Finally, the presidential campaign debates help us form and solidify our images of the candidates. Although the candidate's "image" is often seen as less important than the candidate's position on an issue or the candidate's political philosophy, political image is an important element of the modern presidency. Presidents serve their goals for the nation through their own public relations efforts on behalf of specific programs and approaches to problem solving. To be successful, the president must present an image that commands the trust and acceptance of the people, the nation's allies, and the nation's enemies. We do care about the image of our president and that caring is justified.

DEBATE INFLUENCES: KNOWLEDGE, IMAGE, AND VOTE CHOICE

Several factors make the 1992 campaign and these particular debates so interesting and so important as we try to understand the "new politics." First, there were three true candidates, each with an organized following and national visibility. Second, the candidates, particularly Perot and Clinton, broadened our ideas about campaigning to include radio and television talk shows and electronic town meetings. Third, Perot used his money, his amateur campaign organization, and his "plain talk" style to reach potential voters.

Another important factor of these debates is that three presidential and one vice presidential debates were conducted over a 9-day period and finished just two weeks before the election. From the first debate on October 11, 1992, until a day or two after the final debate on October 19, the debates were the most important political topic in the news and on the minds of the public.

We wanted to investigate how these 1992 candidate debates influenced a sample of potential voters selected from a variety of places around the country. As we had done in 1988 (Lemert, 1993; Lemert, Elliott, Bernstein, Rosenberg, & Nestvold, 1991), we tried to isolate the impact the debates had on our survey sample's political knowledge, image of the candidates, and voting preferences.

Debate Influences on Knowledge

Watching and listening to a candidate debate does increase what we know about the campaign issues. Kraus (1988) reviewed studies of the

1960, 1976, and 1980 debates. He concluded that campaign issues are discussed, that the candidates could be classified in terms of their issue positions, that voters learn about the issues, and that some issues become more salient than others, all because of debate exposure. Hellweg, Pfau, and Brydon (1992) made a similar generalization. Watching the debates has been associated with increased knowledge of the issues and the candidates' positions on the issues in *all* presidential debates.

In a carefully designed study of the first 1992 debate, Zhu, Milavsky, and Biswas (1994) developed 24 issue areas from the news before the debate and found that "8 were addressed by Bush, 9 by Clinton, and 4 by Bush" (p. 317). These 21 items discussed in the debate formed an issue knowledge battery of questions to decide if the debate influenced knowledge. The findings were unambiguous: People who watched the debate knew more after than before the debate, and debate watchers learned more about debated issues than did nonwatchers.

Chaffee, Zhao, and Leshner (1994) also looked at the 1992 campaign to detect the influence of media use on knowledge of party stands on the issues, knowledge of the candidates' stands on the issues, and personal characteristics of the candidates. After controlling for a host of intervening variables (education, age, income, ideology, race, occupation, etc.), they found that newspaper reading and TV news viewing were positively related to each of the knowledge variables. Attention to newspaper campaign information was related to party issue knowledge and candidate personal knowledge, whereas attention to TV news was related to candidate issue knowledge and candidate personal knowledge. For our purposes, the most important finding was that debate viewing was related to party issue knowledge and candidate personal knowledge.

Lemert (1993) found that debate exposure was positively related to increases in political knowledge for both 1988 presidential debates, although exposure to the vice presidential debate did not influence knowledge. This influence held after controls for education, age, income, political interest, gender, network television news viewing, newspaper reading, and discussion of the presidential campaign had been introduced.

Watching a televised presidential debate is not a passive and neutral experience, it is a learning experience.

Debate Influences on Candidate Image

If debates have an influence on knowledge, shouldn't they also have an influence on our "image" of the candidates? The obvious answer seems to be "yes."

All campaign teams strive to present a positive "image" for their candidate. Kraus (1988) noted that the image a candidate manages to create while in office or on the campaign trail is an important factor in converting candidate awareness into a candidate vote. The debates are particularly important in the development of this image. This seems to have been the case in 1960. Hellweg et al. (1992) concluded that the debates were influential in improving Kennedy's image and may have actually harmed that of Nixon.

However, debate influence on image can be selective. Elliott and Sothirajah (1993) found that exposure to the 1988 debates and postdebate analysis for the first 1988 presidential debate influenced the people's evaluations of Dukakis as a debater and his political image. There was little impact on the image of the better known candidate—George Bush. Gallup (1987) added a similar caution. Debates are not particularly related to dramatic swings in image of the candidates but can "stall the momentum of a candidate, . . . dampen the enthusiasm of his or her supporters, and . . . prompt second thoughts" (p. 34).

In support of this latter idea, Zhu et al. (1994) discovered that the first 1992 debate influenced the image of only one candidate, Ross Perot. Watching that debate made people feel better about Perot's integrity and charisma. A similar conclusion was reached in a study by Carter and Stamm (1994). They asked their respondents to provide word associations for the campaign topics of "Bush," "Clinton," and "Perot." Their open-ended responses (word associations) were then analyzed in terms of six possible relationships the words could have with the candidates. Using this innovative "cognigraphics" methodology, the researchers concluded that George Bush was not helped by debates, that Bill Clinton was seen as more consequential after the debates, and that Ross Perot, particularly after the last two debates, showed an improvement in affect that suggested improved credibility.

In summary, can debates improve (or harm) a candidate's image? The answer is yes but that needs to be qualified. Debates have their greatest impact on the image of the candidate(s) we know least about. In 1960 that was Jack Kennedy. Michael Dukakis's image benefited most in 1988's first debate. Who would benefit most from the 1992 debates? Almost certainly, Ross Perot's image had the greatest room to improve. Bill Clinton's was not far behind and should have fared well also. Perhaps the safest bet was that George Bush was in the least favorable position.

Our data will help us answer this question.

Debate Influences on the Vote

For the politician and the campaign staff there is but one important outcome—the vote. It makes little difference to them if the audience is informed on the issues or if it feels comfortable with their images. Getting votes is the bottom line.

Do debates influence the way we vote? This is not easily answered, and sometimes interpretations seem contradictory. For instance, Gallup (1987) reviewed poll results from the 1960, 1976, 1980, and 1984 debates and concluded that debates have a small impact on voting preference, although a strong debate performance can be a decisive factor among undecided or weakly committed voters. Compare this with findings based on the Roper polls (cited in Hellweg et al., 1992, p. 113). The polls estimated that 4 million people changed their voting intention because of the 1960 debates. In a close election, as in 1960, a shift of 4 million votes easily determines the winner.

In a study relevant to this one, Lemert et al. (1991) found that debate exposure did influence the probability of voting for one candidate over another. In a slightly different setting, Schrott (1990) looked at data from West German elections in 1972, 1976, 1980, and 1983. His findings consistently suggested that seeing a candidate as "winning" a debate increased the voter's likelihood of voting for that candidate.

Finally, when Lanoue (1992) analyzed data collected before and after the single 1980 debate between Ronald Reagan and President Carter, he found that approximately 40% of the people who supported Carter before the debate thought he lost in the encounter with Reagan. In contrast, only 20% of Reagan's predebate supporters thought Reagan had lost. And, importantly, voters with low knowledge levels were particularly influenced by debate exposure.

In summary, then, it is reasonable to hypothesize a debate effect on the vote. Such an effect should be strongest for those with the least knowledge of the campaign. Our time-series survey design over the three presidential debates allows us to test for this possible relationship.

METHODS, VARIABLES, AND ANALYSES

We were interested in how the debates might influence knowledge about the campaign, the image of the candidates, and the probability of voting for the candidates. In addition, we wanted to know how potential voters evaluated the performance of each candidate in the three debates. To guide us in developing answers to these questions, we surveyed potential voters about their knowledge, images of the candidates, and voting preferences. Using Multiple Classification Analysis (MCA; described in Chapter 5), we attempted to isolate the influence of the debates on knowledge, image, and voting preference by controlling for other influences.

Methods

For our investigation of debate influence on potential voters, we used a survey analysis beginning on October 11, 1992, immediately after the first debate. (You can see a detailed outline of the design in Chapter 2.) We randomly selected people to interview and called every night through October 22, 1992, three days after the third presidential debate. By structuring our study in this manner, we could investigate the influence of the first debate (October 11), second debate (October 15), and third debate (October 19) on the people in our sample. The people we interviewed were selected in the cities of Philadelphia, Pennsylvania; Indianapolis, Indiana; Carbondale, Illinois; and Eugene, Oregon. Over this 12-day period, we interviewed 1,433 people.

Variables

We know from past studies and from our own experience in doing debate studies that there are many influences deciding what people know about politics and campaigns, their images of the candidates, and how they will eventually vote. Because of these multiple influences on people's ideas, beliefs, and political behavior, we needed several types of variables to determine whether the debate had any measurable impact. We broke these variables down into three groups.

First, there are what we call "control" variables. These variables are known to influence the variables we are interested in but are not the primary concern of this section of the study. The second variable class is labeled "predictor" variables. This classification includes the variable or variables that is of greatest importance to us. The final variable classification is the "dependent" variable group. In our case, these are the variables we think are influenced by debate exposure.

Control variables. We have six variables introduced as controls for this part of the study. Education, the years of formal training in a learning institution, was measured by asking subjects for the total number of years of schooling they had completed. The mean for education was 14.3 years of schooling with a standard deviation of 2.72.

Our measure of campaign interest was a single Likert-item scale asking respondents how interested they were in this campaign. Responses ranged along a 5-point scale from very uninterested (8.9%) to very interested (42.8%) with a mean of 3.99 and a standard deviation of 1.22.

The use of alternative media was indexed by asking individuals to name the talk shows in which they had seen any of the presidential or

Debate Effects on Survey Respondents 151

vice presidential candidates. Each response was recorded for each show as 0 (they had not seen George Bush on *Arsenio Hall*) or 1 (they had). All positive responses were summed to form the alternative media use score. The mean score for this variable was .84 (62.3% had not seen any candidate on alternative media) with a range from 0 to 11. The standard deviation was 1.38.

To determine newspaper use, people were asked how many days per week they read the newspaper. The responses averaged 3.76 days per week with a standard deviation of 2.92. Nearly one fourth (23.4%) of the sample indicated reading no days per week; 36.3% indicated reading seven days per week.

Network television news use was measured by asking how many nights per week the subjects watched network television news. The mean for television news use was 4.04 nights per week with a standard deviation of 2.55. Nearly one third (31%) watched seven nights a week while 14.5% said they did not watch any network television news during the week.

Each person told us which political party he or she identified with. We grouped them, based on their responses, as Republicans, Democrats, and Independent/Others.

Predictor variables. Debate viewing was measured by asking individuals how much of the most recent presidential debate they had watched. Breaking this down over the three presidential debates, we looked at the people we interviewed from October 11 through October 14 for the first presidential debate, at the respondents from October 15 to October 18 for the second presidential debate, and at the respondents from October 19 through October 22 for the third presidential debate (refer to the design diagram in Chapter 2).

Over the October interview period, 30.4% said they had not watched the most recent debate (a score of 0), 5.3% said they had watched "a little" (a score of 1), 11.0% said "some" (a score of 2), 20.2% said "most" (a score of 3), and 31.9% said "all" (a score of 4). The mean was 2.18 with a standard deviation of 1.66.

Dependent variables. Although our primary concern in this portion of the study is debate influence on issue knowledge, candidate image, and voting probabilities, we were also interested in how people evaluated debate performance. We asked each debate viewer to make a series of two-way comparisons. We asked them the following: "Based on what you have heard or seen about (fill in day) debate, would you say that George Bush won by a lot, that George Bush won by a little, that the debate was about even, that Bill Clinton won by a little, or that Bill

Clinton won by a lot?" The same question was asked comparing Bill Clinton versus Ross Perot and Ross Perot versus George Bush.

Issue knowledge was measured by summing respondent's ability to match the proper candidate with a known issue position. For George Bush, the "correct" issue answer was in identifying him as favoring a Constitutional Amendment making abortion illegal. For Bill Clinton, the issue was an increase in the taxes paid by upper income Americans. For Ross Perot, the issue was favoring an increase in the taxes paid on gasoline. Overall, 63.4% of the sample correctly matched George Bush with an abortion amendment, 81.2% matched Clinton to a tax increase for the rich, and 61.6% identified Perot as favoring a gas tax. The mean score for the sum of the three issues was 2.06 with a standard deviation of 1.03. Although only 11.7% were unable to identify a single issue position, 44.8% correctly identified all three positions.

Each candidate's political image was constructed by summing three items into an image scale. The three items were respondent evaluations, on a 0 to 10 scale, of each of the candidates (a) domestic knowledge, (b) character, and (c) understanding of the problems of common people. The mean image score for George Bush was 16.15 with a standard deviation of 7.08. The mean image score for Bill Clinton was 20.37 with a standard deviation of 5.75. For Ross Perot the mean image score was 18.31 with a standard deviation of 6.54.[1]

Finally, the probability of voting for each of the three candidates was measured by asking each respondent how likely it was that he or she would vote for Bush, Clinton, and Perot. In each case, responses ranged from 0 (extremely unlikely) to 10 (extremely likely). The mean voting probability score for Bush was 3.32 with a standard deviation of 3.82. For Bill Clinton the mean probability score was 6.06 with a standard deviation of 4.09. For Ross Perot the mean was 3.16 with a standard deviation of 3.41. Knowledge and image scores were entered into the data analysis as predictor variables for the 0 to 10 probability of voting for each candidate.

The Analysis

To look at the influence of political party on perceptions of debate performance, we relied on cross-tabulations and chi-square statistical tests. The chi-square test tells us whether a distribution of responses differs significantly from the results one might get by chance.

We used MCA as our primary analytical tool when investigating the impact of the debates. This method (see Chapter 5) allows us to gauge the influence of exposure to the debates while simultaneously controlling for the influence of our control variables. This is a powerful technique that allows us to isolate the influence of the debate on the knowledge, images, and voting intentions of the people in our sample.

FINDINGS

Our findings are presented in four sections. In the first section we look at how people evaluated the debate performance of the three candidates. This was done for each of the three debates, and the results are presented in Tables 8.1 to 8.3.

The second section looks at the influence of debate exposure on issue knowledge for each of the three debates. These results are presented in Table 8.4. The third section summarizes our findings about the influence of the debates on the political images of each candidate. These findings are presented for each candidate across the three debates in Tables 8.5, 8.6, and 8.7. The final section looks at the influence of the debates on the probability of voting for each candidate across the three debates. These findings are presented in Tables 8.8 to 8.10.

Debate Performance

Debate 1. The first presidential debate followed the "traditional" debate format with a moderator, a panel of journalists, and the candidates. If anything, George Bush should have had the edge, based on his experiences debating with Geraldine Ferraro as a vice presidential candidate and Michael Dukakis as a presidential candidate. Bill Clinton was also a seasoned debater, necessarily, because of the multiple-debate requirements of the Democratic presidential primary campaign. Ross Perot was the unknown candidate. How would he fare against these two experienced politicians? Our findings, presented in Table 8.1, show that he did very well indeed.

You cannot analyze debate performance perceptions without taking into account the influence of political party. There are no "objective" standards. Since the 1960 debate, and in every debate that has followed, Republicans see the Republican candidates as doing best, whereas Democrats see their own candidate as winning. Independents and others split. You can see that in Table 8.1. Republicans were reluctant to see Clinton getting the best of the debate, with 17.1% saying he won "by a little" and 7.9% saying he won "by a lot." Democrats were unlikely to give Bush any credit. Only 4.3% saw him winning by a little, 2.2% by a lot. Finally, Independents and others gave the nod to Clinton over Bush, with 42.5% saying that Clinton won by a little, 17.8% by a lot.

Table 8.1. Cross-Tabulation[a] of Debate Performance by Party: First Presidential Debate.

Debate Performance Bush vs. Clinton[***]	Republicans %	Democrat %	Ind/Other %
Bush by a lot	15.8	2.2	6.8
Bush by a little	40.8	4.3	11.0
Even	18.4	7.2	21.9
Clinton by a little	17.1	34.1	42.5
Clinton by a lot	7.9	52.2	17.8
N	76	138	73
Clinton vs. Perot[***]			
Clinton by a lot	15.9	27.5	11.0
Clinton by a little	23.2	29.8	15.1
Even	9.8	9.9	15.1
Perot by a little	19.5	19.8	28.8
Perot by a lot	31.7	13.0	30.1
N	82	131	73
Perot vs. Bush[***]			
Perot by a lot	19.5	47.3	40.8
Perot by a little	25.6	29.8	31.6
Even	12.2	5.3	7.9
Bush by a little	17.1	7.6	7.9
Bush by a lot	25.6	9.9	11.8
N	82	131	76

[*]$p < .10$, χ^2 test.
[**]$p < .05$, χ^2 test.
[***]$p < .01$, χ^2 test.
[a]The Chi-square (χ^2) statistic is used to determine if the distribution of responses differs significantly from what might be anticipated by chance alone. In the case of this table, the likelihood that the particular distributions observed would have occurred simply by chance is less than 1 in 100 ($p < .01$). These same findings were observed for Tables 8.2 and 8.3.

Look now at the Perot comparisons. For Clinton versus Perot, 31.7% of the Republicans thought that Perot had won by a lot, 19.5% by a little. Even for the Democrats, 19.8% saw Perot winning by a little, 13.0% by a lot. Independents and others clearly favored Perot, with 28.8% giving him victory by a little, 30.1% by a lot.

Comparing Perot with Bush, the results are even clearer. For Republicans, 25.6% saw Perot winning by a little, 19.5% by a lot. The Democrats gave Perot a wide margin, with 47.3% seeing Perot as the winner by a lot, 29.8% as the winner by a little. Finally, the Independents and others gave Perot a substantial majority, with 40.8% saying that Perot won by a lot, 31.6% that he won by a little.

Clearly, Ross Perot came out on the top after this first debate. True, he did not have to do much. If he just stood there, answered questions, made a few jokes, and appeared equal to the other two, he could not lose. He apparently did more than that. Whatever the party preference of the people we interviewed, Ross Perot came out on top overall. He did well among Democrats when compared with Clinton and well among Republicans when compared with Bush.

Although the day went to Perot, the loser was George Bush. He fared poorly with Democrats and Independent/others when compared to Clinton, and lost badly (Democrats and Independents/others) when compared to Perot. Clinton was in the middle.

Debate 2. The format for the second presidential debate changed. This time a "town-meeting" atmosphere dominated, and average voters were allowed to ask questions directly of the candidates. This was an environment suited to the campaign styles of Bill Clinton and Ross Perot, both of whom had made extensive use of the electronic town meeting during their campaigns. It was a format that would prove to be uncomfortable to George Bush. The candidate-to-candidate comparisons for the second debate are presented in Table 8.2.

Even the Republicans saw Bill Clinton's performance as superior to that of their candidate. For them, 23.4% saw Clinton winning by a little, 27.3% by a lot. The figures are much higher for the Democrats. A majority, 76.1%, saw Clinton as the winner by a lot. Independent/others gave Clinton a substantial victory; 44.4% by a little and 37.0% by a lot. Clinton was also the clear winner against Perot, with 36.4% of the Republicans saying that he had won by a lot. The same finding held for Democrats and the Independent/others with percentages of 59.6% and 30.8%, respectively.

Finally, in the comparisons between Perot and Bush, Perot was seen as winning by the Democrats and the Independent/others and losing by the Republicans, but not by an exceptionally high amount. Again, only this time perhaps even more, George Bush was the big loser. Ross Perot replaced Bill Clinton as the middle person.

Debate 3. The third and final presidential debate, held on October 19, combined two formats: a moderator-only format as used in

Table 8.2. Cross-Tabulation of Debate Performance by Party: Second Presidential Debate.

Debate Performance Bush vs. Clinton***	Republicans %	Democrat %	Ind/Other %
Bush by a lot	9.1	1.8	0.0
Bush by a little	22.1	1.8	9.3
Even	18.2	0.0	9.3
Clinton by a little	23.4	20.2	44.4
Clinton by a lot	27.3	76.1	37.0
N	77	109	54
Clinton vs. Perot***			
Clinton by a lot	36.4	59.6	30.8
Clinton by a little	31.2	30.3	28.8
Even	11.7	0.9	19.2
Perot by a little	15.6	7.3	11.5
Perot by a lot	5.2	1.8	9.6
N	77	109	52
Perot vs. Bush***			
Perot by a lot	11.8	28.8	31.4
Perot by a little	22.4	27.9	33.3
Even	10.5	3.8	11.8
Bush by a little	23.7	27.9	15.7
Bush by a lot	31.6	11.5	7.8
N	76	104	51

*$p < .10$, χ^2 test.
**$p < .05$, χ^2 test.
***$p < .01$, χ^2 test.

the October 13 vice presidential debate, and the traditional moderator/panel of journalists format used in the first presidential debate. For the moderator-only format, experience was on the side of Bill Clinton and Ross Perot, based on their extensive use of talk-show visits as part of their campaign strategy. Based on our results from the first debate, if Perot's "winning" was based on something other than a contrast effect, then this format should benefit Perot. The findings are presented in Table 8.3.

Table 8.3. Cross-Tabulation of Debate Performance by Party: Third Presidential Debate.

Debate Performance Bush vs. Clinton***	Republicans %	Democrats %	Ind/Other %
Bush by a lot	30.9	2.0	14.5
Bush by a little	26.6	6.8	16.9
Even	17.0	13.5	14.5
Clinton by a little	18.1	30.4	28.9
Clinton by a lot	7.4	47.3	25.3
N	94	148	83
Clinton vs. Perot***			
Clinton by a lot	12.1	38.5	23.2
Clinton by a little	25.3	23.6	20.7
Even	11.0	15.5	7.3
Perot by a little	25.3	8.8	25.6
Perot by a lot	26.4	13.5	23.2
N	91	148	82
Perot vs. Bush***			
Perot by a lot	16.1	38.6	39.5
Perot by a little	16.1	24.1	21.0
Even	11.8	13.1	7.4
Bush by a little	23.7	11.7	12.3
Bush by a lot	32.3	12.4	19.8
N	93	145	81

*$p < .10$, χ^2 test.
**$p < .05$, χ^2 test.
***$p < .01$, χ^2 test.

Bush and Clinton came out close to even with perhaps a slight edge, based on the Independents/others' judgments, to Clinton. Of the Republicans, 30.9% saw George Bush winning by a lot. For the Democrats, it was 47.3% who saw their candidate winning by a lot. The Independent/others gave the nod to Clinton, with 25.3% saying he won by a lot compared to 14.5% who thought Bush had won by a lot.

Clinton seemed to have come out about even with Perot. The Republicans saw Perot as getting the best of it, with 26.4% saying he had beaten Bill Clinton by a lot compared with 12.1% of the Republicans who thought Clinton beat Perot by a lot. Democrats clearly saw Clinton as the winner, with 38.5% saying he won by a lot. Independents/others were split almost exactly, with 23.2% seeing Clinton as winning by a lot, 23.2% seeing Perot winning by a lot, 20.7% seeing Clinton winning by a little, and 25.6% seeing Perot winning by a little.

Perot again came out ahead of George Bush. Many Republicans saw him beating George Bush by a lot (16.1%) or a little (16.1%). Democrats favored Perot by a lot (38.6%) as did the Independents/others (39.5%).

Overall, this third debate was about even between Clinton and Perot, with, again, George Bush in third. None of the formats had worked to George Bush's advantage. Based on our October samples, the results of the debates, in terms of perceptions of winners and losers, are clear. Ross Perot won the first debate, Bill Clinton the second, and Perot and Clinton came out even for the third debate. George Bush was third in every debate. Debate winners and losers, however, may have little to do with how debates influence issue knowledge, candidate image, and voting probabilities. We now turn our attention to these variables.

Issue Knowledge

The process of learning about campaign issues is a complex one. We know that there is a relationship between the level of education and almost all types of knowledge. We know also that people who are more interested in a political campaign tend to know more about the issues of the campaign. They also tend to be better educated. It is complicated.

We have a history of finding relationships between media exposure and campaign knowledge, particularly for newspaper reading. In this campaign a third type of media exposure, which we labeled *alternative media*, is considered besides newspapers and network television news as possible sources of information about the issues of the campaign.

In the results presented in Table 8.4, education, campaign interest, exposure to the candidates on alternative media, daily newspaper, and network television news use appear under the *Regression* heading in the table. The numbers in the table are "raw" regression coefficients. (See Chapter 5 for a more complete explanation of regressions and what they mean.)

The *Adjusted Means* heading in the table presents the "adjusted" mean score for each level of debate viewing (none, little or some, most, all) and each category of political party (Republican, Democrat, Independent/Other). (For more explanation of "adjusted" means and how to read MCA tables, see Chapter 5.)

Only two variables had statistically significant effects on issue knowledge for the first debate. Education was positively related to issue knowledge, and debate viewing showed a clear debate exposure impact.

Debate Effects on Survey Respondents 159

Table 8.4. Summary of Multiple Classification Analyses: Influence of Presidential Debate Exposure on Issue Knowledge; Adjusted Mean Scores and Regression Coefficients.

Predictors	Issue Knowledge Debate 1 $M = 2.20$	Issue Knowledge Debate 2 $M = 2.14$	Issue Knowledge Debate 3 $M = 2.13$
Regressions[a]			
Education	.053***	.079***	.066***
Campaign Interest	—	.110***	.100***
Alternative Media	—	—	—
Newspaper Use	—	.039*	.050***
Network TV News	—	—	—
Adjusted Means[b]			
Debate Viewing			
None	1.87***	1.88***	1.87***
Little or Some	2.03	1.96	2.16
Most	2.28	2.14	2.13
All	2.50	2.41	2.37
Political Party	—	—	—
N	396	320	475

*$p < .10$.
**$p < .05$.
***$p < .01$.

[a]The lay reader should pay attention to whether the sign before the regression numbers is + or -; that tells you whether the relationship between the control variable and the dependent variable is positive (as education increases, issue knowledge increases) or negative (as one increases, the other decreases).

[b]The "adjusted means" represent the mean scores for each level of debate viewing or category of political party after simultaneously adjusting for the influence of all other variables in the multiple classification analysis. Basically, these "adjusted means" represent what the mean scores would be if all of the people interviewed were equivalent on the other variables. These procedures are followed for Tables 8.4 through 8.10.

The adjusted mean score for those who did not watch the debate was 1.87 (out of a possible 3), whereas the corresponding means for those who watched a little or some, most, or all of the debate were 2.03, 2.28, and 2.50, respectively. Not only was watching the debate important, but how much of the debate one watched seemed to have an impact.

The pattern of influence for the second debate is similar. This time, three of the control variables—education, campaign interest, and newspaper—use are positively associated with issue knowledge. Again, debate exposure is strongly related to issue knowledge. The adjusted mean scores ranged from 1.88 for those who did not see the debate to 2.41 for those who watched it all.

The third debate nearly mirrors the findings for the second debate. Education, campaign interest, and newspaper use are each positively related to issue knowledge. Debate viewing shows a clear and consistent relationship with knowledge, with the lowest adjusted mean score (1.87) for those who did not watch the debate and the highest score for those who watched it all (2.37). For this debate, there was very little difference in adjusted issue knowledge means for those watching a little or some (2.16) and those watching most of the debate (2.13).

Looking across the three debates, there can be no doubt about the influence of viewing presidential candidate debates and knowing the issues of a campaign. For each debate, viewers knew more than nonviewers, and this persisted after simultaneously controlling for education, campaign interest, media use, and political party (which was not related to issue knowledge).

Although we found some evidence for the influence of newspaper use on issue knowledge in the second and third debate, neither alternative media nor network TV news was significantly related to issue knowledge after any of the debates. That is not particularly surprising in the case of network TV news, because a weak relationship between television news and issue knowledge is often the finding in campaign research. However, given the importance attached to the use of alternative media by the press and by Clinton and Perot, our failure to find a relationship between watching alternative programming and knowledge seems troubling. The explanation for no statistically significant relationship between alternative media use and issue knowledge may lie in the curvilinear nature of the relationship between knowledge and exposure to alternative media (as reported in Table 5.3, Chapter 5). It appears that medium levels of exposure to candidate appearances on alternative media were associated with the highest level of knowledge. Instead of a straight-line relationship (i.e., a linear one) between alternative media exposure and knowledge, we have a curvilinear one. Curvilinearity could easily reduce the size of the regression coefficient in MCA.

Returning to the matter of the debates themselves, other studies have shown that past debates are important sources of information about the issues during a political campaign. Our respondents learned from the 1992 debates. Debate viewers were better informed about some of the issues of the campaign than nonviewers. If we want voting to be based on knowledge of where the candidates stand on the issues, then debates are important sources of information.

Candidate Image

The image measure we developed for each of our candidates combined into a single index what respondents thought about what the candidates knew about domestic problems, their character, and their understanding of the problems of common people. As we had done for issue knowledge, we again used MCA to interpret our results. We also used the same control variables.

George Bush's Political Image. The findings for George Bush's image are presented in Table 8.5. For the first and second debates, the

Table 8.5. Summary of Multiple Classification Analyses: Influence of Presidential Debate Exposure on George Bush's Image; Adjusted Mean Scores and Regression Coefficients.

Predictors	Bush's Image Debate 1 $M = 16.13$	Bush's Image Debate 2 $M = 16.82$	Bush's Image Debate 3 $M = 16.26$
Regressions[a]			
Education	—	—	—
Campaign Interest	.467*	—	.576**
Alternative Media	—	—	—
Newspaper Use	—	—	—
Network TV News	—	—	.360***
Adjusted Means[a]			
Debate Viewing	—	—	
None			16.58*
Little or Some			15.65
Most			17.35
All			15.52
Political Party			
Republican	21.55***	21.35***	20.63***
Democrat	13.35	14.47	13.05
Ind/Other	15.30	14.09	16.73
N	383	308	456

*$p < .10$.
**$p < .05$.
***$p < .01$.
[a]See explanation for "regression" and "adjusted means" in Table 8.4.

primary influence on George Bush's image was political party. For the first debate, George Bush's image was highest for Republicans (21.55), next highest for Independent/others (15.30), and lowest for Democrats (13.35). Campaign interest was also positively related to George Bush's image for this debate. For the second debate, only political party had an impact on George Bush's image. Again, Republicans gave him the highest rating (21.35), whereas Democrats (14.47) and Independent/others (14.09) were about even.

The third debate was the one that was interesting. For this debate, George Bush's image was positively influenced by campaign interest and watching network television news. Debate viewing and political party were also related to image.

The relationship between debate viewing and image was modest ($p < .10$) and not straightforward. For instance, those who watched least had a more positive image of George Bush (16.58) than those who watched "a little or some" (15.65) and those who watched "all" of the debate (15.52). The most positive image was recorded for those who watched "most" of the debate (17.35). The impact of network television news viewing, which tended to be positive toward Bush's performance in this final debate, might have interacted with debate viewing to produce the complex effect we observe. The most likely interpretation, however, is that this is an anomaly, a chance occurrence leading to findings that are difficult to interpret.

Whatever the reason for the outcome for debate viewing, political party again demonstrated its power in influencing image. Republicans were very positive toward George Bush (20.63) followed by Independent/others (16.73) and then Democrats (13.05).

George Bush's image was not helped (nor harmed, apparently) by the debates. In the sense that no gain is a loss, George Bush was unable to use the debates to improve his image in the eyes of potential voters.

Bill Clinton's Political Image. It was interesting to see how Bill Clinton's image improved or was hurt by the debates. The results of debate viewing on his image are presented in Table 8.6. Campaign interest and political party were the significant influences on Bill Clinton's political image during the first debate. The relationship between campaign interest and Clinton's image was positive. In terms of party influence, Clinton's image was highest for the Democrats (22.95) followed by Independent/others (19.90) and then Republicans (17.57). Debate exposure had no significant impact.

This was not the case for the second debate. Recall that Clinton was the clear victor in this debate (see Table 8.2). That performance appears to have transferred to the evaluations of his image. Party still

Table 8.6. Summary of Multiple Classification Analyses: Influence of Presidential Debate Exposure on Bill Clinton's Image; Adjusted Mean Scores and Regression Coefficients.

Predictors	Clinton's Image Debate 1 $M = 20.73$	Clinton's Image Debate 2 $M = 20.75$	Clinton's Image Debate 3 $M = 20.31$
Regressions[a]			
Education	—	—	—
Campaign Interest	.513***	—	—
Alternative Media	—	—	.460**
Newspaper Use	—	—	—
Network TV News	—	—	—
Adjusted Means[a]			
Debate Viewing	—		—
None		19.47**	
Little or Some		20.51	
Most		20.50	
All		21.89	
Political Party			
Republican	17.57***	17.98***	16.36***
Democrat	22.95	23.50	22.97
Ind/Other	19.90	22.58	20.14
N	373	303	453

*$p < .10$.
**$p < .05$.
***$p < .01$.
[a]See explanation for "regression" and "adjusted means" in Table 8.4.

played a major role, with the highest image scores registered by the Democrats (23.50), the next highest by the Independent/others (22.58), and the lowest scores by the Republicans (17.98). Our interest, however, is on the influence of debate exposure.

Clinton's image was lowest for the people who did not watch the debate, with an adjusted mean score of 19.47. Those watching "little or some" or "most" of the debate had nearly identical adjusted mean scores—20.51 and 20.50, respectively. Those who watched all of the debate had the highest image scores for Bill Clinton, with an adjusted mean of 21.89. Bill Clinton's image got a boost from his performance during this debate.

For the third debate, only alternative media use and political party were significantly related to Bill Clinton's image. Alternative media use was positively associated with Bill Clinton's image. Perhaps all of those appearances on radio and television talk shows paid off. Party, again, showed a significant effect on Clinton's image. Understandably, Republicans evaluated his image lowest (16.36), Democrats highest (22.97), and Independent/others in the middle (20.14).

For Bill Clinton, in the first debate, in which he was upstaged by Ross Perot, and in the third debate, in which he and Perot were nearly equal, debate exposure had no statistically significant impact. For the second presidential debate, which Clinton clearly won, debate exposure was significantly related to his image. Clearly, Clinton was not harmed and did benefit from the debates.

Ross Perot's Political Image. Ross Perot had the most to gain from the debates. He had reentered the campaign just before the debates. Many held him in low regard because he dropped out of the campaign. As we have seen, people thought he won the first debate, came out second in the second debate, and was equal to Clinton in the third debate. How did Perot's image fare as a result of the debates?

For each debate, Ross Perot's image benefited as a result of debate exposure (Table 8.7). For the first debate, Perot's image was influenced by newspaper use, debate viewing, and political party. Newspaper use was negatively related to Perot's image, indicating that the more the people we interviewed read the newspaper, the less positive their image was of Ross Perot. Independent/others evaluated Perot's image most favorably (20.09) followed by Republicans (18.65) and Democrats (17.05). Perot's message received its most favorable response from the Independent/others and Republicans.

Debate viewing for this first debate did have an impact. Recall that this was the debate clearly won by Perot. Those who did not watch the debate gave Perot his lowest image score, an adjusted mean of 16.12. For those who watched a "little or some" or "most" of the debate, the scores were higher, with adjusted means of 18.49 and 18.39, respectively. Perot's best image scores were for those who watched all of the debate. Here the adjusted mean score was 19.59.

Perot had done what he needed to do. His overall image mean score for the first debate, 18.24, was ahead of Bush's overall image mean after the first debate (16.13) and behind the overall mean for Bill Clinton at this time (20.73). In terms of his image, he was no longer a curiosity, he was a contender.

Table 8.7. Summary of Multiple Classification Analyses: Influence of Presidential Debate Exposure on Ross Perot's Image; Adjusted Mean Scores and Regression Coefficients.

Predictors	Perot's Image Debate 1 $M = 18.24$	Perot's Image Debate 2 $M = 17.96$	Perot's Image Debate 3 $M = 19.00$
Regressions[a]			
Education	—	—	-.445***
Campaign Interest	—	—	—
Alternative Media	—	—	—
Newspaper Use	-.239*	—	—
Network TV News	—	—	—
Adjusted Means[a]			
Debate Viewing			
None	16.12***	16.29*	17.54***
Little or Some	18.49	17.60	18.07
Most	18.39	18.35	20.10
All	19.59	19.06	20.09
Political Party		—	
Republican	18.65***		18.67***
Democrat	17.05		18.29
Ind/Other	20.09		20.51
N	365	303	440

*$p < .10$.
**$p < .05$.
***$p < .01$.
[a]See explanation for "regression" and "adjusted means" in Table 8.4.

The second debate clearly belonged to Bill Clinton, but Ross Perot's image also benefited. Of all the variables we used in our MCA, only one—debate viewing—was significantly related to Ross Perot's political image. His weakest image was recorded for those who did not view the debate (16.29), followed by those watching a "little or some" (17.60), "most" (18.35), and "all" (19.06). Even finishing second, as was the case for Perot, worked to his benefit.

The third debate showed several influences on Perot's image. The negative relationship between education and Perot's image during this third debate suggests that people might have been evaluating what would actually happen should Perot be elected. Better educated folks had a less positive image of Ross Perot.

Party returned as a factor in this debate. Democrats were the least positive (18.29), Independent/others the most positive (20.51), with Republicans between the two (18.67). Perot scored reasonably well across each group. Compare his 18.67 image score for Republican respondents with their 16.36 image score for Bill Clinton (Table 8.6). Similarly, compare the 18.29 given him by the Democrats with the far less favorable 13.05 image score they gave to George Bush (Table 8.5).

Debate viewing was a strong predictor of the image people held of Ross Perot. The adjusted mean for nonviewers was 17.54, below the mean for those watching "little or some" of the debate (18.07), "most" of the debate (20.10), and "all" of the debate (20.09). Ross Perot had managed to hold or strengthen his position in terms of image. By the time the debates were over, Ross Perot's image was slightly behind Bill Clinton's but ahead of George Bush's.

The pattern of debate influence on Ross Perot's political image over the three debates is clear. After each debate, viewers were more positive toward Perot than nonviewers. Generally, the more viewers watched, the more positive they felt toward Perot. The debates had proven to be an important element in Ross Perot's campaign success. As shown in previous studies, the least-known candidate generally tends to benefit most from debates.

Voting Probability

When everything is taken into account, one factor is most important to the candidate and, ultimately, to the potential voter: the vote. Every four years in November, voters enter their polling booths and indicate their choice. It is a zero-sum game. Voters cannot vote one quarter for one candidate, one half for another, and one quarter for the third. They must select one and vote for only one.

We were a little kinder to the people we interviewed. We allowed them to indicate, on a scale from 0 to 10, the probability they would vote for each candidate. Consequently, they could tell us that there was about a 5 in 10 chance they would vote for Perot, a 1 in 10 chance for Clinton, and a 5 in 10 chance for Bush (the probabilities did not have to sum to 10). In this way, we felt we could better gauge how people were leaning at the time.

We also added four variables to our MCA-regression equations. We already looked at the influence of the debates on issue knowledge and candidate image. To each MCA, we added issue knowledge, Bush's political image, Clinton's political image, and Perot's political image.

This allowed us to test the influence of knowledge and image on voting probabilities as well as the influence of debate exposure.

The Probability of Voting for George Bush. The findings for the probabilities of voting for George Bush are presented in Table 8.8. These results are interesting. First, and most important from our perspective, the debates had no direct influence on the probability of voting for George Bush in any of the debates. This holds as well for the probability of voting for Bill Clinton (Table 8.9) and the probability of voting for Ross Perot (Table 8.10). Does that mean that the debates were unimportant elements in determining voting preferences? We do not think so.

Table 8.8. Summary of Multiple Classification Analyses: Influence of Presidential Debate Exposure on the Probability of Voting for George Bush; Adjusted Mean Scores and Regression Coefficients.

Predictors	Probability for Bush Debate 1 $M = 3.33$	Probability for Bush Debate 2 $M = 3.55$	Probability for Bush Debate 3 $M = 3.36$
Regressions[a]			
Education	—	—	—
Campaign Interest	—	—	—
Alternative Media	—	—	—
Newspaper Use	—	-.095*	—
Network TV News	—	—	—
Issue Knowledge	—	—	—
Bush's Image	.246***	.283***	.282***
Clinton's Image	-.114***	-.206***	-.131***
Perot's Image	—	.046*	.063***
Adjusted Means[a]			
Debate Viewing	—	—	—
Political Party			
Republican	5.71***	4.87***	5.38***
Democrat	2.14	2.61	2.35
Ind/Oth	2.99	3.31	2.86
N	347	276	421

*$p < .10$.
**$p < .05$.
***$p < .01$.
[a]See explanation for "regression" and "adjusted means" in Table 8.4.

We already showed that debate exposure was related to issue knowledge and, in specific circumstances, to candidate image. It is through image and knowledge that debate exposure helped to form the voting probabilities for the candidates. Even if the debates had no direct impact on George Bush's image, as our analysis indicated, they did influence Bill Clinton's image in the second presidential debate and Ross Perot's image in all three.

A second factor is that the probabilities of voting for George Bush remained pretty constant across the debate period. With means of 3.33 for debate 1, 3.55 for debate 2, and 3.36 for debate 3, there is no evidence of a significant shift in voting preference for George Bush. Because he was behind at the start of the debates, this posed a significant problem for his campaign. Time was running out.

The political images of the candidates and political party identification were the most consistent influences on the probability of voting for George Bush. After the first debate, the probability of voting for him was influenced positively by his image and negatively by the image people held of Bill Clinton. Political party was a strong predictor of voting probabilities. Remember that we used a 0 to 10 scale. There was an adjusted mean of 5.71 in the Republican's probability of voting for George Bush after the first debate, compared with adjusted means of 2.14 for Democrats and 2.99 for Independent/others.

The pattern for debate 2 is similar. After this debate, newspaper use was negatively related to the probability of voting for George Bush: his image and the image of Ross Perot were positively related. Bill Clinton's image was again negatively related to voting for Bush, as it had been after the first debate. Voting probabilities by party were as expected. The Bush probability for Republicans was 4.87, for Democrats 2.61, and for Independent/others 3.31.

Nearly the same pattern held for the third debate. Bush's and Perot's images were positively related to the probability of voting for George Bush, whereas Clinton's image showed a negative relationship. Republicans once again were most likely to think they would vote for George Bush, with a probability mean of 5.38. Democrats with a mean of 2.35 and Independent/others with an adjusted mean of 2.86 were far behind.

To the degree that the debates improved the image of Bill Clinton, they reduced the probability of voting for George Bush. And, although the raw regressions are low, there is some evidence that improvement in Perot's image, influenced positively by each debate, indirectly helped George Bush. By themselves, the debates did not cost George Bush the election.

The Probability of Voting for Bill Clinton. A number of variables were significantly related to the probability of voting for Bill Clinton after the first debate. These findings, and the findings for the second and third presidential debates, are presented in Table 8.9.

The nightly use of network television news, issue knowledge, and Bill Clinton's image were positively related to the probability of voting for him. The images of George Bush and Ross Perot had negative relationships to voting for Clinton. As with George Bush, debate viewing had no direct impact on the probability of voting for Bill Clinton.

Party, of course, was a strong predictor. The mean probability given by Democrats was 7.36, for Independent/others 6.52, and for

Table 8.9. Summary of Multiple Classification Analyses: Influence of Presidential Debate Exposure on the Probability of Voting for Bill Clinton; Adjusted Mean Scores and Regression Coefficients.

Predictors	Probability for Clinton Debate 1 $M = 6.41$	Probability for Clinton Debate 2 $M = 6.00$	Probability for Clinton Debate 3 $M = 6.01$
Regressions[a]			
Education	—	—	—
Campaign Interest	—	—	—
Alternative Media	—	—	—
Newspaper Use	—	—	—
Network TV News	.128**	—	—
Issue Knowledge	.360**	—	.343**
Bush's Image	-.137***	-.133***	-.120***
Clinton's Image	.357***	.400***	.394***
Perot's Image	-.075***	-.110*	-.077***
Adjusted Means[a]			
Debate Viewing	—	—	—
Political Party			
Republican	4.66***	4.52***	4.05***
Democrat	7.36	7.24	7.23
Ind/Other	6.51	5.94	6.09
N	347	273	420

*$p < .10$.
**$p < .05$.
***$p < .01$.
[a] See explanation for "regression" and "adjusted means" in Table 8.4.

Republicans 4.66. Note that the 4.66 Republicans gave to Clinton was not a great deal lower than the 5.71 they had given to their own candidate, George Bush, after the first debate (see Table 8.8).

For the second debate, only candidate image and party were significant predictors. Clinton's image was positively linked to the probability of voting for him, whereas Bush's and Perot's images again were negatively associated with voting for Clinton. Democrats supported Clinton strongly with an adjusted mean of 7.24. Independent/others were less enthusiastic, with a mean of 5.94. Both were followed by the Republicans who indicated a 4.52 probability of voting for Clinton after the second debate, the debate in which Clinton performed so well. You might note, once again, that Republican support for Clinton (4.52) was very close to the support (4.87) they had for George Bush after that same debate 2 (see Table 8.8).

Greater issue knowledge, along with Bill Clinton's political image, predicted a higher voting probability for Clinton after the third debate. Again, Bush's and Perot's images were negatively related to the likelihood of voting for Bill Clinton.

Democrats maintained their support for their party candidate, with a 7.23 voting probability for Clinton. Independent/others remained supportive, with a mean of 6.09. Republicans had become somewhat less supportive than in the first and second debates, falling to a 4.05 probability. They may have realized that George Bush was their only candidate. The difference between their support of Clinton (M = 4.05) and Bush (M = 5.38; Table 8.8) had increased after the third debate.

Clinton's support remained reasonably constant across the three debates; 6.41 for debate 1, 6.00 for debate 2, and 6.01 for debate 3. Even though debate viewing had no direct impact on the probability of voting for him, issue knowledge, which was influenced by debate viewing, was a positive influence in debates 1 and 3, and his image worked to his benefit across each debate (as favorable images of his opponents worked against him).

The Probability of Voting for Ross Perot. The expressed probability of voting for Ross Perot remained fairly stable across the three debates, although somewhat more variation can be noted for Perot than for Bush or Clinton. After the first debate, the probability of voting for Ross Perot was 3.10. It fell to 2.85 after the second debate, which was won by Clinton, but climbed to 3.57 after the third debate. If one compares the overall probability for Ross Perot after the third debate (3.57) with the overall probability of voting for George Bush after the third debate (3.36), one would feel that things were going as well or better than anyone prior to the debates might have expected for Ross Perot.

After the first debate, Ross Perot's general image was positively influenced by his political image and negatively influenced by network television viewing, George Bush's political image, and the political image of Bill Clinton. No direct influence of debate exposure was uncovered.

Ross Perot received his strongest support from Independent/others (3.82), followed by Democrats (2.99) and Republicans (2.66). His overall support base, a mean of 3.10, was not very strong, behind Bush's 3.33 (Table 8.8) and Clinton's 6.41 (Table 8.9) after the first debate.

The second debate saw a decrease in Perot's overall mean from 3.10 after the first debate to 2.85 after the second. Recall that this debate was easily dominated by Bill Clinton. The probability of voting for Perot was negatively influenced by campaign interest and Bush's image. Perot's own image had a positive impact. Independent/others remained the most supportive of Perot, with an adjusted mean probability of 3.63. This time, support by Republicans (2.92) was higher than support for Perot by Democrats (2.38). Perot seemed to be making minor headway with the Republican voters.

For the third debate, high issue knowledge and favorability of Bush's and Clinton's images each reduced the probability of voting for Ross Perot. Again, Perot's image was positively related to the probability of voting for him. Independent/others still showed the strongest support for candidate Perot (4.34), although Republicans showed a sharp increase from debate 2 (3.93). Democratic support fell far behind (2.89).

Perot does appear to have benefited after the third debate. His lowest overall voting probability score, 2.85, was recorded after the second debate, which he and Bush clearly lost to Clinton. After the third debate—which the people we interviewed had called a tie between Perot and Clinton—support for Perot was at its highest, at 3.57. Perot, still low in terms of voting probability, had nevertheless been able to improve people's inclinations to vote for him.

SUMMING UP

Where does this leave us regarding the effects of the three 1992 presidential debates on the political process?

First, there were clear winners and losers, at least from the perspective of the people we interviewed. Ross Perot won the first debate, Bill Clinton the second, and Perot and Clinton came in at about even after the third. George Bush finished last in each debate, although the gap was somewhat less after the third debate than after the other two.

Second, the debates were a consistent and significant source of information about the issues of the campaign. For each debate, the

Table 8.10. Summary of Multiple Classification Analyses: Influence of Presidential Debate Exposure on the Probability of Voting for Ross Perot; Adjusted Mean Scores and Regression Coefficients.

Predictors	Probability for Perot Debate 1 $M = 3.10$	Probability for Perot Debate 2 $M = 2.85$	Probability for Perot Debate 3 $M = 3.57$
Regressions[a]			
Education	—	—	—
Campaign Interest	—	-.073**	—
Alternative Media	—	—	—
Newspaper Use	—	—	—
Network TV News	-.145**	—	—
Issue Knowledge	—	—	-.324*
Bush's Image	-.053**	-.070**	-.094***
Clinton's Image	-.123***	—	-.123***
Perot's Image	.287***	.303***	.336***
Adjusted Means[a]			
Debate Viewing	—	—	—
Political Party			
Republican	2.66**	2.92**	3.93***
Democrat	2.99	2.38	2.89
Ind/Other	3.82	3.63	4.34
N	347	275	422

*$p < .10$.
**$p < .05$.
***$p < .01$.
[a]See explanation for "regression" and "adjusted means" in Table 8.4.

degree of debate viewing was positively related to knowing more about the issues of the campaign. Assuming that an informed electorate is desirable in a democracy, the 1992 presidential candidate debates clearly played a significant role.

Third, the images of the candidates can be influenced by campaign debates. When the candidate's image is already well formed, as it was with President George Bush, debate influence is probably minimized unless a major mistake occurs. For a new political personality, like Ross Perot, if performance is judged acceptable, then image will benefit from the debate. Even Bill Clinton's image, which was also pretty well known to the electorate, benefited after the second debate, which he clearly dominated.

Fourth, the influence of the debates on voting probabilities is indirect, at least that is the way it appears in this analysis. We vote based on our images of all of the candidates, on the parameters established by our claims of party membership, and somewhat on our knowledge of the campaign issues, network television news use, and newspaper use. There are obviously other important factors, but these were most important in this study.

Finally, the debates did not cinch the win for Clinton, nor did they doom Bush. The debates are one important element in the way we make our final decisions regarding our voting choices. For 1992, the role of the debates was important, particularly for Perot, who managed to use the debates to support his claim to being president.

By themselves, the debates do not explain all of the reasons people form images of the candidates, learn about the issues, or decide to vote. It is a complex process, and people bring a variety of sources to bear on how they develop their final evaluations of the candidates. One such source is the reaction that journalists have to the candidates in the debates. The "verdicts" they render can influence how people eventually make their decisions. We cover this next in Chapter 9, "News Verdicts and Verdict Effects."

ENDNOTE

1. The internal consistency of each summed scale was measured using Cronbach's alpha. Cronbach's alpha for Bush's image scale was .82; for Bill Clinton .81; and for Ross Perot .78.

REFERENCES

Carter, R.F., & Stamm, K.R. (1994). The 1992 Presidential campaign and debates: A cognitive view. *Communication Research, 21,* 380-395.

Chaffee, S.H., Zhao, X., & Leshner, G. (1994). Political knowledge and the campaign media of 1992. *Communication Research, 21,* 305-324.

Donaldson, S. (1988). On the Dukakis campaign trail. *Gannett Center Journal, 2*(4), 87-118.

Dye, T.R., & Zeigler, H. (1986). *American politics in the media age* (2nd ed.). Monterey, CA: Brooks/Cole.

Elliott, W.R., & Sothirajah, J. (1993). Post-debate analysis and media reliance: Influences on candidate image and voting probabilities. *Journalism Quarterly, 70,* 321-335.

Gallup, G., Jr. (1987). The impact of presidential debates on the vote and turnout. In J.L. Swerdlow (Ed.), *Presidential debates: 1988 and beyond* (pp. 34-42). Washington, DC: Congressional Quarterly.

Hellweg, S.A., Pfau, M., & Brydon, S.R. (1992). *Televised presidential debates: Advocacy in contemporary America.* New York: Praeger.

Jamieson, K. H. (1987). Television, presidential campaigns, and debates. In J.L. Swerdlow (Ed.), *Presidential debates: 1988 and beyond* (pp. 27-33). Washington, DC: Congressional Quarterly.

Kraus, S. (1988). *Televised presidential debates and public policy.* Hillsdale, NJ: Erlbaum.

Lanoue, D.J. (1992). One that made a difference: Cognitive consistency, political knowledge, and the 1980 presidential debate. *Public Opinion Quarterly, 56,* 168-184.

Lemert, J.B. (1993). Do televised presidential debates help inform voters? *Journal of Broadcasting & Electronic Media, 37,* 83-94.

Lemert, J.B., Elliott, W.R., Bernstein, J.M., Rosenberg, W.L., & Nestvold, K.J. (1991). *News verdicts, the debates, and presidential campaigns.* New York: Praeger.

Meadow, R.G. (1983). Televised campaign debates as whistle-stop speeches. In W.C. Adams (Ed.), *Television coverage of the 1980 Presidential campaign* (pp. 89-116). Norwood, NJ: Ablex.

Schrott, P.R. (1990). Electoral consequences of "winning" debates. *Public Opinion Quarterly, 54,* 567-585.

Spear, J.C. (1984). *Presidents and the press: The Nixon legacy.* Cambridge, MA: MIT Press.

Zhu, J., Milavsky, J.R., & Biswas, R. (1994). Do televised debates affect image perception more than issue knowledge? A study of the first 1992 Presidential debate. *Human Communication Research, 20,* 302-333.

9

News Verdicts and Their Effects

James B. Lemert

At least since Gerald Ford's "Eastern Europe gaffe" in 1976, people have believed that media-carried "verdicts" about who did well in presidential debates have been at least as important as the debates themselves. As is true of so many things, the certainty (and plausibility) of this belief outpaced the evidence for it, at least until recently.

Prior to our 1988 study, the best evidence for a news verdict effect came from a study by Steeper (1978), done for the Republican campaign. Steeper showed that a sample of persons watching the "Eastern Europe" remarks live—and the immediate follow-up questions by journalists—did not especially react to the remarks while they were being made, nor to the follow-up questions and Ford's stubborn insistence that yes, he did mean to say that Poland and Eastern Europe were free from Soviet domination. These respondents had ample opportunity to show any reactions because each could punch a "like-dislike" button as many times as wanted. Other respondents, interviewed after the debate, seemed to show the classic "delayed verdict" pattern, in which more of those interviewed later said Carter had won than did those interviewed sooner after the debate. The only major flaws in Steeper's study were that it failed to tie the changed "winner" perceptions to any specific postdebate media content and in effect tried to assume that button pushing during the debate measured the same thing as did poll responses after the debate.

In surveys, verdict effects take time to show up because, by definition, the verdict occurs in news coverage *after* the debate is over. Such verdicts often appear first in postdebate news specials on debate night, and then in newspapers and television's morning and evening news shows the next day. Then it takes some time for awareness of the direction of the verdict to diffuse among the population.

Our study of the 1988 campaign used a powerful time-series survey design that also incorporated sensitive measurements of media content and exposure to that content in order to draw conclusions about the impact of verdicts carried by the news media (Lemert, Elliott, Bernstein, Rosenberg, & Nestvold, 1991). In the time series, we were able to interview samples of people immediately after each debate, thus maximizing the chances that we were interviewing them before exposure to any verdicts. Then we interviewed other samples after the evening news the next night, the night after that, and so on. Unlike the Steeper study, which largely compared electronic button pushing during the debate against survey interviews afterward, we asked the same questions of respondents immediately after the debate, the next night, the night after that, and so on.

Using the time-series design, we were able to demonstrate verdict effects after each of the 1988 debates. The effects varied by debate in longevity and in how many cognitions, beliefs, and attitudes they altered, but they were present after each debate. The longest-lived and most widespread verdict effect seemed to have been for Dan Quayle (negative) and Lloyd Bentsen (positive) in the aftermath of their October 5 debate, but even it began to dissipate as the October 13 final presidential debate loomed. Except for Dan Quayle, 1988 media verdicts seemed to affect the candidate who was defined as doing well, rather than the one defined as the "loser."

Based on our 1988 research, we offer the following tentative generalizations about media verdicts: Media verdicts have their broadest and most long-lasting effects when the news media uniformly present the same verdict(s) and campaign events allow them continually to repeat those verdicts over a continuous period of several days. Debate formats that reduce risk of direct embarrassment to candidates tend to increase the risk that a media verdict effect will occur by making it less obvious to the viewer who was doing better and who was in trouble, thus opening the way for the media to point out "winners" and "losers."

Given the compressed timing of the 1992 debates, the "news verdict" effect that we demonstrated for 1988's widely spaced debates faced a severe challenge for 1992. Among other reasons, it appeared to us unlikely that candidate performance verdicts about a given debate would be sustained long enough in the news—given the onrushing next debate—to spread through the population and be reinforced by repetition.

The varied formats of the 1992 debates also may have made it easier for unaided members of the viewing audience to draw their own conclusions about who "won" or "lost," thus reducing the audience's vulnerability to media-declared performance verdicts. Debate formats in 1992 varied considerably from the one used since the resumption of presidential debates in 1976: no candidate-to-candidate questions allowed, a moderator, and questions from a panel of journalists, with no follow-ups allowed the journalist asking the question. In 1992, the first debate (October 11) followed the conventional format mentioned here, but none of the others did entirely. The October 13 vice presidential debate used a freewheeling moderator-only format that allowed candidates to address—and try to pursue—each other. The October 15 "town hall" debate had a moderator and questions from a studio audience made up of undecided voters. Finally, the last debate (October 19) split time between the old moderator-with-panel format and the more risky moderator-only format.

Arguably, then, the new and different formats should join the compressed schedule of debates in reducing the chances of finding a media verdict effect in 1992. All this does not mean that we didn't expect broadcast news to draw conclusions about who did—and did not—do well in the debates! As we will see, once again broadcast journalists did.

As in our study of the 1988 campaign, we both monitored media content and interviewed survey respondents in a time-series design that helped enable us to match content with possible audience responses to that content. The first part of this chapter discusses our content analysis of network verdicts, replicating our analyses of both network newscasts and postdebate news specials in the 1976 through 1988 campaigns (Lemert et al., 1991, Chapters 3 and 4, respectively). Then, in the second part, we look at the survey evidence about whether any verdict effects occurred.

NETWORK CONTENT

Verdicts about candidate performance in the debates were coded for 1992 using the same coding system as was used in our previous book (Lemert et al., 1991).

ABC and CBS Evening Newscasts

For purposes of replication, we looked at ABC and CBS evening newscasts, as we had done in the previous study. As we feared, however, there was so little time between the debates that, as soon as another debate had intervened, network journalists presented very few newscast performance verdicts about any of these earlier debates. Therefore, unlike our content studies of the 1976 through 1988 debates, we sampled evening news content from one and three days after a given debate, rather than one and four. Even so, the first three (October 11, 13, and 15) debates tended to disappear from the evening news once a more recent debate had occurred. Even the final debate (October 19) frequently was merged by correspondents and anchors with the other debates, a few days later in a kind of generic "the debates."

ABC, CBS, and NBC News Specials

The second portion of our content analyses replicates the "candidate verdicts" and "debates as institutions" parts of our previous study of postdebate news specials. We look only at the candidate verdicts portion in this chapter. As we had done previously, we looked at ABC, NBC, and CBS postdebate news specials. In contrast to previous years, more of those postdebate specials came 24 or more hours after the debate—especially ABC's *Nightline*.

Both sets of 1992 verdicts content were coded by the author, who also was involved in all the coding of 1976 through 1988 news content. The test-retest reliability percentage was .85 for the 1992 evening newscasts and .89 for the postdebate specials.

With both the newscast and the news special data, we can extend a consistent series of network content observations that will stretch back through five presidential elections from 1992 to 1976, and we can analyze what verdicts were happening on network news in 1992, in their own right. We begin with the 1992 verdicts.

Candidate Verdicts in 1992

The 1992 verdict results are based on the combined newscasts and news specials. There were two clear winners, as well as two clear losers.

Winners. In brief, media verdicts declared Ross Perot the big winner in the first (October 11) debate, Bill Clinton the big winner of the October 15 ("talk show") debate, and Bill Clinton very marginally the winner of the final (October 19) debate. As for the vice presidential debate (October 13), neither Dan Quayle nor Al Gore emerged clearly as the winner, with each getting roughly 45% favorable performance verdicts on network news. However, because almost twice as much attention was paid to Quayle's performance, he received almost twice as many favorable performance statements as Gore did. The greater attention paid to Quayle's performance almost certainly reflected the high media curiosity and low expectations created by Quayle's 1988 debate against Lloyd Bentsen, because often he was said to have been very combative and aggressive toward Gore. But these verdicts also contrasted Quayle's aggressiveness with Bush's in the first debate, implying that Quayle's 1988 performance was not the only baseline being used by journalists to assess his performance.

A typical positive verdict about Perot's first debate said that he was funny, at ease, and had a good stock of appealing "one-liners." Often, this description was accompanied by a discounting assertion or implication that Perot still had no realistic chance of winning the election.

A characteristic "town hall debate" verdict about Clinton said he was quite comfortable relating to people in the October 15 format, and there was considerable attention paid to how he moved toward, and looked directly at, people in the studio who asked him questions.

Losers. President Bush was defined as a big loser in the October 11 and 15 debates. Many of these verdicts emphasized his passivity and failure to take advantage of opportunities to take the initiative. Verdicts about Bush's October 15 performance emphasized as well his apparent discomfort with the format—his twice looking at his watch was taken as a symptom of that discomfort—and his alleged inability to understand or relate to questions or requests from the audience. Often the October 15 verdicts mentioned the man who asked Bush to lay off character attacks or the woman who kept asking how the "deficit" (probably she meant the economy) affected Bush "personally."

For the October 19 debate, the distribution of network verdicts about Bush was closer to Clinton's. Bush received a fair amount of praise for his relative improvement over the two preceding debates. Nevertheless, even the October 19 debate showed Bush with slightly more negative (49%) than positive (40%) network news verdicts about his performance. To a certain extent, Bush fell victim to the setting of higher expectations for him than Clinton in the final debate—"Bush's got to hit a home run"—because Bush was behind in the polls.

The other big loser was Admiral James Stockdale in the vice presidential debate, but even he received a lower percentage of *negative* statements about his performance (68%) than Bush did in each of the first two presidential debates (78% negative, October 11; 69%, October 15). Stockdale was portrayed as an exceptionally decent man whom Perot put in a "show biz" spot he could not handle; journalists often used Stockdale's own words (e.g., "Why am I here?") to document that portrayal.

Figure 9.1 presents a summary of these results for the three presidential candidates, graphing the percentages of verdicts that were favorable among all verdicts that each of the men received over the course of the three debates.

Visually, the three patterns in Figure 9.1 are striking. Statistically they are, too: Tests run on each candidate's performance verdicts revealed that all three presidential candidates showed significant variations from debate to debate. Clinton's 91% favorable performance verdicts in October 15's "town hall" debate far exceeded his encouraging but modest (roughly 50%) favorable appraisal rates after the first and last debates. Bush was much more favorably appraised in his final debate than in the two preceding ones, although at 40% he still fell below Clinton's 53% favorable in that debate.

The most interesting media changes were for Perot, whose performance verdicts were very positive (84%) in the first debate, plunging after that in the next, and plunging once again in the last debate. In fact,

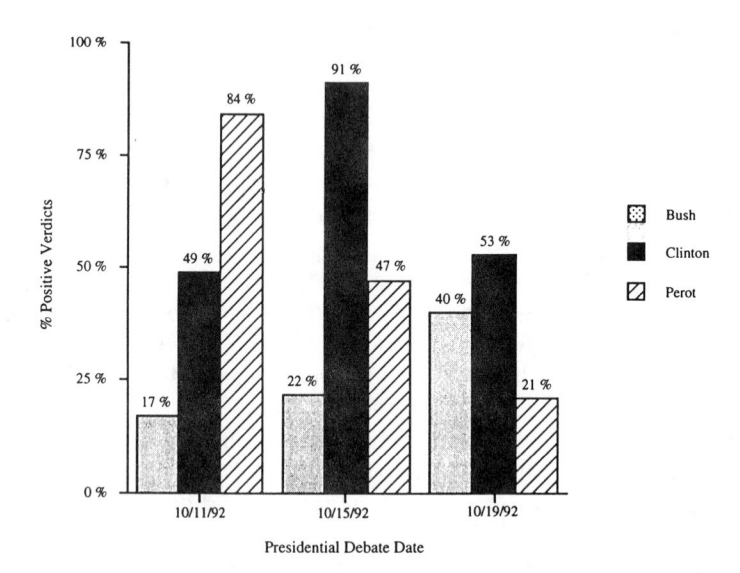

Figure 9.1. Percent positive verdicts by debate and candidate

by the time we reached the aftermath of the final debate, Perot's favorable verdicts comprised only 21% of the verdicts about him, a huge drop from an 84% favorable start.

A fairly typical negative performance verdict about Perot would say that he had not added much to what he had said in the first debate—that he was repeating himself, in other words. Yet Perot's final debate attack on Bush's handling of Iraq before the Gulf War led many evening newscasts the next day, and certainly was a new issue for many viewers.

In any case, not only was there a deep plunge in the rate of favorable verdicts about Perot, there was about as steep a drop in TV journalists' focus on Perot as the object of a performance verdict of any kind. Twice as many verdicts concerned Perot in the first presidential debate as the second, and more than twice as many for the second as the third. In other words, there was a tremendous dropoff in attention paid to Perot's performance on network news after the first debate. (See Chapter 6 for further development of these and other themes.)

Journalists and Other Elites Render Verdicts

Over time, major shifts have occurred in how much weight network journalists have given to politicians to render verdicts, and how much they have taken on themselves.

1976 through 1988. In each presidential year through 1988, journalists have been the most frequent source to render verdicts on postdebate news specials, but not on the evening news. On the evening news, elite political insiders were the dominant sources used. For example, in 1988, journalists were the sources of about 65% of the performance verdicts on postdebate news specials, but only 34% of the verdicts on the evening news. Instead, political elites were the sources of half of all the verdicts on 1988's evening news.

When one thinks about the different production situations for these two types of newscasts, an initially plausible explanation for this discrepancy is that the postdebate analyses often went on the air immediately after the debate, and it was both harder and *riskier* for producers to schedule elite campaign sources for live interviews than it was to tape reaction interviews with them the next day—and then to edit those interviews for the evening news. This undoubtedly explains somewhat the lower reliance on elites in the post-debate analyses, but probably not all of it.

Why not all of it? As the networks have been telling us at least since 1988, hordes of video-fluent "spin doctors" have been made freely available to be interviewed immediately after the debates, so getting articulate campaign sources hardly seems to have been much of a production problem for postdebate analysis shows. Because these spin doctors were all presumably adept at quick, succinct, sound bites, and because they all had elite credentials, risk of "empty" live air and unpredictable statements should have been reduced as debate "spin-doctoring" was institutionalized in the 1980s.

In 1988, the networks reported extensively on the "spin doctor" phenomenon, as we reported in our previous book (Lemert et al., 1991), and journalists made it emphatically clear that they were (and the audience should be) extremely skeptical of what was said after the debate. So this would help explain why the networks resisted using them, despite the growing convenience and predictability of using elites on postdebate news specials.

This still does not explain why the evening news would rely on campaign elites *more* the next day. As we already mentioned, network journalists have time to edit interviews conducted the morning after the debate, and that day-after story has now become more about *reactions* to who did well in the debate—and how the campaign's plans have been affected. Obviously, the prime source for this information would be campaign insiders.

Given the flood of spin doctors—often shown us in 1992's (symbolically significant?) distance shots on network postdebate specials—and given journalists' evident hostility to spin-doctoring, another part of the explanation is that network journalists and producers are satisfied that they made their point to these elites the previous night, so it is then acceptable to use them on the next evening's news.

1992. So far, much of what we've said refers to trends through 1988. What happened in 1992? In 1992, elite insiders again were used much more often roughly 24 hours later—on the next night's evening news (36% of sources used)—than in postdebate news specials (20% of sources used). But comparisons of 1992 with the past show some interesting trends developing: Elites were used less often in either type of show than in most previous years. In 1992, for the first time, elite insiders dropped to second place as a source on the evening news, although they were sources only slightly fewer times than were journalists. Political elites were also used even less often on the 1992 news specials than in any previous year since 1980. Tables 9.1 and 9.2 present these results. The same tables show as well an increase in the use of "voters" as judges of debate performance in 1992.

Voters as Judges of Candidate Performance

Ostensibly, the debates are held to help voters make up their minds. Yet we saw in Tables 9.1 and 9.2 that journalists and elite political insiders easily have been the most common sources of performance verdicts on network news.

Table 9.1. Sources of Candidate Verdicts in ABC and CBS Evening Newscasts.

Year (N)[a]	Journalist (%)	Elite "Insider" (%)	MOS, Polls, Crowds, Etc. (%)	Totals (%)
1976 (241)	38	46	16	100
1980 (143)	21	54	25	100
1984 (441)	27	58	15	100
1988 (410)	34	49	17	100
1992 (236)	40	36	24	100
Totals	32	50	18	100
(N)	(471)	(729)	(271)	(1,471)

[a]The totals exclude a small number of cases each year in which the performance verdict was to be determined "later" (often "on Election Day"). Only 22 cases were excluded from the table on this basis.

Table 9.2. Sources of Candidate Verdicts in ABC, CBS, and NBC Postdebate Specials.

Year (N)[a]	Journalist (%)	Elite "Insider" (%)	MOS, Polls, Crowds, Etc. (%)	Totals (%)
1976 (340)	67	20	14	100
1980 (447)	51	36	13	100
1984 (738)	66	27	7	100
1988 (669)	65	26	17	100
1992 (820)	55	20	25	100
Totals	61	25	14	100
(N)	(1,822)	(761)	(431)	(3,014)

[a]The totals exclude a small number of cases each year in which the performance verdict was to be determined "later" (often "on Election Day"). Only 22 cases were excluded from the table on this basis.

Since 1976, the networks have occasionally used polls, "man-on-the-street" (MOS) interviews, phone-in tallies, interviews with debate studio audience members as they left the scene, crowd and rally reactions in the aftermath, reactions of people hooked up by researchers to a variety of wondrous machines, interviews with special groups of voters assembled in living rooms or elsewhere, and so on.

In our report on the 1988 campaign, we thought there might have been a slight trend upward in network use of sample surveys that year. Nevertheless, with all these techniques available to reflect voter/audience reaction, even by 1988 they constituted only about 1 in 6 verdict sources.

If we assume 1988 did represent a trend upwards in the use of standard polling, did that trend continue in 1992? We expected this to happen for at least two reasons. First, over time more and more technical ability to do "instant" and overnight polling also presumably would lead to a network increase in the use of polls as sources of debate verdicts. Second, 1992 had been billed as the year voters actively took greater control of the campaign information they were receiving. So we wanted to see whether, in this extraordinary Year of the Voter, network attention to the audience as judge would increase.

As Tables 9.1 and 9.2 show, the networks substantially increased their use of nonelite verdict sources (sometimes characterized as "voters"; at other times, "viewers"), regardless of whether we look at evening newscasts (Table 9.1) or postdebate specials (Table 9.2). In each case, roughly 1 in every 4 sources were nonelites.

The only year with a comparable figure was 1980, and that high figure was produced by a now-notorious phone-in poll (people dialed one 900-number if they thought Carter won, another if they thought Reagan did; you could call as many times as you wanted, as long as you could afford the 50-cent per-call charge). ABC emphasized its phone-in "poll" heavily in its 1980 coverage, for reasons that probably had relatively more to do with ratings than with any concern about how voters felt about debate performance. Heavily criticized by the commercial polling industry, ABC did not try that 1980 experiment again. Excluding that anomalous year, no other figure in either table approaches the 1992 figure for the voter as source.

On the surface, CBS tried a similar gambit in 1992. It recruited a presumably random panel of respondents to phone CBS directly immediately after one debate, in which survey interviewers were waiting to interview them. Only the selected respondents were given the phone number to call. Assuming both that the original recruiting and the phone-in follow-up approximated random (unbiased selection) sampling, we can say that this CBS gambit had only a surface resemblance to

ABC's effort in 1980, and was an interesting attempt to find a way to get "instant feedback" from a large number of viewers. We coded this CBS effort as if we knew it to be a scientifically acceptable sample survey.

In any case, we tried to sort out whether the increase in the use of nonelites as sources of verdicts was due to increased technical ability to do "instant polls" or, perhaps, heightened network sensitivity to The Year of The Voter. To do this, we took advantage of the fact that coding of the post-debate analyses separately tallied standard public opinion polls from the many other ways that audience reactions can be reflected on network news.

The surge upward in use of audience members as a source of verdicts clearly was partly the result of expanded polling: About 6% of 1992 sources were based on standard polling, compared to slightly less than 2% in 1988 and even less in 1984 and 1980. In fact, the use of standard polls rises in a straight line from 1976, when none at all were used as a verdict source.

That is not the whole story, though. The broad class of so-called MOS interviews, which includes interviews with viewers assembled by the networks, data from people with "like-dislike" buttons they can punch throughout the debate, and so on, *also* hit the highest rate (13.3% of all verdict sources) ever, more than double the rate in any previous year. In fact, 1992's MOS category had more than twice as many cases as did standard polls.

However, even the polls and MOS categories together do not exhaust the increase in voters as sources. Verdicts embedded in reactions by studio audiences during the 1992 debates—especially the October 15 "talk show" debate—also reached the highest rate ever observed, though this category's contribution to the surge in voters as sources wasn't as great as that from MOS and polls.

In summary, clearly growth in "instant polling" technology and experience may account for part of the upward surge in voters as debate judges, but older, less expensive, and (sometimes) more obvious techniques accounted for more of the surge than did the polls. We conclude that the networks were at least in part responding to their perception (in 1992 at least) that the voters were a major part of the story of the presidential campaign.

A VERDICT EFFECT?

Now that we know more about the media environment surrounding our respondents, it is time to look for any evidence that the media verdicts had an effect. In this section, we look in turn at each debate.

Methodology

As we did in 1988, we use two different ways of indexing exposure to a media verdict. First, our time-series design allows us to interview people immediately after a debate and compare their perceptions with those of other people we interview later. The more time passes after the debate, the more likely respondents will have heard about who did well from media and personal contacts. So we use the day interviewed as one index of exposure to a verdict. The second way to index exposure to a media verdict is simply to ask people whether they watched a given debate and, if so, whether they went on to watch a postdebate analysis show. We then compare the reactions of those who watched only the debate against those who watched both the debate and postdebate analyses. Logically, any difference between the two groups would seem to be due to the influence of the analysis because both groups watched the debate.

An Effect on What? We look at a variety of measures that might reflect a verdict effect. Broadly speaking, these measures boil down into two types: (a) *open-ended questions*, in which respondents put in their own words how they felt about a given debate; and (b) *rating scales*, in which respondents rate the candidates' characteristics or performance, their own chances of voting for that candidate, and so on. In the case of the scales, respondents chose from among the various response categories we offered them; in the case of the open-ended questions, they defined and categorized the situation in their own terms.

In 1988, we found respondents increasingly over time using words to describe Quayle's debate performance that closely reflected media verdicts. When we used rating scales, we also found considerable evidence of verdict effects after each of the 1988 debates.

Our Analytical Strategy. When we use rating scales, we generally use a powerful statistical test that can sort out simultaneously a lot of rival explanations for what we find on the rating scale. This test is called *Multiple Classification Analysis* (MCA).

One major rival to any apparent verdict effect would be the "wishful thinking" or *selective perception* effect: People who prefer a given candidate before the debate tend very strongly to see that candidate as doing well. Virtually every previous study of winner perceptions has found audience members' perceptions to be highly selective by party identification or other indicators of preexisting preferences. We did in 1988 as well, but we found that the verdict effect could indeed modify partisan "wishful thinking." When a verdict goes against a favored candidate, people do modify downward their perception of how well that candidate did; when the verdict goes in favor of the preferred candidate, people modify upward the strength of their belief that their candidate won. The verdict effect in 1988 was not as strong as was wishful thinking, but the MCAs showed that it had a visible and independent impact in its own right.

Because partisan perceptions of winners and losers are such an important and pervasive way in which people relate to the debates, we wanted our analytical strategy to recognize the likely priority of wishful thinking over any verdict effect. We did this by introducing an indicator of partisan preferences—party identification—as an explanatory variable *before* introducing either of our two indices of a media verdict: reported exposure to analysis and date of the interview. In effect, partisanship allows us to extract every bit of explanatory power we can before we allow media verdicts to account for anything in the MCAs. We used party identification as a kind of surrogate of whom people would be rooting for in a given debate, just as we did in our previous book (Lemert et al., 1991). It would be interesting to see, given the presence of Perot in the race, how and whether party identification remained such a good surrogate.

We need to consider other rivals to a news verdict as well. Because personal characteristics (*demographics*) such as education often predict the amount of attention paid to political news, and because attention to postdebate news shows is one of our two ways of reflecting exposure to verdicts, we should eliminate (*control*) such demographics as an explanation for any apparent verdict effect.

Another set of control variables to be introduced to the MCAs before verdict exposure is more psychological than demographic. If we find that, for example, higher interest in the presidential campaign predicts heavier exposure to a given debate, we would want to extract the influence of any such psychological variables before we allow analysis following a given debate any chance to explain the outcome.

Finally, although all of the other respondents in our time series were interviewed only once, during the October 11-22 debate time period, our panelists were interviewed for a second time. Generally, some of the panelists were interviewed after each debate—a different subset of panelists in each case, because no panelist was interviewed more than once during the debate time period. Thus, we need to protect against the possibility that panel members might react differently to the debates than the rest of our respondents; therefore, we entered whether the respondent were a panelist into the MCAs before we allowed the two media verdict variables to try to predict perceptions of debate winners and losers.

All of these rivals to a postdebate verdict effect, then, were given a much better chance to explain reactions to the debates than were exposure to postdebate analysis and "Day"—the time-series variable.

The First Debate

We already saw that the networks defined Ross Perot as the winner of the October 11 debate. We also had some hints in our survey data that a news verdict effect may have occurred for Perot in the aftermath of this debate.

The most direct and initially impressive evidence comes from ratings of Perot's prowess as a debater. MCA results showed that, even after all the demographics and other control variables had been allowed first crack at explaining Perot's rating, both Day and reported exposure to analysis predicted ratings of Perot's abilities as a debater. Those who watched both the October 11 debate and the postdebate analysis rated Perot somewhat ($p = .078$) higher than those who only watched the debate. Beyond that, Day showed that immediately after the October 11 debate, Perot's mean evaluation as a debater was more than a full 2 scale points below any of the subsequent means for October 12 through 14 ($p = .000$).

Impressive as this seemed to be, however, we found an identical pattern for ratings of Bush's debating prowess. That is, Bush's ratings also were far higher on October 12, 13, and 14 than they were on October 11—immediately after the debate. This is exactly the opposite of what the "verdict effect" hypothesis would predict: Bush's ratings should have either stayed the same or gone down, not up, as awareness of Bush's performance verdicts diffused throughout the population.

Could we have been unlucky and either drawn a sample of grouches to interview just after the debate or, for the next three nights after that, a sample of ultragenerous souls who thought everybody did a wonderful job? The most direct way to test this "response set" explanation for the time-series result is to introduce yet another control variable—ratings of Bush's debating prowess—and then see whether Day and/or reported exposure remain standing as predictors for the October 11 debate.

Because both Bush and Perot ratings were higher in the days following the debate, and because Bush ratings seemed to run counter to a news verdict hypothesis, the Bush debater ratings suggest themselves as a "response-set" control when we analyze day-by-day ratings of Perot's debating prowess.

Table 9.3 presents these results. Even after the huge apparent influence of "response set" is extracted from the table, October 11 respondents gave substantially lower ratings for Perot's debate prowess than did those interviewed on October 12, 13, and 14 ($p < .05$). Furthermore, reported exposure to postdebate analysis even improved

Table 9.3. Summary of Multiple Classification Analysis: Influence of the Number of Days Since the October 11 Debate on the Rating [0 (low) to 10 (high)] of Perot as a Debater; Adjusted Mean Scores and Regression Coefficients.

Predictors	Rating of Perot as a Debater
Regressions	
Campaign Interest	—
Bush's Debater Rating	.556***
Education	—
Adjusted Means[a]	
Political Party	
Republican	5.12***
Democrat	6.11
Ind	6.44
Panel or Single Interview	—
Day of Interview (N)	
October 11 (52)	5.05**
October 12 (52)	6.24
October 13 (44)	5.97
October 14 (42)	6.23
Reported Debate Exposure (N)	
Debate Only (83)	5.49*
Both Debate and Analysis (107)	6.13

*$p < .10$.
**$p < .05$.
***$p < .01$.

[a]Means are adjusted for the impact of all preceding variables, such as campaign interest, education, "response set," party, and panel. Only then is this exposure variable allowed to try to explain what variation in ratings remains in the table. The multiple predictors in this table accounted for a very high 41.6% of the variance in ratings of Perot's debating skills.

slightly as a predictor after the introduction of the "response-set" variable, reaching $p = .060$, although it still did not reach the customary acceptable level of less than .05 (i.e., $p < .05$).

Table 9.3 also shows that party identification predicted ratings of Perot's debating ability. Interestingly, party did *not* predict ratings of Perot as a debater until *after* we had introduced the "response-set" control (ratings of Bush's debating skills). In general, party identification was not as powerful a predictor of Perot's debater ratings as it was for that of Bush and Clinton. In any case, the newly adjusted means for party showed Republicans giving Perot a 5.12 rating, Democrats a 6.11, and Independents 6.44. (By *adjusted means* we refer to scores recalculated after the apparent influence of other predictors had been extracted.)

The suggestive evidence in Table 9.3 for an October 11 verdict effect needs to be placed in context. The general findings regarding ratings of debating prowess did not carry over to ratings of who won the specific debate. Neither Day nor reported exposure to analysis predicted ratings of which member of a pair had done better in the October 11 debate, although party of course strongly predicted these ratings whenever Bush or Clinton was involved. After each debate, we used 5-point rating scales to ask respondents to compare all possible pairs of the three debaters. The scales ranged from 1 (debater X by a lot) to 5 (Y by a lot), with 3 meaning the two were even and 2 or 4 meaning a slight edge to X and Y, respectively. Reported exposure also did *not* relate to voting preferences.

On the other hand, reported exposure and/or Day were related to ratings of Clinton's and Perot's abilities to relate to the common people, Clinton's and Perot's character, and Clinton's and Perot's knowledge of domestic policy issues. In every case, reported exposure to analysis was associated with more favorable ratings of both Perot and Clinton, although the differences did not always reach the customary $p < .05$ level of statistical significance.

So we have evidence that there was a verdict effect, but the effect appears to have been limited. It did not extend to judgments of who actually won the October 11 debate, and it did not extend to an intent to vote for Perot, Clinton, or Bush.

The Vice Presidential Debate

Coming two days after the first presidential debate, this confrontation was the only one exclusively to have a moderator-only format and increased opportunities for the candidates to challenge each other. To say the least, Dan Quayle and Al Gore took advantage of those openings. If one looks only at the proportion of candidate verdicts in our earlier content analysis that were positive, Quayle and Gore were pretty even. However, because Quayle was the subject of twice as many performance verdicts, the absolute number of favorable verdicts about him was about double the number Gore received.

The clearest verdict from television news, however, was an almost uniformly negative one about James Stockdale. Many of these negative verdicts, however, were qualified by a comment that Stockdale was a war hero, not a politician, and probably should not have been placed in such a high-pressure situation (an implied criticism of Perot).

Given this media environment, how did our survey respondents react? As with the presidential debaters, we asked respondents to evaluate each of the three possible pairings of debaters: Quayle versus Gore, Gore versus Stockdale, and Stockdale versus Quayle. As before, they did their ratings on a 5-point scale, with the first candidate named at the 1 end and the second in the pair at the 5 end. In addition, we asked respondents to rate each vice presidential candidate on a 0 to 10 scale as a political debater—the same kind of scale used for the presidential candidates. Unlike the presidential candidates, though, no other ratings scales were used—we did not have the vice presidential candidates each rated on their "understanding of the problems of common people," "knowledge of domestic issues," and "character," or the probability of voting for each of them.

One other difference in methodology was that the time series for the vice presidential debate was reduced to only debate night and the next night. In the case of the presidential debates, the shortest time series was debate night plus the next three nights. The effect of this shortening of the vice presidential time series may have been to reduce the power of the Day variable to make a difference, so we placed more emphasis in the vice presidential debate MCAs on reported exposure to postdebate analysis shows.

Ratings of Quayle's prowess as a debater provide the clearest support for a news verdict effect (Table 9.4). Race was the only demographic variable to correlate with attention to the vice presidential debate, so it was included as a control, along with party and whether respondents were panelists. As Table 9.4 shows, race and party significantly predicted ratings of Quayle—and so did whether respondents viewed a postdebate news special. Whites ($M = 6.01$) gave Quayle a substantially higher rating than did non-white respondents (4.51). Republicans gave Quayle an adjusted mean rating of 6.14 as a debater, with Democrats second at 5.38 and Independents lowest at 5.15.

Even after all the preceding predictors had been allowed first crack at explaining Quayle's debater ratings, respondents who said they watched a postdebate analysis gave Quayle a much higher adjusted mean rating (6.50) than those who watched only the debate (5.19) itself. Beyond ratings of Quayle as a debater, there was no evidence of a verdict effect for any of the paired comparisons of the three rival candidates. Nor did exposure to analysis predict voting for Bush-Quayle.

So once again we have some evidence of a verdict effect, but the effect certainly seems more limited and narrow—and in the opposite direction—than was the case for the 1988 Quayle-Bentsen debate. The

Table 9.4. Summary of Multiple Classification Analysis: Influence of Viewing Postdebate Analysis on the Rating [0 (low) to 10 (high)] pf Quayle as a Debater; Adjusted Mean Scores and Regression Coefficients.

Predictors	Rating of Quayle as a Debater
Regressions	
Campaign Interest	—
Adjusted Means[a]	
Race	
White	6.01**
Other	4.51
Political Party	
Republican	6.14***
Democrat	5.38
Ind	5.15
Day of Interview	—
Panel or Single Interview	—
Reported Debate Exposure (N)	
Debate Only (51)	5.19***
Both Debate and Analysis (49)	6.50

*$p < .10$.
**$p < .05$.
***$p < .01$.

[a]Means are adjusted for the impact of all preceding variables, such as campaign interest, race, party, and panel. Only then is this exposure variable allowed to try to explain what variation in ratings remains in the table. The multiple predictors in this table accounted for 22.5% of the variance in ratings of Perot's debating skills.

1988 verdict extended to a wider variety of open-ended and scaled measures than did the 1992 Quayle verdict effect. Another difference worth noting is that the verdict effect extended in 1988 both to the "winner" (Lloyd Bentsen) and to the "loser" (Quayle). In 1992, that verdict effect extended only to Quayle.

The Quayle-Bentsen verdict lasted a relatively long time. Again, it is worth restating that we stopped asking detailed questions about the 1992 vice presidential debate after 24 hours, so we cannot say for sure how long a verdict effect might have lasted this time.

The Richmond "Town Hall" Debate

This October 15 debate featured extended interaction between the candidates and an audience of undecided voters. Network verdicts clearly favored Clinton's performance, with Perot at around half the percentage of favorable verdicts that he had received in the first debate, and Bush continuing to trail badly.

Ratings of Clinton over Perot as the winner of the Richmond debate suggest both a verdict effect and a possible debate effect (Table 9.5). Age, interest in the campaign, and working status (full- or part-time worker, student, homemaker, unemployed worker, etc.) were correlated with attention to the Richmond debate; therefore all were included among the variables given precedence over debate and analysis exposure. However, party was the only control variable to relate significantly ($p < .01$) to ratings of whether Clinton or Perot won.

Both exposure variables—Day and reported exposure—seemed related to these ratings, although reported exposure was both much more weakly related ($p = .088$) and at least as much due to viewing only the debate as it was to postdebate analysis.

The most striking exposure difference was between those who were interviewed immediately after the Richmond debate and those interviewed the next three nights. Unfortunately, because of the lateness of the debate in Eastern and Midwestern time zones, most of the October 15 interviews were done at the University of Oregon. Could the greater tilt toward Clinton as winner over Perot *after* October 15 thus be somehow due to the higher marks given Perot by Oregonians on October 15? In order to test this proposition, we needed to see whether the same increasing tilt toward Clinton over Perot occurred among the Oregon samples on October 16, 17, and 18. If it did, then perhaps we could conclude that no bias was introduced by having mostly Oregonians interviewed on October 15. This check proved somewhat reassuring: The pattern for the Oregon sample was very similar to the overall pattern for those days. The Oregon mean for October 16 through 18 was 1.84—if anything, slightly more tilted toward Clinton over Perot than ratings from the three other sites on those three days. Furthermore, slight day-to-day ups and downs for the Oregon sample matched the overall day-to-day ups and downs for October 16, 17, and 18 in Table 9.5.

Despite the impressive day-by-day similarities between the various sites, there is one worry about the October 15 data that cannot be written off completely: Were there enough interviews done on October 15 for us to feel we have a stable estimate of the mean for that day? Although we did 51 interviews on that day, only 33 had replied to all the variables used in our MCA—a relatively small and perhaps unstable

Table 9.5. Summary of Multiple Classification Analysis: Influence of Day of Interview and Debate Exposure on Comparisons of Whether Clinton (1, 2) or Perot (4, 5) "Did Better" in October 15 "Town Hall" Debate; Adjusted Mean Scores and Regression Coefficients.

Predictors	Comparison Between Clinton Perot
Regressions	
Age	—
Campaign Interest	—
Occupation	—
Adjusted Means[a]	
Political Party	
Republican	2.26***
Democrat	1.70
Ind	2.35
Panel or Single Interview	—
Day of Interview (N)	
October 15 (33)	2.62**
October 16 (80)	1.87
October 17 (66)	2.05
October 18 (68)	1.95
Reported Debate Exposure (N)	
None (18)	2.58*
Debate Only (97)	1.92
Both Debate and Analysis (132)	2.06

*$p < .10$.
**$p < .05$.
***$p < .01$.
[a]Means for both exposure variables have been adjusted for the apparent influence of all control variables. Only then are day and reported exposure allowed to try to explain what variance remains in ratings of whether Clinton or Perot did better in the debate. Total variance accounted for by all predictors in this table: *14.8%*.

number of cases. We compensated for this a little by rerunning the MCA with Day and party as the only two variables, because all the others did not reach statistical significance. These eliminations had the effect of restoring some six additional cases that had a missing value on one or more of the eliminated predictor variables. The mean for October 15 fell from 2.62 to 2.38 with these additional cases, but remained significantly

($p < .05$) more favorable to Perot than for the subsequent days when Clinton gained as the perceived winner.

Still, if the reader feels this evidence for a Richmond debate verdict effect is a little shaky, what other evidence can we present to bolster the case? First, ratings of Clinton's debating skills seemed to reflect exposure to the debate, but exposure to postdebate news specials did not seem to add (or subtract) anything. Those who watched the debate and those who watched both the debate and analysis were almost identical at 7.53 and 7.60, respectively, compared to a much lower 6.77 for those not watching the debate. Day was not related to the ratings. As was almost always the case when Clinton and/or Bush were involved, party strongly predicted how high Clinton's ratings as a debater were, with Democrats giving the highest, Republicans the lowest, and Independents in between. Higher interest in the campaign also predicted higher ratings of Clinton's debating skills. Since the October 15 "town hall" debate clearly was a chance for Clinton to demonstrate his ability to relate to ordinary voters, we used another relevant scale to rate each of the candidates. Using that 0 to 10 rating scale, we had respondents evaluate Perot's and Clinton's "understanding of the problems of common people."

Interestingly, exposure predicted both Perot's and Clinton's ratings, but not quite in the same way. In Clinton's case, exposure to the debate or to debate plus the analysis significantly predicted very high evaluations of Clinton's understanding of ordinary people's problems. The difference for Clinton between debate only and debate plus analysis, although in the right direction (Clinton was the highest for debate plus analysis), did not reach statistical significance ($p = .198$). In contrast, Ross Perot's ratings were indeed significantly higher for debate plus analysis than for debate only. Recall that Figure 9.1 shows Perot getting 47% favorable verdicts after this debate.

The October 15 debate heavily emphasized domestic policy issues such as the economy, the national debt, and jobs. We also asked respondents to evaluate (0 to 10 again) each of the presidential candidates' knowledge of domestic policy issues. Both Clinton and Perot had their highest ratings given them by people who saw a postdebate analysis, which was significantly higher than for those who viewed only the debate. As usual, these exposure findings occurred after all demographic and other controls were exerted.

As was the case for the October 11 and 13 debates, then, we have some intriguing evidence that postdebate analysis had an effect. Perhaps given the unprecedented crowding together of all the debates, we should not be too surprised that the evidence is once again not nearly as robust as we would like it to be.

The Final Debate

This October 19 debate was the one in which the candidates were one on one with moderator Jim Lehrer for the first half, then had a panel of journalists asking most of the questions in the second half. As we saw, the network news portrayed Bush's performance as clearly more active and effective than in the preceding two presidential debates. However, Bush's rate of favorable performance verdicts still fell slightly below those for Clinton, perhaps because performance expectations were higher for Bush—trailing in the polls, he had to "hit a home run" or "score a knockout," as more than one network journalist put it. Perot was almost the missing man in coverage of this last debate, but the few times he was mentioned he hit a new low at 21% favorable verdicts.

If coverage of the October 19 debate focused on Clinton's endgame against Bush (another sports cliche!), our October 19-22 interviews might have been expected to show a verdict effect for ratings of Bush or Clinton as a debater and of the Clinton-Bush winner, with perhaps some spillover to other ratings of Bush's or Clinton's understanding, knowledge, and character.

As we have done throughout the analyses in this chapter, we entered as controls all the demographics that correlated with amount of attention to the debate and analysis. In the case of the October 19 debate, these were education, interest in the campaign, and marital status. Then we entered as further controls party identification and whether the respondent had been interviewed once before in the post-Labor Day period ("Panel").

Once again, we found some slight evidence that there was a limited verdict effect. Ratings of Clinton's debating skills were higher if the respondent watched the debate and the news analysis (adjusted mean = 7.84) than when the respondent watched only the debate (adjusted mean = 7.53). However, this difference ($p = .088$) fell a little short of the customary statistical significance level of $p < .05$. There was no evidence of a verdict effect for Bush's or Perot's debater ratings.

As was true for all debates, party identification dominated all predictions of whom respondents would vote for. In 1992, verdict exposure was unrelated to any of these "bottom line" dependent variables, no matter whether we used rating scales or a simple multiple-choice candidate preference measure.

SUMMARY AND CONCLUSIONS

In the Year of the Voter, network journalists shifted away from quoting and paraphrasing insider elite sources for verdicts as often as in the past, often substituting their own or voter performance perceptions for "spin-doctor" verdicts. The year was marked by a surge upward in the use of polls, a variety of "man-on-the-street" feedback techniques, and, mostly because of the October 15 "talk-show debate," much greater attention to the interaction between audience and debaters. Nevertheless, even with all these signs of increased attention to voters—supposedly the *raison d'etre* of the debates—only 1 in every 4 sources of a performance verdict was a nonelite audience member.

On the evening news, at least, journalists spent more time interviewing each other and proffering their own verdicts than they ever had since 1976, when our videotape records began. For the first time, journalists displaced other elite insiders as the most frequent source of performance verdicts on the ABC and CBS evening newscasts.

The direction and extent of network performance verdicts about each of the three presidential candidates varied enormously from debate to debate. Perot received very high marks in the first debate, with the marks plunging lower and lower in the two successive ones, whereas journalists simultaneously spent increasingly little time talking about his performance. Praise of Bush's debate performances was very low in the first two debates and somewhat more common in the last. Clinton never fared badly in network verdicts about any debate, but more than 9 of every 10 verdicts about him were positive after the Richmond town hall debate, the highest proportion of favorable verdicts we ever recorded.

Because of the compressed schedule of debates, we did not expect that media verdicts would last long enough to have an impact on our survey respondents. Yet, using both the time series variable (Day) and reported exposure to post-debate analyses, we found at least some signs of a verdict effect with each of 1992's four debates. The strongest, most widespread evidence of a verdict effect was found with the October 11, 13, and 15 debates. Day seemed to predict a delayed swing in debater ratings, whereas reported exposure to postdebate analysis most commonly predicted higher candidate characteristic ratings (understanding of common people, knowledge of domestic issues, etc.) for Clinton and/or Perot after the October 11 and 15 debates.

As was true of every debate except Quayle-Bentsen in 1988, verdict effects seemed most visible in 1992 for the candidate deemed by the media to have done well. With the single exception of Quayle in 1988, our results show that negative verdicts in the media have not seemed to "stick" to the target. Unlike 1988, though, the verdict effect did not ever extend to voting preferences. Nevertheless, somewhat to our surprise, there is enough evidence for us to conclude that media performance verdicts did influence voter perceptions of the candidates, especially of Clinton and Perot. Unlike 1988, Dan Quayle seemed to have gained from postdebate analysis, if only in terms of his perceived debating skills.

REFERENCES

Lemert, J. B., Elliott, W. R., Bernstein, J. M., Rosenberg, W. L., & Nestvold, K. J. (1991). *News verdicts, the debates, and presidential campaigns.* New York: Praeger.

Steeper, F. T. (1978). Public response to Gerald Ford's statements on eastern Europe in the second debate. In G. F. Bishop, R. G. Meadow, & M. Jackson-Beeck (Eds.) *The presidential debates: Media, electoral, and policy perspectives* (pp. 81-101). New York: Praeger.

10

Media and Mass Views of the Presidential Debates as a Political Institution

James B. Lemert and James M. Bernstein

Major party presidential candidates have participated in televised debates in every presidential election year since 1976. The number and format of the debates have varied somewhat, but the candidates of the Republican and Democrat parties have always faced each other live before a nationwide audience. In 1980, for example, President Carter refused to participate in a televised debate that included independent candidate John Anderson, but eventually did take part in one debate with Republican challenger Ronald Reagan.

In other years the two major party candidates have faced each other at least twice, sometimes three times, such as in 1992. The 1992 presidential debates marked the first time that debate formats and ground rules varied considerably from the constraints of the past moderator/panel-of-journalists model. Regardless of the year-to-year variations, though, televised presidential debates have become an entrenched part of the presidential election process. Whether reluctantly or enthusiastically, candidates expect to be expected to debate.

HOW DEEP THE ROOTS?

One would think that having debates every election cycle—in effect, institutionalizing them—would give the debates all the legitimacy they need. To some extent, that is the case; in fact, their institutionalization at the national level has probably contributed to expectations that there will be debates in state and local races as well. However, despite the presence of fall debates in the last five presidential campaigns, presidential debates remain a relatively fragile institution. One need only look at the 1992 presidential election campaign for evidence.

That year was the second consecutive time the Commission for Presidential Debates was involved as sponsor. The Commission is independent and bipartisan (its co-chairs are former chairs of the two major parties) and was established in 1987 as an alternative to the League of Women Voters, which had sponsored the debates in 1976, 1980, and 1984. The idea behind the Commission was that it would handle the logistical details of the debates (e.g., locations, formats, and dates) well in advance of the Fall campaign—and then the candidates would sign off on the arrangements. But it has not quite turned out that way. The Bush campaign in both elections has rejected the Commission's proposals (see Bates, 1993). In 1992, that rejection resulted in cancellation of the first two debates scheduled by the Commission.

Ultimately, at the insistence of Bush advisor James Baker, the Clinton and Bush campaigns negotiated directly concerning the terms of the debates, not with and through the Commission. The Commission did, however, agree to sponsor the four debates, which occurred within a span of nine days in October. But as one writer has put it: "This successful outcome was hardly foreordained" (Bates, 1993, p. 8). If the past teaches us anything, the outcome will not be foreordained in 1996 either.

Why should we be concerned about how deep the institutional roots are of presidential debates?

THREE THINGS DEBATES PROVIDE

The most important reasons for holding presidential debates concern the contributions the debates make to the election process. First, televised presidential debates signal an "official" start of the election "season" and suggest a seriousness to the potential audience that can increase attention to the entire campaign (see Jamieson & Birdsell, 1988). Second, debates apparently serve a teaching role, for the vast amount of research evidence shows that exposure and attention to them enhances learning about the candidates and their positions on issues (e.g., Bernstein & Lewis, 1993; Chaffee, 1978; Drew & Weaver, 1991; Kennamer, 1990; Lemert, 1993; Lemert et al., 1983; Sears & Chaffee, 1979). Third, debates can serve to increase voter involvement and turnout. This can happen in one of two ways. A debate can create a sense of system openness and voter involvement, thus producing increased turnout (see Kraus, 1988; Lemert, 1981a; Lemert et al., 1991). But as we suggested elsewhere, "the more plausible route to higher turnout may be through the debates' widely documented effect of reinforcing voter loyalties, since such a reinforcement effect almost certainly increases the individual's motivation to participate" (Lemert, Elliott, Bernstein, Rosenberg, & Nestvold, 1991, p. 82; see also Lemert, 1981b, pp. 93-101).

LEGITIMATION THROUGH DEBATES

A fourth consequence of holding the debates was implied earlier when we suggested that debates might increase turnout by creating a sense of system openness. Whether debates increase turnout, there is a strong sense that, when conducted openly and fairly, they can enhance the legitimacy of the election process. We can only speculate on what might have happened had the debates not occurred in 1992. Our guess is the electoral process itself would have suffered a loss of legitimacy. We believe, however, that even though the debates were held, the political brinkmanship that often seems inevitable when candidates debate over debates can be injurious to the process. As we argued in our book (Lemert et al., 1991) about the 1988 campaign: "If the institutional legitimacy of the debates is threatened, then eventually the legitimacy of the election process itself also may be threatened" (p. 82).

PURPOSE OF THIS CHAPTER

The purpose of this chapter, then, is to measure and reflect on the perception of debates as a political institution in presidential election campaigns. We do this in two ways: by examining the extent to which members of the mass public support the idea of debates as a political institution and by examining news media portrayals of presidential debates.

Although the study does not suggest a cause-and-effect relationship between media and mass perceptions, it compares and contrasts the two over the Fall campaign and tries to explore possible reasons for each. In addition, we take advantage of the fact that we produced and can use comparative data going back to the 1988 campaign for mass perceptions, and to 1976 for media portrayals, of the debates.

For all the research that exists with respect to effects of televised presidential debates, surprisingly little work has dealt with the assessment of the status of the presidential debates as a political institution. Our own work from the 1988 election showed survey respondents relatively supportive of the idea of presidential debates in general, although they may have been somewhat cynical about the number of debates and the motives of the candidates when they appeared on them. Still, the respondents in the 1988 study generally recognized the debates as an opportunity to learn about the candidates, even though they said they were unlikely to use the debates as the basis for their final voting choice (Lemert et al., 1991, especially Chapter 9).

Our previous research (Chapter 5) also showed that, despite the general interest in, importance of, and support for the debates shown by members of the mass public, news coverage of the debates tended to reduce their importance to whether they affected the ambitions of candidates and other elites (including journalists).

The content-analytic findings from 1988 tended to support an argument by Diamond and Friery (1987, p. 51) that voters and viewers are the forgotten participants in news coverage of the debates. One question we ask in this study, then, is whether the news media continue to reduce a debate's importance to whether it affects elite insiders. Put another way, if 1992 was the Year the Voters Revolted (see Germond & Witcover, 1993), did the audience as an important reference figure come to mind more often to the elite journalists covering the debates?

In 1988, we found signs that respondents' interest in, and support for, presidential debates declined as the Fall campaign wore on. In a year in which a man in a ponytail braced the president on live national television and asked him to stick to the issues, how were voters reacting? Did viewing the Richmond and other debates seem to strengthen voter support for the debates as something of their very own?

STUDY METHODOLOGY

Media treatment of the debates is examined in two content analyses. Through our survey data, we look at mass attitudes toward the debates. Our previous work provides us with comparative data from at least one previous presidential election for both the survey data (1988) and content-analytic replication data (each presidential year back to 1976).

The Content Analyses

The News Special Replication. We did two content analyses—the first a replication of our previous work on ABC, CBS, and NBC postdebate specials for the period 1976-88. Using the same coding scheme as the previous work and employing a coder who had worked on the previous content analyses, in essence we tacked the year 1992 onto this series of observations. As was the case before, we analyzed both newscasts obtained from the Vanderbilt Television News Archive as well as some contemporaneous network transcripts and videotapes obtained by us.

As was true in the past, these news specials usually followed the debate immediately or later that same night, but occasionally a network would run a news special 24 or more hours later. In 1992, these delayed news specials were more often true of ABC and its *Nightline* program than of the two other networks. For the news special content analyses, the test-retest reliability figure for the single coder was .89.

The Print-Broadcast Study. The second content analysis was based on a computer search[1] geared only toward 1992 media coverage of the debates as institutions. The search used the keyword *format* to screen out debate stories that focused entirely on the candidates. This strategy succeeded in identifying a population of 319 broadcast and print stories.

A stratified random sample was drawn of these stories by creating six time periods surrounding the debates and then sampling seven stories from each of them. The 42 stories drawn (7 x 6 time periods) produced more than 1,000 implicit or explicit assertions about the 1992 debates as a political institution.

Before the debate agreement. October 2 and earlier represent the period before an agreement to debate was hammered out by the Clinton and Bush camps and a debate invitation to Perot was issued by the two sides. This subpopulation of stories stretched all the way back to early 1992, but the largest single batch of stories occurred during the several weeks prior to the agreement, when each side publicly maneuvered to try to cast blame on the other for holding up an agreement while simultaneously negotiating in private (see Chapter 7). Not surprisingly, given the fact the period stretched over more than nine months, this was the largest subpopulation of stories. Because our interest was in seeing whether treatment of the debates varied between periods, the number of cases selected per period did not reflect the differences between the periods in the number of stories available. As was true within each of the six time periods, each story within the group was numbered, and then the sample of seven items was drawn randomly from that time period.

October 3 until the start of first debate. This was the period when the ground rules and the identities of the debaters were known, but no debate had been held yet.

After the first (October 11) debate but before the October 13 vice presidential debate. This was the period marked by appraisals of the first debate, which used the moderator-cum-panel format that had characterized all previous debates since they resumed in 1976. It also was the period when "advance" stories were being written about the upcoming vice presidential debate, which marked a great departure from formats since 1976—moderator only, with debaters able to address each other directly.

After the October 13 debate but before the October 15 Richmond "town hall/talk show" debate. This was the period during which appraisals of the controversial vice presidential debate were prominent, as well as "advance" stories about the audience-participation Richmond debate.

After the Richmond debate but before the October 19 final debate. This was the time when appraisals of the Richmond format would reach a peak, as well as "advance" stories about what we might anticipate happening in the final debate.

After October 19, through the month of October. We expected that this period would contain a number of appraisals of the final debate as well as overviews of the entire October 11-19 series, plus speculation about whether the debates would make a difference in the election outcome.

In the coding, statements about the candidates were ignored unless there was a connection to debates as institutions. For example, a statement that the debates were becoming increasingly important to George Bush's reelection chances would be included, but a statement saying only that George Bush did not perform very well would not be. The same criterion was used in the network news special replication for deciding whether an assertion concerned the debates as an institution. The test-retest reliability figure (Holsti's R as provided in Budd, Thorp, & Donohew, 1967, p. 68) for this content analysis was .834, slightly lower than for the replication study, but still relatively high.

Similar but not identical lists of variables to be coded were used for both content analyses. In each study, an overall positive-to-negative "verdict" about the debate or debates was coded, as well as whether the debate was characterized as important—and to whom, if it was. Both studies coded whether conflict, interest/entertainment value, and new information were attributed to the debate. As well, both coded whether, regardless of whether the information itself were said to be new, the information produced in the debate was said to have helped voters differentiate between the candidates. In addition, each study coded the source of the assertion.

Although the overlap between the two coding systems was high, we did not directly integrate the data from the two studies because one was of postdebate TV network news specials only and the other was of a much more diverse array of nationally prominent print, radio, and TV items.

The Survey Data

Our survey results come from a random-digit telephone survey obtained over the Fall campaign period in four diverse communities:

- a very large, racially diverse eastern city (Philadelphia),
- a bustling midwestern urban center (Indianapolis),
- a small, rural community (the surrounding environs around the college town of Carbondale, Illinois), and
- a middle-sized, racially homogeneous Pacific Northwest community (Eugene-Springfield, Oregon).

The surveys were gathered in six waves and represented both a *time-series* survey design similar to what we used in our 1988 project and an additional three-interview *panel* study using a smaller number of respondents. For more details of the survey design, see Chapter 2.

RESULTS

Our examination of results starts with how the media portrayed the 1992 debates. In the replication study, we also place the 1992 content into an historical perspective that goes back through the 1976 presidential campaign.

The Network Replication Study

Perhaps the most dramatic finding was the extraordinary turnaround from 1988 in the favorability of verdicts presented on network news specials about the 1992 debates. As Table 10.1 shows, 1988 saw the lowest proportion of favorable verdicts on record, whereas 1992 saw by far the highest proportion (71% favorable) in any year since the presidential debates resumed in 1976. The previous high (53% favorable) was in the aftermath of 1980's single Carter-Reagan debate.

A favorable institutional verdict about the debates was produced in any of several ways. For example:

- a candidate or campaign official calls the debate(s) vital to the campaign plans of candidate(s);
- a voter says he or she learned a lot from the debate(s) or was very interested in it (or them);
- the format of the debate(s) is praised by someone;
- the debate is said to have illuminated differences among the candidates;
- new information about the candidates or their plans is said to have been created during the debate(s);
- the debates are said to be important to the mass audience (e.g., Nielsen ratings show that huge audiences are tuning in);
- the debates are said to help voters in their evaluation of the candidates or to help voters understand and participate in the election campaign; and/or

Table 10.1. Direction of Verdict About Debate by Year of Postdebate Analysis Program.

Year (N)	Positive Verdicts (%)	Neutral Verdicts (%)	Negative Verdicts (%)
1976 (N = 56)	50	12	38
1980 (N = 118)	53	15	32
1984 (N = 95)	47	22	31
1988 (N = 75)	35	24	41
1992 (N = 302)	71	8	21
Total (N = 646)	58	14	28
(N)	(377)	(87)	(182)

$\chi^2 = 51.88$, $df = 8$, $p < .001$.

- someone praises the sponsor, moderator, or other participants who are not candidates (most verdicts about candidate performance thus would be excluded).

Not only did the 1992 debates receive high praise, but 1992's postdebate news specials also saw a relatively large shift away from an exclusive focus on only the candidates, their performance, and their ambitions (Table 10.2). A word of caution here: This was only a relative shift because even in 1992 some 70% of all implicit or explicit assertions about the debate concerned the candidates only. Perhaps the most notable increase from the past concerned *both* the candidate and the debate. An example of such an entry might emphasize how, for example, the Richmond debate format suited Bill Clinton's interactive style or how the moderator-only format in the vice presidential debate allowed the candidates to interrupt each other.

The shift away from an exclusive focus on the ambitions of the candidates shows up again in Table 10.3, in which 1992 shows an increased emphasis on the importance of the debates to voters as well as to both voters and candidates. The biggest increase was in the category of "important to both candidate(s) and voters."

Were these trends attributable to coverage of any of the four debates in particular? Certainly the move toward more focus on the voters as participants in the debate process seems largely to have been the product of the October 15 "town-hall/talk-show" debate, in which "only" 65% of all items focused on the candidates. In fact, the media focus on the candidates (84%) in the first debate was, if anything, more like previous years than 1992 as a whole. The increased emphasis on the

Table 10.2. Object of Statements Made on Postdebate News Specials by Year of Programs.

Year (N)	Candidates (%)	Debate Itself (%)	Both (%)
1976 ($N = 347$)	84	10	6
1980 ($N = 492$)	74	17	9
1984 ($N = 762$)	88	7	5
1988 ($N = 699$)	89	5	6
1992 ($N = 837$)	70	14	16
Total ($N = 3,137$)	81	11	9

$\chi^2 = 153.69$, $df = 8$, $p < .001$.

Table 10.3. Year and Importance of Presidential Debates.

Year	Can't Code Importance (%)	Important to Candidate (%)	Important to Voters (%)	Important to Both (%)	Not Important (%)
1976 (N = 346)	21	61	10	5	3
1980 (N = 492)	8	53	15	21	3
1984 (N = 762)	5	74	6	13	2
1988 (N = 699)	7	71	5	16	1
1992 (N = 802)	1	53	12	30	4
Total (N = 3,101)	7	63	9	19	2

$\chi^2 = 58.15$, $df = 10$, $p < .001$.

category of *both* the candidates and the debate resulted largely from both the vice presidential and October 15 debates, with the increase largely attributable to a discussion of how the format allowed candidates to use certain tactics.

Independent of format variations, though, journalists were very likely to continue to define the importance of the debates in terms of their impact on candidate ambitions. Sources most likely to continue defining importance as importance to *candidates* were unnamed elites (83% of their importance statements focused on the candidates), journalists (74% of importance statements), and named elites (67%). No other group of sources had anywhere near as high a focus on candidate/campaign ambitions. In fact, the next highest figure for importance to candidates was only 18% (public opinion polls).

Literally, then, journalists continued to side with insider elites in their almost exclusive focus on what was important to them—who would win—rather than on what was important to voters (data not tabled; $p = .00000$). Because campaign insiders clearly were trying to make their candidate look good, it is perhaps no surprise that they should try to talk about the debate in terms of its impact on their candidate's chances. What is not so apparent, though, is why, in their own statements, journalists continue to be about as preoccupied with what the candidates got out of the debates rather than what the audience did.

In our previous book (Lemert et al. 1991), we emphasized the consistent finding that, except for the single Reagan-Carter debate in 1980, the postdebate news specials seemed to focus almost exclusively on the importance of the debates to the candidates rather than to the voters. Although there was a major shift in 1992 toward framing the debates in voters' terms, it was still more often than not their importance to the ambitions of the candidates that was emphasized.

The observed shifts to importance-to-voters and importance-to-both-candidates-and-voters seemed to have been driven almost exclusively by the October 11 and Richmond debates, with the vice presidential and final debates doing much to diminish the discrepancies between the 1992 debates as a whole and previous years. In other words, the vice presidential and final debates helped keep the overall focus on importance to candidate ambitions as high as it was.

A very slight increase in the proportion of assertions that the debate was *unimportant* was due almost entirely to the October 11 debate, which used the same format as all previous debates since 1976.

Although we have not tabled these breakdowns by each 1992 debate, the differences among them all were significant at $p = .000$. Similarly, verdicts about each 1992 debate were substantially more often positive about the Richmond debate than the other three, especially when compared to the first and vice presidential debates. However, the sampling procedure used for the print-broadcast content analysis provided us with an additional, and more revealing, mode of analysis. So, instead, we move to that new sample.

The Print-Broadcast Study

As Table 10.4 shows, we obtained roughly the same result as in the network news replication study when we analyzed the direction of media verdicts about each 1992 debate. The first presidential and vice presidential debates received by far the lowest proportions of favorable verdicts, with the proportion for the first presidential debate actually closer to the 1988 percentage for network news specials than to the overall 1992 figure (58%) for this print-broadcast sample. Again, it may be worth reminding the reader that the first debate used essentially the same format as had been used ever since the Fall debates resumed in 1976.

We could do something with this sample that we could not do with the network news replication study. We could compare verdicts about a debate in "advance" stories—done before the debate—with those made in the debate's aftermath. Tables 10.5A and 10.5B show substantial before-after changes in the direction of these verdicts.

Table 10.4. Print and Broadcast News Treatment of the 1992 Candidate Debates.

Debate[a] (N)	Positive Verdicts (%)	Neutral Verdicts (%)	Negative Verdicts (%)
October 11, First Presidential Debate (N = 79)	41	5	54
October 13, Vice Presidential Debate (N = 230)	51	15	34
October 15, Second Presidential Debate (N = 210)	72	16	12
October 19, Final Presidential Debate (N = 50)	62	26	12
Total (N = 569)	58	15	27

$\chi^2 = 71.46$, $df = 8$, $p < .001$.

[a]All cases in which more than one 1992 debate was the object of the verdict are excluded. The most common of such excluded cases was "all of the 1992 debates" for which there were 436 cases. Some 63% of the media verdicts about the object "all the 1992 debates" were favorable, a slightly higher percentage than for the four individual debates, as presented under "Total" at the bottom of the table.

In brief, what might be called "anticipatory" verdicts about the moderator-only vice presidential debate were predominantly positive, but there was a huge increase in the proportion of negative verdicts after the actual debate (Table 10.5A). What this almost certainly means is that journalists and their news sources more often praised the direct, one-on-one format of the debate before the debate occurred than they afterward praised the way the candidates actually had used that format.

In remarkable contrast, a before-after shift went in the opposite direction for coverage of the Richmond debate (Table 10.5B). That is, "advance" stories discussed the debate in more skeptical terms before it occurred, but in highly favorable ones after it was over. Apparently, the early skepticism reflected questions that journalists had about allowing presumably "unsophisticated" voters to lob "softball" questions at the candidates.

No before-after coverage differences were observed for either the first or the last presidential debate. As we had found in our study of the

Table 10.5. Changes in Media Views from Before to After Vice-Presidential and Richmond "Talk Show" Debate.

A. Vice-Presidential Debate

Time of Interview (N)	Positive Verdicts (%)	Neutral Verdicts (%)	Negative Verdicts (%)
Before Oct. 11 Vice Presidential Debate (N = 75)	64	24	12
After Oct. 11 Vice Presidential Debate (N = 155)	45	10	45
Total (N = 230)	51	15	34

$\chi^2 = 26.35$, $df = 2$, $p < .001$

B. Richmond Debate

Time of Interview (N)	Positive Verdicts[a]	Neutral Verdicts[a]	Negative Verdicts[a]
Before Oct. 13 Richmond Debate (N = 28)	46	40	14
After Oct. 13 Richmond Debate (N = 182)	76	13	11
Total (N = 210)	72	16	12

$\chi^2 = 8.91$, $df = 1$, $p < .01$.
[a]Because two of the six cells had expected values of less than 5, Neutral and Negative columns were combined for the purpose of calculating the Chi-square statistic.

1976 through 1988 debates, journalists were least often the source of favorable verdicts about the debates as an institution. Although we tabled the results for the print-broadcast sample (Table 10.6), the same pattern held for the 1992 network replication: Once again, journalists were more often either neutral or negative than were other sources. We should also add that the network replication study also shows that journalists increasingly over time have been playing the role as their own news sources—perhaps as part of a "backlash" against campaign "spin doctors."

Table 10.6. Source by Direction of Verdict About the 1992 Debates.

Source (N)	Positive Verdicts (%)	Neutral Verdicts (%)	Negative Verdicts (%)
Journalists (N = 564)	52	18	29
Polls (N = 18)	83	6	11
"Man-on-the-Street," etc. (N = 72)	63	7	30
Reactions during debate by voter groups (N = 29)	97	3	—
Named Elite (N = 298)	72	9	18
Unnamed Elite (N = 104)	56	27	17
Total (N = 1,085)	60	15	25

$\chi^2 = 58.15$, $df = 10$, $p < .001$.

Survey Results

In every wave of the study, we asked survey respondents several questions that were intended to elicit their views of whether they valued the debates. Not all questions were asked in every wave, although most were.

Format Preferences. In October and then again in the November wave, we asked respondents about their preferred format for presidential debates. Based on our observation of the different formats, it became clear that we should offer respondents more choices than we had in our October questionnaire, which was written before the debate-period time series began. The October question gave respondents the choice of panel, moderator, and both. The November question expanded the options to "panel only," "moderator only," "moderator with questions from the audience," and "combination panel and moderator." The latter corresponded to the debate format used from 1976 through October 11, 1992.

Usefulness Ratings. In the October and November interviews (Waves 2-6), we asked respondents to evaluate, on a 0 to 10 scale, a number of sources of information about the presidential campaign. Each such source was rated in turn on this scale, with 10 being the "most useful" end. Near the middle of the list of such presidential campaign sources were "televised debates." Other sources rated included TV news stories, newspaper stories, talk shows, televised ads, and so on.

Likert Ratings. In all waves, three Likert-type items were asked about the debates. Another debate item was asked in every wave, but its content varied from Wave 1 (September) to all the remaining waves. These four items were interspersed with other items that were not about the debates but had the same Likert-type response alternatives. Each item presented a statement about the debates, and responses could range on a 5-point scale from "Strongly Agree" to "Strongly Disagree." Two of the four debate-related statements always were favorable and two were unfavorable toward the debates:

- Presidential debates are one of the best ways for me to learn where the candidates stand on the issues.
- Presidential candidates seem to avoid answering important questions during the debates.
- All in all, I think the presidential debates are a waste of time.
- Televised presidential debates are one of the best ways for people to make their final voting choice (Wave 1 only).
- I was waiting for the presidential debates to help me make up my mind up about who I will vote for (Waves 2-6).

Organization of Survey Results. The survey results for support of the debates as a political institution are presented in three subsections: (a) after controlling for other factors, the apparent impact of exposure to each debate; (b) changes in support for the debates by panelists; and (c) wave-by-wave differences in debate format preferences.

Debate exposure as a factor. We need to start by taking into account a number of factors besides attention to the debates that could be rivals to the debate as an explanation of mass attitudes toward the presidential debates. These rivals fall into two broad classes.

The first class includes those variables that are strongly related to the amount of attention a person pays to a given debate. If such a rival predicts viewing a given debate, why could it also not predict the amount of support for the debates as an institution? We can certainly identify, for each debate, those demographic and other variables that predict debate attention. For example, such demographics as education, race, marital status, gender, employment status and age might well predict differences in attention paid to a given debate, as well as some other, more psychological variables. Among these other variables, almost by definition, one would expect that interest in the presidential campaign would predict attention to each of the debates.

The second class of rivals includes those variables that probably are a little more closely related to support for the debates than they are to attention. In other words, they may or may not be related to attention, but they would seem to have a good chance of predicting the amount of support for the debates. In essence, they are candidates to rival debate exposure because they already measure something resembling attitudes toward the debates. We use two such variables: the individual's feelings of "Internal" Efficacy, and "External" Efficacy. However, as readers of earlier chapters have already seen, it is more appropriate to use the four efficacy scales separately, rather than adding them together. The four scales are listed under the type of efficacy each represents, but analysis was done by individual scales.

Internal Efficacy feelings, as conceptualized by Craig, Niemi and Silver (1990), refer to feelings of self-confidence that one can understand and participate usefully in politics. The two items were: "Sometimes government and politics seem so complicated that a person like me can't really understand what's going on" (referred to in our tables as "*Complicated*"), and "I feel that I could do as good a job in public office as most other people" (referred to as "*Could do job*"). At least some debate-related items, such as their usefulness in helping the individual to find out about candidates, would seem to somewhat overlap Internal Efficacy items such as "Complicated."

External Efficacy has much less to do with one's own sense of political competence than it does with the political system's interest in, and openness to, citizen participation. Thus, one could have great personal confidence but feel the political system is closed, or just the reverse—one could have confidence in the system but lack it in oneself. And, of course, one could be in high in both types of efficacy—or low in both. The External Efficacy measure especially seems to measure generalized attitudes toward the political system that almost certainly would overlap some with such debate-related items as whether the debates were a waste of time, whether candidates avoided answering questions, and so on. The two External Efficacy items were: (a) "Under our form of government, the people have the final say about how the country is run, no matter who is in office" ("*Say*"); and (b) "If public officials are not interested in hearing what the people think, there is really no way to make them listen" ("*No Listen*").

Respondents used a 5-point Strongly Agree to Strongly Disagree scale. Because two of the four items were worded negatively or critically, a Strongly *Dis*agree response to them would be scored as a high efficacy response and Strongly Agree would be the high efficacy response to the two positively worded questions.

Except for a question about the preferred debate format, our analyses used a procedure called *Multiple Classification Analysis* (MCA), which can simultaneously take into account multiple rival predictors and sort them out according to criteria that the researcher establishes. We chose to give all the rivals to debate exposure "first crack" at explaining the level of support for the debates—*before* we allowed reported exposure to explain anything.

In general, our hypothesis is that exposure to the debates and/or to postdebate analysis shows will predict greater support for the debates as an institution, even after all the other rivals have been allowed first crack at accounting for support for the debates. As we already saw, 1992's postdebate analyses had an unusually high proportion of favorable verdicts about the presidential debates as a political institution, so we wanted to try as well to separately analyze whether the postdebate news specials contributed something more—or less—to debate support than the debates did by themselves. We could separate exposure to postdebate specials from debate exposure for the three presidential debates. Unfortunately, for technical reasons, the vice presidential debate interview schedule forced us to choose either to compare only exposure to nonexposure or to compare only postdebate versus debate-only exposure. We chose the former comparison.

Exposure results. Because exposure to particular debates and their aftermath was most sensitively measured in the October 11-22 period (Waves 2 through 5), much of our analysis focuses on exposure to each of the four debates as a predictor of each of five scales measuring support for the debates. Already, however, you can see that we are talking about reporting 20 complex MCA results for five dependent variables by each of four debates. Rather than the 20 separate tables that just these analyses would generate, we report these results in a summary overview table (Tables 10.7A through 10.7D). What does this overview show?

In 13 of 20 cases, even after controls are exerted for every demographic variable that predicted exposure to that particular debate, and even after controls for interest in the presidential campaign and the four efficacy items, debate exposure predicts higher support for the debates as an institution. In general, the adjusted mean differences for exposure to the debate only and exposure to both the debate and a postdebate analysis do not differ very much. The big difference is between any exposure and none.

As a debate-legitimizing experience, apparently the Quayle-Gore-Stockdale debate had weaker effects than each of the three presidential debates. In the case of the vice presidential debate, exposure predicts greater denial that the debates are a waste of time and, like all the other three debates, higher ratings of the usefulness of presidential debates. In contrast to two of the scales for the vice presidential debate, the first and second presidential debates produced statistically signifi-

Table 10.7A. First Presidential Debate, Summary of Multiple Classification Analyses[a]: Influence of Debate Exposure on Five Measures of Support for Debates; Adjusted Mean Scores and Regression Coefficients

	Scale Items[b]				
Predictors	Was Waiting for Debates	Debates Waste of Time	Avoid Answering Questions	Best Ways to Learn Stands	Usefulness of Debates
Regressions					
Education	-.061***	-.038*	—	-.059***	—
Campaign Interest	-.083*	-.114***	-.142***	.114***	.524***
Efficacy Items					
Complicated	-.116**	-.082*	—	—	—
Could Do Job	—	—	.146***	-.117**	—
Have Say	.105*	—	—	.126***	.263*
No Listen	—	-.199***	-.083*	—	—
Adjusted Means					
Political Party					
Republican	2.69**		3.53**		6.36*
Democrat	2.55		3.53		7.00
Independent	2.96		3.87		6.01

Table 10.7A. First Presidential Debate, Summary of Multiple Classification Analyses[a]: Influence of Debate Exposure on Five Measures of Support for Debates; Adjusted Mean Scores and Regression Coefficients (cont.)

Panel					
Yes	—	2.55**	—	—	—
No		2.31			
Debate Viewing					
No	2.37**	2.65***	—	3.00***	4.56***
Yes, Deb Only	2.81	2.30		3.20	6.93
Yes, Deb & Anal	2.79	2.09		3.43	7.39
N	364	363	364	363	352

*$p < .10$; **$p < .05$, ***$p < .01$.

[a]For more complete instructions on how to read MCA tables, see Chapter 5 and the text for this chapter. MCA is also used in Tables 10.7B, 10.7C, and 10.7D.

[b]The first four items are scaled from 1 = strongly disagree to 5 = strongly agree. The "Usefulness of Debates" is scaled from 0 = low to 10 = high. The same scales are used in Tables 10.7B, 10.7C, and 10.7D.

Table 10.7B. Vice Presidential Debate, Summary of Multiple Classification Analyses: Influence of Debate Exposure on Five Measures of Support for Debates; Adjusted Mean Scores and Regression Coefficients.

Predictors	Was Waiting for Debates	Debates Waste of Time	Avoid Answering Questions	Best Ways to Learn Stands	Usefulness of Debates
Regressions					
Campaign Interest	—	-.136***	-.071***	—	.274***
Efficacy Items					
Complicated	-.084**	-.122***	-.091***	—	.230***
Could Do Job	—	.091**	.070**	-.119**	-.194**
Have Say	—	—	.047	.089***	—
No Listen	-.086**	-.169***	-.076***	—	.191**
Adjusted Means					
Race	—			—	—
White		2.29**	3.79**		
Black		2.57	3.72		
Asian		2.35	3.29		

Table 10.7B. Vice Presidential Debate, Summary of Multiple Classification Analyses: Influence of Debate Exposure on Five Measures of Support for Debates; Adjusted Mean Scores and Regression Coefficients (cont.).

Political Party					
Republican	2.72***	2.43*	—	—	6.66*
Democrat	2.64	2.33			7.14
Independent	2.98	2.21			6.69
Panel	—	—	—	—	—
Debate Viewing					
No	—	2.42*	—	—	6.41***
Yes		2.28			7.13
N	818	829	829	829	811

*$p < .10$.
**$p < .05$.
***$p < .01$.

Table 10.7C. Second Presidential Debate, Summary of Multiple Classification Analyses: Influence of Debate Exposure on Five Measures of Support for Debates; Adjusted Mean Scores and Regression Coefficients.

Predictors	Was Waiting for Debates	Debates Waste of Time	Avoid Answering Questions	Best Ways to Learn Stands	Usefulness of Debates
Regressions					
Age	—	.017***	.006**	-.010***	-.020**
Campaign Interest	—	-.202***	—	—	.300***
Efficacy Items					
Complicated	—	-.197***	-.137***	—	—
Could Do Job	—	.136***	.096**	-.115**	.292**
Have Say	—	-.078*	—	.104**	—
No Listen	-.134**	-.136***	—	—	.308**
Adjusted Means					
Political Party	—	—	—	—	—
Republican					6.79**
Democrat					7.35
Independent					6.02

Table 10.7C. Second Presidential Debate, Summary of Multiple Classification Analyses: Influence of Debate Exposure on Five Measures of Support for Debates; Adjusted Mean Scores and Regression Coefficients (cont.).

Panel					
Debate Viewing					
No	2.18***	—	2.70***	2.76**	5.47***
Yes, Deb Only	2.94		2.24	3.24	7.25
Yes, Deb & Anal	2.77		2.17	3.32	7.14
N	316		316	315	310

*p < .10.
**p < .05.
***p < .01.

Table 10.7D. Final Presidential Debate, Summary of Multiple Classification Analyses: Influence of Debate Exposure on Five Measures of Support for Debates; Adjusted Mean Scores and Regression Coefficients.

Predictors	Was Waiting for Debates	Debates Waste of Time	Avoid Answering Questions	Best Ways to Learn Stands	Usefulness of Debates
Regressions					
Education	-.061***	—	—	-.048***	—
Campaign Interest	—	-.078**	—	—	.292***
Efficacy Items					
Complicated	-.107**	-.071*	—	—	—
Could Do Job	—	.085**	—	-.155**	—
Have Say	—	—	-.078**	.072*	—
No Listen	-.089*	-.176***	—	—	—
Adjusted Means					
Martial Status	—	—	—		—
Single				3.48**	
Married				3.12	
Divorced				3.15	
Separated				2.88	
Living with Other				3.47	
Widow(er)				2.90	

Table 10.7D. Final Presidential Debate, Summary of Multiple Classification Analyses: Influence of Debate Exposure on Five Measures of Support for Debates; Adjusted Mean Scores and Regression Coefficients (cont.).

Political Party	—	—	—	—	—
Republican	2.74**				
Democrat	2.69				
Independent	3.07				
Panel		—	—	—	—
Yes	2.57*				
No	2.85				
Debating Viewing	—	2.67***	—	3.03**	5.57***
No					
Yes, Deb Only		2.19		3.37	7.18
Yes, Deb & Anal		2.19		3.21	7.78
N	434	434	435	435	310

* $p < .10$.
** $p < .05$.
*** $p < .01$.
—not statistically significant.

cant results for exposure on four of the five debate support scales. Exposure to the final presidential debate significantly predicted support on three of the five scales, so even it surpassed the vice presidential debate.

Of the five debate support scales, the statement that the candidates seemed to avoid questions asked of them during the debates was the single item that seemed least affected by debate exposure. Debate exposure never did predict disagreement with this item.

Two scales always were related to exposure after each of the four debates: the debates as a waste of time and the rating of their usefulness. Debate exposure always predicted both more *dis*agreement that debates were a waste and higher ratings of their usefulness. Except for the vice presidential debate, exposure always predicted higher agreement on a third scale—that debates were one of the best ways of learning about the candidates' issue stands.

Interest in the presidential campaign and "Could do job," one of the two Internal Efficacy scales, were the two control variables that most often correlated with the five debate support scales. Higher interest always correlated with two of the five debate scales: *dis*agreement that the debates were a "waste of time" and high "usefulness" ratings. Agreement that one could do the job always correlated positively with agreement that the debates were one of the best ways to find out about the candidates' policy views. Most likely people who have confidence in their own abilities also agree that they can apply their abilities to checking out the candidates on a debate. Disagreement that politicians will not listen ("No Listen") always was related to disagreement that the debates are a waste of time.

Party identification significantly ($p < .05$) predicted level of support for the debates only 7 of 20 times, but those times were revealing. Independents seemed to express the most ambivalent attitudes toward the debates as vehicles for voters. After the vice presidential and the first and last presidential debates, Independents were most likely to agree that they had been waiting for the debates, but at the same time they gave especially lower ratings to debate usefulness after the first debate and joined Republicans in giving lower ratings after the vice presidential debate. Furthermore, Independents had higher mean agreement scores after the first presidential debate that the candidates seemed to avoid answering the questions asked them.

Whether respondents were members of our panel almost never made a difference in their debate support ratings, which is a reassuring sign that the September interview had not affected their October reactions. In the 2 (of 20) cases in which the panel reached at least the $p < .10$ level, panelists showed slightly greater cynicism about the debates than did nonpanelists, a frequency about at what one would expect by chance. Similarly, only 1 in 20 tests reached $p < .05$—also about what one would expect by chance. We conclude that there is no evidence that having been interviewed before had sensitized panelists. Thus, for purposes of these analyses, we merged panelists and time-series respondents.

Panel Results

With that reassurance about the panelists, we took advantage of our panel design by using our respondents as their own controls and using change scores to talk about our debate support measures. Presumably, the panel design gave us the analytical power to analyze change while at the same time our October time-series comparisons reassured us that the panelists were typical of what we would have found had we repeatedly interviewed the larger time-series sample.

If the debate experience itself can be a legitimizing—or delegitimizing, for that matter—experience for the debates, how did our respondents' assessments change over time? Although viewing of a given debate might conceivably cause people to become more suspicious, skeptical, or contemptuous of the debates, our content analyses and the MCA of the apparent effects of exposure strongly suggest that we should predict favorable changes by panelists toward the debates as an institution. Generally, this is what happened. A summary of t-test results for changes on the debate support scales is in Table 10.8. Panelists were interviewed once just after Labor Day, once during the debate time-series period (October 11-22), and finally in early November, just before the election.

In order to preserve the maximum number of cases available for each comparison, we used t-tests of change scores for two of the three groups at a time, rather than a simultaneous analysis of all three groups of scores.

Change from September to October. Let's consider first the comparisons between the same 257 panelists in September and during the October 11-22 debate period. These comparisons are in the second column. Three comparable items (of the 5 rows in the table) were asked both in the post-Labor Day period and during the October 11-22 debate period.

Consistent with our expectations, *dis*agreement rose significantly with our two negative items—that candidates avoid answering questions in the debates, and that debates are a waste of time. Interestingly, though, disagreement also tended to rise ($p < .10$) with the one positive item that was asked both in September and October 11-22: The debates are one of the best ways of learning about candidates' issue stands. As

Table 10.8. A Summary of Changes in Debate Support by Panelists Over Time.[a]

Scale	Comparison of Matched Panelists Between:		
Rating of Debate Usefulness (0 = low to 10 = high)	No comparable measure in Wave 1	No comparable measure in Wave 1	Oct. vs. Nov.[***] Means: Oct. = 6.36 Nov. = 6.88 N = 200[b]
Best way to learn about issue stands (1 = SD to 5 = SA)	Sept. vs. Oct.[*] Means: Sept. = 3.31 Oct. = 3.18 N = 257	Sept. vs. Nov.— Means: Sept. = 3.27 Nov. = 3.21 N = 236	Oct. vs. Nov.[**] Means: Oct. = 3.10 Nov. = 3.24 N = 205
Candidates avoid answering questions (1 = SD to 5 = SA)	Sept. vs. Oct.[***] Means: Sept. = 3.91 Oct. = 3.69 N = 257	Sept. vs. Nov.[***] Means: Sept. = 3.96 Nov. = 3.54 N = 232	Oct. vs. Nov.— Means: Oct. = 3.68 Nov. = 3.56 N = 203
Debates are a waste of time (1 = SD to 5 = SA)	Sept. vs. Oct.[***] Means: Sept. = 2.54 Oct. = 2.34 N = 258	Sept. vs. Nov.[***] Means: Sept. = 2.55 Nov. = 2.63 N = 236	Oct. vs. Nov.[***] Means: Oct. = 2.42 Nov. = 2.24 N = 206

Table 10.8. A Summary of Changes in Debate Support by Panelists Over Time[a] (cont.).

Was waiting for the debates to help me decide who to vote for (1 = SD to 5 = SA)	No comparable Measure in Wave 1	No comparable Measure in Wave 1	Oct. vs. Nov.*** Means: Oct. = 2.47 Nov. = 2.78 N = 206

*$p < .10$, t-test.
**$p < .05$, t-test.
***$p < .01$, t-test.

[a]The September interviews (Wave 1) were conducted from September 7 through September 18. The October interviews (Waves 2 through 5) were conducted from October 11 through October 22. The November interviews (Wave 6) were conducted just before the election on November 1 and November 2.

[b]Numbers vary between Wave 1, Waves 2-5, and Wave 6 groups because of incomplete interviews and no contacts. Because t-test comparisons are only for those respondents who answered the same question on each of the two occasions, means for any one time period will also vary.

we will see, however, the trend is in the other direction when respondents' October ratings are compared with their November ones.

Change from September to November. Because many of the October measurements were obtained before all the debates were actually over, perhaps the November measures provide a clearer retrospective reading of our panel's reactions. These findings are in the third column of Table 10.8. *Dis*agreement with the two negative items rose significantly from September, and no clear trend emerged on the single positively worded item.

Change from October to November. The last column contains results for changes from the October debate period to November. It is now possible to use all five debate support scales. At the top of the last column, the 0 to 10 rating of the usefulness of televised presidential debates showed a significant mean increase in support for the debates. There are now two positively worded scales, and agreement rises significantly on both items—"Best way to learn" and "Was waiting for the debates"—whereas *dis*agreement rose significantly that the debates are a waste of time. Change was toward greater disagreement as well on the second negatively worded item—that the candidates avoid answering questions—but the movement is not large enough to reach even $p < .10$.

Overall, then, change scores usually showed significant increases in panel support for the debates over the Fall campaign period. Of the 8 (of 11 possible) change scores that reached at least the $p < .05$ level, every one of them reflect increased support for the debates. 1992's increased support for the debates stands in some contrast to 1988's apparent declines in support over time (Lemert et al., 1991).[2]

Preferred Debate Format. During the October and November interviews, we asked respondents to indicate their preferences for a presidential debate format. Experience with the October debate format question, as well as with the actual debates themselves, led us to add some alternatives to the format question in November that were not there in October, so we could not easily combine the October and November results, even for panelists who responded in each month.

Nevertheless, we could divide the October 11-22 period into its four waves and see if format preferences change as experience accumulates with each of the different debate formats. As Table 10.9 shows, the most often preferred format in Waves 2 and 3 seems to be the panel of journalists, whereas there is a major shift to the moderator-only format in Waves 4 and 5. Recall that Wave 2 followed the October 11 debate, which used the customary panel-*cum*-moderator format. Interestingly,

Table 10.9. Survey Wave and Debate Format Preferences: Do Preferences Change as Experience Grows?

Wave and Debate Aftermath (N)	Prefer Panel %	Prefer Moderator %	Prefer Combination %	Makes No Difference %
Wave 2: Oct. 11-12 (N = 54)	48	17	2	33
Wave 3: Oct. 13-14 (N = 52)	38	35	—	27
Wave 4: Oct. 15-18 (N = 122)	22	57	1	20
Wave 5: Oct. 19-22 (N = 483)	26	40	5	29
Total (N = 711)	28	40	4	28

$\chi^2 = 58.15$, $df = 10$, $p < .001$.

the moderator-only format used in the vice-presidential debate (Wave 3 follows this debate) did not see much of a shift away from the panel format; that shift occurred in Waves 4 (after the Carole Simpson-*cum*-audience Richmond debate) and 5 (after the split-format final debate). Following the Richmond debate (Wave 4), the moderator-only format received the highest percentage any format would receive during this time period—57%. That percentage fell to a plurality in Wave 4, which followed the mixed moderator-only (first half) and panel-plus-moderator (second half) final debate format. Again, it was probably no accident that 25 of the 27 total respondents who opted for a mixed format said so in the aftermath of the last debate, even though what we meant by "mixed" may not have been what they meant.

The October 15 debate—and favorable media verdicts about the "moderator-audience participation" format—made a strong impression. The swell upward in "moderator-only" choices did not follow the moderator-only vice-presidential debate, as we saw. We interpret the "moderator-only" response as a surrogate for the October 15 format. Read this way, that format got more total choices than either of the other two format choices offered, despite the fact that respondents in Waves 2 and 3 had not yet had the chance to observe the "audience participation" format used.

How much of an impression that October 15 debate made may be even clearer when we look at the Wave 6 data, in which we gave panelists a clearer and more elaborated set of choices—and in which everyone interviewed had had a chance to learn about, and reflect on, all four debates. The question we asked, the choices offered and the percentages for each are presented in Table 10.10.

Now that our question allows respondents to separate moderator-only from moderator-plus-audience-questions format, there no longer was any need to use the moderator-only choice in Table 10.9 as a surrogate.

When we subdivided panelists by whether they had watched a given debate, we found that, regardless of the debate, viewers always gave the moderator-plus-audience-questions format either a majority or just barely under that. Meanwhile, the moderator-only format, often favored by debate "purists," consistently did poorly, even among those who watched the vice presidential debate—the only one to use that format all the way through. Perhaps our panel's negative appraisal of this format, like the changed media verdict we reported earlier about that noisy debate, reflected some of the same confusion between this format and the candidates using it.

Table 10.10. Debate Format Preferences[a].

Format Preference	Preferring Format (%)
Panel Only	10
Moderator Only	12
Moderator and Audience	47
Panel and Moderator	16
No Difference	15
Total (N = 220)	100

[a]Preferences for specific debate formats were determined by responses to the following: 'This year several presidential debate formats were used. One had a panel of journalists, one had a single moderator, one had a moderator and took questions from the audience, and one combined the single moderator and panel formats. Which one did you prefer? The panel, the single moderator, the moderator with questions from the audience, the combination panel and moderator, or didn't it make any difference to you?"

DISCUSSION

Both journalists and our survey respondents seemed to like the 1992 Fall debates, the first since 1976 to depart from the moderator-*cum*-panel format. Perhaps the biggest departure from past formats was the Richmond "town-hall" or "talk-show" debate, a format never before seen in the Fall debates. Both the single-interview time-series respondents and our panelists liked this format. That October 15 debate also received the highest percentage of positive verdicts on both network news specials and in our print-broadcast sample.

The format favored by debate purists—a single moderator with candidates able to address each other directly—received far more positive media verdicts *before* it occurred, when it was possible for media to focus on the format in the abstract, than it did afterward, when the behavior of the rival debaters may have been confused with the potentialities of the format. Perhaps the same confusion of candidate behavior with format happened in survey respondents' minds as well because few favored this format.

Although journalists initially seemed more skeptical of the audience-participation Richmond debate, the actual debate itself seems to have been a triumph in the eyes of both journalists and the audience. As a result, format and actual use of that format seemed once again to merge in the minds of both journalists and the audience, this time greatly helping the cause of the debates—as well as of this format. The character of future presidential debates may have been permanently changed as a result.

ENDNOTES

1. This search for stories focused on the debates as institutions using the keywords *format* and *presidential* or *vice presidential debate(s)* and restricting the search to 1992. The search used the political campaign library of stories on the Nexis service.
2. When we talk about apparent change in 1988, it is worth restating that the data from 1988 were entirely from a time series, in which no respondent was interviewed more than once. Thus we need to qualify any assertions about change in 1988. The 1992 panel provides results that allow less qualified talk of change because the same respondents were interviewed at least two times, and more often three.

REFERENCES

Bates, S. (1993). *The future of presidential debates.* Washington, DC: The Annenberg Washington Program.

Bernstein, J.M., & Lewis, D.S. (1993, May). *Knowledge of candidates' issue positions among first-time and experienced voters: Did talk-show campaigning matter?* Paper presented to the Midwest conference, American Association for Public Opinion Research, St. Charles, IL.

Budd, R.W., Thorp, R.K., & Donohew, L. (1967). *Content analysis of communications.* New York: Macmillan.

Chaffee, S.H. (1978). Presidential debates—Are they helpful to voters? *Communication Monographs, 45,* 330-353.

Craig, S.C., Niemi, R.G., & Silver, G.E. (1990). Political efficacy and trust: A report on the NES pilot study items. *Political Behavior, 12,* 289-314.

Diamond, E., & Friery, K. (1987). Media coverage of presidential debates. In J. L. Swerdlow (Ed.), *The presidential debates: 1988 and beyond* (pp. 45-53). Washington, DC: Congressional Quarterly.

Drew, D., & Weaver, D.H. (1991). Voter learning in the 1988 presidential election: Did the debates and the media matter? *Journalism Quarterly, 68,* 27-37.

Germond, J.W., & Witcover, J. (1993). *Mad as hell: Revolt at the ballot box, 1992.* New York: Warner.

Jamieson, K.H., & Birdsell, D.S. (1988). *Presidential debates.* New York: Oxford University Press.

Kennamer, J.D. (1990). Political discussion and cognition: A 1988 look. *Journalism Quarterly, 67,* 348-352.

Kraus, S. (1988). *Televised presidential debates and public policy.* Hillsdale, NJ: Erlbaum.

Lemert, J.B. (1981a, March 21). *Simple reductionism in the study of media effects: How we got there, and are we stuck with it?* Invited paper presented to the Spring conference, Mass Communication and Society Division, Association for Education in Journalism, Kent, OH.

Lemert, J.B. (1981b). *Does mass communication change public opinion after all? A new approach to effects analysis.* Chicago: Nelson-Hall.

Lemert, J.B. (1993). Do televised presidential debates help inform voters? *Journal of Broadcasting & Electronic Media, 37,* 83-94.

Lemert, J.B., Elliott, W.R., Bernstein, J.M., Rosenberg, W.L., & Nestvold, K.J. (1991). *News verdicts, the debates, and presidential campaigns.* New York: Praeger.

Lemert, J.B., Elliott, W.R., Nestvold, K.J., & Rarick, G.R. (1983). Effects of viewing a presidential primary debate. *Communication Research, 10,* 155-173.

Sears, D.O., & Chaffee, S.H. (1979). Uses and effects of the 1976 debates: An overview of empirical studies. In S. Kraus (Ed.), *The great debates: Carter vs. Ford, 1976* (pp. 223-261). Bloomington: Indiana University Press.

11

Rapid Response Teams

William L. Rosenberg

The 1992 Presidential election, like political campaigns of the past, could easily be characterized as a military operation involving assaults, charges, and countercharges. Each campaign released statements about their own candidate's background as well as challenging or promoting inaccurate statements about the opposition's past record and policies. Campaigns have always sought to position themselves in the most desirable light, whether it be by undercutting the opposition, often with misstatements, or by highlighting or exaggerating their own positions. With the recent rise in negative campaign advertising, rapid response teams were a natural "response." Rapid response teams provided the campaigns with round-the-clock monitoring of the opposition as well as serving to develop informative responses to the public via the media.

Political campaigns must establish protocols to respond to charges and allegations. Some campaigns choose never to respond because they feel that by even commenting they are lowering themselves. Other campaigns feel that not commenting gives the charges some degree of credibility. However, sometimes the charges leveled against a candidate are so significant that the campaign finds that it must respond. The Willie Horton ads of the 1988 Dukakis Presidential campaign are an example. Dukakis failed to adequately respond to this and a number of other charges leveled by the Bush campaign and paid very dearly. The leader of the 1988 Democratic fact patrol—the group responsible for responding to charges by "providing the facts"—was George Stephanopoulos. The Dukakis campaign's failure to act aggressively was not lost on the political operatives of the Clinton campaign of 1992. In order to not suffer a similar misfortune, the Clinton campaign developed its own version of the fact patrols, which they termed the "rapid response team."

In 1992, perhaps because of the continuing and recurrent coverage of the Gennifer Flowers controversy, the Clinton campaign felt that it could not afford to let accusations go unanswered in the press. The consequences of inaction were viewed as potentially too damaging. Hence, the Democrats established their rapid response team version of fact patrols.

Historically, political campaigns have sought ways to manage their information needs. John Kessel, in his book *Presidential Campaign Politics, Coalition Strategies and Citizen Response* (1988), described three key procedures that campaigns use to deal with their information needs. The first is the use of "reference librarians," who have the daunting task of storing and managing information that can be readily made available to the campaign, the media, and the public as needed. Presidential campaigns routinely keep files of their candidate's statements and positions as well as those of the opposition. In this way the campaign can quickly research a charge, assertion or the record of the opposition in order to launch an assault or defend itself.

Betsy Wright, the "Secretary of Defense" for the Clinton rapid response team, was responsible for the record of the Clinton Administration in Arkansas and served as the coordinator of research for the Clinton election campaign team. Wright's informal political information structure of friends of the campaign was so immense that she was able to monitor the activity of out-of-town journalists as they attempted to research stories in Arkansas (Wines, 1992). Her contacts were able to tell her what files the journalists were examining and to whom they were talking. She would contact journalists to let them know that they were "sighted" and offer to provide them assistance in researching their stories.

The second traditional internal information campaign activity is the development of speaker's manuals and issue books. These documents provide the candidate or surrogate with facts and figures, by issue area, and in a format that can be readily presented. These documents provide messages that have at their core the goal of strengthening the speaker's position and authoritativeness while undercutting the opposition.

Finally, campaigns often establish an answer desk, with a well-publicized telephone number. Here political operatives provide responses to questions posed by the caller. This provides the voters with the ability to get answers to their questions and demonstrates the campaign's responsiveness. These three activities, although quite important, are largely reactive methods of political campaigning. However, the activities of the fact patrols of the 1980s were a combination of both proactive and reactive techniques. The fact patrols of the 1980s were designed to correct the factual misstatements made about a campaign as well as to launch assaults. The fact patrols and later rapid response teams built on these functional information demands of campaigns by increasing the output of material, at a faster pace, with more background and through higher technology.

In 1988, the Democratic fact patrols were often members of the U.S. House and Senate. All used their expertise in their specific policy areas to help support their ticket by pointing out the failings of the opposition and providing a response when challenges or charges were leveled. The fact patrols of 1988 often traveled as a six-member team arriving in a city, stumping for their candidate and simultaneously launching a barrage of charges against the opposition. Air travel allows teams to hit several cities in a day, holding half-hour press conferences near the airports and then moving on to the next city on their tour.

The 1988 Dukakis fact patrols were co-chaired by Sen. Barbara A. Mukulski (Maryland) and Rep. Thomas S. Foley (Washington). The Democrats' plan was to use 40 congressional members visiting 56 cities in key states during the final two weeks of the campaign (Schwartz, 1988). The main theme presented in 1988 was that Bush was a man who left "no fingerprints." Furthermore, Bush had accumulated an assortment of failed public missions in such areas as the environment, drug policy, regulatory reform, trade, and terrorism (Borger, Baer, Walsh, Plattner, & Range, 1988). Some members of the teams spoke in their specific area of expertise (Schwartz, 1988). For example, Senator Al Gore, Jr. (Tenn.) pointed out Bush's failings in terms of regulatory reform. Similarly, Rep. Richard A. Gephardt (Missouri) talked about his area of expertise—trade. Gore and Gephardt were often accompanied by Representatives Charles Rangel and Charles Schumer of New York, Dennis E. Eckhart (Ohio), and Dale Bumpers of Arkansas.

EARLY VERSIONS OF THE FACT PATROLS AND RESPONSE TEAMS

Versions of fact patrols have existed for many years. Like the information-retrieval process, public relations and media contacts have played an important role in the development of political campaign strategies.

In 1932, Charles Michelson worked for the Democrats, as did Hill Blackett for the Republicans four years later, as the first modern-era media-public relations persons. Although initially this media-public relations position resided within the political parties, as each political party's strength declined, candidates such as Richard Nixon sought their assistance from Madison Avenue. This shift has undoubtedly served to further weaken the role of political parties in America because the candidates have assumed greater independence.

Typically, presidential campaigns have senior staff publicists from the public relations sector formed as teams to handle these aspects of the campaign. For example, in the 1984 Reagan campaign, James Travis, Gerald Rafshoon, Peter Daily, John Deardourff, and Douglas Bailey formed what was known as the "Tuesday Team," whose purpose it was to manage the media and public relations issues of the campaign. In 1960, the Nixon campaign established the firm Campaign Associates and in the 1972 election the November Group. Reagan formed the "Campaign 80" group for his 1980 presidential bid.

Television has in large part served to increase the role of the media teams. Media consultants have become more and more specialized in their campaign functions. In the 1950s, the public relations teams principally were responsible for space and time acquisition. With television coming of age, the media consultant's role shifted and increased in prominence. According to Kessel, almost everything that was disseminated prior to the television age came from the public relations division of the campaign. In that era, operatives such as Michelson worked on getting their stories—those that supported their candidates—into print in the best light possible. Statements would be sent to prominent party members who had the ability to draw attention, due to their own stature, and who could then reinforce the campaign's message through repetition.

By the 1950s, Michelson's one-person operation had blossomed into an internal public relations firm within the Democratic National Committee, with a number of responsibilities. This internal firm worked with a campaign press that was based in Washington, DC by distributing timely press releases that included all types of campaign information, including candidate speeches and campaign announcements. Michelson's group also released information to reporters traveling with the candidate and party leaders who might use the information as a scripted weapon directed at the opposition. This group also served the press outside the Washington environment who may not have had the resources to maintain a Washington, DC staff, but nonetheless were interested in printing information about the campaign. Recognizing that fact, the campaigns sought to provide prepackaged material to the media, including articles, features, editorials, and photographs. This reduced the burden associated with reporting the material, thus increasing the likelihood that it would remain unedited.

Clearly, then, the roots of the modern rapid response teams can be traced at least as far back in the history of American presidential campaigns as the 1960 Nixon campaign, and probably further back than that. But the lessons learned from the Dukakis-Bush campaign of 1988, plus the tempo of modern American campaign communications, seem to have combined to lead to the formal organization of campaign groups whose specific function is to get the campaign's messages into the media environment at breakneck speed.

THE CLINTON RAPID RESPONSE TEAM

The Clinton campaign's rapid response team set up shop in the former *Arkansas Gazette* offices in Little Rock, Arkansas. The facility housed computer terminals with dozens of staffers under the direction of James Carville. Carville's team searched the media wires and researched databases in an effort to mount a massive political operation aimed at the Republicans. The campaign's 24-hour-a-day operation was established to respond in minutes to any allegation or charge made by Bush or his surrogates. The response team has often been thought of as a military operation (Kelly, 1992), with the meeting offices being referred to by the campaign staff as the "war room."

During the 1992 election, the response teams monitored a variety of communication vehicles that were used to reach voters, including television, both on the airwaves and on cable, newspapers, talk shows, and paid advertising, as well as radio and direct mail pieces. This provided the campaigns with information that was transmitted to the mass public. By monitoring television and print material in the press, the campaigns could position themselves in relation to their opponents as well as respond to any charges or allegations that were brought forward.

Although the television networks and the print media could be monitored by the campaigns without too much difficulty, radio provided an arena for particularly vicious attacks that were often difficult to challenge directly because the radio market is so segmented. The problems in mounting a response included the sheer ability of the campaign to monitor what charges or assertions had been presented, much less to have a mechanism to respond. Similar problems existed with the direct-mail pieces that were distributed directly to voters' homes and that could contain very pointed messages. These two media sources, radio and direct mail, could be the most effectively targeted and most difficult to rebut unless they eventually became an issue in the broad television media or newspaper or magazine press. However, their impact could be dramatic because they were able to reach their desired audience without rebuttal.

The 1988 media group headed by George Stephanopoulos, then Deputy Communications Director, often took the position of turning the other cheek when nasty charges were leveled against Dukakis. Clinton's rapid response team was aggressively headed by James Carville. Carville continually provided Clinton with faxes full of facts and figures that Clinton could use on the stump. Very early in the campaign the Clinton Team took the position that it would let no charge go unanswered in the press. If the Bush campaign released a negative ad, the Clinton Team responded immediately. For example, a particularly negative television ad produced by the Bush campaign depicted a deserted road photographed in black and white. The ad presented one negative image after another, eventually showing a buzzard perched on a stark desert tree. This setting supposedly represented Clinton's home state of Arkansas. The message was that Clinton had doubled the debt of Arkansas and increased taxes. The clip ended with "Bill Clinton wants to do for America what he has done for Arkansas. America can't take the risk." Within hours, the Clinton Team had a response ad running throughout the country (Underwood, 1992). The Clinton campaign was convinced that it should not let an assault such as this remain unanswered.

Carville's approach was "the first law is that the public cannot react to information that they don't have. If all they hear is one thing, you can't expect them to know something else if you don't tell them." Carville's opinion was that "for a long time, people seemed to run campaigns as if someone said: 'Well, we're just not going to answer.' This just leads to inaccurate, low-quality information. We like to provide accurate, high-quality information. This business is very time-intense, very time-compressed. The shelf life of a story is down sometimes to hours, not to an afternoon or morning. The first reaction that comes out is generally the one that carries the day. If you're not in the cycle, you're out of it." Carville further observed that "oftentimes, campaigns want to move at their own pace. But we don't have such a luxury. We have to move at the pace information is disseminated." (All quotes from Smith, 1992, p. B9.)

The Clinton Team met twice daily at 7 in the morning and evening, with representatives from various campaign departments, including Carville, Stephanopoulos, media consultant Mandy Grunwald, research coordinator Wright, and scheduling director Susan Thomases, as well as other staff members. The Republicans had a similar reconnaissance team that monitored information overnight and met each morning at 7 as well. The Clinton Team was well versed in economics, foreign policy, and press relations, as well as practical battlefield politics.

An example of the pace at which the Clinton team operated is illustrated by its response to charges made by South Carolina Republican Governor Carroll Campbell (Smith, 1992). Serving as a Bush surrogate, Campbell began attacking Clinton's economic development record in Arkansas. The Response Team actually produced a letter to Clinton, written by Campbell several years earlier, and placed it in the hands of the reporters *before* Campbell's press conference began. In the letter Carroll praised Clinton's approach and suggested that his initiatives were a model for the South. Carville's approach was similar in many ways to Michelson's of the 1930s. Both sought to be at, or ahead of, the pace of the press of their era.

Stephanopoulos, Communications Director for the Clinton-Gore campaign, said, "We know that if an attack isn't answered, whether it's true or false, it tends to stick. So we block and counter-punch before they have a chance to hit the body. . . . The issue is to have an answer in time for the news cycle. We try to get it in the story" (Black & Lehigh, 1992, p. A1). Republican consultant Eddie Mahe had a similar message, "try whenever possible to get inside your opponent's story each day with your own positive message" (Rosenstiel, 1992, p. A1). Although in the past campaigns used to try to stage media events early in the day to assure the possibility of a news slot, now the activity is much more intense.

The aggressiveness of the Clinton rapid response team was recalled by Susan Zirinsky, Head of the Political Unit for CBS News (Ifil, 1992). She cited an incident in which she was at the Republican National Convention with Dan Rather, awaiting the acceptance speech of George Bush, when her beeper went off. It was George Stephanopoulos letting her know of the availability of Mr. Clinton's response to the speech that Bush had not yet given.

THE BUSH RESPONSE TEAM

The 1992 Bush rapid response team was headed by Alixe Glenn, who was eventually marginally linked as one who shared a house with Elizabeth Tamposi ("Tamposi shared house," 1992). Tamposi, a State Department official, was implicated in the political scandal involved with inappropriately obtaining Bill Clinton's passport. The task of the Republican rapid response team was essentially the same as it was for the

Democrats. The Team provided for coordinated research and tracked statements and positions of the Clinton-Gore campaign. On occasion, this included releasing negative information to the press about Clinton.

Although the Clinton campaign was known for its rapid response team, which, despite its speed, generally engaged in reactive positions, using a subtle approach of personal contacts with targeted opinion leaders in both the political and media arenas, the tone was decidedly different in the Republican camp when they unleashed their "attack faxes." The Clinton campaign also released a daily fax. The Democratic version, titled "Good news of the day," attempted to place favorable information in the public domain about the Clinton record as Governor of Arkansas as well as to present what he would do when in the White House.

The Bush campaign made extensive use of the "attack fax'" process. One of the key operatives in this warfare was Mary Matalin, Deputy Campaign Manager for the Bush Campaign. Matalin had for a week or so been releasing faxes accusing "Boy Clinton" of "riding high in the straddle" as he traveled around the country in his "pander mobile" (Lavin, 1992). Then in early August, Matalin recalled that she was in bed, getting angrier and angrier when she claimed she had a "fax attack." She said she composed the midnight fax—"Sniveling hypocritical Democrats: Stand up and be counted—On second thought, shut up and sit down!"—from two binders of material after failing to go to sleep. However, in doing this, she brought up two of the "no-nos" of the Bush campaign. Those issues were Clinton's past drug use and what was termed his zipper problem that led to the attack fax term, "bimbo eruptions." The assault went so far that Bush distanced himself from the action and Matalin released a public statement acknowledging that perhaps she violated the President's desire to avoid references to Governor Clinton's personal life. However, the damage was done nonetheless. Her associate, Torrie Clark, the Press Secretary for the campaign, initially defended Matalin's actions with regard to the midnight fax. The two have been called the "Thelma and Louise" of the Bush campaign (Grove, 1992a). Later, Clark distanced herself somewhat from the attack. David Axelrod, a Chicago-based Democratic consultant, claimed that Matalin did not write that fax at her kitchen table. He said the Bush campaign put it out there to shake things up but still give Bush plausible deniability. Matalin was a protege of the late Lee Atwater, reputedly one of the "Kings" of dirty tricks within the Republican party.

It should be noted that attack faxes are not limited to cross-party fights. In the 1992 Democratic primary, Harrison Hickman, a Washington-based pollster for Sen. Bob Kerrey, released an attack fax against Clinton's draft record. Sen. Kerrey responded by blasting his own pollster for that action (Grove, 1992b).

In another "attack fax," Matalin used unsubstantiated innuendos about Soviet government involvement in Clinton's visit to Moscow and his participation in nonviolent antiwar activities while he was a Rhodes Scholar in 1969. She went so far as stating that he may have been an "agent of influence" for the former Soviet Union (Farrell, 1992). The Bush campaign dubbed their orchestrated media campaign about Clinton's Rhodes Scholar-period trip to Moscow as the "Red Willie" offensive. Many Republicans who knew Clinton at the time have publicly dismissed these allegations. Prior attempts to smear Clinton focused on the derogatory moniker "Slick Willie," in which questions about his character, style, and commitment to positions were raised ("Mud-faxing," 1992).

THE PEROT RESPONSE EFFORT

Unlike the Clinton and Bush campaigns, Perot did not have an organized rapid response effort. In fact, there was no professional opposition research team or quick-response team at all to combat the efforts of the Bush and Clinton campaigns. The Perot campaign was a very streamlined organization, guided by a few professionals. Much of the work for the campaign was undertaken by volunteers. Part of this lack of organization may have been due to the on-again, off-again, on-again nature of his campaign. However, even if Perot had stayed in the entire race, his personal style may have still dictated the media approach he chose (see Chapter 6).

According to Sharon Warden, Press Secretary to the Perot '92 Campaign, the campaign did not have the time to put out the fax of the day as the Democrats and Republicans did. She said, "There was no staff to handle that effort." The campaign "just never got on top of that function" (Holman, personal communication, August 11, 1994).

Overall, Perot did not have a good relationship with the media. He did not hold press conferences nor face the traditional media. Rather, he sought out free and alternative media that included talk shows and electronic town meetings, in which he felt he could talk directly to the people. Therefore, he did not use a typical response-team approach. Instead, he went directly to the American people via alternative media, bypassing news media gatekeepers.

POLITICAL ADS WITHIN THE RAPID RESPONSE TEAM FUNCTION

The ads of the 1992 campaign were clearly viewed as central to victory. By September, James Baker had left the State Department and become

White House Chief of Staff. In his new position he assumed responsibility for reorganizing the White House and campaign staffs. What was once a group campaign process, involving Republican National Committee Chairman Richard Bond, Deputy Campaign Manager Matalin, and Press Secretary Clarke, now was organized under Baker. Alixe Glen was brought on board to run the campaign's communications, and the original campaign chairman, Robert Mosbacher, was delegated to raise money through the Republican National Committee to pay for party ads and get-out-the-vote drives. Baker also placed a trusted confidant, Mitchell Daniels, to serve as the liaison between the campaign's political elements and the Madison Avenue types who were jointly working on the production of the Bush ads. The leaders of the agency—The November Group—formed to produce the Bush ads favored the "feel-good" approach such as those used to sell automobiles and Coca Cola. The political types favored attack ads directed at the Democrats. Daniels served in the role of arbiter ("Mud-faxing," 1992).

Clinton's media campaign was managed by Washington media consultants Mandy Grunwald and Frank Greer. They were joined by the ad team, Deutsch, Inc., as well as others from the Madison Avenue community.

By August, the Clinton campaign decided that it was not enough to simply respond; it had to attack first (Page & Clifford, 1992). By using bus trips throughout the country the Clinton-Gore campaign would capitalize on the populist nature of their campaign and the sense that Bush was out of touch with the voters. As Fall approached, the Clinton campaign began using more traditional campaign modes to reach voters, which included flying to key cities and holding press conferences, as well as using modern technology to hold satellite-linked town meetings. Similarly, Bush and Quayle made extensive use of satellite-based television interviews in key media markets. Often satellite feeds to local television stations were used to counteract the effect of a Clinton-Gore local campaign visit. Both campaigns trolled the skies, searching satellite feeds to organizations as well as the news media to keep informed of the other's positions.

August saw the arrival of the first negative campaign ads. In response to negative statements issued by the Bush campaign, the Clinton campaign launched its own negative ads. These ads were released by Ron Brown, the Democratic National Chairman and a Clinton surrogate, who was in Houston during the Republican National Convention to respond to GOP attacks. The ads ran in Washington, DC and Houston and were placed in the middle of the Republican's convention broadcast coverage (Mandel, 1992). Both campaigns decided that campaign surrogates were an effective tool to counteract the effects of the opposition. By placing Brown at the site of the Republican Convention, he would be in a position to hold press conferences and provide rebuttals to the Republicans. The negative ads had a similar effect by being positioned at both the media market sites, the Republican convention, and the nation's capital, where consumption would be high among politicians and the media.

The first ad presented by the Democrats during the Republican convention began with, "And now a short break for the facts. On November 5, 1990, George Bush signed the second biggest tax increase in American history. Under Bill Clinton, Arkansas has the second lowest tax burden per person in the country. Those are the facts. Back to the show." The Democrats' second ad used the following script: "More facts. Under George Bush, America has had no growth in private-sector jobs and wages have fallen. This year, under Bill Clinton, Arkansas leads the nation in job growth and incomes have grown [at] twice the national rate. Those are the facts. Back to the show" (Mandel, 1992).

The Republican surrogate, Governor Carroll Campbell of South Carolina, countercharged that Ron Brown "took a quick break from the truth." Campbell asserted that "not only has Bill Clinton proposed the largest tax increase in history. In 1986, in Arkansas he pledged not to raise taxes. And since that time he has had 36 tax increases in Arkansas." He went on to point out that low-income persons in Arkansas have shouldered much of the burden of these increases. Then Campbell provided Labor Department statistics countering Clinton's ads about job growth during the Bush Administration (Mandel, 1992, p. 1).

SUMMARY

The development of rapid response teams was a central feature of both the Democratic and Republican candidate organizations that were created to run their respective 1992 campaigns. No evidence was uncovered that the Perot campaign ever developed a similar team. Because so much of Team activity by the Republicans and Democrats was pointed toward controlling what was presented to voters through the news media, and since Perot clearly tried to do an end run around the news media (see especially Chapter 6), perhaps we should not be surprised by this contrast between Perot and his rivals.

New communications technologies (e.g., satellites, cheap videotape production facilities, computer links through modems, the fax machine) helped drive the markedly more speedy struggle to control what appeared in the mainstream news media that themselves were operating with these new technologies. Undoubtedly, the perceived failures of the 1988 Dukakis campaign also had a lot to do with the drive toward "instant" rebuttals, attacks, and countercharges. Apparently, we are well past the day when the Democrats and Republicans feel they can wait to let the facts sort themselves out in the next news cycle, 24 hours later.

REFERENCES

Black, C., & Lehigh, S. (1992, August 13). Attack and counterattack: Clinton team masters striking back, and hard. *The Boston Globe*, p. A1.
Borger, G., Baer, D., Walsh, T., Plattner, A., & Range, P.R. (1988, October 24). Can Dukakis come back? *US News and World Report*, p. 22.
Farrell, J. A. (1992, October 6). GOP labels Clinton a communist dupe. *The Boston Globe*, p. 14.
Grove, L. (1992a, August 18). The Bush women, calling the shots. *The Washington Post*, p. D1.
Grove, L. (1992b, February 18). The campaign crush. *The Washington Post*, p. D1.
Ifil, G. (1992, September 1). The Clinton team's utility infielder is becoming a major-league hitter. *The New York Times*, p. A15.
Kelly, M. (1992, August 11). The 1992 campaign: The Democrats; Clinton's staff sees campaign as a real war. *The New York Times*, p. A16.
Kessel, J. H. (1988). *Presidential campaign politics, coalition strategies and citizen response* (3rd ed.). Chicago: Dorsey Press.
Lavin, C. (1992, August 25). The President's pit bull. *Minneapolis Star Tribune*, p. E1.
Mandel, S. (1992, August 19). National issue. *Investor's Daily*, p. 1.
Mud-faxing: Clean up your act, Mr. President. The Clinton attack memo besmirches your campaign. (1992, August 4). *Newsday*, p. 34.
Page, S., & Clifford, T. (1992, September 6). Heat is on; Bush, Clinton begin stretch run for White House. *Newsday*, p. 6.
Rosenstiel, T. B. (1992, August 7). In politics, the defense never rests. *Los Angeles Times*, p. A1.
Smith, M. (1992, August 18). Clinton team's forte; rapid fire responses. *The Houston Chronicle*, p. B9.
Tamposi shared house with Bush aide. (1992, November 20). *Reuters Limited*, PM Cycle.
Underwood, J. (1992, November 12). A run for their money: Political advertising for the US presidential elections. *Marketing*, p. 16.
Wines, M. (1992, April 15). Clinton: Mission; Keeping track of those keeping track. *The New York Times*, p. A24.

12

Media and Voters React to the 1992 Presidential Ads

James B. Lemert

The 1992 presidential ads, like many other aspects of the Fall presidential campaign, mixed genuine innovation with a mere extension of the past. George Bush's attack ads against his Democratic opponent actually increased in number in 1992 but, unlike 1988, he did not settle on a small number of attack ads and keep repeating them. In a way, Bush's 1992 effort resembled that by Dukakis in 1988: Lots of money was spent producing—and rejecting—ads, with relatively less spent on actually airing them (see Devlin, 1989, 1993). Both Dukakis in 1988 and Bush in 1992 seemed to want to be their own advertising planner, putting a slightly new twist on the old adage about the man who is his own attorney having a fool for a client. One interesting new Bush ad series featured two with a purported morning-after debate "verdict" (presumably to help offset anticipated debate verdicts on the news) from people supposedly intercepted in a shopping mall somewhere. These "people-in-the-mall" respondents in the series actually were Republicans recruited by the Bush campaign to come to the shoot.

Meanwhile, an innovative Clinton team went to school on what happened in 1988, organized "quick response" ad rebuttal teams, gathered intelligence on new Bush ads to come, and geared itself both to produce "quickie" rebuttal ads almost overnight and to fax rebuttal news releases in time to stimulate same-day news stories. The Clinton attack ads relied heavily on actual news footage—especially the several "Read My Lips: No New Taxes!" spots featuring Bush's pledge in the 1988 campaign—to redirect hostility away from Clinton as the source of his attack ads. The use of actual news footage to attack Bush was very reminiscent of how the Bush campaign in 1988 attacked the Michael Dukakis defense credentials by using actual news footage of Dukakis looking silly as he bounced around in a rapidly moving tank.

Then there was Ross Perot, with his low-budget production team, his high-budget, densely packed October and November airplay, and his "talking head" infomercials that "experts" thought virtually invited the audience to desert him. Because the "infomercials" were long enough to be listed on the TV schedule—unlike the "modern" 15-, 30- and 60-second campaign spots, in which exposure would be both accidental and frequent—people could easily avoid them, experts warned. Yet Perot's first infomercial, telecast during the first week in October, outdrew NBC's *Quantum Leap* with about 16.5 million viewers and a 20% share of all homes using television (Garrett, 1992). The size of Perot's 30-minute infomercial audience—even on replay—continued to surprise journalists throughout Perot's media blitz. Eventually, major American newspapers began to debate whether Perotmercials should be highlighted in TV listings of candidate "appearances" on talk shows and the like, with *USA Today* and *The Philadelphia Inquirer* deciding to highlight them and *The New York Times* and *The Washington Post* deciding only to list them in the program grid (McKibben, 1992).

ANOTHER "ECHO CHAMBER" IN 1992?

Media Coverage in 1988

Our study of the Bush-Dukakis campaign came up with a startling finding regarding the 1988 advertising war: Network news had become a giant echo chamber for those ads, rebroadcasting an unprecedented 62 excerpts of them during the 1988 campaign, with the combined networks attempting only a single "Ad Watch" or "Fact Patrol" story accompanying them. These 62 sound bites represented three times as many "free media" replays as had ever occurred in the Vanderbilt University videotape holdings of presidential campaign newscasts that extend through Carter-Ford in 1976.

Some 44 of these ad stories replayed the ads of only one of the 1988 candidates; 27 of these single-candidate replays (61%) were ads done on behalf of Bush, including the infamous "Willie Horton" ad that now has become embedded in media and campaign folklore. Many of our 1988 survey respondents reported seeing the "Willie Horton" ad. Given the placement of this ad by a Bush front group called the Presidential Victory Committee, our Eugene-Springfield, Philadelphia and Carbondale respondents almost certainly saw this spot on the news, not as a paid ad.

A Third-Person Effect?

We think that national journalists' belief that the Bush attacks were powerful and persuasive led them to make a very common error among elite decision makers: Journalists changed what they did in the 1988 campaign because they believed the Bush ads must have been persuading voters. One of the changes that journalists made in how they covered the 1988 campaign was to produce an extraordinary number of stories about those ads. Even the 27 stories that clearly replayed only Bush ads exceeded the previous high of 21 combined total replays in 1980. In the communication research literature, the formal label for this kind of elite behavioral change is the third-person effect.

When the third-person effect occurs, an elite decides that a message must be having a powerful impact on the masses and therefore changes his or her own behavior to try to take account of that perceived effect (see especially Davison, 1983). Typically, when the third-person effect occurs, the elite decision maker changes behavior before there is any evidence whether the message really was all that powerful. When a politician suffers from a third-person effect, there are political mechanisms in place (including the news media) to evaluate the wisdom of the action taken, but there are rather few such mechanisms available to have the news media account for such misjudgments.

A "Cheap News" Explanation?

To be sure, other factors might well have contributed to 1988's extraordinary rise in ad replays. Increasing "bottom-line" cost-containment pressures on news departments could have encouraged them to use the ad tapes to take the easy—and inexpensive—way out, when they could, in their campaign coverage. The Bush and Dukakis campaigns were, of course, all too eager to supply videotape copies of their ads to the networks. All the reporter had to do, then, would be to decide which segments to play, then write and shoot a script about the ad. In 1988, all but one of these ABC, CBS, and NBC scripts merely discussed the tactical purposes of the specific ad(s) and, perhaps, what the other side might do. To have provided a story that checked the factual claims made in the ads—or to have covered the ads with a fresh perspective—would have cost more, both in time and money.

1992 Coverage: Rival Predictions

So we now have the background to set up some rival predictions about how network news might treat 1992's Fall presidential ads.

Rival Predictions on 1992's Replays. Those "bottom-line" pressures clearly did not go away in 1992; if anything, they may have become more intense (see Rosenstiel, 1993). So, if cost containment were the chief factor, we might expect even *more frequent* use of advertising sound bites in 1992.

On the other hand, some prominent national journalists began not to assume that the 1992 Bush and Clinton attack ads necessarily achieved their purpose (e.g., Kurtz, 1992). If the third-person effect explains 1988's network fascination with ad replays, but the prevailing wisdom among network journalists were at least noncommittal about whether 1992 attack ads worked, then we might expect to find fewer ad replays in 1992 than 1988.

Rival Predictions on "Ad Patrols." Potentially, we might also find a proportional increase in media "ad patrols" on network news, regardless of how many total ad replays there were. After the 1988 presidential election, influential political columnist David Broder called on his print and broadcast colleagues to report aggressively on the accuracy of presidential campaign ads. Many journalists (see, e.g., the Freedom Forum series on the 1992 campaign: Freedom Forum, 1992, 1993) asserted that they and colleagues responded to Broder's call by beefing up their ad-watch coverage. CNN correspondent Brooks Jackson (1992, p. 51) described himself as being a member of the "Ad Police" and warned campaign managers that the police will not stand for "any retouching of the truth for political advantage." Policing examples cited by Jackson involved network and local broadcasters during the primaries. Presumably, such energetic police work would carry over to the Fall, and Cappella and Jamieson (1994, p. 344) observed that ABC, NBC, CBS, and CNN each developed and used ad-watch pieces in the Fall campaign. Arguably, another reason why network ad patrolling might rise in the Fall campaign is that the Clinton campaign made it cheaper to do. The Clinton campaign's "quick response" operations were specifically designed to feed journalists with documented facts about truth claims made in Bush attack ads, thus knowingly reducing somewhat the costs of doing an ad-watch piece on network news.

However, because more work—especially independent confirmation—still would be required to do such fact checking, to the extent that holding down costs drove campaign coverage in 1992, we might expect at most just a slight increase from the extremely low proportion of 1 "fact patrol" out of 62 ad stories in 1988.

What Network News Did in 1992

So did network news continue to act like a Greek Chorus, repeating presidential ads and extending their reach to locations where they would never otherwise be seen? Furthermore, regardless of how many ad replays there were on the news, did the networks change the way they covered those ads? To answer these questions, we examined the Vanderbilt Television News Archive Index for the months of September, October, and November 1992, using the same technique that we used in our previous book (Lemert, Elliott, Bernstein, Rosenberg, & Nestvold, 1991). Table 12.1 presents these results for the same three networks (ABC, CBS, and NBC) we studied in 1988 and before.

Ad replays were indeed down from 1988, and ad-watch segments were up, at least a little. Nevertheless, only 6 of the 28 stories replaying presidential ad segments attempted to provide a "consumer protection" assessment of the ads. The remaining 22 of those 28 stories continued to provide only an insiders' perspective about the ads: what they meant to the campaigns, what their tactical purposes were, and so on.

The 28 replays from September 1 through Election Day were second only to 1988's 62 and considerably above the previous high of 21 in 1980. The networks hardly seem to have stopped using the ads to do a number of "cheap news" stories about the presidential campaign. Although a number of newspapers embarked on ad watches in response to Broder's 1990 call to arms and/or to a general sense of embarrassment (see Jamieson, 1992, p. 156), it is noteworthy that in only one month CNN's Brooks Jackson alone matched the combined total of six for the entire Fall campaign done by the three older networks. In the period September 26-October 26, Jackson did at least six distinct ad-watch pieces on considerably more than a dozen Bush and Clinton ads.[1]

In other words, ABC, CBS, and NBC did not come very far toward what many critics would term a more *professional* standard in covering the advertising campaign, at least not in comparison to CNN and Jackson.

Table 12.1. Number of Network News Stories Using Presidential Ad Sound Bites and Number of "Ad Watch" Segments[a] in Those Stories, by Fall Campaign Year[b].

Year	Stories Using Sound Bites and "Ad Watch"
1976	3
1980	21
1984	8
1988	62
	(1 "Ad Watch" Component)
1992	28
	(6 "Ad Watch" Components)

[a]For a story with an ad sound bite to be regarded as having an "Ad Watch" component, the story must have done any of several things, such as examining the truth claims made in the ad, critically examining what was not said in the ad, reporting inconsistencies between the ad and the candidate's entire career, and so on. Only ads from the 1988 and 1992 campaigns were examined for an "Ad Watch" component in network stories about them.

[b]Stories that used ads from previous presidential campaigns were not included if they used no ads from the current presidential campaign. Two such popular 1992 "remembrance of things past" news replays were the anti-Goldwater "Daisy Girl" ad from 1964 and the "Willie Horton" ad from 1988, rapidly becoming an "instant classic" in media circles.

What would a *professional* ad-watch standard be like? Research by Jamieson (1992), Cappella and Jamieson (1994), and Pfau and Louden (1993) suggests that whether ad-watch pieces serve the audience may depend on how the pieces are produced. Their research suggests that the correspondent should be visually dominant, with the ad itself visible but shown on a monitor situated a few feet behind the correspondent. Otherwise, they suggest, the ad content may overpower the corrections, commentary, and context being provided by the correspondent. (We agree; we believe a monitor in the background should provide at least enough visual content to allow audience members to recognize the ad when they see it, but neither the ad's audio nor its visuals should dominate.) The Cappella-Jamieson and Pfau-Louden results were based on experiments involving somewhat artificial viewing conditions and a very small number of commercials. Nevertheless, they present highly promising clues for television newspeople who want to do ad-watch stories that do what they are supposed to do—call attention to the claims and methods used in the ads.

IMPACT OF "ATTACK" ADS

After we review again a second major surprise about presidential ads from our 1988 study, we turn to our survey data to see what effects, if any, Clinton, Bush, and Perot ads might have had.

1988's Attack Ads: A Surprise

In 1988, the prevailing media and "insider" wisdom was that the Bush attack ads against Dukakis were devastatingly effective. In fact, at least one writer (Barone, 1988) asserted that the Democrat's failure to respond to the Bush ads was a revealing demonstration of his lack of fitness to be president because it showed Dukakis was out of touch with the questions Americans had about him. The belief in the success of the Roger Ailes-managed ad campaign against Dukakis was not limited to journalists and campaign insiders either. Some campaign scholars may have jumped to that conclusion, too, but fortunately at least one (West, 1993) tried to present some evidence in support of that conclusion. It is on the grounds of the quality of the evidence that we prefer to conduct this argument, an argument that we made at some length in Chapter 1. In essence, we asserted that West's evidence about 1988 was critically flawed because he apparently was unable to compare reactions to Bush's campaign attack versus positive ads. Such a comparison in effect holds the candidate constant while comparing the attack tactic versus the alternative. Instead, West's evidence seemed highly selective, comparing reactions to only one specific ad to the absence of that specific ad, when many more obvious comparisons seemed more warranted. Even this understates the problem because West's most common technique for the 1988 ads apparently was to use the amount of exposure to presidential ads as his key variable. I never could find a clear explanation by West of whether his 1988 comparisons merely took into account different amounts of exposure to any of the Bush ads or even to the ads of both sides. Clearly, neither of these alternative analyses provides a satisfactory basis to decide whether Bush's attack ads worked. Lumping Bush attack and positive ads together cannot tell us whether his attack ads, his positive ads, or both were what helped Bush defeat Dukakis. The second alternative, using exposure to anybody's ads, would produce a circular chain of evidence: Somebody, after all, is going to "win." No matter which candidate wins, we then can look for ad exposure to "explain" that outcome because at least some of the ads were for the winner.

The basic problem may have been that West tried to reanalyze survey data collected by others for other purposes. In neither this nor our previous book are we handicapped by that problem. Our own data about the 1988 campaign ads allowed us to make direct comparisons between negative and positive ads, holding the sponsoring candidate constant. Contrary to the media (and some scholarly) wisdom—and somewhat to our own surprise—we found that the Bush attack ads actually seemed to backfire with the mass audience (Lemert et al., 1991). Beyond that, even Dukakis negative ads, which actually outnumbered those produced by Bush, but did not come close to getting as much airplay, seemed to backfire as well when compared to the Dukakis positive ads.

A 1992 Replication

Our analysis in this chapter uses an approach similar to what we did in our previous book (Lemert et al., 1991). Although we knew when the debates were scheduled and thus could organize a time series around each debate, the schedule of ads obviously was not fully determined by each campaign very far in advance—and would not willingly have been made available to us even if it had been. So we had to be content to ask our survey respondents to tell us the presidential ads they remembered seeing, just as we did during our 1988 interviews.

The information we gathered about the 1992 ads, though, was considerably more detailed than in the 1988 study. Instead of just one ad, we asked our October respondents to recall three presidential campaign ads. More important, we asked them to describe the ads to us—their content, their appearance, and so on—thus allowing us to match descriptions with a list of the campaign ads that we had developed. We found this technique of matching descriptions with our list of ads allowed us more definitively to identify the ad's sponsor. (We found in 1988 that occasionally respondents were very confused about who sponsored certain ads. This seemed especially true of some Dukakis ads, especially one that tried to caricature and otherwise make fun of Bush campaign managers.) Finally, we also asked respondents to tell us whether they thought the ad mostly praised its own candidate or criticized the opponent.

POSSIBLE WEAKNESSES IN STUDY DESIGN

Given that we are measuring exposure to presidential ads by asking respondents to recall them, we need to address two possible criticisms of this approach.

Low Recall. First, if there are very low levels of recall of television news stories (e.g., Robinson & Levy, 1986), why should we expect that respondents will be able to recall televised presidential ads? A basic principle of learning is that repetition enhances recall. Therefore, recall of the ads should be much higher, we think, because the ads are repeated, although network journalists would not be caught dead repeating a given news story. Further working against news recall (but not so much that of advertising) is the fact that television news stories are more deeply embedded in a newscast context in which the next and preceding stories compete with the "target" story for attention and recall. Often these competing news stories are grouped together in sets of related topics, thus enhancing the prospects of mutual interference. In addition, within a given news story, television news conventionally uses techniques that actually interfere with learning, such as using visuals that can distract from the audio content (see Graber, 1993; Robinson & Levy, 1986).

In their study of the 1972 presidential campaign, Patterson and McClure (1976, p. 110) reported that only 21% of their respondents failed to recall anything about a specific campaign ad. Some 52% of their sample were able to recall very specific details about an ad, remarkably close to the 53% who were able to do so in our study of the 1988 campaign (Lemert et al., 1991; see also West, 1993, Chapter 2). As we will see, recall of specific ads was even higher in our 1992 study when we used a slightly more sensitive procedure.

Bias in Ad Recall. The second criticism concerns possible bias in a recall measure. Critics might argue that both the 1988 and 1992 ad effects studies use a survey technique that might attribute too much of an effect to the ads. This criticism proceeds as follows. Because respondents were recalling the ads for us, what is to prevent the recall itself from being selective? Suppose the 1988 attack ads only *seemed* to backfire? Suppose, in other words, people who had absolutely no intention of voting for Bush tended to remember his attack ads because they made them angry? Suppose, as well, people who had no intention ever of voting for Dukakis tended to remember only the Democrat's attack ads? We would then have gotten what appeared to have been a "backlash" effect, when all that was really going on was a widely observed phenomenon called *selective recall.*

In 1988, we found no evidence that recall of *attack* ads was selective: Republicans were as likely as Democrats to recall Bush attack ads; they were also equally likely to recall Dukakis attack ads (Lemert et al., 1991).

We did, however, find evidence that recall of *positive* ads—the kind that praise the sponsoring candidate—was selective. Democrats were more likely to recall Dukakis positives and Republicans Bush positives. Thus, one might still argue that selective recall could have contributed to the appearance of a backlash: Although a candidate's attack ads were recalled by everybody, we were actually comparing attack ads with positive ads by that same candidate, and those positive ads were, indeed, selectively recalled.

Given this mixed and partial support for the selective-recall explanation, the next step we took in our analysis of the 1988 data was to introduce party identification as a "control" variable. In addition, we also controlled for race, gender, income, locale of the interview, and interview date—all *before* we allowed recalled ad exposure to explain anything. Thus, any selective recall related to party and to all the other control variables was extracted from the results before the nature of the ad had any chance to predict the likelihood of voting for Dukakis and Bush. Even after all these controls, attack ads invariably and powerfully worked against the interests of the sponsoring candidate—no matter whether we measured the likelihood of voting for Dukakis or for Bush.

ATTACK ADS IN 1992

We used a similar approach for the three-way race in 1992. Presumably, if we found the same pattern of selective recall in 1992, adherents of the "selective recall" explanation (if they chose not to believe that our controls had eliminated the selective-recall effect) would assert that we should again find attack ads appearing to backfire against both Clinton and Bush. Adherents of a selective-recall explanation would be in trouble if it turned out that attack ads backfired for one candidate but not the other.

Which Ads Were Recalled Most in 1992?

Among our 1,433 October 11-22 respondents,[2] 61% were able to recall both the ad's sponsor and enough detail about the ad to enable us to identify it with a particular ad (e.g., Perot's "diagnosis infomercial"). Roughly another 6% were able to identify both the sponsor and enough content to allow a general identification (e.g., a 30-minute Perot "infomercial" or a Bush "attack" ad). Based on survey respondents' open-ended descriptions of the ads, we were able to match the description with our list of the ads used by the Bush, Clinton, and Perot campaigns.

Ads on behalf of George Bush were recalled most often, followed fairly closely by Perot ads, with Clinton a distant third. So although many campaign insiders noted the sophisticated ad tactics developed by the Clinton campaign, the actual Clinton ads did not come as quickly to people's minds as did both Bush and Perot ads. A second thing to notice is that, although Bush actually had less money for airplay of his ads than either Clinton or Perot (Devlin, 1993), more people recalled his ads than they did those of Perot. And those Bush ads were seen to be attacks (on Clinton).

Bush ads mentioned first were led by the *Time Magazine* cover (81) spot, later withdrawn when *Time* threatened to sue (the cover contained the words, "Why voters don't trust Clinton"). Next most often recalled was the "two-faced Clinton" spot with the blurs obscuring each face (72), then a general reference to an ad attacking Clinton's "draft dodging" (29).

Although Perot's long infomercials were mentioned frequently, it was often difficult to determine from the respondent's description which one it was. The single most commonly identified Perot ad actually was the short "the storm is coming" spot (47 mentions), followed by Perot's first infomercial—the "diagnosis" infomercial (43)—then a short spot about Perot's being loaned a veteran's Purple Heart medal (35), and then a generic reference to a 30-minute infomercial (28).

Among Clinton ads, the most frequently mentioned was one of the several "read my lips" attack spots (52 mentions) that featured Bush's vow to the Republican National Convention in 1988.

Attack Ads in a Three-Way Race

Unlike 1988, 1992 was a three-way presidential race. Another of the bits of campaign wisdom is that if two candidates attack each other in a three-way race, the one who benefits is the one who stays away from running attack ads (e.g., Kurtz, 1992). Bush and Clinton ads clearly took aim at each other. Perot ads were often highly critical of ideas and government performance, but not nearly as often of his opponents personally. In his final infomercial, Perot did make some cracks about whether Clinton's experience—as governor of a state in which chickens were the main industry—qualified him to run the United States. But in general Perot stayed away from personalized attack ads. Our survey questions about presidential ads confirm our impression that Perot stayed away— and even more important, was *seen by our respondents* as staying away— from negative advertising.

Perceptions of "Who Went Negative?"

Table 12.2 presents these results for just the first ad reported by respondents, although the results are overwhelmingly the same regardless of whether they are for the first, second, or third ad. Bush is the candidate who "went negative," our respondents believed.

Table 12.2. Clinton, Bush and Perot Ads: Nature of First Ad Recalled.

Sponsor (N)	Praised Candidate (%)	Criticized Opponent (%)	Praised and Criticized (%)
Saw, but don't know sponsor (N = 109)	45.9	34.9	19.3
Clinton (N = 193)	46.1	45.6	8.3
Bush (N = 390)	15.9	79.2	4.9
Perot (N = 306)	79.1	12.7	8.2

$\chi^2 = 340.57$, $df = 6$, $p < .001$.

If respondents reported a Perot ad, almost 80% of them perceived the ad as primarily praising Perot, rather than attacking an opponent. The percentages of Perot positive ads were even higher for the second (84%) and third mentions (88%).

In marked contrast to Perot, almost 80% of those who reported seeing a Bush ad said the ad primarily criticized an opponent. Clinton fell somewhere in the middle of these two perceived extremes—roughly as many recalled ads praising as criticizing. If we restrict the comparison from Table 12.2 only to Clinton and Bush ads, we find respondents citing attack ads significantly more often for Bush than Clinton ($p < .001$).

Selective Exposure/Recall?

Did it occur: In a word, yes, although perhaps not as strongly as one might expect. In almost every group of voters, Bush ads most often were the first to be mentioned. This was true for both Republicans and Democrats. The only exception was among respondents who described themselves as Independents, and then it was very close: 42.7% mentioned Perot ads first, followed by 39.4% mentioning Bush ads. Clinton ads were mentioned least often by Republicans and Independents, and even Democrats mentioned Bush ads more often (39.7% of all ads mentioned by Democrats, compared to just under 25% of Clinton ads; Perot ads trailed Clinton's among Democrats).

Despite these similarities across party lines, Clinton ads were mentioned somewhat more often by Democrats than by Republicans or Independents. Bush ads were mentioned slightly more often by Republicans than by Democrats and Independents, and Perot ads were mentioned more often by Independents and Republicans than by Democrats (data not tabled; $p < .05$, by chi-square test).

When we used our other questions to break down the ads by type, the tendency toward selective recall got stronger (data not tabled; $p < .002$, by chi-square test). As in 1988, we found that party identification made little or no difference concerning whose negative ads were recalled, but we found big differences regarding whose *positive* ads were. Democrats accounted for nearly two thirds of the mentions of Clinton's positive ads; Republicans accounted for less than 15%. As for Bush positive ads, Republicans accounted for more than 57% of all those mentions, compared to less than 26% by the Democrats. Interestingly, at this more detailed level of analysis there were almost no signs of selective recall of Perot ads. Recall of Perot's ads was fairly evenly distributed across the three party identification groups. Although all of Perot's ads were generally perceived as positives, we also found no evidence that recall of subgroups of Perot ads (e.g., the "storm" spot, the "diagnosis" infomercial, etc.) was selective by party identification groups.

Unlike Republicans and Democrats and their selective recall of their candidate's positive ads, Independents did not exhibit any patterns of selectivity with regard to anybody's ads.

In brief, then, what evidence there was of selective recall concerned who mentioned Bush and Clinton *positive* ads, not who mentioned their negative ads. In other words, we found for 1992 exactly the pattern we observed for 1988—selective recall only for the positive ads done for Democratic and Republican candidates.

The *Bystander* Hypothesis

Perhaps we have the preconditions to test what we might call the *bystander* hypothesis. Based on respondent perceptions, we had two candidates attacking each other, out in front of everybody, while the third lurked in the neighborhood, out of the fray. Did Clinton and Bush hurt each other, then, with their attack ads and thus benefit "bystander" Perot?

We turn now to the October 11-22 data set for evidence concerning the apparent effects of each candidate's ads.

APPARENT EFFECTS OF THE ADS ON CANDIDATES

We start with the most direct and straightforward way to measure effects: voting choice. Table 12.3 relates voting choices to Bush and Clinton attack versus positive ads.

Table 12.3. Bush-Clinton Ad Exposure and Presidential Vote Choice.

Sponsor, Ad Type (N)	Voting Choice (October 11-22)		
	Bush (%)	Clinton (%)	Perot (%)
Clinton Attack Ad (N = 98)	14.3	64.3	21.4
Clinton Positive Ad (N = 80)	17.5	77.5	5.0
Bush Attack Ad (N = 299)	25.8	65.6	8.7
Bush Positive Ad (N = 49)	59.2	32.7	8.2

$\chi^2 = 53.28$, $df = 6$, $p < .001$, for entire table.
$\chi^2 = 13.68$, $df = 2$, $p < .01$, when comparing only Clinton attack versus Clinton positive ads.
$\chi^2 = 22.22$, $df = 2$, $p < .001$, when comparing only Bush attack versus Bush positive ads.

Here we have our first clue that the "bystander" hypothesis might have some support, at least with regard to the Clinton attack ads. Although only 11% of all respondents in this table intended in October to vote for Perot, 21% of those exposed to Clinton attack ads did. Meanwhile, notice in Table 12.3 that people who reported exposure to Bush attack ads were twice as likely to say they would vote for Clinton as those who reported exposure to Bush's positive ads. So our first look suggests that Bush attack ads may have backfired against him—helping his Democratic Party opponent, just as they did in 1988—and that Clinton attack ads may have hurt Bush slightly but clearly helped Perot.

Recall, however, that party identification predicted reported recall of both Clinton and Bush positive ads. Obviously, then, we need at least to control for party before we attach much weight to the Table 12.3 results for Bush and Clinton ads. If we can hold party identification constant and still find that Bush attack ads seemed to backfire whereas Clinton ads helped Perot and hurt Bush, we will have shown that party identification cannot account for all of what is going on. When we tried to do this, however, we quickly ran into a fairly common problem with the Chi-square statistic: It is very vulnerable to low numbers of cases when we divide the cases in a larger table into three—Republican, Democrat, and Independent. Although we have 140 Republicans, 239 Democrats and 105 Independents for each of these less well-populated versions of Table 12.3, at least half the 12 cells in each of these tables suffer from problems resulting from low numbers. With that warning about possible instabilities in the findings, let us summarize what these tables showed.

Among Republicans, the Bush vote was considerably lower, Clinton's slightly higher, and Perot's much higher for a Clinton attack ad. Republicans who reported exposure to a Clinton positive ad were very much more likely to vote for Bush. This pattern for Clinton ads even more emphatically echoes what we saw for the larger sample in Table 12.3. As for the Bush ads, exposure to his attack ads was associated with slightly lower Bush and slightly higher Clinton and Perot voting—the same pattern as in Table 12.3, but just a faint echo of it for the Republicans.

Among Democrats, Clinton attack ads were associated with a very high Clinton vote, no votes at all for Bush, and only one vote for Perot. In contrast, Democrats who reported exposure to positive Clinton ads were more likely to vote for either Bush or Perot than their counterparts who reported exposure to Clinton attack ads. Exposure to Bush attack ads, which was almost as high for Democrats as for Republicans, was associated with a higher rate of Clinton voting than when the Democrat reported exposure to a Bush positive ad. In brief, the larger patterns in Table 12.3 for Bush ads and Clinton ads were clearly echoed among Democrats, with the single exception that it was Clinton, not Perot, who was helped by Clinton attacks ads.

Among Independents, Clinton attack ads may have hurt Bush, but they probably helped Perot among Independents much more than they did Clinton. Not a single Independent who saw a Clinton attack ad would vote for Bush. But only 47% of Independents who reported exposure to a Clinton attack ad would vote for Clinton, compared to 79% of Independents who first mentioned a positive Clinton ad. How did the Bush ads seem to play? As was true of the Democrats and, more weakly, of Republicans, Bush attack ads seemed to produce a higher Clinton vote and lower Bush vote than did Bush's positive ads. In general, Independents fully echoed the findings for Bush attack ads (see Table 12.3), but Clinton's attack ads may have damaged both Bush and Clinton among Independents while giving Perot a big boost.

In summary, when we ran exposure to Bush and Clinton ads against voting choice, controlling for party identification, Bush attack ads seemed to hurt Bush and help Clinton in each of the three party groups. Clinton's attack ads seemed to hurt Bush and help Perot among Republicans and Independents. Among Democrats, Clinton's attack ads seemed to hurt Bush and help Clinton, not Perot.

These results, partly based as they are on potentially unstable numbers and using only party as a single control, need to be tested with more powerful analytic tools. Fortunately, we can do that.

ANALYZING VOTING INTENSITY

The tables to follow use an analytic procedure called Multiple Classification Analysis (MCA). MCA becomes available to us when we shift away from voting choice—a categorical variable, with values of "Bush," "Clinton," "Perot," "Don't Know," and so on—to a scale that measures the intensity of voting preferences. This intensity measure asked respondents to rate, on a 0 to 10 scale, their likelihoods of voting for each of the three presidential candidates. We can then use MCA simultaneously to control for party identification and as many as eight other predictors.

What MCA allows us to do is statistically to extract the influence of a number of "control" variables—such as political party identification—before we allow ad exposure to explain voting likelihoods. In other words, ad exposure as a variable only gets the "leftovers." If reported ad exposure stands up against all these rival predictors, a much more convincing case can be made that the type of ad seen does affect likelihoods of voting for each of the respective candidates. (Chapter 5 provides more information about how to "read" MCA tables.)

Possible Multiple Controls

What are these control variables, then? We control *Party* identification, of course, because it predicts recall of Bush and Clinton positive ads. Other controls we can exert may predict either or both whose ad—and what type—is mentioned and voting intensity for Bush, Clinton, or Perot.

Education is an obvious control to exert because we saw in our other results that education is related to candidate choice (as education declines, voting for Perot and Bush rises) as well as recall of political ads (as education rises, the number of ads recalled also rises).

We suspect that *Internal and External Efficacy* feelings may well predict, at the very least (see Chapter 6), voting for both Bush and Perot. We used two Internal and two External Efficacy scales as controls, bringing us to a total of six controls so far.

Campaign Interest may very well predict either/or both ad recall and the intensity of support for any of the three presidential candidates.

We know from results bearing on Perot (see Chapter 6) that the intensity of support for Perot grew over time in the fall campaign. So we also tried interview *Wave* as another control. Because this part of our analysis was based on our large October 11-22 data set, we are talking about Waves 2 through 5 here: October 11 and 12 (Wave 2); October 13 and 14 (Wave 3); October 15, 16, 17, and 18 (Wave 4); and October 19, 20, 21, and 22 (Wave 5). That already brings us to eight controls.

Panel is a variable describing whether or not the October respondents had been interviewed in September. Most had not, but if we were to combine October panelists with our large October sample in order to maximize the number of cases, we should protect against the possibility that the September interview had sensitized panelists, so we introduced that as a control as well (nine controls so far).

Sex is another potential control variable; we know from other analyses (Chapter 6) that women were less likely to vote for Perot than were men (that's 10 controls).

Locale of the interview is strongly related to voting, with residents of Indianapolis much more likely to vote for Bush than residents of the other three areas. In addition, because the Clinton campaign placed more of its ads on a local—rather than national—basis, we might want to control locale anyway. That way, we could guard against the effects of possible discrepancies among the ads shown in each market. Furthermore, given racial and other demographic differences among the four interviewing sites, we could use locale as a kind of last-ditch, surrogate control for several other demographics that we did not otherwise control. So that is control 11. Unfortunately, the MCA procedure[3] limits us to a maximum of 10 predictor variables—nine controls plus the political ad variable.

Eliminating Superfluous Controls. We have 11 plausible control variables, 2 more than we can accommodate in any single MCA once we add our twelfth predictor—ad exposure. Thus, in order to pare our list down to the maximum of 10, we had to run various combinations of 10 predictors in order to see which produced the most clearcut and powerful analyses. Always, the ad variable was entered as the last of the 10 predictors.

One rule of thumb in eliminating predictors was that if any of them did not relate to the dependent variable in any of our MCAs, it could be discarded to make room for one that did. A second rule of thumb was that we tried to keep in all three of our analyses any variable that predicted at least two of the three candidate voting likelihood ratings. Finally, all else being equal, we used the MCA solution that explained the greatest amount of variation on the 0 to 10 voting likelihood measures.

Whether or not October respondents were a panelist made no difference in their ratings of voting preferences for any of the three candidates, so that control was eliminated. Once controls for education, campaign interest, and efficacy were exerted, interview wave no longer predicted voting likelihood for any of the candidates, so wave was eliminated from the MCAs. Sex strongly predicted voting likelihood only for Perot, so it was kept as a control variable only for the Perot voting measure. The four efficacy measures—"Politics Too Complicated," "I Could Do as Good a Job" (both measures of Internal Efficacy), "the People Have the Final Say," and "Politicians Won't Listen" (both External Efficacy)—had mixed success as control variables but were retained for all analyses.

Does Ad Exposure Predict Voting Likelihood?

Tables 12.4 (Clinton), 12.5 (Bush), and 12.6 (Perot) present the full MCA results for the odds of voting for each of the respective candidates.

Clinton. As years of education increased, so did the odds of voting for Clinton (Table 12.4). As the respondent's agreement rose that he or she could do as good a job in public office as most people, the likelihood of voting for Clinton also rose. Under locale, note how much less likely the Indianapolis residents were to vote for Clinton. As we certainly expected, Democratic Party identification strongly predicted voting for Clinton, even when party was placed relatively low in the hierarchy of predictors. Given the least favorable position of all, ad exposure nevertheless strongly predicted the rated odds of voting for Clinton. Among those able to report exposure to a specific ad, the highest three means for voting Clinton were: Clinton attack ads (6.84), Clinton positive ads (6.72), and Bush attack ads (6.34). Note as well that the lowest odds of voting for Clinton (adjusted mean of 4.13) were for a small number of people who reported seeing a Bush ad, but could not remember more than that about it. Interestingly, the next lowest odds were among people who reported seeing Perot's first infomercial—the "diagnosis" infomercial.

Bush. Table 12.5 presents results for Bush. All but one of the control variables significantly predicted Bush voting odds. As respondents' years of education and confidence that they could do a reasonably good job in public office declined, the odds of voting Bush went up. Similarly, those who agreed that sometimes politics seemed too complicated for them to understand were more likely to vote for Bush. In essence, then, as scores on each of the Internal Efficacy scales went down, the odds of voting Bush went up. In remarkable contrast, however, both External Efficacy measures were positively related to Bush voting. As disagreement that politicians would not listen to the people increased (i.e., respondents gave the high External Efficacy answers), the rated odds of voting for Bush went up. And as agreement increased that the people have the final say, the odds of voting for Bush also went up.

Once again, locale made a big difference, with Indianapolis respondents most likely to vote for Bush. Not surprisingly, Republican identification also strongly predicted the odds of voting for Bush; note that Republicans were the only group in the entire table to have a mean rating at 5.0 or above on this 0 to 10 scale.

Table 12.4. Summary of Multiple Classification Analysis[a]: Political Ad Exposure and Probability of Voting for Bill Clinton October 11-22 ($N = 965$); Adjusted Mean Scores and Regression Coefficients.

Predictors	Probability of Voting for Bill Clinton
Regressions	
Education	.094**
Efficacy Items	
Too complicated	—
Do good job	.208**
Final say	—
Won't listen	—
Campaign Interest	—
Adjusted Means	
Locale	
Carbondale, IL	6.24***
Eugene, OR	6.23
Philadelphia, PA	6.32
Indianapolis, IN	5.38
Political Party	
Republican	2.63***
Democrat	8.53
Ind	5.88
First Ad Mentioned (N)	
Think saw, don't know who (45)	5.61***
Saw, don't know who (109)	6.64
Clinton's attack ad (87)	6.84
Clinton's positive ad (74)	6.72
Bush, don't know more (12)	4.13
Bush's attack ad (280)	6.34
Bush's positive ad (43)	5.40
Perot's infomercial (85)	5.34
Perot "storm" (39)	5.98
"Diagnosis" infomercial (40)	4.93
Perot other (147)	5.67

*$p < .10$.
**$p < .05$.
***$p < .01$.
[a]For a more complete discussion of how to read MCA tables, see Chapter 5.

Table 12.5. Summary of Multiple Classification Analysis[a]: Political Ad Exposure and Probability of Voting for George Bush October 11-22 (N = 965); Adjusted Mean Scores and Regression Coefficients.

Predictors	Probability of Voting for George Bush
Regressions	
Education	-.078**
Efficacy Items	
Too complicated	.221***
Do good job	-.290
Final say	.391
Won't listen	-.198**
Campaign Interest	—
Adjusted Means	
Locale	
Carbondale, IL	3.31***
Eugene, OR	3.08
Philadelphia, PA	3.38
Indianapolis, IN	4.08
Political Party	
Republican	6.87***
Democrat	1.35
Ind	2.94
First Ad Mentioned (N)	
Think saw, don't know who (45)	3.94***
Saw, don't know who (109)	2.86
Clinton's attack ad (87)	2.90
Clinton's positive ad (74)	3.83
Bush, don't know more (12)	4.73
Bush's attack ad (280)	3.37
Bush's positive ad (43)	4.48
Perot's infomercial (85)	3.28
Perot "storm" (39)	3.38
"Diagnosis" infomercial (40)	3.79
Perot other (147)	3.45

*$p < .10$.
**$p < .05$.
***$p < .01$.
[a]For a more complete discussion of how to read MCA tables, see Chapter 5.

Table 12.6. Summary of Multiple Classification Analysis[a]: Political Ad Exposure and Probability of Voting for Ross Perot October 11-22 ($N = 965$); Adjusted Mean Scores and Regression Coefficients.

Predictors	Probability of Voting for Ross Perot
Regressions	
Education	-.110*
Efficacy Items	
Too complicated	—
Do good job	.208**
Final say	—
Won't listen	.375***
Campaign Interest	—
Adjusted Means	
Locale	—
Political Party	
Republican	3.33***
Democrat	2.58
Ind	4.25
Gender	
Female	2.84***
Male	3.64
First Ad Mentioned (N)	
Think saw, don't know who (45)	2.91***
Saw, don't know who (109)	3.06
Clinton's attack ad (87)	3.70
Clinton's positive ad (74)	2.50
Bush, don't know more (12)	2.25
Bush's attack ad (280)	2.72
Bush's positive ad (43)	2.64
Perot's infomercial (85)	4.25
Perot "storm" (39)	3.27
"Diagnosis" infomercial (40)	3.87
Perot other (144)	3.88

*$p < .10$.
**$p < .05$.
***$p < .01$.
[a] For a more complete discussion of how to read MCA tables, see Chapter 5.

Finally, ad exposure again made a significant (p = .042) difference, with Bush ads ("can't describe any further") and Bush positive ads having by far the highest odds and the odds for Bush attack ads more than a full rating unit below. Among those able to recall a specific ad, the lowest odds of voting for Bush were for Clinton attack ads, again suggesting that Clinton attacks against Bush seemed to hurt Bush, whereas Bush's own attack ads were counterproductive.

We turn now to the results for Ross Perot (see Table 12.6).

Perot. As was true of Bush voting, the *lower* the years of education, the greater the odds the respondent would vote for Perot. Unlike Bush voting, though, the greater respondents' confidence that they could do as good a job as most people in public office, the higher the odds of voting Perot. Also unlike Bush voting, lower External Efficacy (high agreement that politicians will not listen) predicted stronger odds of voting Perot. (Recall that lower Internal and higher External Efficacy predicted higher odds of voting for Bush.) Interestingly, locale made no difference in Perot voting odds, very much unlike the rated odds for either Clinton or Bush.

Democrats were substantially less willing to vote Perot and Independents more, with Republicans in between. Women were far less willing to vote for Perot than were men. (As mentioned previously, Perot was the only candidate for whom gender related to voting odds.)

Finally, exposure to presidential ads strongly predicted the odds of voting Perot ($p = .001$). The greatest odds (4.29 on a 0 to 10 scale) were associated with having seen one of the Perot infomercials, but Clinton's attack ads (3.66) also fell comfortably in the middle of the other Perot commercials, which ranged from a low of 3.26 to 3.95. This finding confirms earlier findings that the Clinton attack ads helped Perot as the "bystander."

Although party identification was strongly related to each of the voting likelihood measures, the multiple predictors collectively accounted for a considerably smaller share of respondent-to-respondent variance in the Perot ratings than in Clinton's and Bush's. And this occurred despite the fact that Perot ratings had one more predictor—gender—than the Clinton and Bush ratings did. The unique absence of a relationship to locale only for Perot—and Perot's uniquely national TV campaign—may provide a clue to part of the explanation. On the other hand, though, Perot's actual voting percentages varied considerably among the 50 states.

A Closer Look at Attack Ads. We can visualize the apparent impact of the Clinton and Bush attack ads more easily by isolating them and running another set of MCAs. Table 12.7 presents these results in two subtables. Table 12.7A presents the MCA comparison for Bush attack versus positive ads. Even after all the controls present in the larger

MCAs have been exerted, we find the odds of voting Bush are significantly lower when the Bush ad is a negative one.

Table 12.7B presents the results for Clinton's ads. Once again, we find confirmation that Clinton attack ads damaged Bush and helped Perot, while leaving the voting odds for Clinton essentially the same.

PANEL RESULTS

For a variety of reasons, including panel attrition and especially attrition in the numbers of viewers who recalled seeing the specific ad groupings used in Tables 12.3 to 12.7, our best evidence on voting impact of the ads comes from the much larger October 11-22 data set.

Table 12.7. Attack vs. Positive Ad Tactics Comparisons for George Bush and Bill Clinton: Multiple Classification Analysis Adjusted Mean Scores[a].

	A. George Bush Ads		
Bush Ad Type	Probability of Voting for Bill Clinton	Probability of Voting for George Bush	Probability of Voting for Ross Perot
Attack	6.30	3.39[b]	2.65
Positive	5.59	4.52	2.53

	B. Bill Clinton Ads		
Clinton Ad Type	Probability of Voting for Bill Clinton	Probability of Voting for George Bush	Probability of Voting for Ross Perot
Attack	6.84	2.91[b]	3.71[b]
Positive	6.72	3.42	2.45

[a]The adjusted means reported in this table will sometimes differ slightly from those in Tables 12.2 through 12.4 because many cases used to adjust for the effects of control variables in those previous MCA tables have been lost from the MCAs used to adjust (and test) the means in this table. In all cases, however, each of the control variables that were potent predictors in Tables 12.2 through 12.4 remained potent in these smaller MCAs.

[b]Means for attack vs. positive ad tactics used by this candidate differ at $p < .05$ for the 0 to 10 rating of odds that the respondent will vote for the candidate listed at the top of this column. Thus, Bush attack ads are compared with Bush positive ads; Clinton attack ads are compared with Clinton positive ads.

However, there were enough panel cases for us to break down October-November changes in ratings of the presidential campaign ads as an information source.[4] Interestingly, although never highly rated in comparison to other presidential campaign information sources, presidential ads were rated significantly more useful in November (mean of 3.81 on a 0 to 10 scale) than they were in October (3.22). Can we link these generally more favorable ratings to the ads themselves? Some 153 of the 199 panelists who rated the ads both in October and November were able in November to recall the most memorable presidential ad they had seen and to describe it in enough detail to be categorized. (Note that the form of this ad exposure question differs slightly from that asked in October, in which we just asked respondents, in turn, each to recall an ad they had seen, up to a maximum of three.)

The number of cases for each specific category of ad varied from a low of 3 (Perot's "diagnosis" infomercial) to a high of 27 (a tie between Bush and Clinton attack ads), so we decided to combine a few of the categories in order to get more stable estimates of mean changes for each advertising group. (These combinations did not change the patterns of mean changes.)

If people did not like attack ads, we might expect that exposure to Clinton and Bush attack ads would not be associated with a growth in support of ads as an information vehicle. In contrast, reported exposure to Perot ads (overwhelmingly seen as positive) and to positive Bush and Clinton ads should predict rising support for these polispots as information sources.

Table 12.8 presents these results for October-November changes in ad ratings. The table uses MCA to control for campaign interest, each of the four Internal and External Efficacy scales, party identification, and locale. Interestingly, none of the control variables predicted *change* in ad usefulness ratings, but the ad cited did. The greatest improvement in ratings was for Clinton's positive ads (+2.46, on a 0 to 10 scale). A very intriguing finding was that even the Bush positive ads were associated with *negative* change in ad usefulness ratings, followed closely by Bush attack ads. In other words, if Bush ads came to mind, it did not matter whether they were positive or negative. No other ad groups were associated with a drop in the evaluation of the ads, not even Clinton attack ads, which showed a very slight improvement in the value placed on presidential campaign ads as an information source. In general, Perot's infomercials were especially linked to an increase in rated usefulness of the ads.

Although these more detailed comparisons were not tabled, we used the same MCA technique to compare only Clinton attack and positive ads, only Bush attack versus positive ads, and all Perot ads combined versus the other ads.

Table 12.8. Summary of Multiple Classification Analysis[a]: Political Ad Exposure and October-November Changes in Value Placed on Presidential Ads as Information Sources; Adjusted Mean Scores and Regression Coefficients.

Predictors	Value of Presidential Ads
Regressions	
Campaign Interest	—
Efficacy Items	
Too complicated	—
Do good job	—
Final say	—
Won't listen	—
Adjusted Means	
Locale	—
Political Party	—
Ad Mentioned (N)	
Clinton's attack ad (27)	+ 0.23***
Clinton's positive ad (14)	+ 2.46
Bush's attack ad (27)	- 0.40
Bush's positive ad (14)	- 0.68
Perot don't know more (8)	+ 0.89
Perot's infomercial (25)	+ 1.61
Perot "storm" (4)	+ 1.12
Perot other (26)	+ 0.40

*$p < .10$.
**$p < .05$.
***$p < .01$.
[a]For a more complete discussion of how to read MCA tables, see Chapter 5.

Clinton Attack versus Positive Ads

If November panelists recalled seeing a Clinton attack ad, ratings of the value of presidential ads actually went down slightly when the adjusted means were calculated for this minitable, whereas if they recalled a Clinton positive ad, ratings of the ads went up by almost a full 3 points. These changes by Clinton ad type differed significantly at $p < .02$.

Bush Attack versus Positive Ads

Inspection of Table 12.8 already suggests that the tone of the Bush ad made no difference. In each case, ratings of the value of presidential ads went down from October to November. This result was confirmed by a comparison of only the two types of Bush ads.

Perot Ads Combined

Although Table 12.8 showed some slight variations among the Perot ads, in general the Perot ads seemed to make people reporting exposure to them feel better about the value of presidential ads. This impression was confirmed ($p < .001$) when we combined all the Perot ads, left the rest of Table 12.8 as it was, and tested for any differences. Only the Clinton positive ads were associated with a greater improvement than the Perot ads.

SUMMARY AND CONCLUSIONS

Although many commentators seem to have concluded that the news media did a much better job of being the Ad Police in the 1992 presidential campaign, network news seems to have left much room for improvement. In only one month, a single reporter for CNN matched the total ad watches by ABC, CBS, and NBC, *combined*, for the entire Fall campaign. Among newspapers, *USA Today*, the *St. Louis Post-Dispatch*, and the *Portland Oregonian* were not listed as prominently as they should have been as presidential Ad Police. Because policing television ads may be easier when you do not have to replay the ads, and because the corrections and perspectives can be clipped out and consulted again, perhaps newspapers may actually have an advantage over TV news here, especially if the TV Ad Police put the actual ad in the foreground of the report. A printed photo of an identifying moment in the ad should allow the voter to recognize the spot when it is on television, analogous to playing only the visual of an identifiable segment of the ad on a TV monitor located behind the correspondent.

Despite the fact that Bush ads received somewhat less paid airplay than did those of Clinton, and despite the fact that Perot spent more money on airplay than either of his rivals, Bush attack ads dominated recalled exposure to presidential ads.

It is often said that people recall attack ads more easily than positive ones. Yet Perot ads usually were not seen as negative, and recalled exposure to his ads was second only to that for Bush. Clinton ads, although often mentioned by critics and political junkies as "state of the art," were not recalled nearly as often as the Bush and Perot ads.

Early in this chapter, we raised and tried to answer concerns about relying on recall of ads to index exposure to them. We pointed out that recall of presidential ads is rather high—and not as selective as one might expect. Both in 1988 and in 1992, there was no party-related selective recall of attack ads. There also seemed no relation between party identification and recall of the various Perot ads. However, there was selective recall (by Republicans and Democrats only) of positive ads for their respective party standard bearers—both in 1988 and in 1992. This finding compelled controlling for party identification before we tried to draw any conclusions about ad effects, and in the MCAs we introduced a large number of other controls before we allowed reported ad exposure to explain anything. What we found was that the Bush attack ads seemed to hurt Bush and help his Democratic rival—a classic repeat of 1988, in other words. But Clinton attack ads did not work the same way. They appeared to hurt Bush and help Perot, who unlike his two major party rivals generally was not seen as running attack ads and thus seemed *selectively* to benefit from the "bystander" phenomenon. Why selective? Because Perot benefited from Clinton attack ads, not Bush ads. Only Clinton seemed to gain from Bush's attacks on him. In general, Perot ads seemed to help only him, without any carryover to either Bush or Clinton, although there was some suggestion that his "diagnosis" infomercial was associated with lower odds of voting Clinton.

We found solid evidence that attack ads made as big a difference in 1992 as in 1988. By the way, our questions about exposure to ads came very early in the October questionnaires, and the voting intent questions came near the end, 20 minutes later. There was no evidence of any selective recall of the Perot ads, but exposure to them seemed to help Perot.

Despite all this, perhaps diehard adherents of a "biased recall" explanation might wish to continue to say that people who always intended to vote for Bush would tend to recall Bush positive ads. Even if that were true for Bush in 1988 and in 1992, how could these adherents explain the marked differences in reactions to the 1988 Dukakis attack ads and to the 1992 Clinton attack ads? In 1988, both major party candidates seemed to be affected the same way by their own attack ads; in 1992, each seemed affected by his own attack ads in different ways. Each year, Bush was the only candidate whose own attack ads seemed to hurt him and help his Democratic opponent. In contrast, Clinton's attack ads seemed to achieve their purpose of damaging their target's election prospects, but they also intensified support for Perot. Furthermore, unlike 1988, the Democrat's attack ads were not associated with a comparatively weaker preference for him. In other words, for the two major party candidates, we had an identical (although relatively weak) pattern of selective recall in each year, yet the relationships between recalled ad exposure and voting differed radically from 1988 to 1992.

Here is another difference. There was considerable evidence in 1988 that exposure to either Bush or Dukakis attack ads dismayed respondents about the "mudslinging" quality of that campaign. In 1992 it was primarily Bush ads—whether they were negative or positive—that were associated with a drop in the already low value respondents had for presidential campaign ads. Overall, the rated value of the ads as information sources actually increased among panelists recalling Perot and Clinton ads.

Given the same pattern of selective recall in 1992 and 1988 for the two major party candidates, it is hard to see how any adherent of a biased-recall explanation could account for the quite different array of effects apparent in 1992 compared to 1988.

Why did only Bush attack ads backfire against him and help his opponent? And why was it that only the Bush ads were associated with a decline in the perceived information value of presidential ads? A narrow answer to the first question would point to the differences between Clinton and Bush ad tactics in 1992.

Clinton attack ads often relied on using sound bites from actual news footage, with minimalist audio commentary, thus making Bush and what he was saying the issue—not Clinton, not the editing, and not the voice-over script. In contrast, when Bush tried to use "actual" footage, it was in the form of a manifestly altered, edited, and speeded-up montage of Arkansas Governor Clinton signing various alleged "tax and spend" bills, with no audio content at all from Clinton.

Other Clinton spots used the familiar device of the newspaper or magazine reprint, lending independent credence to a Clinton rebuttal of Bush charges. But when Bush tried to use the *Time* Magazine cover, with its line about why citizens do not trust Clinton, the magazine moved quickly and with much publicity to force Bush to stop using its cover, thus snatching away whatever documentation the ad had (this was the single most frequently recalled Bush attack ad, by the way) and leaving Bush vulnerable to charges that he had tried to misrepresent *Time's* position on Clinton.

A broader answer might cover both the Bush attack ad backfire and the apparent impact of both the positive and negative Bush ads on the perceived information value of 1992's presidential ads. If Americans resented the 1988 advertising campaign—and they did, according to our *News Verdicts* results for that campaign—perhaps they were "primed" by memories of that experience to look closely at whether Bush would try to do again what he did in 1988. This "priming effect" may also explain why it was that Bush ads were recalled by more people than were those by either of his competitors, despite the fact that both his competitors spent more money on paid airplay than Bush was able to do.

ENDNOTES

1. All these stories appeared on CNN's Inside Politics from September 26, 1992 to October 26, 1992. The counts for the three older networks covered the period from September 1 through the day of the election, November 3.
2. This number includes both panelists and our single-interview respondents because panelists and single-interview respondents did not differ in their ability to recall the ads, and there was also no evidence that they differed in their voting preferences for each of the three candidates.
3. This limitation occurs with the SPSSX statistical package.
4. Because the September question about presidential ads differed importantly from the way the question was asked in October and November, we could not use the September ratings in any analysis of change.

REFERENCES

Barone, M. (1988, October 11). These Dukakis ads just don't work. *The Washington Post*, p. A19.

Cappella, J.N., & Jamieson, K.H. (1994). Broadcast adwatch effects. *Communication Research, 21*, 342-365.

Davison, W.P. (1983) The third-person effect in communication. *Public Opinion Quarterly, 65*, 91-106.

Devlin, L.P. (1989). Contrasts in presidential campaign commercials of 1988. *American Behavioral Scientist, 32*, 389-414.

Devlin, L.P. (1993). Contrasts in presidential campaign commercials of 1992. *American Behavioral Scientist, 37*, 272-290.

Freedom Forum. (1992, 1993). *A series of special election reports.* New York: The Freedom Form Studies Center, Columbia University.

Garrett, M. (1992, October 8). Perot's no Roseanne, but he gets into millions of homes anyway. *The Washington Times*, p. A4.

Graber, D.A. (1993). Failures in news transmission: Reasons and remedies. In P. Gaunt (Ed.), *Beyond agendas: New directions in communication research* (pp. 75-89). Westport, CT: Greenwood Press.

Jackson, B. (1992, September). Gotcha!: How to avoid getting busted by the ad police. *Campaigns & Elections*, p. 51.

Jamieson, K.H. (1992). *Dirty politics: Deception, distraction, and democracy.* New York: Oxford University Press.

Kurtz, H. (1992, October 26). Negative ads appear to lose potency. *The Washington Post,* p. A1.

Lemert, J.B., Elliott, W.R., Bernstein, J.M., Rosenberg, W.L., & Nestvold, K.J. (1991). *News verdicts, the debates, and presidential campaigns.* New York: Praeger.

McKibben, G. (1992, November 2). Should newspapers print the time of a candidate's tv ad? *The Boston Globe,* p. 13.

Patterson, T., & McClure, R.D. (1976). *The unseeing eye.* New York: Putnam.

Pfau, M., & Louden, A. (1993, November). *The effectiveness of television news adwatch formats in deflecting the influence of campaign polispots.* Paper presented at the meeting of the Speech Communication Association, Miami, FL.

Robinson, J.P., & Levy, M.R. (1986). *The main source: Learning from television news.* Beverly Hills: Sage.

Rosenstiel, T. (1993). *Strange bedfellows.* New York: Hyperion.

West, D.M. (1993). *Air wars: Television advertising in election campaigns, 1952-1992.* Washington, DC: Congressional Quarterly.

13

The Role of Polls and Polling in the '92 Campaign

William L. Rosenberg

Polls are a central feature of modern election campaigns. We can distinguish between three users of surveys or polls: polls done by and for the news media, polls done by and for the presidential *campaign organizations*, and surveys (academics prefer the words "sample survey") done by academics. Most surveys done by academics—such as the ones done by us for this book—have much more relaxed deadlines for release and generally involve many more questions and more intense analysis. Almost always, both the news media polls and those done for campaign organizations are completed and used before the election is over, for obvious reasons. The campaigns are conducting research that is proprietary. They wish to understand who supports them and who does not. They also seek to understand the issues that are sensitive to the voters so that they can position their campaigns appropriately. The media use opinion research to guide their coverage and, presumably, to inform the public about the candidates and issues. The academic community uses opinion research to address the underlying questions of how and why certain phenomena present themselves within public's opinion structure and knowledge base.

This chapter concentrates on polling done for the 1992 Bush and Clinton presidential campaign organizations and for the news media.

POLLING FOR THE CAMPAIGNS

History

Internally, campaigns have used survey research for a number of years. Until the 1960 election the use of polls was rather simple and not taken seriously by the campaigns themselves. The political leadership was largely not familiar with the techniques nor the consequences of using "modern analysis." Throughout the early 1960s the analysis that was done was often rudimentary frequencies—the percentage who chose one response versus another—and "cross-tabs"—the comparison of specific groups (e.g., males and females) on a variable such as whom the individual planned to vote for. One early example of the more sophisticated campaign use of scientific opinion research was in the 1960 campaign. The Kennedy campaign, using faculty from MIT, Yale and Columbia, developed the Simulates Project. This project involved the use of 130,000 survey responses collected between 1952 and 1959. The purpose behind the project was to conduct "what if" analysis, that is, trial balloons that could be tested against already collected survey results in order to predict voter reactions to various policy positions. The reliability of the early polls was generally thought to be guaranteed by having large sample sizes and reporting only frequencies or simple cross-tabulations (e.g., candidate support by party; see Kessel, 1988, pp. 139-140).

In the 1964 campaign, Barry Goldwater's staff sought to undertake three national surveys that were under the supervision of a bright but recent graduate of Stanford Law school who had had no training at all in survey research. The third survey was not even fielded because the campaign felt that the information from the first two was not producing positive findings. Over the next few years, politicians became more dependent on the polls. By 1976, pollsters even began to have prominent positions within the campaign organizations. Pollsters such as Robert Teeter of Market Opinion Research for the Republicans and Pat Cadell for Jimmy Carter became central fixtures in the campaigns. By 1984, Teeter and Richard Wirthlin of Decision Making Information were directing much of the Republican's strategy, whereas Peter Hart and Pat Cadell were doing likewise for the Democrats. It is interesting that the backgrounds and training of these skilled individuals were still limited in terms of formal training. Peter Hart had no formal academic training at all in the field of survey research, but rather had cut his teeth in the field by simply doing it. As he produced results that were considered correct, he gained stature and thus "became expert" (Hart, personal communication with William L. Rosenberg, 1978).

Over time the pollsters increased the usefulness of the information they provided to the campaigns beyond the rudimentary descriptive statistics and cross-tabs. In the 1980 campaign, Richard Wirthlin and Richard Beal built on an "MIT-like model" similar to the one used by the 1960 Kennedy campaign. They developed the Political Information System (PINS), which utilized an extensive bank of survey data that was then used as the basis to simulate "what if" strategies that the Reagan campaign might wish to consider. By having expert systems and professional analysts involved in the central core of advisors, the "making of the president" took on a whole new dimension.

Today, all Presidential campaigns maintain large-scale survey research teams to conduct opinion research using both focus groups and large samples of voters. These data are closely held by the campaigns, in contrast to the public surveys conducted by the media organizations and those in the academic community. By 1980, CBS researchers had determined that there were at least 147 public polling organizations at the state or regional level, with almost a third established between 1978 and 1980 (Dionne, 1980).

Bush and Clinton Campaigns

The Bush and Clinton campaigns, unlike the Perot campaign, were heavily involved in opinion research. The Bush team's efforts were directed by Fred Steeper, whereas Clinton's barometer was Stan Greenberg of the Analysis Group. During the campaign both sides undertook national as well as cross-sectional surveys. They also monitored media coverage of national and state opinion polls, as well as candidates' polls of their party members running in the states.

As Election Day drew near, both camps were monitoring their respective "tracking polls" and relevant political research to determine their strengths and weaknesses. A tracking poll is a poll that is done on a daily basis, which serves to provide updated opinion data so that campaigns can judge how they are doing at a particular point in time, especially in connection with events as they occur during the campaign. The purposes of tracking polls are similar to the time-series survey design in our own study: We built a time series around each of the debates in an effort to trace reactions as they developed each day after the debate (see Chapter 2).

Both campaigns used survey research to prioritize which states were winnable, toss-ups, or hopeless. On the basis of this determination the campaigns adjusted their political strategy and resources. According to Greenberg (Clinton's pollster), the Clinton campaign was targeting states in which it had a lead of 8% or more, with a total of at least 370

Electoral College votes, well over the minimum needed. The Democrats did not want to waste resources on states in which they were either running even or losing, but rather sought to cement their lead in the states that they felt were in their camp. The Republicans devised a rank-order system based on their opinion data from 29 states. This list contained those states that the Republicans felt they needed to win in order to reach the minimum winning level of 270 Electoral College votes. As it turned out, the Democrats eventually won 10 of the bottom 11 states on the Republican's 29-state listing ("Hotline electoral scoreboard," 1992).

Both Steeper and Greenberg used national polls. Steeper also used aggregated trend lines and decided that the actual poll numbers would be the average of all of the six national quality polls ("Hotline conference call," 1992). A week before the election Greenberg was working primarily from two databases. The first was a series of two-day surveys, whereas the second was a national simulated model based on state polls. Greenberg indicated that if they did not have a poll of their own, they used the most conservative poll available, that is, the one with the lowest Clinton estimate of strength. He found that the Clinton numbers were at a high of +13% after the October 15 Presidential debate. That lead then began to dwindle quickly to +11% then +9% and eventually to +7%. By the October 26-27 survey, the Clinton lead was +5%, based on approximately 10,000 interviews. Greenberg's national simulated model, based on state data, was +7% at that time. The actual vote difference between Clinton and Bush was 5% on election day ("Hotline conference call," 1992).

NEWS MEDIA POLLS

History

Very early in our history as a country, American news media were doing what were called "straw polls." Bernard Hennessy (1981) has provided an excellent review of the origin and development of polling in America. The origin of polls may well have come from a root of the Greek term *polis*, or city. In Middle English, the word *polle* means "head." Early polls were designed to count heads in order to establish taxes, determine the population, and identify voters (Nelson, 1992, p. A20). The notion of the straw polls that were conducted by the newspapers of the early 1800s, according to Claude Robinson (1937, p. 417), was to provide "an unofficial canvass of the electorate to determine the division of popular sentiment on public issues or on candidates for public office." The word *straw* probably referred to the idea that "unofficial canvasses" might detect, very early, the straws in the wind that were blowing toward an electoral outcome.

Although the news media displayed a very early interest in doing straw polls, nevertheless, during the middle of the 20th century, and especially as the methodology of "scientific" polls began to be perfected, the more prominent media-reported polls were by George Gallup, Archibald Crossley, Lou Harris, and other independent commercial organizations. In the last 20 years, though, a major shift has taken place in who is doing campaign polls intended for public release in the media. Now the major news media themselves have largely taken over the field.

The networks have had national efforts to gather election information since the 1960s. In 1968, CBS News launched a survey effort for the Presidential election, largely due to the fact that candidates would release internal polls to the press that were inaccurate and often purposely misleading. The CBS Poll lasted for a few years and then was scrapped. In 1975, the Poll was resurrected through a collaboration with *The New York Times* in order to monitor the 1976 election and has remained in place since (Franckovic, personal communication with William L. Rosenberg, January 12, 1994).

Since 1990, the NES (the News Election Service), an organization representing the networks and some newspapers, provides cooperatively sponsored exit poll information to each of its members. This permits an economy of scale that provides a greater degree of reliable data collection while at the same time reducing the costs to each news agency.

Polls and Media Self-Promotion

With the exception of the NES exit polls and cross-media polling during the campaign (e.g., CBS-*New York Times*), generally the news media tend to emphasize the polls they do while not giving much play to those their rivals do. Given the increasing expense of doing these polls, and given competitive pressures, perhaps this should not be a surprise. These media polls often seem to be a device for self-promotion.

One symptom of this self-preoccupation was 1992 news media inattention to a valuable state-by-state polling resource. During the election of 1992, a weekly compilation of the publicly available trial-heat survey results done at the state level—the *Hotline Electoral Scoreboard*—was available to all media subscribers (Page & Clifford, 1992). Just as an example, for the week during and just after the Republican Convention, the sampling error ranges were from 3 to 5 percentage points, thus indicating that the sizes of these state samples ranged roughly from 400 to

1,200 respondents. This admirable resource received very little news coverage. The probable reason for this was that the product of the scorecard was a collaborative activity that reported the results from all credible sources, including those from rival polls.

The polls that the major news organizations produce give them a chance to enhance their own source credibility by providing a "scientifically" gathered exclusive story. By reporting only their own polls or, at best, referring simply to "other polls," they were able to present themselves as the News Authority. This approach works toward the marketing goal of having the audience seek their channel or product in order to remain "informed."

In fairness, we should mention that during the 1992 Presidential campaign *The New York Times* published a regular feature, "Poll Round-Up," covering the most recent six or so public polls available from a number of sources. Also, both *The New York Times* and *The Washington Post* did report other organizations' polling data—usually horse race figures—when relevant to their stories. However, at both papers the bulk of the coverage still was based on their "own" survey data.

Rich Morin, Director of the News-Polling Division at *The Washington Post*, claims that a primary reason the paper does polls is that their polls support news projects at *The Post* (Morin, personal communication with William L. Rosenberg, September 13, 1994). Some weeks *The Post* did not even report the findings of the weekly horse-race poll, according to Morin. He indicated that if you examine the poll reporting costs by inches published alone, the price is very costly. Other news organizations outside the prestige presses, according to Morin, conduct regional, statewide, or national polls to demonstrate that they are indeed a "player." He argues that *The Washington Post* and *The New York Times* are two examples of papers that have no such need to project a "player" image.

Horse-Race Pressures in Polling

The media metaphor for a campaign—"the race"—immediately suggests a mind-set about how journalists will report their preelection polls: Who is ahead as they come down the home stretch?

One of the prices paid for this use of the polling data is that this coverage tends to limit—and perhaps even displace entirely—the amount of more valuable survey analysis that could provide the audience with insights into the nature of the candidates' bases of support, the reasons why a candidate is supported or opposed by other voters, what potential voters know—and do not know—about each candidate, and so on. Instead, what we get is a very temporary snapshot of who is leading, and by how much. Soon another snapshot will come, and there will be no reason to remember the current one. Meanwhile, the insights that could have been provided also could have lingered long past the snapshot.

It is an understatement to say that there is nothing new about this media preoccupation with the "straws in the wind," of course, and it is hard for even the elite media pollsters—increasingly sophisticated as they are becoming—to resist using the polls to call the "horse race." The 1992 campaign was a case in point. Despite vows to put its polls to higher and better use, for example, *The Washington Post* felt forced to return to calling the race.

According to Sharon Warden, staff writer in the News-Polling Division at *The Washington Post*, the original editorial intention of the paper was to focus more on issues and less on horse race coverage (Warden, personal communication with William L. Rosenberg, August 26, 1994). According to her, the paper wanted issues to drive its poll coverage. However, she indicated that campaign developments, principally changes in the composition of the field of candidates during both the primary and general election campaigns, drove the issues focus from the newspaper's polls. Warden cited in particular the effect of Perot changing his mind about running. On the other hand, she indicated that, in 1992, *The Post* had originally planned to conduct weekly horse race polls as it had in the 1988 election. In 1992, though, these polls were to start much earlier—in June rather than on Labor Day as they had in 1988—so the newspaper could gauge reactions during the political party conventions. The policy at *The Post* was to imbed the weekly tracking poll in its daily election coverage to support the story presented.

Be that as it may, even if a major media poll develops new insights for some readers or viewers through a less superficial approach to analyzing the presidential preferences of voters, the media practice of promoting only their own polls serves as an impediment to other media carrying those analyses and insights. On a somewhat more hopeful note, if there were enough time left in the campaign for the rival polls to retool their questionnaires and analyses because of what the first poll was reporting, perhaps similar insights might reach the readers or viewers of the "copy cat" media.

A Different Kind of Newspaper. One major Eastern newspaper, *The Philadelphia Inquirer*, is almost unique among metropolitan newspapers in its refusal to do—or even commission others to do—its own polling. According to Executive Editor James Naughton (personal communication with William L. Rosenberg, September 13, 1994), the newspaper will fully report polls done by others, but only if the poll findings support a story that is usually already in the works.

The Inquirer claims that it would rather concentrate on issues. The paper has a policy that it will reprint polling information developed by other sources, if it is newsworthy. However, the fundamental editorial policy of the paper is that if polling information is used in a story, the reader must be given some clue as to the scientific basis of the results. The American Association of Public Opinion Researchers (AAPOR) has a set of professional standards they promote within the media. *The Inquirer's* standards are virtually those of AAPOR.

According to John Brumfield (personal communication with William L. Rosenberg, September 12, 1994), an editorial assistant at *The Philadelphia Inquirer*, the paper may also run a story about the findings of the poll as news rather than as a polling story. In this case, the results of the poll often are presented because they are contrary to popular expectations.

The CNN-USA Today "Horse Race" Controversy

An example of the potential for self-promotion with polls may have been the controversy that swirled around the CNN-*USA Today*/Gallup Poll just days before the election. Until that point Clinton was generally seen as the front-runner, with a lead in some cases up to 10%, depending on the poll. Suddenly, just five days before the election, the CNN-*USA Today* poll announced that the election was a dead heat between Clinton and Bush, a major departure from the horse race reports of a day before. The reason for the change was that the CNN-*USA Today* poll had suddenly started reporting on "likely voters," rather than "registered voters," as they had been doing. This startling new reading of the horse race was treated as evidence that Bush finally was making a surge.

The controversy surrounding the CNN poll is more complicated than it might at first appear. In reality, the poll result that received so much attention because it showed a much narrower gap between Bush and Clinton than all the other polls might conceivably have been an artifact of sampling error, which is often about 3% in national opinion polls, except for the fact that the sample presented had been changed. The larger issue was the fact that it was not readily apparent to readers and viewers, particularly those who obtained the results from other news sources, that the basis of the CNN-*USA Today* sample had been changed. The press focused on the headline statement that Bush seemed to be closing on the front runner rather than the fact that apples (proportionately more "likely" voters) and oranges (registered voters) were being compared.

However, the problem was compounded by the fact that the new poll was presented on CNN using the same graphics that contained CNN's earlier polls. This new finding was then widely reported as a startling new development by other news media. The finding gave the appearance that Bush could win the election. According to Marvin Kitman (1992, p. 51), "The surge for Bush was totally false. Future historians will see this as a classic example of what Big Brother, or Ted Turner, can do manipulating a few numbers. . . . [T]he damage . . . , despite the change in methodology, is not done by the poll itself, but how the poll is interpreted."

William Schneider, CNN's director of polling, did come forward on several CNN news shows to explain the distinction between the two samples, as well as a decision on how the poll allocated undecided voters. The first distinction, likely versus registered voters, is an important issue in polling interpretation. In effect, each respondent is handicapped, like horses at the races, to determine how likely each is to vote. The second distinction that Schneider had to present was the procedure for dealing with those who are likely to vote but unsure of whom they will support. Schneider very adequately pointed out on several occasions that Gallup's research showed that undecideds are more likely to vote with the challenger.

However, he chose to explain the apparent closing of the gap between Bush and Clinton with a discussion of sampling error. According to David Chandler (1992) of *The Boston Globe*, Schneider claimed that the CNN results were really not inconsistent with the other nationwide polls. Schneider's defense of the findings in terms of sampling error masked the much larger issue of a changed sample definition. However, the explanation Schneider chose ended up generating much press coverage. The problem was that it was being reported inaccurately.

According to Morin at *The Washington Post*, he did not "jump as quick and deep" into the coverage of the CNN poll story showing a dead heat because his newspaper had its own weekly horse race data for likely voters and was comfortable relying on its own numbers. Many other news organizations were not in this enviable position. Morin (personal communication with William L. Rosenberg, September 13, 1994) suggests that the biggest abuses are probably associated with the secondary uses of polling information. The major media polls are very rich in information. The news wires often pick up the horse race information and do not cover the more important information that was also addressed in the survey. Too often the press relied on the statement—"Other polls have found . . ."—without citing the actual source, but nonetheless giving the horse-race-type polling information.

Technology's Effects on Poll News. Stories move over the wires and in databases, such as Lexis/Nexis, whereas graphics generally do not. Therefore, it is more important to place results in the text of the story if broader circulation through other media is the goal. In the case of CNN's poll, though, the graphics actually were misleading, implying there had been no change in approach. Unfortunately, CNN's textual material describing the shift to likely voters that reached Nexis/Lexis probably was not clearly enough explained to alert many newsrooms to the significance of the changed sample base.

Evaluation. In reality, what the CNN-*USA Today* poll did, in terms of analysis, may well have been the correct move. As we got closer to Election Day, it became more accurate to discuss likely voters as a proxy for the intended population of actual voters. It is true, however, that there is considerable variation among the national polls about how to identify, and weigh, voting likelihood. Often they are unwilling to share with others the precise techniques they use to do this. In any case, however, it is the clear responsibility of the media at least to report such major details as whether the sample of people were identified as likely voters and whether that represented a change in sample criteria. That responsibility rests as much with other media reporting such startling "new findings" in someone else's poll as it does when it's in their own. As for CNN, although it was true its reports mentioned the new sample criterion, its presentation of both "old" and "new" percentages in the same graphic was highly misleading, as was its deemphasis (by Schneider and others) of the possibility that the change in criterion might indeed be the cause of the startling "drop" in Clinton's lead. It appeared CNN felt it had a Big Story and ran with it.

A MAJOR FLAW IN NATIONAL PRESIDENTIAL POLLS

A fundamental flaw in the presentation of almost all of these horse race polls is their failure to address the fact that the national percentages they present are almost irrelevant to the issue of who will win the presidential election.

The presidential election is essentially 50 state elections (see Appendix D). All of the elections are held at the same time with the purpose of chosing electors to the Electoral College. Each of these 50 elections is a winner-take all-situation. Even candidates winning a state by one vote receive that state's entire Electoral College vote, and the other candidates receive none, even though they may have won millions of popular votes in that state.

On only a few occasions during the campaign do some media polls actually conduct large enough samples to segment each state's vote in order to predict electoral college outcomes. Hence, the results of most media election polls are quite unrepresentative of the presidential election, even though they might accurately project popular sentiment. A rare example of appropriate presentation of polling data was the *Hotline Electoral Scoreboard* (1992) which used state polls to predict electoral college voting. On November 3, the Hotline showed Clinton leading in 36 states with 395 electoral votes. This was significantly above the 270 required for winning the presidency. At that time Bush had 116 electors and Perot had none.

The national media do on occasion attempt to deal with the problem of the sample versus the Electoral College by polling in specific swing or questionable states so that reasonable predictions can be made. According to Jeff Alderman, Director of Polling at ABC News, ABC has been conducting presidential polling on a state-by-state basis since 1984. The 1992 effort included almost 20,000 individuals and screened out unlikely voters to yield a likely voter pool of approximately 10,000. Although there was some variation in sample sizes, even for the smaller states, the likely voter sample sizes were generally 150 or more. ABC recognized that the sample sizes were small on a state-by-state basis, but it did not release the horse race numbers for each state. The approach was to generate a probability model that would predict the odds that the poll leader would win that state. The network used a 90% probability threshold to project a candidate as "firmly" ahead and 75%-90% to label the state as "leaning" to the leading candidate. Polls with margins lower than these threshold levels were considered "toss-up" states. Based on these categories, electoral votes were assigned. ABC also used the combination of the states to determine the national horse-race figures. According to Alderman (personal e-mail communication with William L. Rosenberg, October 22, 1994) both the national horse race figures and the electoral college voting model were very accurate.

THE FUTURE ROLE OF CAMPAIGN POLLS

All cf the modern techniques and computers in the world will not change that fact that the fundamentals of choosing what to ask and how to ask it remain paramount. In many ways, the surveys of today are still the straw polls of yesteryear. The continual focus on the horse race—who is winning and who is behind—is often the centerpiece of most polling analysis presented in the media. Often coupled with that is the theme of expectations. Is the front-runner doing as well as he should be, or is a distant challenger doing better than expected? The ying and the yang of contemporary media polling coverage often rests on three central points: the horse race, the expectation's game, and the big "MO," the momentum that is referred to often by political pundits. Rarely are campaign issues a central point in media reporting of presidential election survey results. Although the encouragement of issue debates between candidates is often discussed, election surveys continually go back to what the media, the candidates, and the audiences are familiar with—the horse race.

The horse race use of polls also may tend to drive the other stories about the presidential campaign. One can almost hear it again, "Buoyed by his comeback in the polls, President Bush campaigned today in an upbeat mood."

REFERENCES

Chandler, D.L. (1992, November 2). The methods behind the madness. *The Boston Globe* [Section: Science and Technology], p. 35.

Dionne, E.J., Jr. (1980, February 16). 1980 brings more pollsters than ever. *The New York Times*, p. 10.

Hennessy, B. (1981). *Public opinion* (4th ed.). Monterey, CA: Brooks/Cole.

Hotline conference call: Clinton and Bush pollsters. (1992, November 5). The Hotline. American Political Network.

Hotline electoral scoreboard. (1992, November 3). The Hotline. American Political Network.

Kessel, J.H. (1988). *Presidential campaign politics, coalition strategies and citizen response* (3rd ed.). Chicago: Dorsey Press.

Kitman, M. (November 9, 1992). Polls, predictions and politics. *Newsday* [Section: Part II; The Marvin Kitman Show], p. 51; [Other Edition: City], p. 49.

Nelson, C. (1992, September 24). Who's ahead, Who's behind? Who's asking? What you need to know about opinion polls. *Minneapolis Star Tribune*, p. A20.

Page, S., & Clifford, T. (1992, September 6). Heat is on; Bush, Clinton begin stretch run for White House. *Newsday*, p. 6.

Robinson, C.E. (1937). Straw votes. *Encyclopedia of the Social Sciences, 14*, 417.

14

Summary and Conclusions

William R. Elliott

Almost everyone agrees that the 1992 campaign for the presidency was different, that it represented some type of watershed in American politics. Initially, the campaign assumed a gloomy air characterized by a general malaise, what we have termed a *politics of disenchantment*. People seemed discouraged with political parties, with their candidates, and with the ways the press covered campaign activities. It did not look like a good year.

Then, on February 20, 1992, something happened. A Texas billionaire named Ross Perot appeared on *Larry King Live*. He matter-of-factly told Larry King and the viewing audience that he would run for president if his name appeared on the ballot of all 50 states. Disenchantment with "politics as usual" became the focus of Ross Perot's campaign. Local support groups formed across the nation. On September 18, Ross Perot's name was placed on the ballot of the 50th state.

Ross Perot made 1992 different. He tapped into the discontent felt by many voters. He provided a counterpoint to "politics as usual." He may not have been a "voice in the wilderness," but his message resonated with the concerns, hopes, and fears of many Americans.

This campaign was anything but "typical." Characterized by unexpected events—the entry, departure, and reentry of Ross Perot—and changing media use by candidates and voters alike, Campaign '92 signaled a change in American politics.

PURPOSE OF THE STUDY

This is our second major presidential campaign study. Our first study, of the 1988 campaign (Lemert, Elliott, Bernstein, Rosenberg, & Nestvold, 1991), explored the effects of presidential campaign debates and news media verdicts on voter perceptions and attitudes, the use and impact of "attack ads," and the news media and voter support of the presidential debates as a political institution.

In 1992, we reexplored these issues; however, we added the "new media" of political communication—the radio and television talk shows and the electronic town meetings—to our inventory of possible campaign influences. Within this area, we wanted to explore how traditional media responded to new information sources, how the public responded, and how the candidates, particularly Ross Perot, were able to integrate new media activities into their campaign strategies.

As in all campaigns since 1976, presidential and vice presidential candidate debates have played an important role. In 1992, the role of the debates was amplified. For this campaign, the debates gave Ross Perot a chance to get his message to the people. The debates offered a chance for George Bush to reinvigorate a failing campaign and provided Bill Clinton an opportunity to solidify his lead. The debates were the news story for nearly two weeks in mid-October, two critical campaign weeks! We investigated the influence of these debates, news verdicts about the debates, and the status of presidential debates as a political institution.

Candidates use advertising because they can control the message. In 1992, however, advertising claims faced new challenges. The press reviewed and evaluated campaign charges. Candidates were put on notice that misleading claims would be corrected. Rapid response teams were created by the Clinton and Bush campaign staffs to answer campaign charges immediately.

How did the voters and the media respond to "attack ads"? Conventional wisdom, supported in several major works (Jamieson, 1992; West, 1993), suggests that negative campaign advertising works even though it is disliked by the voters, many candidates, and the press. Based on our evidence, we thought that this conventional "wisdom" was wrong about the 1988 campaign (Lemert et al., 1991). We wanted again to test our findings in 1992.

Campaign polls are campaign news. The press track who is ahead and who is behind. We are informed, almost daily, that someone is gaining or losing momentum—the big "Mo," as George Bush referred to it in 1988. As with debates and advertising, polling has become a source of campaign information, supplying us with the "horse race" aspect of each campaign.

OUR METHODOLOGY

We wanted to look at Campaign '92 from several perspectives. Rather than relying on a single way of studying Campaign '92, we used a variety of research tools to unravel what was taking place in the campaign. Interviews with campaign decision makers were supplemented by a series of content analyses looking at how the mainstream press responded to the talk-show appearances by the candidates and how television networks covered presidential campaign debates.

We used both a repeated-interview panel-survey design and a "trend"/time-series design. The panel interviews allowed us to identify specific changes when they occurred, and the time-series surveys allowed us to examine the impact of specific campaign communications, such as the debates, postdebate analysis, the talk shows, and political ads.

Furthermore, because each type of survey design had different strengths and weaknesses, using each type of survey enabled us to check results produced by the other, lending extra confidence when those survey results converged. Therefore, we sought to provide a rounded picture of the 1992 campaign through interviews with campaign decision makers, content analyses (some of them tracing back through 1976), and two complementary survey designs.

THE FINDINGS

Our findings cover many areas of campaign activity. First, we studied how talk shows and other alternative media influenced the campaign. Second, we again investigated the role of the presidential and vice presidential debates, looking at their influence on information about the campaign issues and the images of the candidates, how debate verdicts influence viewer verdicts, and how the mass public views the debates as an institution. Our last major area of investigation looked at advertising and polling, particularly the response of the public and the press to the "attack" ads of 1992. Our summary of these findings follows.

The New Media and the Old Media: Point-Counterpoint

Throughout the campaign, mainstream media were critical of talk-show appearances by the candidates. Journalists such as Elizabeth Drew, Ted Koppel, and Robert Novak thought that the questions asked by talk-show hosts and audiences were lightweight. Academics and journalists, particularly, were likely to criticize talk-show campaigning. After the election, a "revisionist" mentality took over and judgments about the role of the talk shows became more positive.

The people who watched the candidates on the talk shows were well educated, had high internal efficacy, knew more about the issues than nonwatchers, paid more attention as well to conventional news sources about the campaign, and rated the talk shows as more valuable than conventional news sources for campaign information. From the voter's point of view, the talk shows were important parts of the campaign. Audiences appreciated them. Everyone may remember Clinton's saxophone performance on *Arsenio Hall*. People who actually watched the program know that Clinton used the program to discuss substantive issues with the host and with the audience.

That the talk shows both contained substantive information and extended that information to people who might not otherwise have learned it were confirmed by our finding in Chapter 5 that people with moderate levels of exposure to candidate talk shows learned a great deal about what policy proposals each of the candidates had made. These results held up even after controls for interest, education, exposure to the debates, and numerous other variables. Because viewers of the most talk shows also paid the most attention to the most other campaign sources, they had more sources of this information than did those who had viewed at most one or two of the candidate talk shows. As a result, when we controlled for exposure to these other sources, we found that it was the much more numerous viewers of one or two talk-show appearances whose knowledge seemed most enhanced by watching and listening to the candidates on these alternative media.

The cumulative audience for the talk shows was very large, even though spread thinly across dozens of viewing opportunities. By the time of their November interview, some 65% of our panelists said they had seen at least one candidate talk-show appearance, a considerable increase over the percentages observed in September and October interviews.

Talk-show appearances helped some of the candidates. For Clinton and Perot, the more people saw one of them on talk shows, the more likely these same people would vote for that specific candidate. This was not true for George Bush. Viewing Bush on talk shows did not, by itself, predict the odds of voting for him. Instead, as respondents' viewing rose of talk-show appearances by any of the three presidential candidates, the *lower* the odds of a vote for Bush. Clearly, one cannot explain this finding purely in terms of Bush's performance on the talk shows, because if that were the explanation, then higher Bush viewing should have predicted lower odds of voting for Bush. One plausible explanation might be that viewing of more than one candidate allowed some of our respondents to compare Bush's approach to the talk shows with that of Clinton, Perot, or even that of both Clinton and Perot.

The New Candidate

Ross Perot was not just a new candidate, he was a new kind of candidate. With unlimited financial resources, a volunteer army, and a recognition that many Americans were upset with "government as usual," Perot became a contender, even though his supporters knew he would not win. That did not matter.

Perot appealed to many of the people who voted for Bush in 1988 but would not vote for him again. Perot supporters were relatively young and knew less about the issues than Bush or Clinton backers. They thought they personally could influence the political system. For most of them, being active in politics was new stuff. They were novices. Perot supporters started the campaign discouraged about politics. They changed. The debates especially seemed to help them come out of the campaign less cynical about American politics.

The media responded to Perot. Initially, Perot was treated lightly. Later, when his numbers started to grow in the polls, he was treated more seriously. Perot was always uncomfortable in dealing with the mainstream press. He decided to do without it. His supporters, also suspicious of how the mainstream press treated their candidate, felt comfortable seeing him on talk shows, in the debates, and in his "infomercials." Perot did not need the traditional press.

Perot posed a difficult problem for the mainstream press. Even while recognizing his accomplishments, they would qualify these successes. His appearance in the first presidential debate prompted twice as much attention from network news as he received in the second debate. In the third debate, Perot received even less media attention, even though our survey findings indicate that respondents thought he and Clinton performed equally well in that debate. Although the networks praised his wit and "one-liners," they also pointed out that he had no chance to win the election. From the network perspective, Perot was not a candidate. Many in the mass public did not share that belief, at least not entirely.

The Debates

Just as Campaign '92 was different, so were the 1992 debates. Multiple formats were tried: the traditional panel of journalists, a single moderator, a town-hall meeting, and a combination of moderator and panel.

The three candidates differed clearly in terms of debate performance. Perot, helped by his darkhorse" and "spoiler" image, emerged as the clear winner of the first debate. His ability to joke, adlib, and stand up to his better known opponents won the respect of the voters and press alike.

Clinton demonstrated an ability to touch people in the second presidential debate. When he moved away from the podium and talked with the audience, assuring them that he understood their problems and pain, he had set himself apart from the other candidates.

Bush was unable to master any of the debate formats—the traditional panel of journalists, the town hall, the mixed moderator and panel—and, consequently, was evaluated as least effective in each of the debates by the people we interviewed. In the second debate, instead of generating an image of understanding and compassion, Bush appeared incapable of grasping people's problems and concerns. He needed to strike some responsive chord in the audience to boost his reelection chances. The chord was missed.

The debates were related to the image of the candidates. Perot's image, as with lesser known candidates from the past, benefited most from his debate appearances. Even Clinton, who by October was a well-known personality, benefited from the second debate, the debate he so clearly dominated. Whether Bush's image was too well formed by then or whether his debate performances were too weak, his image was the only image that did not benefit from any of the presidential debates.

Exposure to postdebate analysis, the verdicts rendered by journalists and others immediately after the debates, continued to predict perceptions of debate performance, as it had done in our 1988 study (Lemert et al., 1991). Network commentators favored Perot after the first debate, were positive toward Quayle after the vice presidential debate, and heavily favored Clinton after the second presidential debate. People who saw both the debate and the postdebate analysis gave correspondingly higher debater prowess ratings—Perot after the first, Quayle after the vice presidential debate, and Clinton after the second presidential debate—than people who watched the debate only or people who did not watch at all. In an apparent reaction against the 1988 campaign "spin doctors," network journalists reduced the use of verdicts from campaign insiders, increasing the use of themselves and a variety of "public opinion" indicators as sources.

The new debate formats worked, at least from the perspective of the viewers. The "town-hall" format used in the October 15 presidential debate was judged a success by the press. Initially skeptical about questions from the audience, they recognized the importance of the "town-hall' concept. The press did not respond in the same way to the vice presidential debate. This innovative format, using a moderator only, was widely criticized after the debate because of the way the vice presidential candidates used the format.

In marked contrast to the 1988 debates, the networks seemed more aware of the voters as a reference group, although the importance of the debates to the candidates and their campaigns remained the central preoccupation of network journalists. In general, print and broadcast journalists seemed much more supportive of the debates as a political institution than in 1988. Nevertheless, they remained less supportive than other news sources in statements about the debates.

With the exception of the vice presidential debate, respondents approved of the debates, and popular support grew after each presidential debate. This was particularly true for the Richmond "town-hall" format. Perot supporters particularly became more supportive of the debates as a political institution as the Fall campaign went on.

Advertising and Polling

David Broder (1990) was an active critic of the role of the press in the 1988 campaign. He was particularly concerned about the responsibility of the press to counter misleading claims made in political advertising. In general, the mainstream press supported Broder's ideas and made plans to establish "truth squads" to police the candidates.

Despite their promises, the television networks policed only slightly better in 1992 than they did in 1988. Compared with other campaign coverage, their performance was not particularly good. For instance, Brooks Jackson of CNN did as many "ad watch" pieces during a 1-month segment as ABC, CBS, and NBC combined put together over the entire Fall campaign.

Attack ads had backfired, according to our study of the 1988 campaign (Lemert et al., 1991). Neither George Bush nor Michael Dukakis was helped by the attack ads they used. In 1992, the Democratic candidate's attack ads hurt Bush, helped Perot, and may have helped Clinton, but only among Democratic voters. Once again, Bush's attacks on his Democratic opponent backfired, harming him instead of hurting Clinton. It is possible that the experience of the 1988 campaigned "primed" many voters to interpret Bush attack ads as "mudslinging" and "dirty politics." Among our November panelists, only the people recalling a Bush ad showed a negative change in the value they placed on presidential ads as an information resource.

One of the reasons for this may have been the "quick response" teams put together by the candidates. Dukakis had been criticized for not answering Bush attack ads in 1988. Clinton took no chances. He had prepared a response to Bush's acceptance speech at the Republican National Convention *before* that speech was delivered.

Attack faxes were added to the political communication vocabulary by the Bush campaign organization. Although the Bush and Clinton camps elected to use attack ads, Perot adopted a different campaign strategy. He took the high ground, avoiding attack ads. It seemed to have worked, improving his chances of getting a person's vote.

IMPLICATIONS

Campaign '92 was full of surprises, drama, and lessons. We think that this campaign established a baseline for the campaigns to come, at least for campaign '96. Some of the implications we see from Campaign '92 follow.

Fundamental or Incidental Shifts in the Use of the Media

Changes in the media mix for presidential campaigns have their positive and negative implications.

Positives. The "new media" may help to democratize American politics. Besides providing candidates with a direct communication link to the voters, talk shows and town meetings provide information for Americans who do not read a newspaper regularly or watch network television news. In simple terms, the new media have opened new information channels. More information about the campaign, the candidates, and the issues was available in 1992 than in 1988. That is on the plus side.

Larry King, partly responsible for the landslide of new media channels opened up in 1992, speculated on the importance of alternative media sources for campaigns. He said that "there may be too much information too quickly. But we're always better served—the more you know, the better" ("The father," 1994, p. 137).

Lemert (1994) suggested another benefit. The new media provide checks on the accuracy of the old media. Candidate debates are a form of talk show in which the audience gets to observe the candidates directly, without sound bites or editors. New information opportunities—the talk shows, town meetings, e-mail addresses, 800- and 900-

phone numbers—provide alternatives to the "gatekeepered" systems of the past. Our audiences found talk shows and debates more useful than print or broadcast news programs. That is a significant and potentially beneficial change.

Negatives. There are downsides. For the successful candidate, talk shows do not stop with the election. They continue. Bill Clinton, champion of the new media during the campaign, has become Bill Clinton, *critic* of the new media. Campaign '92 demonstrated that Americans are still interested in politics, that they will follow it, and that they may see it as entertaining. Rush Limbaugh and others have discovered the same thing. What was so helpful to Clinton, the candidate, has grown into a continuous chorus of criticism of his policies as president. The genie is out of the bottle.

In the past, a function of the mainstream media was to provide an "objective" forum in which people could, and sometimes did, believe what they read, saw, and heard. People are not as accepting or trusting today, perhaps with good reason. They are cynical. They feel left out of the process. They feel powerless. With the loss of trust and the proliferation of alternative sources of information, how can information be evaluated? Do we believe the candidate, *The Washington Post*, or the people on Oprah Winfrey?

The old idea of "objectivity" needs to be balanced with the new ideals of one-on-one communication. Evaluation, deliberation, clarification, and balance, the characteristics of "objectivity," confront needs for openness, spontaneity, concern, and contact. Talk shows and town hall meetings provide one alternative to the mainstream press and to traditional ideas of "objectivity." Beverly Jackson ("Assessing the press," 1994, p. 31), a senior producer at NBC, noted that the town hall meeting "is an empowering experience for the audience: their chance to hold someone accountable, to talk to someone they would rarely get a chance to talk to or to call on the carpet."

Overall. If the cost of better contact with our leaders is at the expense of "objectivity," then maybe we need to pay the price. We see nothing in the changes in political information that necessarily works against a healthy and democratic marketplace of political ideas. Contact with the mass public by politicians at all levels will improve the level of political knowledge. Each of our studies has documented this. Extending political discussion through a variety of channels brings more of us to the podium for discussion.

We have remarked on the concerns and dangers. When the press "watchdog" turns into the "backbiter," democracy is not well served. Cynicism replaces skepticism. Patterson (1994) feels the press has already gone beyond the "skeptic" phase, seeking conflict over accuracy. By portraying politicians as untrustworthy, the press creates public distrust. When politicians, particularly presidents, see the press in the cynic's role, it is not surprising that they turn to alternative ways to reach the people.

As a nation, we will have to learn to deal with more voices in the political marketplace. Cable channels devoted exclusively to talk shows are hoping to duplicate the popularity of "talk radio." More voices will be heard. More hosts will be seen. Traditional concepts of "accuracy" and "objectivity" become difficult, perhaps impossible, to apply. Journalistic standards will not be followed by all media commentators. The audience will have to learn to evaluate on its own. When it does, some politicians, some members of the press, and some talk-show hosts will come out on the short end.

All of this is new. We will learn.

Debates: A Better System

When we looked at the preferences of the people we interviewed in 1988 (Lemert et al., 1991), we found that they wanted to reduce candidate control of the debates. In 1992, that seems to have happened. Based on a variety of debate formats offered in 1992, the people had clear preferences. We think that the variety of formats offered in 1992 should be continued.

The advantages of a variety of debate formats was noted by Jamieson and Birdsell (1988). They saw multiple formats as a way to ensure that voters would receive different kinds of information from the debates. They also noted that the variety of formats makes a more even playing field for all candidates. Although a town hall meeting might benefit one candidate, another candidate might do better with single moderator, another with a panel of journalists. As our study of the 1992 debates indicated, no single candidate excelled across the three formats.

The timing and duration of the debates is also important. In 1992, the debates took place over a 9-day period, finishing just two weeks before the election. The debates became the most significant campaign news at a critical juncture. By organizing the debates over a short time period, people were able to focus on what was said, relate the first debate to the second, the second to the third, and use the debates as a source of information about the campaign. By continuing this type of organization, presidential debates will remain a major voter decision-making tool.

We have two general recommendations for the 1996 debates: First, we recommend that the three 1992 formats—panel of journalists, single moderator, town hall meeting—be continued. One of each type of format—panel of journalists, single moderator, town hall meeting—will maximize variety and information while collectively minimizing "performance" differences among the candidates. Second, we think it would be in the best interests of the voters to maintain the debates as a central part of the campaign, positioning them near the end of the campaign. This provides an opportunity for them to see the candidates side by side and to judge their answers and positions when many are still deciding how they will vote. Mid-October is an optimal time.

FUTURE RESEARCH NEEDS: PREPARING FOR 1996

By the start of 1994, the campaign for the presidency in 1996 was well underway. Republicans began looking for support, determining issues they could use, and planning how to retake the White House. Democrats did the same. They had a candidate but needed issues and positions. Ross Perot remained relatively quiet but not invisible, his options open.

Researchers are preparing to look at the 1996 campaign to see how it compares with 1992. As a team of researchers that has looked carefully at two presidential campaigns, we have some suggestions for studying the next one:

- We are convinced that multiple methodologies improve our understanding of the campaign process. Whether done by a single team or worked through the integrated efforts of several researchers, we feel that this is the best way to come to grips with the complex process of political campaigning.
- Complementing multiple methodologies, we know it is important to conduct multiple time-point studies. Studies confined to a brief portion of any campaign suffer because they cannot track day-to-day, week-to-week, and month-to-month trends. With appropriate funding, studies could be conducted over a longer period of time, including critical events during the primary campaigns. For an individual researcher or a research team to do this would be difficult. For groups of researchers, sharing their ideas and results electronically, it might not be so difficult. Just as the "new media" appear to have benefited the voter, we think they can benefit the researcher.
- Was 1992 a unique event, something unlikely to be repeated, or was it a new form of campaigning that would have developed independently of the entry of Ross Perot into the race? We think that 1992 was a new form of campaigning and that it will

continue in 1996. Ross Perot's candidacy certainly increased interest in the campaign and certainly increased an awareness of the role of the new media. However, it was Bill Clinton as much as Ross Perot who saw these new media as political tools available for his use. How candidates will use these media, when they will start using them, and how the media themselves will limit or expand access to candidates (think of the primary season) pose interesting questions for 1996.

- For the 1996 campaign, candidates for the presidency, particularly President Clinton, will have to handle the attacks they receive from radio talk shows. Part of the "handling" has started in 1994, as the Clinton Administration complained about unfair and inaccurate statements made by radio talk show host Rush Limbaugh. New media themselves might become an issue in 1996.
- We need a better and more direct tie between the issues of the campaign, what the people know about the issues, and where they get their information. We made a reasonable attempt to get to some of that in this study. Our particular method could have been improved along the lines used by Zhu, Milavsky, and Biswas (1994). We encourage innovative designs like this.
- It may be, in 1996, that the concepts of "old" and "new" media will change. The differences between entertainment, news, and advertising are no longer distinct. With the possibility of 500-channel cable systems, dedicated talk-show channels, and increased awareness of the importance of new media as a campaign tool, further blurring of these differences will accelerate.
- How will campaign advertising be conducted and will the institutionalization of rapid response teams and truth squads take place? What role will attack ads assume in 1996?
- Will ABC, CBS, and NBC News more vigorously join CNN as the Ad Police in 1996? Will the trend toward media policing of political ads continue to spread to more newspapers as well?
- Finally, we need to remember that our November vote in 1996 for president and vice president represents but a small percentage of the decisions we make in our polling places. We look at funding measures, local and statewide candidate races, and initiatives that have direct impact on our lives as citizens, not as researchers. We have not yet addressed how new media techniques and local debates impact these elections. Perhaps it is time that we all did.

REFERENCES

Assessing the press and Clinton in the new media age: An expert roundtable. (1994). *Media Studies Journal, 8*(2), 27-41.

Broder, D. (1990, January 3). Democracy and the press. *The Washington Post*, p. A15.

The father of "talk show democracy": On the line with Larry King. (1994). *Media Studies Journal, 8*(2), 123-137.

Jamieson, K.H. (1992). *Dirty politics: Deception, distraction, and democracy.* New York: Oxford University Press.

Jamieson, K.H., & Birdsell, D.S. (1988). *Presidential debates.* New York: Oxford University Press.

Lemert, J. B. (1994). Adapting to Clinton and the new media reality. *Media Studies Journal, 8*(2), 53-58.

Lemert, J.B., Elliott, W.R., Bernstein, J.M., Rosenberg, W.L., & Nestvold, K.J. (1991). *News verdicts, the debates, and presidential campaigns.* New York: Praeger.

Patterson, T.E. (1994). Legitimate beef: The presidency and a carnivorous press. *Media Studies Journal, 8*(2), 21-26.

West, D.M. (1993). *Air wars: Television advertising in election campaigns, 1952-1992.* Washington, DC: Congressional Quarterly.

Zhu, J., Milavsky, J.R., & Biswas, R. (1994). Do televised debates affect image perception more than issue knowledge? A study of the first 1992 Presidential debate. *Human Communication Research, 20,* 302-333.

Appendix A

Wave 1 Questionnaire

1992 PRESIDENTIAL CAMPAIGN QUESTIONNAIRE

Predebate Questionnaire   Location: 1. IL   2. PA   3. OR   4. IN
                            Interview No: 1   Panel:
                                                (Fill in at end, 0 = No, 1 = Yes)
1992 Campaign Study   Questionnaire No. at this location _____
Attempts (Allow 8 Rings)   Date   Time
                            (Record date   1._____   _____
                            and time of   2._____   _____
Telephone   -   attempt)   3._____   _____
                                            4._____   _____

Hello, my name is _____, and I'm calling from the Mass Communication Research Center at Southern Illinois University.

We are doing a survey about the 1992 presidential election campaign and, because this is a scientific sample, I need to speak to someone who is at least 18 years old, who is in your house right now, and who has the next birthday coming up. (IF NECESSARY, REPEAT ABOVE INTRODUCTION OF YOURSELF TO PERSON WHO COMES TO PHONE NEXT.)

NEXT SAY THIS IF A NEW PERSON: This interview is part of a national study, dealing with the presidential campaign. It will take ten to fifteen minutes to answer all of the questions. (IF THEY SAY THIS ISN'T A GOOD TIME, MAKE AN APPOINTMENT AND GET THEIR FIRST NAME.)

Call back on: Day_____Time of Day_____ First Name_____

Your participation is completely voluntary and you may quit the interview at any time. All information will be kept strictly confidential.
This research has been reviewed and approved by the Carbondale Committee for Research Involving Human Subjects. Should you have any questions about this project, please call Professor William Elliott at the School of Journalism at Southern Illinois University at Carbondale or the Chairperson of Committee for Research Involving Human Subjects. I can give the phone numbers if you wish. (*If they ask, it is xxx-xxxx for Professor Elliott, xxx-xxxx for the Committee.*)

We'd like to ask you some questions about your media use during this campaign.

First, some questions about television.

1. I would like to ask you about network television news programs. Think back carefully over the past week. How many of the seven nights of the week did you watch at least part of the evening network television news programs?
    ___ (0 to 7 nights)
    (8) Don't know
    (9) Refused

2. Within the last two weeks, do you recall seeing any paid political advertisements for George Bush or Bill Clinton on television?
    (1) Yes (Go to Q 2a)   (8) Don't know (Go to Q 3)
    (2) No (Go to Q 3)   (9) Refused (Go to Q 3)

    2a. Think of the ad you remember best. Was it for Bush or Clinton?
        (1) Bush   (8) Don't know (Go to Q 3)
        (2) Clinton   (9 Refused (Go to Q 3)

    2b. (If "BUSH" to 2a) Would you say that this ad mainly praised George Bush, criticized Bill Clinton, or both praised Bush and criticized Clinton?
        (1) Praised Bush   (8) Don't know (Go to Q 3)
        (2) Criticized Clinton   (9) Refusal (Go to Q 3)
        (3) Praised Bush and Criticized Clinton

    2c. (If "BUSH" to 2a)What was this Bush ad about? Did it deal with questions about either candidate's character, about the candidate's record, about a specific issue, or something else? Describe the ad as clearly as you can. (Probe: Can you remember anything else?)

___

2d. (If "BUSH" to 2a) Of the ads you saw, do you remember seeing any for Bill Clinton?
- (1) Yes (Go to Q 2e)
- (2) No (Go to Q 3)
- (8) Don't know (Go to Q 3)
- (9) Refused (Go to Q 3)

2e. (If "BUSH" to 2a) Think of the Clinton ad you remember best, would you say it praised Bill Clinton, criticized George Bush, or both praised Clinton and criticized Bush?
- (4) Praised Clinton and Criticized Bush
- (5) Criticized Bush
- (6) Praised Clinton
- (8) Don't know (Go to Q 3)
- (9) Refusal (Go to Q 3)

2b. (If "CLINTON" to 2a) Would you say that this ad mainly praised Bill Clinton, criticized George Bush, or both praised Clinton and criticized Bush?
- (4) Praised Clinton and Criticized Bush
- (5) Criticized Bush
- (6) Praised Clinton
- (8) Don't know (Go to Q 3)
- (9) Refusal (Go to Q 3)

2c. (If "CLINTON" to 2a) What was this Clinton ad about? Did it deal with questions about either candidate's character, about the candidate's record, about a specific issue, or something else? Describe the ad as clearly as you can. (Probe: Can you remember anything else?)

___

2d. (If "CLINTON" to 2a) Of the ads you saw, do you remember seeing any for George Bush?

- (1) Yes (Go to Q 2e)
- (2) No (Go to Q 3)
- (8) Don't know (Go to Q 3)
- (9) Refused (Go to Q 3)

2e. (If "CLINTON" to 2a) Think of the Bush ad you remember best, would you say it praised George Bush, criticized Bill Clinton, or both praised Bush and criticized Clinton?

(1) Praised Bush
(2) Criticized Clinton
(3) Praised Bush and Criticized Clinton
(8) Don't know (Go to Q 3)
(9) Refusal (Go to Q 3)

3. Have you seen or heard any of the candidates—either Bush, Clinton, Gore, or Quayle—on talk, morning, or late night shows such as Larry King, Phil Donahue, the Today Show, or Arsenio Hall?

(1) Yes (Continue with Q 3)
(2) No (Go to Q 4)
(8) Don't know (Go to Q 4)
(9) Refused (Go to Q 4)

Which show or shows did you see with the presidential or vice presidential candidates? (Check each show the respondent mentions. Do not volunteer the names of the show. Probe: Any others?)

3a. ____ Today Show
3b. ____ Good Morning America
3c. ____ This Morning (CBS)
3d. ____ Donahue
3e. ____ Oprah Winfrey
3f. ____ Larry King Live
3g. ____ Nightline
3g. ____ Nightline
3h. ____ Arsenio Hall
3i. ____ Tonight Show
3j. ____ C-Span
3k. ____ Radio talk show
3l. ____ Other (Specify): _____

4. Now I would like to ask you about newspaper reading. Think back carefully over the past week. How many of the seven days of the week did you read at least part of the main news section of the newspaper?

____ (0 to 7 days)
(8) Don't know
(9) Refused

5. On a scale running from **zero** (0) to **ten** (10), where zero means that you pay **no attention at all** and ten means you pay **full attention**, indicate how much attention you have paid to the following sources of information about this **PRESIDENTIAL** campaign: (Enter 00 for zero, 01 for one, . . ., 09 for nine, 10 for 10, 88 for Don't remember, and 99 for refusal)

5a. Televised talk shows such as Larry King Live _____
5b. Late night news shows such as Nightline _____
5c. Televised Town Meeting broadcasts _____
5d. Late night talk shows such as Arsenio or Letterman _____

5e. Morning news shows such as The Today Show
5f. Daytime talk shows such as Oprah or Donohue
5g. Televised presidential and vice presidential debates
5h. Network news broadcasts
5i. Televised political advertisements
5j. Newspaper news stories
5k. Conversations with family and friends
5l. Democratic National Convention
5m. Republican National Convention
5n. Presidential campaign literature
5o. Other (Specify)

Now some questions about politics and about this presidential campaign.

6. First, do you consider yourself a Republican, Democrat, Independent, or what?
   (1) Republican
   (2) Democrat
   (3) Independent
   (4) Other
   (8) Don't Know
   (9) Refusal

7. Where would you place yourself on a scale running from **zero** (0) to ten (10), where zero means **extremely liberal**, **five** means **middle-of-the-road**, and ten means **extremely conservative**? (Enter 00 for zero, 01 for one, . . ., 09 for nine, 10 for 10, 88 for Don't remember, and 99 for refusal) _____

8. Which of the following best describes you? Are you **registered to vote**, are you a **U.S. citizen but not registered** to vote, or are you a **citizen of another country** and not eligible to vote in this election?

   (1) Registered to vote
   (2) US citizen but not registered
   (3) Citizen of another country (Enter "77" in Q9)
   (8) Don't know
   (9) Refusal

9. On a scale from zero to ten, where **zero** means that you **definitely will not vote**, **five** means there is a **50-50 chance**, and **ten** means you are **absolutely certain you will vote**, what would you say the odds are that you might or might not vote in this presidential election? (Enter 00 for zero, 01 for one, . . ., 09 for nine, 10 for 10, 77 for non-US citizens, 88 for Don't remember, and 99 for refusal) _____

10. At this time we'd like to ask you some questions about some of the things that people are doing or have done during this presidential campaign.

10a. Have you donated any money to one of the presidential candidates?
 (1) Yes (8) DK
 (2) No (9) NR

10b. Have you worn a campaign button, displayed a bumper sticker, or put up a lawn sign for one of the presidential candidates?
 (1) Yes (8) DK
 (2) No (9) NR

10c. Have you worked in the presidential campaign as a volunteer?
 (1) Yes (8) DK
 (2) No (9) NR

10d. Have you discussed the presidential campaign with friends?
 (1) Yes (8) DK
 (2) No (9) NR

10e. Have you tried to persuade someone else to vote for one of the presidential candidates?
 (1) Yes (8) DK
 (2) No (9) NR

10f. Have you attended a presidential campaign speech or rally?
 (1) Yes (8) DK
 (2) No (9) NR

10g. Have you tried to get campaign information about where the presidential candidates stand on the issues?
 (1) Yes (8) DK
 (2) No (9) NR

10h. Have you spent a lot of time reading newspaper or magazine articles about the presidential candidates and their positions?
 (1) Yes (8) DK
 (2) No (9) NR

10i. Not counting programs just about the debates, have you watched any recent television news specials about the presidential campaign?
 (1) Yes (8) DK
 (2) No (9) NR

Appendix A

11. As far as **you** are **personally** concerned, what are the one or two most important issues in this presidential campaign? Begin with the issue you think is most important. (Probe after the first issue: Is there anything else?)

    11a. Most Important Issue: _____

    _____

    _____

    _____

    11b. Second Issue: _____

    _____

    _____

    _____

12. Now, I'm going to read you several statements about Ross Perot. Tell me whether you **strongly agree, agree**, are **neutral, disagree**, or **strongly disagree** with each statement about Ross Perot.

	SA	A	Neu	D	SD
12a. Before he dropped out, I was seriously considering voting for Ross Perot.	(5)	(4)	(3)	(2)	(1)
12b. I don't think I would have voted for Perot, but I did agree with a lot of the things he was saying.	(5)	(4)	(3)	(2)	(1)
12c. I may still vote for Ross Perot if neither Bush nor Clinton looks good to me.	(5)	(4)	(3)	(2)	(1)

13. Next, I'm going to read you several statements about presidential debates and ask you whether you **strongly agree, agree**, are **neutral, disagree**, or **strongly disagree** with each statement.

	SA	A	Neu	D	SD
13a. Presidential debates are one of the best ways for me to learn where the candidates stand on the issues.	(5)	(4)	(3)	(2)	(1)
13b. Presidential candidates seem to avoid answering the important questions during the debates.	(5)	(4)	(3)	(2)	(1)
13c. All in all, I think the presidential debates are a waste of time.	(5)	(4)	(3)	(2)	(1)

13d. Televised presidential debates are the best way
for people to make their final voting choice. (5) (4) (3) (2) (1)

14. Again, relying on what you know and what you have read, seen, and heard about the candidates, how would you rate each of them in terms of the following characteristics? Use a scale running from zero to ten, where **zero** means that the candidate is **very weak** and **ten** that the candidate is **very strong**. (Enter 00 for zero, 01 for one, . . ., 09 for nine, 10 for 10, 88 for Don't remember, and 99 for a Refusal)

14a. Bill Clinton's knowledge of domestic issues. . . . _____
14b. George Bush's knowledge of domestic issues. . . . . _____
14c. George Bush's character . . . . _____
14d. Bill Clinton's character . . . . _____
14e. George Bush's understanding of the problems of common people . . . . _____
14f. Bill Clinton's understanding of the problems of common people . . . . _____
14g. Bill Clinton's knowledge of foreign and defense policy . . . . _____
14h. George Bush's knowledge of foreign and defense policy. . . _____
14i. George Bush's ability as a political debater . . . . _____
14j. Bill Clinton's ability as a political debater . . . . _____

Next, a few evaluations of the vice presidential candidates. How would you rate each of them in terms of the following characteristics? Use a scale running from zero to ten, where **zero** means that the candidate is **very weak** and **ten** that the candidate is **very strong**.

14k. Al Gore's ability to lead the country . . . . _____
14l. Dan Quayle's ability to lead the country . . . . _____
14m. Dan Quayle's ability as a political debater . . . . _____
14n. Al Gore's ability as a political debater . . . . _____

Now some questions about this political campaign.

15. Can you tell me where the Democratic convention was held?
    (1) New York City   (8) Don't Know
    (2) Someplace else   (9) Refusal

16. Can you tell me where the Republican convention was held?
    (1) Houston, Texas   (8) Don't Know
    (2) Someplace else   (9) Refusal

Appendix A

17. Who is the Republican candidate running for the U.S. Senate?
    (1) Williamson (Illinois) (8) Don't Know
    (2) Someone else (9) Refusal

18. Who is the Democratic candidate running for the U.S. Senate?
    (1) Braun (Illinois) (8) Don't Know
    (2) Someone else (9) Refusal

Next, I am going to read you a series of statements about some of the issues in this presidential campaign. For each statement I read, tell me whether you think George Bush agrees with the statement, disagrees with the statement, or if you don't know Bush's position. After you answer for George Bush, then I would like you to tell me if Bill Clinton agrees, disagrees, or if you don't know Clinton's position.

19. There should be a Constitutional amendment outlawing abortion. Does George Bush agree, disagree, or don't you know his position?
    19a. (1) Bush agrees (9) Refusal
    (2) Bush disagrees
    (3) Don't know Bush's position

    Does Bill Clinton agree, disagree, or don't you know his position?
    19b. (1) Clinton agrees (9) Refusal
    (2) Clinton disagrees
    (3) Don't know Clinton's position

20. There should be a tax increase *only* for the wealthiest Americans. Does George Bush agree, disagree, or don't you know his position?
    20a. (1) Bush agrees (9) Refusal
    (2) Bush disagrees
    (3) Don't know Bush's position

    Does Bill Clinton agree, disagree, or don't you know his position?
    20b. (1) Clinton agrees (9) Refusal
    (2) Clinton disagrees
    (3) Don't know Clinton's position

21. The government should take the responsibility for establishing a national health care program. Does George Bush agree, disagree, or don't you know his position?
    21a. (1) Bush agrees (9) Refusal
    (2) Bush disagrees
    (3) Don't know Bush's position

Does Bill Clinton agree, disagree, or don't you know his position?
21b. (1) Clinton agrees (9) Refusal
(2) Clinton disagrees
(3) Don't know Clinton's position

22. US taxpayers should be allowed to use up to 10% of their Federal income tax to reduce the federal deficit. Does George Bush agree, disagree, or don't you know his position?
22a. (1) Bush agrees (9) Refusal
(2) Bush disagrees
(3) Don't know Bush's position

Does Bill Clinton agree, disagree, or don't you know his position?
22b. (1) Clinton agrees (9) Refusal
(2) Clinton disagrees
(3) Don't know Clinton's position

23. A law should be passed creating a national waiting period for handgun purchases. Does George Bush agree, disagree, or don't you know his position?
23a. (1) Bush agrees (9) Refusal
(2) Bush disagrees
(3) Don't know Bush's position

Does Bill Clinton agree, disagree, or don't you know his position?
23b. (1) Clinton agrees (9) Refusal
(2) Clinton disagrees
(3) Don't know Clinton's position

24. At this stage of the 1992 campaign, how would you describe your interest in the presidential campaign? Would you say that you are very uninterested, uninterested, neutral, interested, or very interested in the presidential campaign?
(1) Very uninterested (8) Don't know
(2) Uninterested (9) Refusal
(3) Neutral
(4) Interested
(5) Very interested

25. Next, I am going to read a series of statements people have made about politics. For each statement, tell me if you strongly agree, agree, are neutral, disagree, or strongly disagree.

SA A Neu D SD

Appendix A

25a. I often don't feel sure of myself when talking with other people about politics and government. (I-)(5) (4) (3) (2) (1)

25b. Under our form of government, the people have the final say about how the country is run, no matter who is in office. (E) (5) (4) (3) (2) (1)

25c. I consider myself well qualified to participate in politics. (I) (5) (4) (3) (2) (1)

25d. People like me don't have any say about what the government does. (E-) (5) (4) (3) (2) (1)

25e. I feel that I could do as good a job in public office as most other people. (I) (5) (4) (3) (2) (1)

25f. If public officials are not interested in hearing what the people think, there is really no way to make them listen. (E-) (5) (4) (3) (2) (1)

25g. Sometimes politics and government seem so complicated that a person like me can't really understand what's going on. (I-) (5) (4) (3) (2) (1)

25h. There are many legal ways for citizens to successfully influence what the government does. (E) (5) (4) (3) (2) (1)

26. Based on a scale from zero to ten, where **zero** means that you **definitely would not vote** for the candidate and **ten** that you **definitely would vote** for that candidate, what describes your likelihood of voting (Enter 00 for zero, 01 for one, . . ., 09 for nine, 10 for ten, 88 for Don't remember, and 99 for refusal).

26a. for Bill Clinton? .... _____

26b. for George Bush? .... _____

26c. for Ross Perot? .... _____

27. Suppose the election were between Dan Quayle and Al Gore, what would you say, from zero to ten, describes your likelihood of voting (Enter 00 for zero, 01 for one, . . ., 09 for nine, 10 for ten, 88 for Don't remember, and 99 for refusal).

27a. for Dan Quayle? .... _____

27b. for Al Gore? .... _____

28. If you had to vote today for one of the candidates, who would you vote for?
    (1) Bush
    (2) Clinton
    (3) Perot
    (4) Someone else
    (5) Wouldn't vote
    (8) Don't know
    (9) Refusal

29. Now I'm going to read you several statements about this presidential campaign. Tell me if you strongly agree, agree, are neutral, disagree, or strongly disagree with each statement.

	SA	A	Neu	D	SD
29a. This campaign has relied too much on mudslinging and name calling.	(5)	(4)	(3)	(2)	(1)
29b. I don't think I know enough about any of the candidates to make an intelligent voting choice.	(5)	(4)	(3)	(2)	(1)
29c. From what I've learned so far about the candidates, I'm not sure I want to vote for anybody.	(5)	(4)	(3)	(2)	(1)

We're just about through. Let me ask a few of questions about your background.

30. How old are you ? _____ (Write in present age)

31. What was the last year in school that you completed?

    0 1 2 3 4 5 6 7 8 9 10 11 12 13 14 15 16 17 18 19, 19+

32. Which of the following best describes your current occupational status? (Read the list)

    (1) Full-time employed
    (2) Part-time employed
    (3) Full-time student
    (4) Retired
    (5) Homemaker
    (6) Unemployed at the moment
    (8) Don't know (Don't read)
    (9) Refusal (Don't read)

Appendix A

33. What is your total yearly household income range? Under $10,000? $10,000 to $20,000? Over $20,000 but less than $30,000? $30,000 to $50,000? or more than $50,000?

    (1) < $10,000
    (2) $10,000 to $20,000
    (3) > $20,000 but < $30,000
    (4) $30,000 to $50,000
    (5) > $50,000
    (8) Don't know
    (9) Refusal

34. What is your race? White, Black, Asian, Hispanic, American Indian, or other?

    (1) White
    (2) Black
    (3) Asian
    (4) Hispanic
    (5) American Indian
    (6) Other
    (8) Don't Know
    (9) Refusal

35. We are going to be doing several additional questionnaires over the remainder of the campaign. As part of the study, we are going to interview some people two more times. Would you be willing to be interviewed about the campaign two more times before the campaign is finished?

    (1) Yes (Go to 3a)
    (2) No (Read: Thank you for your assistance. We truly appreciate it.)

    35a. In order that we can be sure to reach you when we call again, can you give us a nickname you go by or the initials of your mother's maiden name?

    _____ (Write nickname or initials)

Thank you very much for your help. We appreciate it.

INTERVIEWER CIRCLES SEX OF RESPONDENT.   (1) Female   (2) Male

Appendix B

Waves 2-5 Questionnaire

1992 PRESIDENTIAL CAMPAIGN QUESTIONNAIRE

First Debate Questionnaire   Location: 1. IL   2. PA   3. OR   4. IN
                             Interview No: 1   Panel:
                                               (Fill in at end, 0 = No, 1 = Yes)
1992 Campaign Study   Questionnaire No. at this location _____
Attempts (Allow 8 Rings)   Date   Time
                             (Record date   1. _____   _____
                             and time of   2. _____   _____
Telephone   -   attempt)   3. _____   _____
                                             4. _____   _____

Hello, my name is _____, and I'm calling from the Mass Communication Research Center at Southern Illinois University.
We are doing a survey about the 1992 presidential election campaign and, because this is a scientific sample, I need to speak to someone who is at least 18 years old, who is in your house right now, and who has the next birthday coming up. (IF NECESSARY, REPEAT ABOVE INTRODUCTION OF YOURSELF TO PERSON WHO COMES TO PHONE NEXT.)
NEXT SAY THIS IF A NEW PERSON: This interview is part of a national study,

dealing with the presidential campaign. It will take ten to fifteen minutes to answer all of the questions. (IF THEY SAY THIS ISN'T A GOOD TIME, MAKE AN APPOINTMENT AND GET THEIR FIRST NAME.)

Call back on: Day _____ Time of Day _____ First Name _____

Your participation is completely voluntary and you may quit the interview at any time. All information will be kept strictly confidential.
This research has been reviewed and approved by the Carbondale Committee for Research
Involving Human Subjects. Should you have any questions about this project, please call Professor William Elliott at the School of Journalism at Southern Illinois University at Carbondale or the Chairperson of Committee for Research Involving Human Subjects. I can give the phone numbers if you wish. (If they ask, it is 453-3267 for Professor Elliott, 453-4533 for the Committee.)

We'd like to ask you some questions about your media use during this campaign.

First, some questions about television.

1. I would like to ask you about **network television** news programs. Think back carefully over the **past week**? How many of the seven nights of the week did you watch at least part of the evening network television news programs?

    ____ (0 to 7 nights)
    (8) Don't know
    (9) Refused

2. Within the last two weeks, do you recall seeing any paid political advertisements about George Bush, Bill Clinton, or Ross Perot on television?
    (1) Yes (Go to Q 2a)   (8) Don't know (Go to Q 3)
    (2) No (Go to Q 3)   (9) Refused (Go to Q 3)

    2a. Think of the ad you remember best. Was it about Bush, Clinton, or Perot?
    (1) Bush   (6) Clinton and Perot
    (2) Clinton   (7) All three
    (3) Perot
    (4) Bush and Clinton   (8) Don't know (Go to Q 3)
    (5) Bush and Perot   (9) Refused (Go to Q 3)

Appendix B

2b. Tell me as much as you can about this ad. Include everything you can remember about it. (Probe: Can you remember anything else?)

_____
_____
_____

2c. Would you say that this ad mainly **praised** the person it was about, **criticized** the person, or **both** praised and criticized?
    (1) Praised   (8) Don't know
    (2) Criticized   (9) Refusal
    (3) Praised and criticized

2d. Do you remember seeing a second ad about Bush, Clinton, or Perot?
    (1) Yes   (8) Don't know
    (2) No   (9) Refused

2e. Who was it about, Bush, Clinton, or Perot?
    (1) Bush   (6) Clinton and Perot
    (2) Clinton   (7) All three
    (3) Perot
    (4) Bush and Clinton   (8) Don't know (Go to Q 3)
    (5) Bush and Perot   (9) Refused (Go to Q 3)

2f. Tell me as much as you can about this ad. Include **everything** you can remember about it. (Probe: Can you remember anything else?)

_____
_____
_____

2g. Would you say that this ad mainly **praised** the person it was about, **criticized** the person, or **both** praised and criticized?
    (1) Praised   (8) Don't know
    (2) Criticized   (9) Refusal
    (3) Praised and criticized

2h. Do you remember seeing a third ad about Bush, Clinton, or Perot?
    (1) Yes   (8) Don't know
    (2) No   (9) Refused

2i. Who was it about, Bush, Clinton, or Perot?
    (1) Bush   (6) Clinton and Perot
    (2) Clinton   (7) All three
    (3) Perot
    (4) Bush and Clinton   (8) Don't know (Go to Q 3)
    (5) Bush and Perot   (9) Refused (Go to Q 3)

2j. Tell me as much as you can about this ad. Include **everything** you can remember about it. (Probe: Can you remember anything else?)

_____

_____

2k. Would you say that this ad mainly **praised** the person it was about, **criticized** the person, or **both** praised and criticized?
   (1) Praised
   (2) Criticized
   (3) Praised and criticized
   (8) Don't know
   (9) Refusal

3. Have you seen or heard any of the candidates—Bush, Clinton, Perot, Gore, Quayle, or Stockdale—as guests on any television talk shows or televised town meetings?
   (1) Yes (Continue with Q 3)
   (2) No (Go to Q 4)
   (8) Don't know (Go to Q 4)
   (9) Refused (Go to Q 4)

Which candidates did you see and which shows were they on? (Check each show and each candidate he respondent mentions. Do not volunteer the names of the show. Probe: Any others? B=Bush, C=Clinton, G=Gore, Q=Quayle, P=Perot, DK=Don't remember who it was)

3a. Today Show	B ___	C ___	G ___	Q ___	P ___	DK ___
3b. Good Morning America	B ___	C ___	G ___	Q ___	P ___	DK ___
3c. This Morning (CBS)	B ___	C ___	G ___	Q ___	P ___	DK ___
3d. Donahue	B ___	C ___	G ___	Q ___	P ___	DK ___
3e. Oprah Winfrey	B ___	C ___	G ___	Q ___	P ___	DK ___
3f. Larry King Live	B ___	C ___	G ___	Q ___	P ___	DK ___
3g. Nightline	B ___	C ___	G ___	Q ___	P ___	DK ___
3h. Arsenio Hall	B ___	C ___	G ___	Q ___	P ___	DK ___
3i. Tonight Show	B ___	C ___	G ___	Q ___	P ___	DK ___
3j. C-Span	B ___	C ___	G ___	Q ___	P ___	DK ___
3k. Town Meetings	B ___	C ___	G ___	Q ___	P ___	DK ___
3l. Don't remember/Other	B ___	C ___	G ___	Q ___	P ___	DK ___

4. Now I would like to ask you about **newspaper reading**. Think back carefully over the past week? How many of the seven days of the week did you read at least part of the **main news section** of the newspaper?

   ___ (0 to 7 days)
   (8) Don't know
   (9) Refused

5. On a scale running from zero (0) to ten (10), where **zero** means that it is **not useful** to you at all in informing you about the presidential candidates and **ten** means it is **extremely useful**, indicate how useful each of the following sources of information about this PRESIDENTIAL campaign have been: (Enter 00 for zero, 01 for one, . . ., 09 for nine, 10 for 10, 88 for Don't remember, and 99 for refusal)

5a. Televised political advertisements _____
5b. Televised talk shows where the audience can ask the candidates questions _____
5c. Televised debates _____
5d. Televised news stories about the presidential campaign _____
5e. Newspaper stories about the presidential campaign _____
5f. Televised interviews with the candidates by journalists on programs such as This Week with David Brinkley _____
5g. Special news programs about the campaign on network television or CNN _____

Now some questions about politics and about this presidential campaign.

6. First, do you consider yourself a Republican, Democrat, Independent, or what?
   (1) Republican   (4) Other
   (2) Democrat   (8) Don't Know
   (3) Independent   (9) Refusal

7. Overall politically, do you consider yourself a liberal, a moderate, or a conservative?
   (1) Liberal   (8) Don't Know
   (2) Moderate   (9) Refusal
   (3) Conservative

8. Which of the following best describes you? Are you **registered to vote**, are you a **U.S. citizen but not registered to vote**, are you **not yet registered** but planning to vote, or are you a **citizen of another country** and not eligible to vote in this election?
   (1) Registered to vote   (8) Don't know
   (2) US citizen but not registered (9) Refusal
   (3) Not registered but planning to vote
   (4) Citizen of another country (Go to Q 11)

9. In 1988, did you vote for Dukakis or Bush?
   (1) Dukakis   (8) Don't Know
   (2) Bush   (9) Refusal

(3) Someone else
(4) Didn't vote
(5) Didn't vote, not eligible

10. On a scale from zero to ten, where **zero** means that you **definitely will not vote**, **five** means there is a **50-50 chance**, and **ten** means you are **absolutely certain you will vote**, how likely are you to vote in this presidential election? (Enter 00 for zero, 01 for one, . . ., 09 for nine, 10 for 10, 77 for non-US citizens, 88 for Don't remember, and 99 for refusal)

———————————

11. At this time we'd like to ask you some questions about some of the things that people are doing or have done during this presidential campaign.

11a. Have you donated any money or volunteered to work in anybody's presidential campaign?
    (1) Yes   (8) DK
    (2) No   (9) NR

11b. Have you discussed the presidential campaign with friends?
    (1) Yes   (8) DK
    (2) No   (9) NR

11c. Have you worn a campaign button, displayed a bumper sticker, or put up a lawn sign for one of the presidential candidates?
    (1) Yes   (8) DK
    (2) No   (9) NR

11d. Have you tried to persuade someone else to vote for one of the presidential candidates?
    (1) Yes   (8) DK
    (2) No   (9) NR

11e. (**Ask from October 15 to October 22**) Did you watch the first presidential debate on Sunday, October 11?
    (1) Yes (Go to Q 11f)   (8) DK (Go to Q 11g)
    (2) No (Go to Q 11g)   (9) NR (Go to Q 11g)

11f. Who do you think won that debate?
    (1) George Bush   (6) Clinton and Perot
    (2) Bill Clinton   (7) All Won
    (3) Ross Perot   (8) No One Won
    (4) Bush and Clinton   (9) Don't Know/Refused
    (5) Bush and Perot

Appendix B   321

11g. (**Ask from October 15 to October 22**) Did you watch the vice presidential debate on Tuesday, October 13?
    (1) Yes (Go to Q 11h)   (8) DK (Go to Q 11i)
    (2) No (Go to Q 11i)   (9) NR (Go to Q 11i)

11h. Who do you think won that debate?
    (1) Dan Quayle   (6) Gore and Stockdale
    (2) Al Gore   (7) All Won
    (3) Jim Stockdale   (8) No One Won
    (4) Quayle and Gore   (9) Don't Know/Refused
    (5) Quayle and Stockdale

11i. (**Ask from October 19 to October 22**) Did you watch the second presidential debate on Thursday, October 15?
    (1) Yes (Go to Q 11j)   (8) DK (Go to Q 12)
    (2) No (Go to Q 12)   (9) NR (Go to Q 12)

11j. Who do you think won that debate?
    (1) George Bush   (6) Clinton and Perot
    (2) Bill Clinton   (7) All Won
    (3) Ross Perot   (8) No One Won
    (4) Bush and Clinton   (9) Don't Know/Refused
    (5) Bush and Perot

12. As far as you are **personally** concerned, what is the **most important issue** in this presidential campaign? (Probe after the first issue: **Is there anything else?**)

12a. Most Important Issue (Issue One): _____

12b. Second Issue (Issue Two): _____

12c. If they mention more than two issues, record the number of additional issues beyond issue 1 and issue 2 (Circle as mentioned)

    3   4   5   6   7   8   9

12d. Total number of issues (0 if no issues mentioned, 1 if Issue One only, 2 if Issue One and Issue Two, and the highest number circled from Q 12c if more than two issues were mentioned)

0   1   2   3   4   5   6   7   8   9

13. Did you watch or listen to (**Give day of debate**)'s presidential debate between Clinton, Bush and Perot?
(1) Yes (Go to Q 14a)   (2) No (Go to Q 13a)

13a. (**Ask of respondents who did not watch** or listen to the debate) Even though you didn't watch the debate, have you seen or heard anything about the debate?
(1) Yes (Go to Q 13b)   (2) No (Go to Q 15 October 13 & 14; Otherwise go to Q 16)

13b. Would you say that what you have learned about (**Give day of debate**)'s debate came primarily from television news, from family or friends, from radio, from newspapers, from the TV analysis after the debate, or from some other source?
(1) Television news   (5) Newspapers
(2) Family and friends   (6) Other source
(3) Radio   (8) Don't know
(4) TV analysis   (9) Refusal

We'd like to ask you to compare how well you think each of the candidates did in (**Give day of debate**)'s debate.

13c. How would you compare **George Bush** and **Bill Clinton** in (Give day of debate)'s debate? Which of the two men did better?
Bush (ask question below)   (8) Don't know (Go to Q 13d)
(3) They were about equal (Go to Q 13d) (9) Refusal (Go to Q 13d)
Clinton (ask question below)

Was that by a lot or just a little?
(1) Bush by a lot
(2) Bush by a little
(4) Clinton by a little
(5) Clinton by a lot

13d. How would you compare **Bill Clinton** and **Ross Perot** in (Give day of debate)'s debate? Which of the two men did better?

Clinton (ask question below)   (8) Don't know (Go to Q 13e)

(3) They were about equal (Go to Q 13e) (9) Refusal (Go to Q 13e)
Perot (ask question below)
Was that by a lot or just a little?
(1) Clinton by a lot
(2) Clinton by a little
(4) Perot by a little
(5) Perot by a lot

13e. How would you compare **Ross Perot** and **George Bush** in (<u>Give day of debate</u>)'s debate? Which of the two men did better?

Perot (ask question below)   (8) Don't know (Go to Q 13f)
(3) They were about equal (Go to Q 13f) (9) Refusal (Go to Q 13f)
Bush (ask question below)
Was that by a lot or just a little?
(1) Perot by a lot
(2) Perot by a little
(4) Bush by a little
(5) Bush by a lot

13f. Was there any one issue or topic that came up during the debate that you think will influence which candidate people will vote for in November? (If No, Don't Know, or Refuse: Go to **Q 15 October 13 and 14; Otherwise go to Q 16**.)
(1) Yes (Go to Q 13g) (8) Don't know
(2) No   (9) Refusal

13g. Can you describe what that was? (Probe: Ask for specifics.)

_____
_____
_____

13h. Which of the three candidates do you think came out best on that issue? (Go to Q 15 October 13 and 14; Otherwise go to Q 16.)
(1) Bush   (8) Don't know
(2) Clinton (9) Refusal
(3) Perot
(4) Everyone
(5) No one

14. (**For respondents who saw the debate**, YES to Q 13a)

14a. How much of the debate itself would you say you watched or listened to? All of it, most of it, some of it, or a little of it?
(4) All of it   (8) Don't know
(3) Most of it   (9) Refused

(2) Some of it
(1) A Little

14b. While you were watching the debate, how much attention did you pay to the debate itself. Would you say you paid a lot of attention, some attention, or that you paid just a little to the debate?
(3) A lot   (8) Don't know
(2) Some   (9) Refused
(1) Just a little

14c. Did you watch any of the television news programs that analyzed the debate **right after the debate was over**?
(1)   Yes   (8)   Don't remember
(2)   No   (9)   Refusal

14d. While you were watching the analysis, how much attention did you pay to the analysis itself? Would you say you paid **a lot** of attention, **some** attention, or that you paid **just a little** to the analysis right after the debate?
(3) A lot   (8) Don't know
(2) Some   (9) Refused
(1) Just a little

We'd like to ask you to compare how well you think each of the candidates did in (**Give day of debate**)'s debate.

14e. How would you compare **George Bush** and **Bill Clinton** in (**Give day of debate**)'s debate? Which of the two men did better?

Bush (ask question below)   (8) Don't know (Go to Q 14f)
(3) They were about equal (Go to Q 14f)   (9) Refusal (Go to Q 14f)
Clinton (ask question below)

Was that by a lot or just a little?

(1) Bush by a lot
(2) Bush by a little
(4) Clinton by a little
(5) Clinton by a lot

14f. How would you compare **Bill Clinton** and **Ross Perot** in (**Give day of debate**)'s debate? Which of the two men did better?

Clinton (ask question below)   (8) Don't know (Go to Q 14g)
(3) They were about equal (Go to Q 14g) (9) Refusal (Go to Q 14g)
Perot (ask question below)
Was that by a lot or just a little?

(1) Clinton by a lot
(2) Clinton by a little
(4) Perot by a little
(5) Perot by a lot

14g. How would you compare **Ross Perot** and **George Bush** in (<u>Give day of debate</u>)'s debate? Which of the two men did better?

Perot (ask question below)   (8) Don't know (Go to Q 14h)
(3) They were about equal (Go to Q 14h) (9) Refusal (Go to Q 14h)
Bush (ask question below)

Was that by a lot or just a little?

(1) Perot by a lot
(2) Perot by a little
(4) Bush by a little
(5) Bush by a lot

14h. Was there any **one** issue or topic that came up during the debate that you think will influence which candidate people will vote for in November? (**If No, Don't know, or Refusal: Go to Q 15 October 13 and 14; Otherwise go to Q 16.**)
(1) Yes (Go to Q 14i)   (8) Don't know
(2) No   (9) Refusal

14i. Can you describe what that was? (Probe: Ask for specifics.)

_____
_____
_____

14j. Which of the three candidates do you think came out best on that issue? (Go to Q 15 October 13 and 14; Otherwise go to Q 16.)
(1) Bush   (8) Don't know
(2) Clinton   (9) Refusal
(3) Perot
(4) Everyone
(5) No one

15. (VICE PRESIDENTIAL DEBATE: **Ask October 13 and 14**) Did you watch or listen to Tuesday's vice presidential debate between Dan Quayle, Al Gore and Jim Stockdale?
(1) Yes (Go to Q 15a)   (2) No (Go to Q 16)

15a. How much of the vice presidential debate itself would you say you

watched or listened to? **All** of it, **most** of it, **some** or it, or **a little** of it?
(4) All of it
(3) Most of it
(2) Some of it
(1) A Little

(8) Don't know
(9) Refused

15b. Did you watch any of the television news programs that analyzed the vice presidential debate **right after the debate was over**?
(1) Yes
(2) No

(8) Don't remember
(9) Refusal

We'd like to ask you to compare how well you think each of the vice presidential candidates did in Tuesday's debate.

15c. How would you compare **Dan Quayle** and **Al Gore** in Tuesday's debate?
Which of the two men did better?
Quayle (ask question below)   (8) Don't know (Go to Q 15d)
(3) They were about equal (Go to Q 15d) (9) Refusal (Go to Q 15d)
Gore (ask question below)

Was that by a lot or just a little?

(1) Quayle by a lot
(2) Quayle by a little
(4) Gore by a little
(5) Gore by a lot

15d. How would you compare **Al Gore** and **Jim Stockdale** in Tuesday's debate?
Which of the two men did better?
Gore (ask question below)   (8) Don't know (Go to Q 15e)
(3) They were about equal (Go to Q 15e) (9) Refusal (Go to Q 15e)
Stockton (ask question below)

Was that by a lot or just a little?

(1) Gore by a lot
(2) Gore by a little
(4) Stockdale by a little
(5) Stockdale by a lot

15e. How would you compare **Jim Stockdale** and **Dan Quayle** in Tuesday's debate?
Which of the two men did better?
Stockton (ask question below)   (8) Don't know (Go to Q 15f)
(3) They were about equal (Go to Q 15f) (9) Refusal (Go to Q 15f)

Quayle (ask question below)

Was that by a lot or just a little?

(1) Stockdale by a lot
(2) Stockdale by a little
(4) Quayle by a little
(5) Quayle by a lot

15f. Was there any one issue or topic that came up during the debate that you think will influence which candidate people will vote for in November?
(1) Yes (Go to Q 15g)   (8) Don't know (Go to Q 16)
(2) No (Go to Q 16)   (9) Refusal (Go to Q 16)

15g. Can you describe what that was? (Probe: Ask for specifics.)

_____

_____

15h. Which of the three candidates do you think came out best on that issue? (Go to Q 16 after they answer)
(1) Quayle   (8) Don't know
(2) Gore   (9) Refusal
(3) Stockdale
(4) Everyone
(5) No one

16. Using a scale from 0 to 10, where **zero** means that the candidate is **very weak** and **ten** that the candidate is **very strong**, how would you rate each of them in terms of the following characteristics? (Enter 00 for zero, 01 for one, . . ., 09 for nine, 10 for 10, 88 for Don't remember, and 99 for a Refusal)

16a. Bill Clinton's knowledge of domestic issues . . . . ____
16b. George Bush's knowledge of domestic issues . . . . ____
16c. Ross Perot's knowledge of domestic issues . . . . ____
16d. George Bush's character . . . . ____
16e. Ross Perot's character . . . . ____
16f. Bill Clinton's character . . . . ____
16g. Ross Perot's understanding of the problems of common people . . ____
16h. George Bush's understanding of the problems of common people . ____
16i. Bill Clinton's understanding of the problems of common people . . ____

(Ask Q 16j to Q 16o from October 19 to October 22)
16j. George Bush's ability as a political debater . . . . ____

16k. Ross Perot's ability as a political debater .... ____
16l. Bill Clinton's ability as a political debater .... ____
16m. Dan Quayle's ability as a political debater .... ____
16n. Al Gore's ability as a political debater .... ____
16o. Jim Stockdale's ability as a political debater .... ____

Now some questions about this political campaign.

17. At this stage, how would you describe your interest in the presidential campaign? Would you say that you are very uninterested, uninterested, neutral, interested, or very interested in the presidential campaign?
    (1) Very uninterested (8) Don't know
    (2) Uninterested (9) Refusal
    (3) Neutral
    (4) Interested
    (5) Very interested

18. I'm going to read you a series of statements about this campaign, about presidential debates, and about politics in general and ask you whether you strongly agree, agree, are neutral, disagree, or strongly disagree with each statement.

	SA	A	Neu	D	SD
18a. This campaign has relied too much on mudslinging and name calling.	(5)	(4)	(3)	(2)	(1)
18b. I was waiting for the presidential debates to help make my mind up about who I will vote for.	(5)	(4)	(3)	(2)	(1)
18c. Under our form of government, the people have the final say about how the country is run, no matter who is in office. (E)	(5)	(4)	(3)	(2)	(1)
18d. All in all, I think the presidential debates are a waste of time.	(5)	(4)	(3)	(2)	(1)
18e. Sometimes politics and government seem so complicated that a person like me can't really understand what's going on. (I-)	(5)	(4)	(3)	(2)	(1)
18f. Presidential candidates seem to avoid answering the important questions during the debates.	(5)	(4)	(3)	(2)	(1)
18g. From what I've learned so far about the candidates, I'm not sure I want to vote for anybody.	(5)	(4)	(3)	(2)	(1)
18h. If public officials are not interested in hearing what the people think, there is really no way to make them listen. (E-)	(5)	(4)	(3)	(2)	(1)

	SA	A	Neu	D	SD
18i. I feel that I could do as good a job in public office as most other people. (I)	(5)	(4)	(3)	(2)	(1)
18j. Presidential debates are one of the best ways for me to learn where the candidates stand on the issues.	(5)	(4)	(3)	(2)	(1)
18k. Now that Ross Perot is a candidate again, this is a better campaign.	(5)	(4)	(3)	(2)	(1)
18l. I agree with many of the things Perot has said.	(5)	(4)	(3)	(2)	(1)

19. (**Ask October 19 to October 22**) This year two presidential debate formats were used. One had a panel of journalists and one had a single moderator. Which one did you prefer? The panel, the moderator, or didn't it make any difference to you?
    (1) Panel
    (2) Moderator
    (3) Combination panel & moderator
    (4) Didn't make any difference
    (8) Don't Know
    (9) Refusal

I am going to read you a series of statements about some of the issues in this presidential campaign. For each statement I read, tell me whether you think **George Bush, Bill Clinton**, and/or **Ross Perot** agrees with the statement, or tell me if you don't know.

20. Which candidate, George Bush, Bill Clinton, or Ross Perot says he favors a Constitutional amendment outlawing abortion?
    (1) Bush favors
    (2) Clinton favors
    (3) Perot favors
    (4) Bush and Clinton or Perot favor
    (5) Clinton and Perot favor
    (6) All favor
    (7) None favor
    (8) Don't know
    (9) Refusal

21. Which candidate, George Bush, Bill Clinton, or Ross Perot, favors a 10 cent per gallon increase in the gas tax every year for the next five years?
    (1) Bush favors
    (2) Clinton favors
    (3) Perot favors
    (4) Perot and Bush or Clinton favor
    (5) Bush and Clinton favor
    (6) All favor
    (7) None favor
    (8) Don't know
    (9) Refusal

22. Which of the **major** party candidates, George Bush or Bill Clinton, favors increasing taxes for American families making more than

$200,000 per year?
- (1) Bush favors
- (2) Clinton favors
- (6) Both favor
- (7) None favor
- (8) Don't know
- (9) Refusal

23. Based on a scale from zero to ten, where **zero** means that you **definitely would not vote for** the candidate and **ten** that you **definitely would** vote for that candidate, what describes your likelihood of voting (Enter 00 for zero, 01 for one, . . ., 09 for nine, 10 for ten, 66 for not voting, 77 for not a US citizen, 88 for Don't remember, and 99 for refusal)

    23a. for Bill Clinton? .... _____
    23b. for George Bush? .... _____
    23c. for Ross Perot? .... _____

24. If you had to vote today for one of the candidates, who would you vote for?
    - (1) Bush
    - (2) Clinton
    - (3) Perot
    - (4) Someone else
    - (5) Wouldn't vote
    - (8) Don't know
    - (9) Refusal

We're just about through. Let me ask a few of questions about your background.

25. How old are you ? _____ (Write in present age)

26. What was the last grade or year in school that you completed?
    0 1 2 3 4 5 6 7 8 9 10 11 12 13 14 15 16 17 18 19, 19+

27. Which of the following best describes your current occupational status? (**Read the list**)
    - (1) Full-time employed
    - (2) Part-time employed
    - (3) Student
    - (4) Retired
    - (5) Homemaker
    - (6) Unemployed at the moment
    - (8) Don't know (Don't read)
    - (9) Refusal (Don't read)

28. What is your marital status? Are you single, married, divorced, separated, living with a significant other, or are you a widow or widower?
    - (1) Single (Go to Q 30)
    - (2) Married (Go to Q 29)
    - (5) Living with a significant other (Go to Q 29)
    - (6) Widow or widower (Go to Q 30)

Appendix B

(3) Divorced (Go to Q 30)   (8) Don't know (Go to Q 30)
(4) Separated (Go to Q 30) (9) Refused (Go to Q 30)

29. Which of the following best describes your spouse's or significant other's current occupational status? (Read the list)
    (1) Full-time employed   (5) Homemaker
    (2) Part-time employed   (6) Unemployed at the moment
    (3) Student   (8) Don't know (Don't read)
    (4) Retired   (9) Refusal (Don't read)

30. What is your total yearly **household** income range? Under $10,000? $10,000 to $20,000? Over $20,000 but less than $30,000? $30,000 to $50,000? or more than $50,000?
    (1) < $10,000   (5) > $50,000
    (2) $10,000 to $20,000
    (3) > $20,000 but < $30,000 (8) Don't know
    (4) $30,000 to $50,000   (9) Refusal

31. What is your race? White, Black, Asian, Hispanic, American Indian, or other?
    (1) White   (5) American Indian
    (2) Black   (6) Other
    (3) Asian   (8) Don't Know
    (4) Hispanic   (9) Refusal

Thank you very much for your help. We appreciate it.

INTERVIEWER CIRCLES SEX OF RESPONDENT.   (1) Female   (2) Male

Appendix C

Wave 6 Questionniare

1992 PRESIDENTIAL CAMPAIGN QUESTIONNAIRE

Pre-Election Questionnaire   Location: 1. IL   2. PA   3. OR   4. IN
                             Interview No: 1   Panel:
                                          (Fill in at end, 0 = No, 1 = Yes)
1992 Campaign Study   Questionnaire No. at this location _____
Attempts (Allow 8 Rings)   Date   Time
                             (Record date   1. _____   _____
                             and time of   2. _____   _____
Telephone   -   attempt)   3. _____   _____
                                            4. _____   _____

Hello, my name is _____, and I'm calling from the Mass Communication Research Center at Southern Illinois University.
We are doing a survey about the 1992 presidential election campaign and, because this is a scientific sample, I need to speak to someone who is at least 18 years old, who is in your house right now, and who has the next birthday coming up. (IF NECESSARY, REPEAT ABOVE INTRODUCTION OF YOURSELF TO PERSON WHO COMES TO PHONE NEXT.)
NEXT SAY THIS IF A NEW PERSON: This interview is part of a national study,

dealing with the presidential campaign. It will take ten to fifteen minutes to answer all of the questions. (IF THEY SAY THIS ISN'T A GOOD TIME, MAKE AN APPOINTMENT AND GET THEIR FIRST NAME.)

Call back on: Day _____ Time of Day_____ First Name_____

Your participation is completely voluntary and you may quit the interview at any time. All information will be kept strictly confidential.

This research has been reviewed and approved by the Carbondale Committee for Research Involving Human Subjects. Should you have any questions about this project, please call Professor William Elliott at the School of Journalism at Southern Illinois University at Carbondale or the Chairperson of Committee for Research Involving Human Subjects. I can give the phone numbers if you wish. (If they ask, it is xxx-xxxx for Professor Elliott, xxx-xxxx for the Committee.)

> We'd like to ask you some questions about your media use during this campaign.

1. We'd like you to think back over the whole presidential campaign.
1a. Think of the presidential campaign ad you remember best. Who was that ad about?
   Was it about Bush, Clinton, or Perot?
   (1) Bush
   (2) Clinton
   (3) Perot
   (4) Bush and Clinton
   (5) Bush and Perot
   (6) Clinton and Perot
   (7) All three
   (8) Don't know (Go to Q 2)
   (9) Refused (Go to Q 2)

1b. Tell me as much as you can about this ad. Include everything you can remember about it. (Probe: Can you remember anything else?)

_____
_____
_____

1c. Would you say that this ad mainly **praised** the person it was about, **criticized** the person, or **both** praised and criticized?
   (1) Praised
   (2) Criticized
   (3) Praised and criticized
   (8) Don't know
   (9) Refusal

2. Have you seen or heard any of the candidates—Bush, Clinton, Perot,

Gore, Quayle, or Stockdale—as guests on any television talk shows or televised town meetings?

(1) Yes (Continue with Q 2) (8) Don't know (Go to Q 3)
(2) No (Go to Q 3) (9) Refused (Go to Q 3)

Which candidates did you see and which shows were they on? (Check each show and each candidate he respondent mentions. Do not volunteer the names of the show. Probe: Any others? B=Bush, C=Clinton, G=Gore, Q=Quayle, P=Perot, DK=Don't remember who it was)

2a. Today Show	B ___	C ___	G ___	Q ___	P ___	S ___
2b. Good Morning America	B ___	C ___	G ___	Q ___	P ___	S ___
2c. This Morning (CBS)	B ___	C ___	G ___	Q ___	P ___	S ___
2d. Donahue	B ___	C ___	G ___	Q ___	P ___	S ___
2e. Oprah Winfrey	B ___	C ___	G ___	Q ___	P ___	S ___
2f. Larry King Live	B ___	C ___	G ___	Q ___	P ___	S ___
2g. Nightline	B ___	C ___	G ___	Q ___	P ___	S ___
2h. Arsenio Hall	B ___	C ___	G ___	Q ___	P ___	S ___
2i. Tonight Show	B ___	C ___	G ___	Q ___	P ___	S ___
2j. C-Span	B ___	C ___	G ___	Q ___	P ___	S ___
2k. Town Meetings	B ___	C ___	G ___	Q ___	P ___	S ___
2l. Don't remember/Other	B ___	C ___	G ___	Q ___	P ___	S ___

3. On a scale running from zero (0) to ten (10), where **zero** means that it is **not useful** to you at all in informing you about the presidential candidates and **ten** means it is **extremely useful**, indicate how useful each of the following sources of information about this PRESIDENTIAL campaign have been: (Enter 00 for zero, 01 for one, ..., 09 for nine, 10 for 10, 88 for Don't remember, and 99 for refusal)

3a. Televised political advertisements
3b. Televised talk shows where the audience can ask the candidates questions ___
3c. Televised debates ___
3d. Televised news stories about the presidential campaign ___
3e. Newspaper stories about the presidential campaign ___
3f. Televised interviews with the candidates by journalists on programs such as This Week with David Brinkley ___
3g. Special news programs about the campaign on network television or CNN ___

___

Now some questions about politics and about this presidential campaign.

4. On a scale from zero to ten, where **zero** means that you **definitely**

4. On a scale from zero to ten, where **zero** means that you **definitely will not vote**, **five** means there is a **50-50 chance**, and **ten** means you are **absolutely certain** you will vote, how likely are you to vote in this presidential election? (Enter 00 for zero, 01 for one, . . ., 09 for nine, 10 for 10, 77 for non-US citizens, 88 for Don't remember, and 99 for refusal) _____

5. At this time we'd like to ask you about the presidential and vice presidential debates.

   5a. Did you watch the first presidential debate on Sunday, October 11?
   (1) Yes   (8) DK
   (2) No   (9) NR

   5b. Did you watch the vice presidential debate on Tuesday, October 13?
   (1) Yes   (8) DK
   (2) No   (9) NR

   5c. Did you watch the second presidential debate on Thursday, October 15?
   (1) Yes   (8) DK
   (2) No   (9) NR

   5d. Did you watch the final presidential debate on Sunday, October 19?
   (1) Yes   (8) DK
   (2) No   (9) NR

6. Overall, how well you think each of the candidates did in the presidential debates?

   6a. How would you compare **George Bush** and **Bill Clinton** over the presidential debates? Which of the two men did better?
   Bush (ask question below)   (8) Don't know (Go to Q 6b)
   (3) They were about equal (Go to Q 6b)   (9) Refusal (Go to Q 6b)
   Clinton (ask question below)

   Was that by a lot or just a little?

   (1) Bush by a lot
   (2) Bush by a little
   (4) Clinton by a little
   (5) Clinton by a lot

   6b. How would you compare **Bill Clinton** and **Ross Perot** over the presidential debates? Which of the two men did better?
   Clinton (ask question below)   (8) Don't know (Go to Q 6c)

Appendix C

(3) They were about equal (Go to Q 6c)   (9) Refusal (Go to Q 6c)
Perot (ask question below)

Was that by a lot or just a little?

(1) Clinton by a lot
(2) Clinton by a little
(4) Perot by a little
(5) Perot by a lot

6c. How would you compare **Ross Perot** and **George Bush** over the presidential debates? Which of the two men did better?
Perot (ask question below)   (8) Don't know (Go to Q 7)
(3) They were about equal (Go to Q 7)   (9) Refusal (Go to Q 7)
Bush (ask question below)

Was that by a lot or just a little?

(1) Perot by a lot
(2) Perot by a little
(4) Bush by a little
(5) Bush by a lot

7. Which of the vice presidential candidates, **Dan Quayle**, **Al Gore** or **Jim Stockdale**, do you think came out best in the vice presidential debate?

   (1) Dan Quayle   (7) All equal
   (2) Al Gore   (8) No one won
   (3) Jim Stockdale   (9) Don't Know/Refusal
   (4) Quayle and Gore equal
   (5) Quayle and Stockdale equal
   (6) Gore and Stockdale equal

8. Using a scale from 0 to 10, where **zero** means that the candidate is **very weak** and **ten** that the candidate is **very strong**, how would you rate each of them in terms of the following characteristics? (Enter 00 for zero, 01 for one, . . ., 09 for nine, 10 for 10, 88 for Don't remember, and 99 for a Refusal)

8a. Bill Clinton's knowledge of domestic issues . . . .
8b. George Bush's knowledge of domestic issues . . . . _____
8c. Ross Perot's knowledge of domestic issues . . . . _____
8d. George Bush's character . . . . _____
8e. Ross Perot's character . . . . _____
8f. Bill Clinton's character . . . . _____
8g. Ross Perot's understanding of the problems of common people . . _____
8h. George Bush's understanding of the problems of common people . . . _____

8h. George Bush's understanding of the problems of common people .. _____
8i. Bill Clinton's understanding of the problems of common people ... _____
8j. George Bush's ability as a political debater .... _____
8k. Ross Perot's ability as a political debater .... _____
8l. Bill Clinton's ability as a political debater .... _____
8m. Dan Quayle's ability as a political debater .... _____
8n. Al Gore's ability as a political debater .... _____
8o. Jim Stockdale's ability as a political debater .... _____

Now some questions about this political campaign.

9. At this stage, how would you describe your interest in the presidential campaign? Would you say that you are **very uninterested, uninterested, neutral, interested,** or **very interested** in the presidential campaign?
   (1) Very uninterested   (8) Don't know
   (2) Uninterested   (9) Refusal
   (3) Neutral
   (4) Interested
   (5) Very interested

10. I'm going to read you a series of statements about this campaign, about presidential debates, and about politics in general and ask you whether you **strongly agree, agree,** are **neutral, disagree,** or **strongly disagree** with each statement.

	SA	A	Neu	D	SD
10a. This campaign has relied too much on mudslinging and name calling.	(5)	(4)	(3)	(2)	(1)
10b. I was waiting for the presidential debates to help make my mind up about who I will vote for.	(5)	(4)	(3)	(2)	(1)
10c. When they report the polls, the media concentrate too much on who is winning and not enough on the reasons people feel the way they do.	(5)	(4)	(3)	(2)	(1)
10d. All in all, I think the presidential debates are a waste of time.	(5)	(4)	(3)	(2)	(1)
10e. Generally, the news media have done a good job in covering this campaign.	(5)	(4)	(3)	(2)	(1)
10f. Presidential candidates seem to avoid answering the important questions during the debates.	(5)	(4)	(3)	(2)	(1)
10g. From what I've learned so far about the candidates, I'm not sure I want to vote for anybody.	(5)	(4)	(3)	(2)	(1)

10h. The press seems more concerned about dirt than they are about the substance of the campaign. (5) (4) (3) (2) (1)
10i. People can learn more about the candidates from talk-shows than they can from daily news reports. (5) (4) (3) (2) (1)
10j. Presidential debates are one of the best ways for me to learn where the candidates stand on the issues. (5) (4) (3) (2) (1)
10k. Now that Ross Perot is a candidate again, this is a better campaign. (5) (4) (3) (2) (1)
10l. I agree with many of the things Perot has said. (5) (4) (3) (2) (1)

11. This year several presidential debate formats were used. One had a panel of journalists, one had a single moderator, one had a moderator and took questions from the audience, and one combined the single moderator and panel formats. Which one did you prefer? The panel, the single moderator, the moderator with questions from the audience, the combination panel and moderator, or didn't it make any difference to you?
    (1) Panel only   (8) Don't Know
    (2) Moderator only   (9) Refusal
    (3) Moderator with questions from the audience
    (4) Combination panel and moderator
    (5) Didn't make any difference

12. Based on a scale from zero to ten, where **zero** means that you **definitely would not vote for** the candidate and **ten** that you **definitely would** vote for that candidate, what describes your likelihood of voting (Enter 00 for zero, 01 for one, . . ., 09 for nine, 10 for ten, 66 for not voting, 77 for not a US citizen, 88 for Don't remember, and 99 for refusal)

12a. for Bill Clinton? .... ____
12b. for George Bush? .... ____
12c. for Ross Perot? .... ____

13. If you had to vote **today** for one of the candidates, who would you vote for?
    (1) Bush   (5) Wouldn't vote
    (2) Clinton   (8) Don't know
    (3) Perot   (9) Refusal
    (4) Someone else

14. I'm going to read you four reasons people have given us for voting

for president. As I read them, tell me whether or not the statement applies to you. (Read each below and check if they apply)

14a. Not voting (Go to Q 15) _____

14b. I'm voting to help my presidential candidate win the election. _____

14c. I'm voting to keep the other presidential candidates from being elected. _____

14d. My vote is an expression of my true political views. _____

14e. My vote is really a protest vote. _____

15. What do you think the odds are for each of the candidates to actually be elected?

15a. Would you say that George Bush's chances of being elected are nearly zero, less than 50/50, about 50/50, better than 50/50, or that it is almost certain that George Bush will be elected?
   (1) Nearly zero   (8) Don't know
   (2) Less than 50/50   (9) Refusal
   (3) About 50/50
   (4) Better than 50/50
   (5) Almost certain

15b. Would you say that Bill Clinton's chances of being elected are nearly zero, less than 50/50, about 50/50, better than 50/50, or that it is almost certain that Bill Clinton will be elected?
   (1) Nearly zero   (8) Don't know
   (2) Less than 50/50   (9) Refusal
   (3) About 50/50
   (4) Better than 50/50
   (5) Almost certain

15c. Would you say that Ross Perot's chances of being elected are nearly zero, less than 50/50, about 50/50, better than 50/50, or that it is almost certain that Ross Perot will be elected?
   (1) Nearly zero   (8) Don't know
   (2) Less than 50/50   (9) Refusal
   (3) About 50/50
   (4) Better than 50/50
   (5) Almost certain

Appendix C

16. Recently, Ross Perot made some accusations against the Republicans about why he dropped out of the campaign in July. Can you tell me what the accusations were about?
    (1) No (Go to Q 17)
    Yes (**Ask about specific accusations and circle the appropriate response below**)
    (2) Indicated story about daughter's wedding, dirty tricks, wire taps
    (3) Something else
    (8) Don't remember
    (9) Refusal

    We're just about through. Let me ask just one question so we can be sure we have matched you correctly.

17. How old are you? _____ (Write in present age)

Thank you very much for your help. We appreciate it.

INTERVIEWER CIRCLES SEX OF RESPONDENT.   (1) Female   (2) Male

Appendix D

State-by-State 1992 Presidential Election Poll Results

STATE	BUSH	CLINTON	PEROT	POLLSTER/DATE/ MARGIN OF ERROR
AL (9)	38	+39	14	ANNISTON STAR, 10/24-25, +/- 3.5%
	+45	38	14	BIRMINGHAM NEWS, 10/26-31, +/- 4%
AK (3)	+37	30	23	Cromer Group (D), 10/25-26, +/- 4.4%
AZ (8)	33	+37	21	ASU/KAET-TV, 10/24-25, +/- 4%
AR (6)	31	++52	10	ARK. DEM-GAZETTE, 10/16-18, +/- 3.5%
CA (54)	29	++45	23	Field Inst., 10/25-28, +/- 3.1%
CO (8)	32	++41	19	DENVER POST, 10/29-31, +/- 4.9%
	32	+39	17	Ciruli/9 News, 10/25-28, +/- 4.7%
CT (8)	29	++37	18	HART. COURANT, 10/23-30, +/- 3%

DE (3)	36	+42	18	NEWS-JOURNAL, 10/28-31, +/- 3.2%
DC (3)	17	++71	8	News 4/PMR, 10/12-14, +/- 4.5%
FL (25)	+39	37	21	FL Opinion, 10/24-27, +/-3.5%
GA (13)	38	+44	12	ATL CONST./WSB-TV, 10/19-21, +/-4%
HI (4)	30	++40	19	HON. ADVERTISER, 10/25, +/- 4.5%
ID (4)	++35	25	28	KTVB-TV/PMR, 10/22-24, +/- 3.5%
IL (22)	30	++46	14	DAILY HERALD/News 7, 10/26-29, +/-3%
	28	++45	12	CHICAGO TRIBUNE, 10/26-28, +/-3%
	37	+44	12	PMR/COPLEY, 10/27-28, +/- 3.5%
IN (12)	+41	37	15	INDIANAPOLIS STAR, 10/28-31, +/- 3.1%
	31	+35	17	JOURNAL-GAZETTE, 10/22-28, +/- 3.1%
IA (7)	32	++41	19	D.M. REGISTER, 10/25-30, +/- 3.4%
KS (6)	33	33	22	Tpka CAPITAL-JOURNAL, 10/26-29, +/-3%
KY (8)	38	+45	12	LEX. HERALD-LEADER, 10/27-29, +/-4%
LA (9)	36	+41	11	SHREVEPORT TIMES, 10/23-24, +/-3.5%
ME (4)	21	++30	21	PRESS HERALD, 10/23-27, +/- 4%
MD (10)	31	++48	15	GWU/GSPM, 10/20-24, +/- 4%
MA (12)	23	++44	22	Becker Inst., 10/23-25, +/-5%
MI (18)	33	++43	17	DETROIT NEWS, 10/26-28, +/- 4%
	32	+41	18	OAK. PRESS/WDIV, 10/28-30, +/- 4.5%
MN (10)	28	++44	18	Minn. STAR-TRIBUNE, 10/27-30, +/- 3%
MS (7)	+41	37	11	NATCHEZ DEMOCRAT, 10/23-24, +/- 3.4%
MO (11)	27	++42	20	POST-DISPATCH/KMOX, 10/25-29, +/-3.7%

Appendix D 345

MT (3)	29	++41	19	Eastern MT College, 10/16-19, +/- 4%
NE (5)	++38	29	17	WORLD-HERALD, 10/20-22, +/-3.2%
NV (4)	30	+35	27	KLAS-TV/PMR, 10/23-24, +/- 3.5%
NH (4)	29	++44	18	ARG, 10/27-28, +/- 4%
	33	+35	21	CONCORD MONITOR, 10/25-26, +/- 3.5%
NJ (15)	30	++42	18	STAR-LEDGER, 10/23-29, +/- 3.5%
	29	++36	12	ASBURY PARK PRESS, 10/29-31, +/- 3.1%
NM (5)	33	++40	11	ALBUQUERQUE TRIBUNE, 10/27-29, +/- 3%
NY (33)	29	++51	16	Marist Inst., 10/25-26, +/- 4%
NC (14)	38	+39	9	Grnsbro N&R, 10/26-27, +/- 3.5%
	32	+40	10	Raleigh N&0, 10/25-28, +/- 4%
ND (3)	+37	36	20	G.F. HERALD, 10/29-30, +/- 4.2%
	++41	30	17	PMR, 10/27-28, +/- 5%
OH (21)	40	+41	19	COLUMBUS DISPATCH, 10/26-29, +/- 3%
	36	+42	18	BEACON JOURNAL, 10/26-31, +/- 3.5%
OK (8)	+37	31	16	Kielhorn/KWTV, 10/26-28, +/- 4%
OR (7)	24	++42	20	OREGONIAN, 10/22-26, +/- 4%
	30	++39	22	REGISTER-GUARD/PMR, 10/25-26, +/-3.5%
PA (23)	36	++45	11	KDKA/PMR, 10/27-28, +/- 3.5%
RI (4)	27	++48	18	WPRI-TV, 10/23-25, +/- 5%
SC (8)	+43	40	13	Columbia STATE, 10/26-28, +/- 3.9%
SD (3)	31	+35	20	ARGUS LEADER, 10/21-22, +/- 3.5%
TN (11)	39	+44	10	PMR, 10/25-26, +/- 3.5%
TX (32)	++43	35	15	Mason-Dixon, 10/26-28, +/- 3.5%
UT (5)	++37	24	13	S.L. TRIBUNE, 10/26-30, +/- 3%
VT (3)	26	++43	16	BURL. FREE PRESS, 10/20-22, +/- 3.5%

VA (13)	++40	33	13	TIMES-DISPATCH, 10/26-29, +/- 3%
	+43	38	10	Mason-Dixon, 10/28-29, +/- 3.5%
WA (11)	31	++40	21	POST-INTELLIGENCER, 10/26-27, +/- 4%
	34	+39	15	KOMO/JRNL-AMERICAN, 10/27-28, +/-4.9%
WV (5)	31	++40	14	CHARLESTON GAZETTE, 10/26-28, +/-4.2%
	30	++48	11	WV Poll/ DAILY MAIL, 10/26-28, +/-4.2%
WI (11)	35	+38	20	MIL. JOURNAL, 10/29-30, +/- 4%
WY (3)	+35	32	23	CASPER STAR-TRIB, 10/22-24, +/- 3.5%

Source: Hotline electoral scoreboard (1992, November 3). American Political Network.

Author Index

A

Abramson, J.B., 51, *54*
Albright, J., 5, 22, 105, *124*
Alter, J., 3, 22, 54, *55*
Apple, R.W., Jr., 107, *124*
Arterton, F.C., 51, *54*
Asard, E, 78, *99*
Auletta, K., 3, 4, 22
Avery, R.K., 52, *55*

B

Baer, D., 235, *244*
Bagdikian, B., 48, *55*
Barone, M., 251, *273*
Bates, S., 200, *232*
Bennett, W.L., 4, 22, 75, *99*
Berelson, B., 35, *40*
Bernstein, J.M., 2, 6, 7, 10, 13, 14, 15, 17, 22, 23, 25, 29, *40*, 43, 47, *55*, 70, 71, 75, 80, *99*, 106, *125*, 141, *142*, 146, 149, *174*, 176, 177, 182, 187, *198*, 201, 209, 228, *232*, 249, 252, 253, 274, 288, 292, 293, 296, *299*
Birdsell, D.S., 201, *232*, 296, *299*

Biswas, R., 22, 24, 147, 148, *174*, 298, *299*
Black, C., 49, *55*, 239, *244*
Borger, G., 235, *244*
Broder, D., 54, *55*, 70, 71, 293, *299*
Brownstein, R., 4, 22
Brydon, S.R., 147, 148, 149, *174*
Budd, R.W., 204, *232*
Bury, C., 74, 75, *99*

C

Campbell, D.T., 28, *40*
Cappella, J.N., 248, 250, *273*
Carter, B., 9, 22
Carter, R.F., 148, *173*
Chaffee, S.H., 14, 22, 24, 147, *173*, 201, *232*
Chandler, D.L., 283, *286*
Chen, E., 46, *55*
Chen, H., 29, *40*
Chomsky, N., 27, *40*
Clifford, T., 242, *244*, 279, *286*
Cook, T.D., 28, *40*
Craig, S.C., 19, 23, 80, *99*, 214, *232*

D

Daily, K., 29, *40*
Davison, W.P., 16, *23*, 247, *273*
Devlin, L.P., 245, 255, *273*
Devroy, A. 49, *55*
Diamond, E., 202, *232*
Dillin, J., 104, *124*
Dionne, E.J., Jr., 277, *286*
Donaldson, S., 145, *173*
Donohew, L., 204, *232*
Drew, D., 75, *99*, 201, *232*
Drew, E., 4, *23*, 74, *99*
Dugger, R., 5, *23*, 105, *124*
Dye, T.R., 145, 173

E

Eller, J., 46, *55*
Elliott, W.R., 1, 2, 6, 7, 10, 13, 15, 17, 22, *23*, 25, 29, *40*, 43, 47, *55*, 70, 71, 75, 80, *99*, 106, *125*, 141, *142*, 146, 148, 149, *174*, 176, 177, 182, 187, *198*, 201, 209, 228, *232*, 249, 252, 253, 274, 288, 292, 293, 296, *299*
Entman, R.M., 54, *55*
Evarts, D.R., 77, *100*
Eveland, W.P., Jr., 76, *99*

F

Farrell, J.A., 241, *244*
Firestone, D., 106, *125*
Freedom Forum Media Studies Center, 3, *23*, 51, *55*, 54, 73, *99*
Friery, K., 202, *232*

G

Gallup, G., Jr., 148, 149, *174*
Garrett, M., 246, *273*
Gaudet, H., 35, *40*
Gergen, D., 4, *23*, 103, *125*, 135, *141*
Germond, J., 58, *71*
Germond, J.E., 6, *23*
Germond, J.W., 75, *99*, 202, *232*
Graber, D.A., 253, *273*

Greider, W., 48, *55*
Groer, A., 128, *141*
Grove, L., 240, *244*
Guo, Z., 29, *40*

H

Hamilton, B., 101, *125*
Hellweg, S.A., 147, 148, 149, *174*
Hennessy, B., 278, *286*
Herman, E., 27, *40*
Hines, C., 4, *23*, 104, *125*
Horowitz, E., 29, *40*
Huang, H., 29, *40*

I

Ifil, G., 239, *244*

J

Jackson, B., 248, *273*, 295, *299*
Jamieson, K.H., 6, *23*, 144, *174*, 201, *232*, 248, 249, 250, *274*, 288, 296, *299*
Jennings, P., 129, 138, 139, *141*

K

Keen, J., 106, *125*
Kelly, M., 237, *244*
Kennamer, J.D., 201, *232*
Kessel, J.H., 234, *244*, 276, *286*
King, L., 76, *99*, 103, *125*
Kitman, M., 283, *286*
Koppel, T., 4, *23*, 74, 75, *99*
Kraus, S., 129, *142*, 145, 146, 148, *174*, 201, *232*
Kurtz, H., 248, 255, *274*

L

Lanoue, D.J., 149, *174*
Lasorsa, D.L., 16, *23*
Lavin, C., 240, *244*
Lazarsfeld, P.F., 35, *40*
Lebel, G.G., 9, 13, 14, *23*
Lehigh, S., 239, *244*
Lemert, J.B., 1, 2, 6, 7, 10, 13, 14, 15, 17, 22, *23*, 25, 29, *40*, 43, 47, *55*,

70, *71*, 75, 80, *99*, 106, 121, *125*, 141, *142*, 146, 147, 149, *174*, 176, 177, 182, 187, *198*, 201, 209, 228, 232, 249, 252, 253, *274*, 288, 292, 293, 294, 296, *299*
Lengel, L., 77, *100*
Leshner, G., 147, *173*
Levy, M.R., 253, *274*
Lewis, D.S., 201, *232*
Liasson, M., 74, *99*
Lippmann, W., 48, *55*
Lipset, S.M., 11, *23*
Louden, A., 250, *274*

M

Mandel, S., 242, 243, *244*
Marelius, J., 135, *142*
Mattley, C., 77, *100*
McCain, T.A., 52, *55*
McClure, R.D., 75, *100*, 253, *274*
McCombs, M.E., 28, 29, *40*
McGrory, M., 5, *23*
McKibben, G., 246, *274*
McLeod, D.M., 76, *99*
Meadow, R.G., 51, *55*, 144, *174*
Mealiea, W., 101, *125*
Means, M., 109, *125*
Meserve, J., 109, *125*
Milavsky, J.R., 22, *24*, 147, 148, *174*, 298, *299*
Miller, C.B., 76, *100*
Morganthau, T., 6, *23*, 106, *125*

N

Nathanson, A.I., 76, *99*
Nelson, C., 278, *286*
Nestvold, K.J., 1, 2, 6, 7, 10, 13, 14, 15, 17, 22, 23, 25, 29, *40*, 43, 47, *55*, 70, *71*, 75, 80, *99*, 106, *125*, 141, *142*, 146, 149, *174*, 176, 177, 182, 187, *198*, 201, 209, 232, 228, 249, 252, 253, *274*, 288, 292, 293, 296, *299*
Newhagen, J.E., 83, *100*

Niemi, R.G., 19, *23*, 80, *99*, 214, *232*
Nolan, M.F., 129, *142*
Novak, R., 4, *24*, 74, 75, *100*

O

Orren, G.R., 51, *54*

P

Page, S., 242, 244, 279, *286*
Patterson, T.E., 58, 59, *71*, 75, 76, 90, *100*, 110, *125*, 253, *274*, 296, *299*
Pease, E.C., 3, 5, *24*
Pfau, M., 147, 148, 149, *174*, 250, *274*
Plattner, A., 235, *244*

R

Rafaeli, S., 52, *55*
Range, P.R., 235, *244*
Ranney, A., 54, *55*
Rarick, G.R., 1, *23*, 25, *40*
Reese, S.D., 26, *40*
Ridout, C.F., 76, *100*
Robinson, C.E., 278, *286*
Robinson, J.P., 253, *274*
Rook, S., 108, *125*
Rosen, J., 45, *55*
Rosenberg, W.L., 2, 6, 7, 10, 13, 14, 15, 17, 22, 23, 25, 29, *40*, 43, 47, *55*, 70, *71*, 75, 80, *99*, 106, *125*, 141, *142*, 146, 149, *174*, 176, 177, 182, 187, *198*, 201, 209, 228, 232, 249, 252, 253, *274*, 288, 292, 293, 296, *299*
Rosenstiel, T.B., 69, *71*, 102, *125*, 239, *244*, 248, *274*

S

Sandell, K.L., 77, *100*
Schrott, P.R., 149, *174*
Schudson, M., 52, *55*
Scott, W.A., 63, *71*
Schwartz, 235, *244*
Sears, D.O., 14, 22, *24*, 201, *232*

Shaw, D., 3, *24*
Shoemaker, P.J., 26, 28, *40*
Silver, G.E., 19, 23, 80, *99*, 214, *232*
Smith, M., 238, 239, *244*
Sothirajah, J., 15, 23, 148, *174*
Spear, J.C., 143, *174*
Stamm, K.R., 148, *173*
Steele, C., 29, *40*
Steeper, F.T., 175, *198*
Stempel, G.H. III., 26, *40*
Stencel, M., 103, *125*

T

Taylor, P., 54, *55*
Thorp, R.K., 204, *232*
Topping, S., 3, *24*

U

Underwood, J., 238, *244*

W

Walsh, T., 235, *244*
Weaver, D.H., 201, *232*
West, D.M., 7, 8, *24*, 251, 253, *274*, 288, *299*
Wines, M., 234, *244*
Witcover, J., 6, *23*, 58, *71*, 75, *99*, 202, *232*

Y

Yang, J.E., 106, *125*

Z

Zeigler, H., 145, *173*
Zhao, X., 147, *173*
Zhu, J.H., 22, *24*, 147, 148, *174*, 298, *299*
Ziyati, A., 77, *100*

Subject Index

A

ABC Evening News, content analysis, 178
ABC News, 32, 43, 138, 285, 293
ABC post-debate news specials, 32, 33, 178; *see also Nightline*, content analysis of, 178, 184
abortion issue, 87, 112, 113, 152
adjusted means, explained, 83, 84, 190
"Ad Police," media performance as, 8, 9, 44, 246, 248-250, 270, 288, 293, 298
ad recall, 252-254, 271, 272
 party identification and, 253, 254, 256-267, 271
 whose ad first, 10, 254-257, 270
 whose ad most often, 16, 254-257
ad replays, 1988, 246-248, 250
ad strategies, 22, 241, 242
ad type, measurement of, 252
ads; *see also* attack ads
 exposure measurement, 7, 8, 252-254, 271
 flaws in measuring effects, 7, 8, 251
 "infomercials," 10, 246, 254, 255
 1950s style in 1992, 2, 9, 246
 Perot's, 10, 246, 254-268, 270-272
 rapid response teams and, 241, 243
 usefulness ratings, 94, 268, 269, 294
affiliates stampede network coverage of Gennifer Flowers, 43
age
 debate support and, 213
 debater performance perceptions and, 194
 knowledge and, 147
 Perot support and, 147, 291
 vote factor, as, 111
agenda control by
 candidates, 45, 47
 loss by traditional media, 44, 45, 47
Albright, Joseph, 105
Alderman, Jeff, 285
Allen, Frank, 29

Alter, Jonathan, 17, 54n
alternative media sources, 17, 21, 26, 27, 41-53, 57, 77, 115-117, 123, 288, 294-296; *see also* audience; talk shows; disenchantment with conventional media; voters regain control
  information accessibility increased by, 51, 52
  Clinton's use as President, 98, 123
  dangers of, 295, 296
  debates as, 144
  effects on attitudes toward old media, 53, 115-117
  exposure measurement; *see* talk show exposure measurement
  increase in available information, 51, 52
  news treatment of; *see* talk shows
  Perot's use of, 47, 49, 50, 59, 109, 110, 131, 241, 288, 297, 298
  voter empowerment by; *see* voters regain control
Ailes, Roger, 6, 12
Anderson, John, 12, 130, 133
Arsenio Hall show, 30, 31, 42, 43, 151, 290
attack ads, 1988
  Bush, 6, 7, 8, 10, 12, 16, 17, 234, 237, 242, 246, 247, 251, 253, 254, 271, 293
  Dukakis, 10, 17, 234, 251, 253, 254, 271, 272, 293
  news replays of, 6, 16, 246-250
  recall of, 252, 253, 271
attack ads, 1992, 2, 6, 7, 12, 16, 242, 270
  Bush's, 245, 254-256, 262-273, 293
  Bush campaign disagreements about using, 242
  "bystander" hypothesis and, 257-267
  Clinton's, 246, 254-256, 262-272, 293
  Clinton campaign's first use against Bush, 242, 243
  Clinton rapid response to, 238, 241-243
  compared to positive ads, 7, 10, 253-267, 269-273
  conventional wisdom about, 6, 7, 10, 12, 16, 17, 247, 248, 250, 251, 288
  direct mail and, 238
  effects of, 6, 7, 10, 252-269, 271-273, 289, 293
  journalists' overestimation of power, 16, 17, 247, 248, 289
  news replays of, 6, 16, 246-250, 289
  radio and, 237, 238
  three-candidate race and, 255; *see also* "bystander" above
  viewer attitudes toward, 6, 7, 10, 268
  voting choice and, 257-267
  who voters believe is using, 255, 256, 270-273
"attack faxes," Bush campaign, 240, 294
audience; *see* voters
Atwater, Lee, 240
Axelrod, David, 240

B

Baker, James, 133, 135, 136, 200, 241
Bailey, Douglas, 236
Beal, Richard, 277
Bennett, W. Lance, 75
Bentsen, Lloyd, 15, 16, 145, 179, 192
"bimbo eruptions," 240

Subject Index

Blackett, Hill, 236
Bond, Richard, 242
Boston Globe, The, 138, 283
"Boston Harbor" ad, 1988, 6
Broder, David, urges coverage reform, 44, 70n, 293
Brown, Jerry, 45
   his "800" phone number and, 46, 59
Brown, Ron, 242, 243
Bruno, Hal, 138
Buchanan, Pat, 131
Bury, Chris, 74, 75
Bush, George
   abortion policy, 87
   ad strategy disagreement, 242
   ad tactics, 272
   ads in 1988, 6, 7, 8, 9, 12, 245, 247, 251, 253, 254, 272
   ads in 1992, 238, 242, 245, 246, 254-273
   campaign advisors, 29, 30
   candidacy at end of primaries, 43
   "Chicken George" and; *see* "Chicken George"
   debate invitation to Perot, 107, 136, 203
   debate goals, 288
   debate negotiations, 127, 130-135, 140, 141, 203
   debate performance and, 148, 149, 153-158, 175-182, 188, 189, 196, 197, 292
   debate tactics, 109, 110
   debate verdict ads, 9, 245
   debates, 1988, 131, 153
   debates, 1992, 9, 13, 18, 19, 107, 127, 130-133, 139, 148, 149, 178, 179, 292
   "goes negative," voters perceive, 255, 256, 293
   "image" and debate viewing, 161-166, 292
   knowledge of his supporters, 112, 113
   loss of voters to Perot, 20, 109, 110
   negotiating position, 1988 debates, 131, 132, 140, 141, 200
   negotiating position, 1992 debates, 127, 129, 131-136, 140, 200
   nomination acceptance speech, Clinton rebuts, 239
   performance, talk show, 49
   Perot and, 101, 109, 136
   poll standing, 1992, 11, 104, 109, 131, 133, 135, 282, 283, 285
   rapid response team, 22, 288
   Richmond debate format and, 139, 155
   surrogates attack Clinton, 243
   talk show appearances, 3, 17, 19, 29, 30, 50, 73, 94, 95, 98
   talk show audience size, 78
   talk show strategy, 48
   talk shows and voting, 95, 96, 290, 291
   "two-faced" Clinton ad, 255
   voter characteristics, 95, 96, 112-114, 122, 123
   voter disenchantment with, 10, 58
   voting preference and, 152, 166-171, 173
Bush-Quayle campaign, 1992
   "attack faxes," 240
   rapid response team, 239-241
   satellite technology use, 242
Bush voters
   campaign ratings by, 119, 120
   debates and, 118, 119
   newspaper ratings by, 113
   similarities to Perot voters, 122, 123

Subject Index

talk show ratings by, 117
TV news ratings by, 117
"bystander" hypothesis about attack ads, 247-267

C

Cadell, Pat, 276
California primary, 1992, 104
Campaign Associates, 1968, 236
Campaign & Elections Magazine, 101
campaign strategists'
   use of new media technologies, 242, 243
   views of talk shows, 21, 26, 29, 30, 41, 45, 46, 49, 50, 57, 67-69
campaign surrogates, 242, 243
campaigns' "answer desks," 235
campaigns' "fact patrols,"
   Dukakis, 1988, 234, 235, 237, 238
   history of, 236, 237
campaigns'
   control of debate panel selection, 138
   media teams, 236
   "opponent files," 234, 235, 240
   rapid response teams, 233-244
   speaker's manuals, 234
   speaker's teams, 235
   strategic goals, 233
Campbell, Carroll, 239, 243
candidate image, measurement of, 152
candidate preferences; *see* voting preferences
candidates' responsiveness to questions from
   journalists, 76
   citizens, 76
Cantor, Mickey, 135, 136
Carter, Jimmy, 130, 145, 149, 199, 206, 209, 276
Carville, James, 238, 239
CBS Evening News content analysis, 178
CBS News, 43, 248, 249, 270
CBS post-debate news specials, 32, 33, 178, 184, 185
CBS-*New York Times* poll, 279
CBS Poll, 279
Chandler, David, 283
Charlotte Observer, 18
"cheap news" explanation for ad replays, 247-249
"Chicken George," 133
Christian Science Monitor, 104
Clark, Torrie, 29, 49, 240, 242
Clinton, Bill
   ad tactics, 272
   ads, 8, 9, 22, 246, 254-272
   Arsenio Hall appearance, 30, 31, 42, 43, 151, 290
   "attack faxes" against, 240, 241
   biographical film, 22
   "bystander" hypothesis, 257-267
   campaign advisors, 30, 45
   campaign sophistication, 45
   candidacy at end of primaries, 43
   character issue, 240, 241
   character ratings, 190
   "Chicken George" tactic, 134
   debate goals, 288
   debate negotiations, 127, 129, 134, 136; *see also* Clinton negotiating position, below
   debate performance and, 148, 153-158, 175-182, 193, 195, 196, 198, 292
   debate tactics and, 109, 110, 292
   debate with Jerry Brown on *Donahue*, 45
   Donahue audience rejects host's questions, 45
   draft record, 240
   economic summit following

Subject Index

election, 62
Gennifer Flowers, damaged by, 43, 44
"image" and debate viewing, 161-166, 292
invitation to Perot to debate, 107, 109
income tax policy, 87
knowledge of "common people," 190
knowledge of supporters, 112, 113
local press conferences, 243
losses of votes to Perot, 20, 110
negotiating position on 1992 debates, 131-134, 136, 140, 200, 203
nomination acceptance speech, 105
passport illegally examined, 239
Perot, treatment of, 101, 106
poll standing, 11, 76, 104, 109, 282, 285
press conferences, 242, 243
"read my lips" ads, 255
"Red Willie" charge against, 241
Republican charges against, 243
Richmond debate format and, 139, 179, 292
satellite-linked town meetings, 242
"Slick Willie," 241
talk show appearances, 3, 19, 30, 45, 46, 48, 69, 73, 76, 94, 95, 97, 98, 110, 290
talk show audience size, 78
talk show/town hall strategy, 45, 46, 48, 53, 69, 74, 75, 124, 242, 290, 298
talk shows, voting and, 95, 96, 290, 291
"tax and spend" record, 243
treatment of Perot, 101, 108, 109

voting preference measure and, 152, 166-171, 173, 262
Clinton-Gore campaign,
bus campaign, 242
rapid-response team, 9, 22, 234, 237-239, 246, 288, 294
satellite message intercepts, 242
Clinton voters
campaign evaluations by, 119, 120
characteristics, 95, 112-114
debates and, 118, 119
ratings of newspapers, 117
ratings of TV news, 117
ratings of talk shows, 117, 118
Clintons appear on *60 Minutes*, 44
CNN, 43, 248, 249, 270, 273n, 282-284, 293; see also *Inside Politics*
CNN-*USA Today* poll controversy, 282-284
Commission on Presidential Debates,
creation of, 140
debate proposal, 1988, 132, 140, 200
debate proposal, 132-137, 140, 200
League of Women Voters and, 140, 141, 200
Compton, Ann, 138
Congress and NAFTA agreement, 110
content analyses, 1988, 31, 32, 201, 206
content analyses, 1992, 20, 21, 26-30, 36, 289
before vs. after debate comparisons, 30, 209, 231
combined print-broadcast sample, 30, 33, 34, 203, 209-212, 231n
debates, media support for, 202-212

design, evening newscasts, 32, 178
design, post-debate specials, 33, 178, 203
evening newscasts, 30, 32, 178
historical comparisons, 30, 31, 33, 178, 203-209, 289
network verdicts, 177-185
post-debate specials, 30, 32, 177-185, 203, 206
qualitative, 26
quantitative, 20, 25, 26, 27, 30, 31
reliability, 33, 63, 178, 203, 204
talk-show sampling frame, 31, 60-62, 71n
control variables, 150; see also specific variable names
conventions, nominating, 69
convergent research methods, 20, 21, 289, 297
"conversational ideal" in alternative media, 52
cross-tablulations/Chi square tests, 152
Crossley, Archibald, 279
Cox News Service, 105
Current Affair, A, 44

D

Dailey, Peter, 236
"Daisy Girl" ad, 1964, 250
Daniels, Mitchell, 242
Deardourff, John, 236
debate effects, 13, 14, 22, 144, 145-149, 151, 161-166, 172, 173
debate format, 2, 10, 13, 14, 74, 137-141
 audience preferences for, 212, 228-231, 296
 Bush negotiating team and, 132-136, 138, 141
 changes in, 2, 13, 14, 136-140, 199, 228, 229, 231, 292, 293, 296

Clinton negotiating team and, 133-136, 138
information limits caused by, 144, 145
institutional support and, 208, 209, 293
keyword search, 203
moderator only, 132, 136-138, 140, 155-158, 190, 196, 210, 212, 228-231, 292
moderator with panel, 212, 228-231
October 11 debate, 138, 153-155, 229
October 19 debate, 137, 140, 155-158, 229
panel of journalists, 132, 135-138, 140, 144, 153-158, 196, 212, 228, 292
performance perceptions influenced by, 177, 207, 292
preference question, November interviews, 212
preference question, October interviews, 212
recommendations concerning, 296, 297
Richmond "Town Hall" format, 74, 136, 137, 139, 155, 179, 193, 207-209, 212, 228-231, 292, 293
vice presidential debate, 138, 139, 228, 229, 293
debate viewing
 control variable, as, 88, 290
 knowledge and, 87, 89
 measurement, 150, 151
 talk show viewing and, 86, 89
debates, contribution to campaign, 200-202, 293
debates, history of, 127-131, 144, 146, 147, 199
debates, 1980, 199
debates, 1988, 147, 288

Subject Index

Bush-Dukakis, 17, 130, 145, 206
 coverage of, 47
 effects, 148
 format preferences, 296
 Quayle-Bentsen, 15, 16, 145, 179, 192
 time series survey and, 196, 252
debates, 1992 presidential, 1, 2, 10, 13, 14, 22, 30, 33, 34, 150, 151
 audience "rediscovered" by media, 207; *see also* voters
 audience size, 19, 78, 138, 139, 141, 151, 206
 Bush voters and, 118, 119
 candidate "image" effects, 144-149, 151, 161-166, 172, 173, 289
 candidate "image" measurement and, 152, 153
 Clinton voters and, 118, 119
 direct communication with voters, 144
 "equal-time" provision and, 129, 130
 exposure and support of debates, 213-223
 final, 1992, 14, 150, 151, 155-171, 178, 179, 196-198, 204, 210, 215, 222-224
 first, 1992, 150, 151, 153-171, 178, 179, 188-190, 204, 209, 210, 216, 217
 importance, 208, 209
 institutional support by voters, 14, 19, 118, 119, 201-203, 212-231, 289, 294, 295
 institutional support by voters, measurement of, 212, 213
 institutional treatment by media, 1, 10, 14, 22, 30, 33, 34, 178, 201-212, 231
 institutionalization, 18, 19, 21, 22, 127, 135, 136, 140, 141, 199-201, 288
 knowledge effects; *see* knowledge
 limitations, 144
 news sources about, 70, 181-185, 211
 Nielsen ratings, 206
 performance perception, measurement of, 151, 152, 176, 195
 performance perceptions by voters, 15, 141, 148, 149, 151, 152-158, 289, 292
 performance verdicts by media and, 13, 14, 32, 108, 109, 129, 145, 175-179, 183-185, 188-198, 289, 292
 Perot voters and, 20, 118, 119, 123, 124, 291, 293
 Richmond "Town Hall," 13, 14, 62, 74, 76, 92, 110, 139, 150, 151, 155, 159-166, 169-171, 178, 193-195, 202, 204, 207, 210, 211, 215, 220, 221, 228-231
 schedule, 1992, 136-140, 296
 limits on verdict effect, 177, 178, 197
 schedule, 1992 vs. 1988, 15, 16, 31, 32, 136-140, 146
 schedule, recommendations concerning, 296, 297
 usefulness ratings of, 94, 212, 216-223, 224, 295
 vice presidential, 150, 151, 178, 179, 190-192, 204, 209-211, 292
 vice presidential and debate support, 215, 218, 219, 224
 verdicts about candidates; *see* verdicts and debates; performance verdicts
 verdicts about, 30, 33, 34, 203-210
 voter use of, 14, 19, 47, 77, 86, 129, 206, 207
 votes, effects on, 148, 149, 151, 166-173

debates, 1976, 145
decision-makers, interviews with;
  see elite interviews
Democratic Party contenders' use of new media, 1992 primaries, 59
Democratic National Committee, 236, 237
Democratic Party convention, 69
"democratization" effects of alternative media, 51
Deutsch, Inc., 242
Dewey, Tom, 128
Dillin, John, 104
direct mail, as attack vehicle, 238
deficit, Federal, and Perot, 5
disenchantment, voter
  attack ads, with, 6, 10; see also attack ads
  candidates, with, 287
  conventional media, with, 3, 4, 17, 77, 98, 115-117, 122, 123, 287; see also voters regain control
  parties, with, 287
  reinvigorates campaign, 2
Dole, Bob, 130
Donahue, Phil, questions rejected by studio audience, 45, 75
Donahue show, 30, 31, 42, 43, 45, 73, 103
Douglas, Stephen A., 128, 129
Drew, Elizabeth, 74, 290
Dukakis, Michael, 6, 10, 112, 130, 153, 246
  ads, 245, 251, 253, 254
  fact patrol, 235
  failure to rebut attacks, 234, 237, 238, 244, 251, 294
  first 1988 debate, 148
  "Dead Kitty" question, 145
  negotiating position on 1988 debates, 130, 131, 140, 141
Dow Jones Fund, 29

E

"Eastern Europe" gaffe, 175
economy
  Bush's handling of, 11, 58
  voter concerns about, 70n
education
  campaign evaluations and, 119, 120
  candidate preference and, 95, 96, 111, 115
  debate support and, 213, 216, 222
  debates and, 150, 158-160, 196
  efficacy feelings and, 113
  interest in campaign and, 119
  knowledge and, 87, 88, 147, 158-160, 290
  measurement, 150
  media usefulness ratings, 116, 117
  talk show usefulness ratings, 90, 116, 117
  talk show viewing and, 82, 83, 86, 290
  verdict effect and, 187
  voting preferences and, 260, 262-266
efficacy feelings; see internal efficacy; external efficacy
Eisenhower, Dwight D., 129
Electoral College and polls, 284, 285
elite interviews in research, 21, 26, 27, 29, 181, 289
  limitations and strengths, 27
elite interviews, 1988 study, 29, 181-183
elitism in campaign journalism, 47, 48; see also alternative media; audience; disenchantment; news sources; talk shows; voters regain control
Eller, Jeff, 30, 45, 46

Subject Index

employment status as control variable, 213
"equal-time" provision and debates, 129, 130
external efficacy, 20
   Bush voters, 96, 97, 114
   campaign evaluations and, 119, 120
   Clinton voters, 95, 114
   debate support and, 214-216, 218, 220, 222, 224
   media ratings and, 115-117
   Perot voters, 19, 20, 95, 113-115, 123
   scales, 80, 98n
   talk show viewing, 80-83, 95, 97
   voting choice and, 260, 262-266, 268-270

F

Ferraro, Geraldine, 153
Flowers, Gennifer, 43, 44
Ford, Gerald, 145, 175

G

Gallup, George, 279
Gallup Organization, 110, 139, 149
Gantt, Harvey, campaign ads, 7
gasoline tax issue, 87, 112, 113, 152
gender
   control variable, as, 105, 111, 213
   gap, Perot, 105, 111, 265, 266
Gergen, David, 103, 135
Gibbons, Jean, 140
Glenn, Alize, 239, 242
Goldwater, Barry, 129, 130, 276
Good Morning America as talk show, 17, 73
Gore, Al
   debate performance verdicts about, 179, 190
   debate with Quayle, Stockdale, 138, 139, 179, 190

NAFTA debate with Perot, 102, 109
   talk show audience size, 78
"Governor Moonbeam," 46
Greenberg, Stan, 277, 278
Grunwald, Mandy, 238, 242
Greer, Frank, 242
Greider, William, 48
Gulf War
   Bush popularity and, 131
   topic in debates, 109

H

Harris, Lou, 279
Hart, Peter, 276
health care, voter concern about, 70
Helms, Jesse, campaign ads, 7
Holman, Sharon, 30
Hickman, Harrison, 240
"horse-race" coverage of campaign, 47, 51, 59, 75, 76, 115, 124, 280, 281, 289
Hotline, The, 103, 279, 280, 285
Hussein, Saddam, 109

I

ideology and Perot vote, 111
"image" as control variable, 166-171
Imus, Don, 45
income, knowledge and, 147
income tax issue, 87, 112, 113, 152
"infomercials," Perot; *see* Perot, Ross
interest,
   campaign, 1, 9, 50-52, 53, 75, 81-83, 95, 97, 119, 158-160, 167-171, 187, 196, 202, 213, 215, 216, 218, 220, 222, 224, 260, 290
   measurement, 150
Inside Politics, 103, 107, 273n
internal efficacy, 20
   Bush voters, 95, 96, 114

Subject Index

Clinton voters, 95, 114
  debate support and, 214-216, 218, 220, 222, 224
  knowledge and, 87
  new media and, 52
  Perot voters and, 19, 20, 95, 113, 114, 115, 123, 124
  scales, 80, 81, 98n, 113
  talk show viewers, 79-83, 85-89, 95-97, 290
  voting choice and, 260, 262-266, 268-270
interview wave, control for, 260

J

Jackson, Brooks, 249, 250, 293
Jennings, Peter, 129
Johnson, Lyndon, 130
Jordan, Hamilton, 105
journalistic interview; *see* elite interviews
journalists as own sources about
  debates, 211, 212
  talk shows, 67, 68
journalists' questions vs. citizens', 76

K

Kefauver, Estes, 128
Kennedy, John F., 129, 130, 143, 145, 148
Kennedy-Nixon debates, 128, 129, 136, 143, 148, 149
Kerry, Bob, 240
Kessel, John, 234
knowledge
  Bush voters and, 112, 113
  campaign, 1
  Clinton voters and, 112, 113
  controlling for, 166-171
  debates effects on, 14, 22, 144, 146, 147, 151, 158-160, 171, 201, 289
  demographics and, 147
  education and, 86-88, 147
  measurement, 152
  new media and, 52, 53
  newspaper reading and, 86-89, 147
  Perot voters and, 112-113
  talk shows and, 21, 76, 79, 86-89, 97, 112-113, 290, 295
  TV viewing and, 86-89, 147
Koppel, Ted, 74, 107, 290

L

Larry King, 76, 294
Larry King Live show, 31, 47, 49, 50, 61, 73
  Bush audience size, 78
  Perot appearances on, 103, 104, 109, 131, 287
  proposed debate on, 134
  Quayle and abortion controversy, 61
League of Women Voters, 140
  interviews about 1988, 29
learning; *see* knowledge
Lehrer, Jim, 138, 140, 196
Lexis/Nexis; *see* Nexis/Lexis
Limbaugh, Rush, 295
Liasson, Mara, 74
Lincoln, Abraham, 128, 129
local journalists, perceived competence, 54n
locale of interview as control variable, 261-266, 268, 269
"Looking Glass" effect, journalists and, 121, 124n
Los Angeles Times, The, 43

M

Madison, James, 128
Mahe, Eddie, 239
Mahui, Abolfath, 105
marital status as control variable, 111, 196, 213, 222, 223
Mashek, John, 138

Subject Index

Matalin, Mary, "attack faxes," 240-242
Means, Marianne, 109
Meet the Press, 104
Michelson, Charles, 236
Michigan State University, Clinton shows up alone, 133
Mondale, Walter, 130, 144, 145
Monroe, James, 128
Moody, Blair, 129
Morgenthau, Tom, 106
Morin, Richard, 280, 283
Morning news shows, shift format to talk, 17, 49
Mosbacher, Robert, 242
Moyers, Bill, 106, 107
MTV, as alternative to reach voters, 42, 43, 51
"mudslinging" attitude scale, 119, 120
Multiple Classification Analysis, logic of, 82-84, 149, 152, 153, 166, 167, 186-188, 214, 215, 260-262

N

Nashville Network, the, 51
Nation, The, 105
Naughton, James, 281
NBC evening news content analysis, 178
NBC News, 32, 43, 248, 249, 270, 293
NBC post-debate news specials, 32, 33, 178
negative ads; *see* attack ads
network news; *see also* ABC, CBS, CNN, NBC News
  "ad policing"; *see* ad police
  ad replays, 6, 16, 246-250
  coverage of debates as institution, 206-209
  debate carriage as public service symbol, 144
  Gennifer Flowers coverage, reluctance, 43
  verdicts about debate performances, 175-198
  viewing, as control variable, 82, 84, 87, 151, 158, 160
  viewing overlap with talk show viewing, 82, 84, 85
new era in presidential campaigns, 2, 10, 12, 22, 58, 131, 146, 287, 288, 294-298
New York primary, and Clinton alternative media appearances, 45
  Don Imus, 45
New York Times, The, 43, 246, 280
News Election Service (NES), 279
news interview shows vs. talk shows, 19
news media, conventional
  attitudes toward; *see* lose information monopoly, below
  awareness of alternative media threat, 17, 27, 46-48, 57-61, 63, 64, 69, 75, 80
  bias toward Perot, 122
  changes over time in talk show treatment, 64-66, 69, 70
  coverage improvement leads to campaign use of new media, 43, 44
  commitment to coverage plans, 18, 58
  coverage of Perot "infomercials," 108, 109
  debates, as way around, 144
  delayed reaction to new media reality, 62, 66
  "horse race" coverage, 47, 51, 59, 75, 76, 115, 116, 281, 289
  lose information monopoly, 3, 9, 10, 15, 17, 18, 42-47, 50-52, 57-60, 63, 66, 69, 75-77, 98, 115-

Subject Index

.17, 123, 124, 241, 288, 294-296
verlook Perot early, 4, 103
react to talk shows, 3, 4, 17, 18, 21, 27, 30, 31, 54, 58-70, 80, 110
role mismatch, 58
usefulness ratings, 212
willingness to adjust to new media reality, 57, 58, 60
news media coverage of
ads, 6, 7, 9, 10, 16, 17, 108, 246-250, 270
conventions, 69, 70
debater performance, 30, 31, 107-109, 181-185, 189, 190, 194, 195
debates, 10, 14, 16, 17, 22, 109
debates as political institution, 30, 33, 34, 201-212
1988 campaign, 44
Perot, 5, 21, 102-105, 108, 110, 121, 122
Perot's 19% vote, 6, 19
Perot's importance, 3-6, 9, 101, 121, 122
Perot's N.A.A.C.P. speech, 5
Perot's return to race, 107
Perot's use of talk shows, 59, 102-104, 110
Perot's withdrawal in July, 105-107
talk shows; *see* talk show, talk shows
voter questions on talk shows, 63, 64, 65
news sources
evaluations of debaters, 181-185, 292
evaluations of debates, 208, 211, 212
evaluations of talk shows, 62, 64-70
"insiders" as, 181, 182, 197, 208, 212

journalists interview each other, 197
journalists' reliance, 70, 181, 182
voters as, 183-185, 197, 212
news verdicts; *see* verdicts
newspaper reading
control variable, 87, 151, 158-160, 167-171
talk show viewing, and, 82, 84, 85
Newsweek, 17, 43, 104, 106, 110
Nexis/Lexis, 124n, 231n, 283, 284
Nightline, 32, 33, 107, 203
Nixon, Richard, 129, 135, 143, 148, 236
non-traditional media; *see* alternative media; talk shows
Novak, Robert, 74, 290
November Group, 1972, 236
November Group, 1992, 242

O

occupation as control variable, 194
Oprah show, 31, 295

P

panel survey design, 20, 21, 28, 35-39, 205, 225, 231, 289
attrition in, 29
costs, 29
time series complements, 28, 29
panelists
ad ratings, changes in, 268-270
campaign evaluation and, 119, 120
campaign ratings, changes in, 119, 120
control, use as, 83-88, 95, 187, 189, 192, 194, 196, 217, 219, 220, 223, 224
debates, changes in attitudes toward, 225-230
Perot's return and, 120, 121
talk show evaluations, 92, 93,

Subject Index

117
talk show viewing, 93, 117
talk show viewing increase, 91-93
talk show viewing, by November, 79, 91-93
voting choice intensity, 121
voting choice reasons, 121
party identification as control, 83, 87, 90, 95, 96, 111, 151, 153-158, 166-171, 186, 187, 189, 190, 192, 194, 196, 216, 219, 220, 223, 224, 254, 263-267
  ad recall and, 253, 254, 256-258, 262-266, 268, 269, 271
passport, Bill Clinton's, 239
Perot, H. Ross, 178-181, 287
  ad spending, 102, 246, 270
  ads, 8, 9, 102, 105, 108, 109, 246, 254-272
  avoidance of press, 47, 102, 241, 291
  avoidance of crowds, 102
  "bystander," benefits from, 257-267
  candidacy at end of primaries, 43
  candidacy ignored by news media, 4, 103, 181
  candidacy, 1992, 2, 4-6, 11, 12, 19
  character, 101, 105, 106-108, 110, 190
  debate invitation to in 1992, 107, 109, 132, 136, 203
  debate performance perceptions, 153-158, 188, 193, 292
  debate performance verdicts, 108, 175-178, 180, 188-190, 193-198, 291, 292
  debates and, 6, 108, 109, 113
  debates legitimize candidacy, 123, 148, 288

"Diagnosis" infomercial, 255, 268, 271
disenchantment with, 11, 12
effect on Bush vote, 20, 106, 111-112
effect on Clinton vote, 20, 106, 109, 111, 112
effects on campaign, 4, 5, 9, 11, 12, 19, 20, 46, 106, 107, 123, 188, 281, 287, 298
"electronic Caesar," 5
efficacy and, 113, 114
followers, media disinterest in their views, 5, 103, 104, 122
followers, frustrated by his withdrawal, 106
future of, 121, 122
gender gap toward, 105, 111, 265, 266
hostility toward press, 5, 20, 102, 122, 241
"image" and debate viewing, 161-166, 292
infomercials, 77, 108, 109, 246, 254, 255
investigations of by media, 5, 102, 105
Jordan, Hamilton, and, 105
knowledgeability ratings, 190
Larry King Live and, 6, 103, 104, 109, 131, 287
party identification and, 187, 189, 190
poll standing after return, 107-109, 285
poll standing before withdrawal, 4-6, 11, 104-106, 291
press treatment of, 5, 20, 101-106, 109, 110, 121, 122
"Purple Heart" ad, 255
qualifies for ballot, date of, 287
rapid response team, lack of, 241, 243

Subject Index

returns to race, 5, 6, 12, 102, 104, 120, 121, 288
Richmond debate format and, 139
Rollins, Ed, and, 105
"Storm" ad, 255
talk show appearances, 3, 6, 30, 46, 47, 49, 59, 94, 95, 97, 98, 102, 103, 109, 110, 115-117, 131, 290
talk show strategy, 53, 131, 241, 290, 298
talk shows and voting, 95, 96, 290, 291
underestimation by journalists, 101, 102, 107
United We Stand, 107
verdicts about NAFTA debate with Gore, 109
volunteers; see Perot followers
voter characteristics, 95, 111-115, 291
voters, 19, 95, 97, 101, 105, 110-115, 123, 293
  ratings of campaign, 119, 120
  ratings of newspapers, 117, 122, 123
  ratings of talk shows, 117, 122, 123
  ratings of TV news, 117, 122, 123
votes, 19, 112, 152
voting probability, 152, 166-173, 190, 265, 266, 290
wealth, 140
withdrawal, 5, 11, 12, 102, 103, 105, 106, 288
Philadelphia Inquirer, The, 246, 281, 282
phone-in polls
  ABC, 1980, 184
  CBS, 1992, 184, 185
political efficacy; *see* internal efficacy; external efficacy
Political Information System (PINS), 277
polls
  academic, 275
  Bush campaign and, 277
  campaign-commissioned, 275-278
  Clinton campaign and, 277
  CNN-*USA Today* poll controversy, 282, 283
  Electoral College and, 284, 285
  Goldwater campaign and, 276
  history, 276-279
  "horse-race" coverage of, 47, 115, 280-286, 289
  Kennedy campaign use, 276
  media, 22, 104, 110, 111, 115, 275, 277-286, 289
  post-debate coverage and, 183, 185, 197
Portland *Oregonian, The*, 270
positive ads; *see* attack ads
post-debate newscasts, content analysis of; *see* content analysis
predictor variables, 150, 151; *see also* debates, talk shows
presidential campaign ads; *see* ads, attack ads
presidential debates; *see* debate, debates
Presidential Victory Committee "Willie Horton" ad, 6, 247
primaries, 1992 sampling frame, 62, 66
"priming" effect, 1988 Bush ads, 272, 273

Q

Quayle, Dan, 15, 16, 131
  "daughter's abortion" controversy, 61
  debate performance, 1988, 179, 192

Subject Index

debate performance, 1992, 179, 190-192
debate tactics, 190
debate with Gore, Stockdale, 138
Quayle-Bentsen debate verdict effect, 15, 16, 145, 179, 192, 197
Quantum Leap, 246
questionnaire
  length in minutes, 35
  variables asked about, 35
questionnaires
  Wave 1, Appendix A
  Waves 2-5, Appendix B
  Wave 6 (panel only), Appendix C
questions to candidates from citizens, 50, 52, 63, 67, 68, 74, 76
  Bush comfortable with, 49
"quick response" teams; *see* under candidate name
Quindlen, Anna, 106

R

race as control variable, 192, 213, 218
radio as attack vehicle, 237
Rafshoon, Gerald, 236
Ranney, Austin, 54n
Rather, Dan, 239
"Read my lips," Clinton ads, 246
Reagan, Ronald, 130, 135, 149, 199, 206, 208
  debate tactics, 145
regression figures, explained, 83-85
Republican National Committee, 242
Republican national convention, 69, 279
  Clinton ads and, 242, 243
research recommendations, 1996, 297, 298
"response set" in debater ratings, 188, 189
"Revolving Door" ad, 1988, 6, 7
Robinson, Michael J., 75
Rook, Susan, 140
Roosevelt, Franklin, 35

S

satellite downloading, Clinton campaign, 242
Schneider, William, 283, 284
sex; *see* gender
Shaw, Bernard, and "Dead Kitty" question, 145
Simpson, Carole, 139
Simulates Project, 276, 277
60 Minutes, Clintons appear on, 44
"softball" questions on talk shows, 64, 66, 77, 79
"sound bite" campaign, 44
sources; *see* news sources
"spin doctors," 181, 192, 211, 292; *see also* news sources
Stanton, Frank, 129
Star, The, and Gennifer Flowers, 44
Stassen, Harold, 128
Steeper, Fred, 277, 278
Stephanopoulos, George, 234, 238, 239
Stevenson, Adlai, 128, 129
St. Louis Post-Dispatch, 270
Stockdale, James
  debate performance, 108, 179, 180, 190, 191
  debate with Quayle, Gore, 138, 179, 180
"straw" polls, 278, 279
survey design, 1988 study, 25
survey design, 1992 study, 20, 21, 25-28, 35-38, 150, 205, 289
survey questionnaires; *see* questionnaires
survey samples
  demographics, 38-40

Subject Index

size, 36-39

T

tabloid journalism, effects on campaign, 43-45

talk show
 appearances by candidates; *see* under candidate's name
 coding scheme, 62, 63
 hosts evaluate their shows, 66, 67, 69
 hosts, poll support for, 75
 hosts, questions they ask, 64-66, 75

Talk shows,
 future of, 295, 298
 radio, 298

Talk shows in 1992 campaign, 2, 3, 4, 10, 17, 20, 41, 42, 47-50, 58, 59, 73, 110, 115-117
 as alternative information source, 3, 4, 17, 46, 48, 50, 60, 69, 75, 77, 98, 115, 158-160
 as "marketing" device, 4, 74, 75
 audience attitudes toward, 3, 4, 17, 19, 21, 60, 75, 115-117, 290
 audience characteristics, 77, 79-82, 86, 97
 audience overlap with other media, 79, 82, 84-86, 89, 90, 97, 98, 290
 audience size, 17, 19, 21, 50, 78, 92, 97, 141, 290
 audience size growth, 91, 92, 290
 callers, 98n, 103, 104
 candidates use to reach voters directly, 42-48, 50, 57-59, 63, 73, 75, 103, 104
 controlling for, 158-160, 167-171
 criticisms of, 74-79, 86, 290
 debate viewing and, 86, 87, 89, 290
 evaluation of, 90-92, 94, 95
 evaluation of, compared to rival media, 94, 97
 evaluation of, Richmond debate effect on, 92, 94
 exposure measurement, 78, 150, 151
 index, 98n
 information value, 64, 66, 74-76, 86, 90, 98
 "latecomers" to, 91, 92
 "never viewers," 91, 92
 news content about, 30, 31, 58, 60-70, 80
 news content codes, 62-63
 news content sampling frames, 31-34, 60-62
 news media reactions to, 3, 4, 17, 46-48
 Perot equated with, 59, 109
 Perot voters and, 20, 95, 97, 98
 politicians' evaluations, 66, 69
 primaries and, 59, 66
 questions asked by citizens on, 50, 52, 63, 67, 74, 76
 Richomd debate similarities, 62, 76, 92
 scholarly opinion of, 4, 67-69, 70, 73, 75, 290
 usefulness ratings of, 212, 295
 vote choice and, 94-98, 110, 290, 291
 voter use of, 19, 21, 48, 50, 52, 60, 74, 75, 77, 79, 90, 98, 290, 295

Tamposi, Elizabeth, 239
"Tank" ad, 1988, 6
Taylor, Paul, 54n
Teeter, Robert, 276
television news, usefulness ratings, 94, 116, 117
third-party candidate, recovery of momentum, 2, 19
third-person effect, 1988 ads and

Subject Index

journalists, 16, 17, 247, 251
This Morning, shift to talk format, 17, 73
This Week with David Brinkley, viewing of by talk-show viewers, 86
Thomas, Helen, 140
Thomases, Susan, 239
Time-CNN Poll, 104
time series survey design, 15, 20, 21, 28, 36-38, 149, 176, 177, 187, 188, 191, 197, 205, 252, 277, 289, 297
    content analysis supplements, 176, 177
    costliness, 29
    panel complements, 28, 29
    verdict exposure and, 186-188
Time, 43, 103
Times-Mirror polls, 74, 75
Today Show
    Clinton call-in appearance, 49
    format shift to talk, 17, 73
"town hall" debate; *see* debates
town hall meetings, 3; *see also* talk shows
tracking poll; *see* time series
traditional media; *see* news media, conventional
Travis, James, 236
trend study; *see* time series
Tsongas, Paul, 46
Turner, Ted, 283
turnout, voter, 1988 vs. 1992, 2

U

U.S. News & World Report, 43
USA Today, 106, 246, 270

V

Vanderbilt Television News Archives, 32, 33, 246
Vanderbilt Television News Index, 16

Vanocur, Sander, 138
verdict effects, 1988, 15, 186, 187, 191, 192, 288
verdict effects, 1992, 1, 13, 15, 22, 175-177, 185, 188-198, 288
    format effects on; *see* debate format
    negative vs. positive, 197
    schedule effects on, 13, 15, 16
verdict exposure measures, 186, 197-198
verdicts about debater performance, 1, 13, 30-32, 107-108, 130, 175-179, 185, 188-198, 292
verdicts about debates themselves, 30, 33, 34
verdicts, voter dependence on, 13, 15, 16, 188-198, 292
vice presidential debate, 131-138
    proposal by Commission, 133
    verdict effects in, 190-192
voter disenchantment; *see* disenchantment
voter knowledge; *see* knowledge
voter turnout; *see* turnout
voters, journalists forget about, 10, 13, 14, 47, 48, 183-185, 197, 202, 208, 209
voters regain control of information resources, 2-4, 10, 15, 17, 45-48, 50, 52, 53, 57, 58, 60, 63, 69, 76, 77, 79, 90, 98, 115, 123, 288, 294-296
voting preference
    ads effects on, 257-267
    debate effects on, 148, 149, 153, 166-171, 173, 190, 196-198
    measurement of probability, 152, 260
    reactions to Perot's return and, 120, 121
    reason given for, 121
    talk shows and, 77, 94-98, 110

W

Wall Street Journal, 43
Washington Post, The, 43, 103, 246, 280, 281, 283, 295
Warden, Sharon, 241, 281
"War Room," Clinton campaign, 237
West, Darrell M., evidence about ad effects, 6-8, 251

Wichita Eagle, 18
Wilhelm, David, 58
Wilkie, Wendell, 35
"Willie Horton" ad, 1988, 6, 234, 247, 250
Wirthlin, Richard, 276, 277
Wright, Betsy, 234, 239

Z

Zirinsky, Susan, 239

JK 526 1992 P